GROWING UP
TO COWBOY

GROWING UP TO COWBOY

A Memoir of the American West

BOB KNOX

SUNSTONE PRESS

SANTA FE

Sunstone books may be purchased for educational, business, or sales promotional use.
For information please write: Special Markets Department, Sunstone Press,
P.O. Box 2321, Santa Fe, New Mexico 87504-2321.

Library of Congress Cataloging-in-Publication Data:

Knox, Bob, 1930–
    Growing up to cowboy: a New Mexico memoir / by Bob Knox.
    p. cm.
    ISBN: 0-86534-352-7 (hardcover) –ISBN: 0-86534-353-5 (paper)
       1. Knox, Bob, 1930– 2. Cowboys–New Mexico–Biography. 3. Ranch life–New Mexico.
    4. New Mexico–Social life and customs–20th century. 5. New Mexico–Biography.
    I. Title.

F801.4. K58 K58 2002
636.2' 13' 092–dc21
[B]   2002017642

Published in

SUNSTONE PRESS
Post Office Box 2321
Santa Fe, NM 87504-2321 / USA
(505) 988-4418 / *orders only* (800) 243-5644
FAX (505) 988-1025
www.sunstonepress.com

**For the inspiration
and my reason for writing this book,**

I wish to dedicate it to:

My kids: RC, Myrna, and Lee

My Grandkids: Lee, Lisa, Felice, Shanna,
Laura, Brooke, and Jamie.

My Great Grandkids: Coy, Mariah, and Trey.

Acknowledgements

To my partner, friend, lover and wonderful wife Bettye for your help, encouragement, support and believing that this could become a reality, my love and thanks to you.

To RC and Lee Ann, always encouraging, you seemed to know when I needed a little boost. You always laughed at my stories whether they were funny or not. You were more help than you know. Thanks so much!

To Bill Quinn for the great workshops and guidance in putting this all together. Thanks Bill, your help is deeply appreciated.

To Joan MacNeish for the great job of sorting through my rough language and crude first draft, great job! For your enthusiasm and excitement, I'm ever grateful.

To the many cowboys I talk about in this story, thanks men, for letting me be part of your lives.

1

Shopping

About the only time in my life I didn't think about being a cowboy was my first six or seven months of age, when I was in an orphanage in Denver, Colorado. Then most of my thoughts were about when someone was going to feed me or change me.

Lyle and Anna Knox were a young married couple living in Springfield, Colorado, in 1930. Lyle was a livestock brand inspector and deputy sheriff, working for the State of Colorado. Anna was a housewife, busy with homemaking. Lyle received a call from the livestock board in Denver to come in for a meeting of all state brand Inspectors. This trip to Denver was exciting for Anna, as she seldom got the opportunity to go to the big city, and she had a lot of shopping she wanted to do.

While Lyle was busy with meetings, Anna took in the main shops, really having a good time. She had lived in Denver a few years, before meeting and marrying Lyle, so she knew her way around the big city.

After a couple days, Lyle was ready to head back home and get out of this big town, as he was kind of a small-town fellow, it didn't take him long to get enough of the big city!

As they were getting in their old car, all packed and ready to head home, Lyle asked Anna if she had any more shopping to do before they left. She said there was one more stop she would like to make, and she wanted him to go with her.

"All right," Lyle said. "Where do you want to go?"

"The orphanage," Anna replied, a smile lighting up her pretty face.

Lyle was a little taken back by this request, but being the kind of man he was, he didn't say much; just figured she might have a friend working there. So they drove out to the orphanage.

As they drove up to the old, red brick building, Lyle gave Anna a questioning look.

She had a big smile on her face and a twinkle in her eye as she asked him to come in with her. Lyle wasn't very comfortable with this situation, but he reluctantly followed her in.

Anna introduced herself and Lyle to the lady, who seemed to be in charge.

"We would like to see some of the children who are available for adoption," Anna said, as Lyle gave her a questioning look. They had talked some about maybe adopting a baby. Looked like Anna might be getting serious about getting a little one!

The lady asked what age she was interested in. Anna told her a baby under a year. She showed Anna and Lyle where these little ones were, and told them to go ahead and look around. If they saw one they were interested in, she would give them the child's story.

Anna moved up and down the aisle, looking and baby talking to all these little kids. They had a pretty good assortment; various sizes, shapes and colors.

Anna was doing some serious talking to these little ones, as Lyle followed her up and down the aisle with his hat in his hand, wondering what he had gotten into.

"Look at this one, Lyle!" Anna exclaimed.

The little one had lost his bottle, and was trying to find it in the wrinkled blanket he had kicked down to the end of the crib. Anna reached down to help the little guy get his bottle up to where he could get a drink.

"He couldn't reach his bottle. He needs me! Do you like him, Lyle?"

Lyle agreed the little guy looked like he might need a friend. If he had been asked what he thought of a horse or a cow, Lyle could have given a pretty good appraisal; but, this was a little out of his line.

"He looks all right to me," Lyle answered. "Go ahead and get him, if that's the one you want."

The lady in charge asked if they had found one they liked.

"Yes," Anna said. "I think we want this one. Tell us about him."

The lady gave them her best sales pitch, ending up by saying he had been there since shortly after birth, around six or seven months, and appeared healthy.

They wrapped me up in a blanket, got my bottle, signed the papers, and I became Robert Lee Knox. Heading out to Springfield, Colorado,

Lyle was grinning all over! He had just gotten himself a son. Anna was one happy new mother and I was one lucky little kid!

I have always been grateful to Anna and Lyle for picking me that day. I don't know how I came to be there in that orphanage; that's not important to me. A loving couple chose me out of a bunch of kids, loved me, and cared for me many years. They never failed me, always standing by me, even when I did some pretty stupid things. That's what is important. My thanks and love to you, Mom and Dad.

Charles Lyle Knox, Father

Anna Ruby Knox, Mother

Anna and Lyle Knox with new
baby, Bobby

Anna and Lyle Knox 1929

2

My New Family

As I relate some of these happenings of my childhood, it is appropriate to tell a little about the family I grew up in.

Lee Lord Knox was Dad's father, born June 25, 1857, in Charleston, Wisconsin. Grandad was one of the first brand Inspectors hired by the State of Colorado. He also served as a deputy U.S. marshal and deputy sheriff. He died at age 71, in Springfield, Colorado, on December 29, 1928. Dad didn't talk much about him and I regret that I never learned much about his life. I'm sure it was interesting.

Dad's mother was Evesta Ellen Bickel, born September 15, 1861, in Amherst, Wisconsin. Grandmother was a small lady, standing about five feet on tip toe, weighing around 95 pounds. What she lacked in size she made up for in heart and grit! She was tough as a boot and loving as any grandmother could be. I called her my "Baby" Grandma.

Lee and Evesta married and came out to Kansas in 1880. In 1883, they moved into Baca County, Colorado, where they homesteaded and started the family ranch on Horse Creek, northwest of Springfield. She and Grandad raised seven kids on the old home ranch in times when the living wasn't so easy. Grandmother died on January 7, 1944, at the age of 83.

They had three daughters, Ellen, Rhoda, and Tina. I never got to know Ellen or Rhoda, but I knew Aunt Tina pretty well. I won't say much about my aunts, but I'll say some about my three uncles, as they were the ones who played a big part in my growing up.

Dayton Erastus was born December 10, 1886, in Murdock, Kansas. Uncle Dayton was the oldest of the Knox brothers. He was a sure enough hard twisted cowboy. As a young man he worked for some big outfits in southeastern Colorado. If you wanted a fist fight right quick, you just called him Erastus! He kept that name pretty well hidden! Dayton was probably the tallest of the Knox family, until I came along, standing around five foot six and weighing around a hundred and thirty. He never married; don't know if by choice or if he couldn't find a lady who would put up with him! He was pretty ornery in his younger years.

The drought of the 1930s forced Dayton and Grandmother to sell the old home place in Baca County. They moved to a small place on the western slope of Colorado between Hotchkiss and Paonia. They lived there several years, and as I got a little older, I spent many a happy summer there with them. Dayton and I got along real good. He taught me a lot about being a cowboy, some of which got me in trouble sometimes! We were pretty close friends.

Dayton was sure handy with a pocket knife. Out of wood, he carved a horse and rider leading a pack string of four mules and a stagecoach with four horses. The detail in these carvings was near perfect, as he had been there and done that! I wish I knew what happened to these carvings. Dayton was truly a master carver. His trademark was hand-carved wooden chains. One continuous chain, over twenty feet long, hung over the back bar at the old Ranch Bar in Cimarron for many years. Dayton died July 25, 1972, in Grand Junction, Colorado at the age of 86.

Dad was born Charles Lyle Knox on September 27, 1889, in Minneapolis, Colorado. Raised on a ranch, Dad became a good cowboy at an early age.

Dad joined the U.S. Army when World War 1 broke out. He had to try three physical exams before he passed and was accepted. At five foot four he barely made the minimum height requirement, but couldn't make the weight requirement the first two tries. He said he never ate so much in his life as he did trying to gain a few pounds to make the minimum weight requirement! Finally getting into the Army he served honorably in France and Germany. Wounded in battle, he suffered from the effects of mustard gas and was honorably discharged. He returned in 1918 to Colorado, quite a hero.

Dad, like his father, took the job of brand inspector, also serving as a deputy sheriff, working the southeastern part of Colorado. He soon had the reputation of being a pretty tough brand inspector and lawman. He helped break up several gangs of horse thieves and cattle rustlers. Although he wasn't very big, physically but he was damn sure a tough little man!

Being small in stature, an excellent and fearless rider, Dad was in demand to ride racehorses at racemeets around southeastern Colorado, Kansas, Oklahoma, and New Mexico. He sure liked riding racehorses. Once, at the racemeet in Las Vegas, New Mexico, his horse fell with him during a race. He was pretty banged up from this spill. He had his eye on a young lady who convinced him to quit riding racehorses, shortly after that spill he and Mom were married.

Ray Lord Knox, was born September 19, 1896, at Minneapolis, Colorado. Uncle Ray was a cowboy, a lot like Dayton. He stood about five foot five, had a big barrel chest, and a round face. He had a tendency to get a little heavy. As a youngster, Ray worked for several big outfits in southeastern Colorado. He must have been like a cat, with nine lives! He had more close calls than anyone I ever knew. As a teenager, while riding a bronc, the horse bucked off into a deep arroyo with Ray, landing upside down on top of him. They weren't found until three days later. The bronc was dead. Ray was unconscious, pinned under the horse. Dad and Dayton packed Ray off to the house on a horse, where he lay some twenty days before regaining consciousness. Ray recovered from this wreck and went on to have many more!

Surprising a band of cattle rustlers one night, Ray was hit over the head with a pistol, doused with kerosene and set on fire. Several years later, a horse, tangled in barbed wire, bucked him off and dragged a long strand of barbed wire across his neck. It took over fifty stitches to sew him up, and another time, when an old gal got mad at him and poisoned him, and he dang near died in the hospital! That's just a few of his close encounters!

Ray spent several years up at Eagle Nest where he kept a few horses to rent for tourists to ride. Ray was pretty mean and hard on horses. Guess that's why he and I never got along very good. As a kid I spent several summers with Ray and Dayton.

Like Uncle Dayton, Ray never married. He had moved over to Jemez Springs, New Mexico, where his luck ran out, and he died in a bunkhouse fire in April,1980, at the age of 84. He is buried at Grand Junction, Colorado.

Robert Lynn Knox was born April 8, 1904 in Minneapolis, Colorado. Uncle Bob was my favorite uncle. He stood about the same height as his brothers, always staying pretty trim and physically fit. He was around where we lived when I was small and we grew very close. Bob was sure a good cowboy and had a special knack for training dogs and horses. He taught me a lot and was always my hero. I wanted to grow up and be a cowboy just like Uncle Bob!

I was fortunate to have worked a few ranches with Uncle Bob, when I first left home and started cowboying. I always admired him and his way with livestock. He could sure ride a pretty rough bucking horse in his old slick-forked N. Porter saddle and he was always there to give me words of encouragement and advice. Bob married late in life and he and Lillian had three children. I guess maybe Bob was a little to old to try to raise children, anyway he had a pretty dysfunctional family. He settled in Grand Junction, Colorado where he went on to the big round-up in 1985, at the age of 81. Uncle Bob is buried in Grand Junction.

That was Dad's side of the family that I grew up with. Growing up around cowboys, horses and cattle fit right into my plan of growing up to be a cowboy. I don't have any record of Mom's father except her telling me that he was a US Marshal, killed in a gun fight, in Indian Territory, Oklahoma, in 1895.

Her mother was born Lena Potts in Mississippi in 1864. They lived in Tecumseh Indian Territory (now Oklahoma), where Mom was born Anna Ruby Crank on May 9, 1894. She had one older brother, Perry Crank. Perry spent his life working for the railroad, living in Livingston, Montana.

Mom, her mother and brother moved to Denver, Colorado, in the late 1890's. Grandma went to chiropractic school and became one of the first licensed lady chiropractors in Colorado. She had a chiropractic practice in Denver for several years, while Mom and Perry went to school. After finishing school, Perry went to work for the railroad and Mom married a young man from Ohio. A couple months after Mom was married, her husband went into the Army and died from the big influenza epidemic while in basic training, leaving Mom a young widow.

In 1919 Grandma left Denver and went to Baca County, Colorado and filed on a homestead. This was a pretty good undertaking for a single woman to file on a homestead, alone. But Grandma proved up on her homestead and got title to the land from the Government! She was a pretty tough lady.

After Mom lost her husband, she came out to see her mother and decided to homestead herself. She filed on and proved up a homestead, also, next to her mother's.

Grandma lived on her homestead for several years, in a dugout with a rock front. Grandma and Mom got enough money to buy some lumber and

16

built a two room house and got to move out of the dugout. (A dugout was a cave like room dug back into a dirt bank with a wood or rock front on it).

A big ranch was buying up a lot of homesteads in that area and had tried to get Grandma and Mom to sell their homesteads to them. Mom gave her homestead to Grandma and Grandma refused to sell.

Shortly after they had built their new wood house, they needed some supplies, so they hooked up their team of horses to the wagon and went into Springfield for these supplies. This was a two-day trip. When they returned home all that was left of their new house was a big pile of ashes. It had burned to the ground.

Mom saw a lot of shod-horse tracks in the yard around where the house had been. She and Grandma didn't have any shod horses. Mom saddled her horse and rode into Springfield to report this to the sheriff. The sheriff came out and looked around, agreed it looked a little suspicious, but nothing could be proven about it being arson. So Grandma said she would just build another house!

The word spread about the tough lady chiropractor and her determination. Neighbors from miles around turned out to help, and it wasn't long before Grandma had another house. This time they built her new house out of rock! Grandma lived out there many years and never did sell out.

As a little kid, I sure hated to go out and visit Grandma! I called her my "Big" Grandma, as she was a large lady. She would whip a little chiropractor treatment on me, and I sure dreaded that! As I got a little older, I was pretty self-conscious of my height and started getting round-shouldered. Grandma took care of that! She made a harness for me that went around my shoulders and drew them back straight. This contraption tied in the back and, when they got it tied on me, it was kinda like a straight jacket. I was darn sure straightened up. Almost pulled me over backwards! I thanked her later, but at the time I thought it was just her way of torturing me!

Grandma would get a headlock on me so she could hold me still, then run her thumb up my spine, popping all the vertebrae in my back like a row of dominoes! I would yell and holler, trying to get away from her. But she would work on my back until she was satisfied with the way it was lined up. She would set me down in the kitchen chair, and standing behind me, she would get one hand under my chin and the other hand on top of my head. Holding my head in her vise-like grip, she would tell me, "Relax!"

But she kept moving my head back and forth. "Relax!" Are you kidding! I knew she was fixing to twist my head clean off!

Sure enough, she would give my head a violent twist first one way and then the other trying, I was sure, to twist it off! Something would "pop," but somehow my head stayed on. Boy, I dreaded those chiropractor treatments!

Grandma had three husbands in her lifetime. I was best man at one of her weddings! Not many people can claim that distinction. She was surely a tough pioneer lady. She passed away in Lamar, Colorado, on January 29, 1957 at the grand old age of 93.

So that's a little history of the family I found myself in when Lyle and Anna took me to raise. I was a pretty lucky kid. I was loved and cared for, not mistreated. (At times I thought I was!) It was a great family to be raised in.

Knox ranch on Horse Creek, Baca County Colorado, late 1890s

Lee Lord Knox, Grandfather

Evesta Ellen Knox, Grandmother

Lena (Garner) Crank, Grandmother

"Baby" Grandma Knox

Grandma Crank in front of rock house on homestead

Mom on homestead early 1920s

Grandma Crank feeding colt on homestead, Baca County, Colorado

Uncle Bob, cowboy picture
taken in early 1930s

Uncle Dayton, cowboy picture taken
early 1900s

Uncle Ray, cowboy
picture taken 1920s

Grandma Knox with uncles Ray, Dayton, and Bob, with Granddad in back

3

My First Horse

Mom and Dad were sure proud new parents when they got back to Springfield. Dad's brothers soon got the word that Lyle had a son and they all came over to see this new addition to the Knox family. They came on horseback, as none of them had cars then. Of course, I got set up in front of them to get a horseback ride. The riding was great, but getting me off was a different matter! I would wrap my legs around the saddle horn and yell for all I was worth when they tried to get me down from the saddle! Wherever we were, if there was a horse around, I had to get taken for a ride.

When my third birthday rolled around, Uncle Bob decided I should have a horse of my own. To my surprise and delight he gave me my first horse. She was a little brown and white paint filly, about 18 months old. Her name was Betty. She was pretty gentle, about half starved, as was most of the livestock in Baca County, Colorado, during the drought in the early 1930s. We were right in the middle of the dust bowl; a pretty tough time in the history of Colorado, when hundreds of cattle and horses were killed to keep them from starving to death.

We had a small acreage on the edge of Springfield, with a set of corrals and a little barn. Dad managed to buy enough feed to soon get Betty up in good shape, and she slicked off to become a real classy little filly.

She was real gentle natured and with lots of help and coaching from Dad and Uncle Bob I was soon riding her around the corral.

Uncle Bob was Dad's younger brother. He was cowboying around southeastern Colorado then, but being between jobs he was staying with us and he had lots of time to work with me and Betty. I couldn't have had a better teacher. Getting my own horse couldn't have been better, 'cause I sure had the cowboy bug at an early age.

Dad had a business trip to Pueblo, shortly after I got Betty. Mom and I got to go with him and, while there, we went by R.T. Frazier Saddle Company. To my delight, there was a little silver horned kid's saddle in the window of the saddle shop. It had little silver spots mounted all around the skirts and down the stirrup fender. It was a pretty stout made little outfit and it didn't take long to talk Mom and Dad into getting it for me. I knew it would sure look good on Betty, and I figured it just didn't get any better than this!

I started riding Betty around the corral and soon had made enough progress that we got to ride out of the corral and around the yard. It didn't take too long until the wide open spaces started beckoning to me. I left the familiar circle of the yard and started down the dirt road that went by our house.

I knew I wasn't supposed to leave the yard, but I figured just a short ride would be all right. This was all new to Betty, and she sure didn't want to leave her familiar yard. She whirled around and started back to the corrals, not wanting to go down the road. I was trying to turn her around, but she ducked out from under me, leaving me sitting in the dusty road, wondering what happened! I got up, unhurt, except for my pride, and went to the house crying to Dad about how Betty had bucked me off and wouldn't go down the road.

Dad wasn't very sympathetic, since I wasn't supposed to leave the yard in the first place. He figured it might be a good time for a little more education.

He said, "You understand you are not to leave the yard again without my permission! Now, let's see if we can get Betty to go where you want her to."

He reached in his pocket and pulled out his pocket knife, and cut a switch off a tree limb, as we walked down to the corral. Betty was waiting at the gate, wanting back in the familiar corral.

I looked at the sturdy switch Dad had cut and I envisioned him getting on Betty and giving her a good switching, and making her go down the road. He would show her who was boss! We walked up to Betty and caught her, but Dad didn't get on her!

"O.K. son, you get back on her. Ride down the road and if she tries to turn and come back, use this switch on her rear end, or I'm going to use it on yours!" Dad said.

This little deal had backfired on me pretty bad! I sure wasn't expecting this turn of events and I wasn't too anxious to get back on Betty. I could see Dad meant business and I didn't think much of the idea of getting a switching myself.

I got back on Betty, a little hesitantly. Dad walked along beside us and encouraged me and showed me how to take hold of my reins and pull

Betty's head around if she wouldn't neck rein. She soon saw I meant business. When she whirled and headed back to the corral, I managed to pull her head around and whacked her across the butt with the switch.

She was sure surprised at this treatment, but she trotted down the road the way I wanted to go. Betty had to try to turn back a few more times, but with Dad coaching me, I soon had enough confidence to spank her with the switch when I had to. I kept her headed down the road and just threatening her with the switch was enough to keep her going where I wanted to go.

I sure felt bad about hurting Betty with that switch, but Dad and Uncle Bob assured me no harder than I was switching her she sure wasn't getting hurt much!

Betty and I were both learning pretty fast. I didn't need the switch very often, but when I did have to use it on her I figured it was better for her to get the switching than me!

It wasn't long before I got rid of the switch as Betty liked to go exploring around as much as I did. She was always more than willing to go wherever I turned her.

Uncle Bob had a couple of his saddle horses at our place then and he would saddle up one of his horses and take Betty and me for some pretty long rides out across the prairie. There weren't many fences then, and we could ride about anywhere we wanted. He would tell me stories about cowboying and sure taught me a lot. He really got me hooked on the cowboy life, and guess I never did out grow it! He spent a lot of time with me, and I wanted to grow up and be just like Uncle Bob!

Uncle Dayton and Ray would come by occasionally to visit Mom and Dad. I would rush them down to the corrals and saddle Betty and show them how well I could ride her.

I would try to talk them into taking me with them to the ranch where they were working so I could cowboy with them. Mom just didn't understand! She figured since I was only four or five, I might ought to stay around home for awhile before I took off with them!

Uncle Dayton and Grandma were living at the old Knox home ranch. Dad, took Mom and me out to visit them. I couldn't take Betty, but I knew Uncle Dayton had lots of horses. Maybe I could ride one of his.

Soon as we got to the ranch I ran down to the corral to find Uncle Dayton and see if he had a horse I could ride. He had just ridden in when we got to the ranch.

"Can I ride your horse, Uncle Dayton?" I hollered my greeting to him, as I rushed up to the corral.

"Don't think you can ride this one, Bobby," he replied.

"Can I lead him?" I pleaded.

"You don't give up very easy, do you kid?" Dayton laughed. "I guess you can lead him. His name is Pardner."

He handed me the bridle reins, and I started leading Pardner around the yard. Everyone had gone into the house. As I circled the yard with Pardner following me, he was probably wondering what the heck was going on! He was used to getting fed and turned out, not led all around the yard by a little kid!

I had worked up a pretty big appetite after all of this horse leading. The wonderful smell of fresh baked bread that Grandma had taken out of the oven drifted out the kitchen door.

I decided to take Pardner with me to see if we might get a piece of that fresh baked bread. The old rock ranch house had a big wooden porch across the front, with two steps leading up to the porch. I climbed up the steps to the porch. Pardner followed up the steps right behind me. When he got all the way up on the porch, he stopped. Looking around kind of unsure of his footing, he blew his nose right loud, snorted in my ear and nickered real loud. I had never heard a horse do all that, especially that close to my ear and it just scared the pee out of me! Literally! I just stood there and peed my pants! Dayton heard the commotion and came out to see what I was up to. He saw my predicament and called Mom. He took Pardner down to the corral and unsaddled him, while Mom took me in and I got some dry britches. Boy was I embarrassed! Took a long time to live that one down.

◊   ◊   ◊

The dust storms in southeastern Colorado were pretty bad in those days. Huge clouds of dust would roll in, blocking the sun in midday so that it seemed like night time. I can remember riding down the old dirt roads with Dad driving and Mom peering anxiously out the side window to warn him if he was getting to close to the ditch! The dirt and dust were so thick Dad couldn't see down the road ahead of us, so he would watch out of his side window for the bar ditch on his side! We would all have handkerchiefs tied over our noses and mouths to filter the dust. I would imagine we were the Knox gang of bank robbers with our masks on, going to town to rob a bank! Mom suggested I think of another game to play, as she didn't really want to be a bank robber.

Dust storm, Springfield, Colorado, 1931

Dust storm, Pritchett, Colorado, 1931

4

Trains Whistles and Wild Cattle

Dad took me with him at times to inspect cattle being shipped to market from the big ranches. There were no cattle trucks then, as we know them today. All the cattle being shipped went by train.

Most of the land in Baca County was unfenced at that time. Large numbers of cattle would be gathered off the open range and penned at large corrals, or railheads, as they were called, located along the railroad tracks. Dad's job was to inspect all the cattle being shipped for the proper brand, proving ownership. Most of the large herds of cattle were wearing one common brand, but Dad sure had an eagle eye and was able to spot a "stray" quicker than anyone. The "strays" were cattle that weren't branded, or having someone else's brand on them, not belonging to the rancher that was shipping at that time. They were cut back and the brand checked to see whose brand the animal was wearing. Then the proper owner was notified to come get his cattle. The unbranded cattle were sold, with the proceeds going to the state, unless ownership could be proven. Most of these strays were honest mistakes, as the cattle roamed large areas, and it was fairly common for them to get mixed up. The ranchers all appreciated Dad's job and his skill at spotting brands, as this helped them all, since most of them were honest ranchers.

These railheads were well built, consisting of several large corrals, smaller corrals and a big crowding pen, which funneled the cattle up a long loading chute. The railroad had a siding on the railroad tracks at these stockyards, where they could drop off boxcars that hauled the cattle, leaving the main track clear for other trains to pass while the cattle cars were being loaded. When all the cattle cars were loaded the train would pick them up from the siding and they would become part of the long line of railroad cars.

Without the train engine there to move the boxcars for loading, the cowboys used long pry bars to pry up between the boxcars wheels and the rail, inching the boxcar along the track. Each boxcar had a hand brake on it so it could be stopped. An empty boxcar would be rolled up to the loading chute until it was in line with the loading chute. A heavy plank ramp would be slid from the front of the chute into the boxcar. This ramp provided a bridge from the chute over to the boxcar for the cattle to walk across as they loaded into the big boxcars. Swinging gates from the chute extended out to the boxcar, keeping the cattle from falling or jumping off the ramp.

Then with lots of hollering, cussing, and prodding, the cattle would go up the chute, across the ramp, and into the boxcar. The ramp would be slid back on top of the chute platform. The sliding doors on the boxcar would be closed, and the cattle were ready for a free train ride to Denver, Kansas City, or sometimes Chicago, to the main markets.

These boxcars would hold around 100 head, depending on how big the cattle were. When a boxcar was loaded, it would be rolled on down the siding track, and an empty boxcar would be rolled up to the chute. I liked this part, because I got to help push those big boxcars.

These shippings brought a lot of cowboys together, lots of horses and cattle. What better place could I have possibly found? Dad was well known and respected by all the cowboys, so I guess that's why they put up with me pestering them with, "Can I ride your horse, mister?" I would ask them all, but the answer was usually the same, "Nope" or maybe a grin and "Maybe, when you get a little bigger".

Then I would try another approach, "Since I can't ride your horse, mister, can I lead him?" This usually got a chuckle and quite often a cowboy riding a pretty gentle horse would give in, and I would get to lead his horse. This, of course, wasn't near as good as riding, but at least I was "leading him!" I would walk around leading the cowboy's horse, imagining myself on a big cattle drive and I would entertain myself while Dad was busy checking the cattle for brands.

Once when Dad was going out to the stock yards near Walsh, Colorado, to inspect a large number of cattle I got to go with him. I was excited because he told me there were going to be lots of cattle to inspect and that meant lots of cowboys and horses. Maybe I would get lucky and get to ride one of the cowboys horses!

There were sure a lot of cowboys there that morning, but my efforts to get a ride or even a horse to lead proved fruitless. Just didn't seem to have any luck that morning.

I was sitting on the top rail of the corrals watching the cowboys at work, drifting the steers by Dad so he could read the brands. There were probably 1,000 to 1,200 big steers in the corrals. These steers were pretty wild, having just been gathered off the open range, and not used to being crowded together in a corral.

The railroad tracks went along the west side of the corrals. I was sitting on the south fence, watching the action going on in the corrals. From my vantage point up on top of the corral fence, I could see a passenger train coming down the track.

I stood up on the top rail so I could get a better view of the passing train and wave at the engineer as the train passed. I waved my hat at the engineer as the train rumbled by. The engineer reached up and blew the train whistle as he returned my wave.

The train going by was enough to spook the cattle, but when the whistle blew the steers hit the east fence in a panic. Seemed like a big wave of cattle hit the corral fence all at one time. The corral fence disappeared under the sudden onslaught of the frightened steers. Then they were gone in a wild stampede, running as fast as they could, away from the frightening noise of the passing train and loud whistle.

Several cowboys were on horseback, sorting and working the cattle in the corrals. The rest of the cowboys' saddle horses had been tied or hobbled on the south side of the corrals, and the cowboys that weren't mounted made a mad dash to their mounts. All the cowboys got mounted and took off at a dead run to try and turn the stampeding steers that were leaving Baca County in one big hurry.

The shipping had to be put off several days while the whole east side of the corrals was put back up and the steers gathered again. They had sure scattered in every direction.

Dad said if the cowboys hadn't been so busy running after the cattle they would probably have caught up with the train and hung the engineer for blowing the train whistle and causing the stampede.

I was sure glad I wasn't out there leading some cowboy's horse around! Maybe I had more luck that day than I had thought!

I always wondered: as the train went by and I stood up on the top rail of the corral and waved my hat at the engineer and he waved back and blew the train whistle real loud: did he blow it for my benefit? I never told anybody I waved at the engineer!

Another time, Dad took me to a big shipping and the locomotive engine was setting on the siding ready to take the long line of loaded cattle cars. I had managed to get over by the big engine and the engineer had gotten down and was visiting with me about the big engine. I asked him if I could ride his big train. As it was going through Springfield and had to stop there anyway, he said it would be all right, if Dad agreed. Dad said okay, and I scrambled up in the big black engine, so excited I could hardly stand it.

The fireman showed me how to shovel coal into the giant burners, and I set to work, shoveling coal and then rushing over to look out the window to see if there was anyone around to wave at. I nearly wore the train whistle out, blowing it full blast, but not around any stockyards! Dad met the train in Springfield, and I got off, thanking the engineer and fireman for the great time. I nearly gave up my dream of being a cowboy.

That had sure been fun, shoveling coal and blowing the train whistle! I quickly got back to the real world when we got home where Betty was waiting in the corral for me to come feed her. I gave up the idea of railroading!

5

Denver

Dad got transferred to Denver in 1936. Mom and Dad bought a small acreage out north of Denver. The place had a nice barn and a good set of corrals, with several acres so Betty had a good pasture.

Dad was appointed chief brand inspector for the big Denver stockyards, a pretty big promotion and a lot of responsibility, with the thousands of cattle coming through the stockyards daily. Dad had several brand inspectors working with him, and they sure stayed busy, making sure all the cattle were branded and proper ownership was proven. Swift, John Clay and Co., Cudahy, and several other big beef packing plants were located up on a big hill above the stockyards. Denver stockyards then, as today, were one of the major cattle markets for the western states.

I always enjoyed going to the stockyards when I could. There was an overhead walkway above the stockyards, extending about a mile. You could go up on the walkway and go to the area of the stockyards you wanted to, without walking down in the alleys and through the corrals. There were stairs going down to ground level at regular intervals.

This walkway was a good place for me to play. I could watch all the activity going on in the corrals below. As the cattle were inspected for brands and buyers sorted cattle, I could watch without getting in the way or run over!

I started school that fall of 1936. I was six. I went to a little two room school house about three miles from our place. First through the twelveth grades, all in two rooms! There was a little set of corrals behind the school for kids who came to school on horseback, so I got to ride Betty to school, when the weather was good. I was kind of a fair weather rider then! When it was cold and snowing I sure didn't mind Mom or Dad taking me.

◊　　◊　　◊

Uncle Bob came to stay with us for a while, and he and Dad bought eight dairy cows. Mom had a big cream separator, and I was always amazed at how that machine knew how to separate the cream from the milk! Mom made butter and sold the extra milk and cream.

Uncle Bob figured I was ready to go to work, so I got the job of milking two cows every morning and night. I soon learned how to milk a cow and would sure be proud when I got my bucket full. I wasn't too excited about this new career, but since Uncle Bob was milking cows too, I figured it must be okay for a cowboy to milk cows!

The best part of this venture were the calves these cows produced. They soon grew big enough for me to try and ride. Uncle Bob would rope one of the calves, snub it up to a fence post, put a loose rope around the calf and I would get on, putting my hand through the loose rope. Uncle Bob would pull the rope up tight around the calf and I would grip the rope. Pulling my hat down tight, Uncle Bob would turn us loose! I had lots of bloody noses, got skinned up here and there, but Uncle Bob said I was sure having fun! Later Uncle Bob would complain, "That darn kids got every calf on the place broke to ride!"

◊   ◊   ◊

For Christmas that year, I got a new pair of chaps. They were shotgun style, laced all the way down the back of the leg, with three rows of heavy leather lacing across the front. Dad took the heavy leather lacing out of my new chaps, replacing it with one single light thong. He explained that if I ever got this thong hung over the saddle horn I would want something that would break and turn me loose so that I wouldn't get drug by my horse.

Heck, I wasn't going to get this thong hung over the saddle horn! I took it out and put the three thick thongs back in. They sure looked better with the three heavy thongs!

◊   ◊   ◊

While I was at school and Dad was working, Mom enjoyed riding Betty. She would saddle Betty and ride over to visit a neighbor. This neighbor lady lived a couple miles from our place. Mom would ride down to the crossroad below our house, turn left, and continue on up to the neighbor's. This was a pretty regular visit, and Betty got used to making the turn at the crossroad to go on up to Mom's friend's place. When spring came and the weather warmed up nice, several kids came by our place to play and ride Betty. Some of them had bicycles, and we were all taking turns riding bikes and Betty.

One of the kids had a new bike, and he was sure proud of it. He was bragging about how fast it would go.

"Heck, it may be fast, but I bet me and Betty are faster!" I bragged.

"Bet I can beat you down to Billy's house!" he challenged.

Billy was a little kid who lived about a quarter mile down the road from our place, past the crossroad. He had ridden his bike up to play with the rest of us.

Well, I was sure ready to match Betty against this bicycle, so we agreed on the race course. Straight down the road, passed the crossroad, and finish at the turnoff to Billy's house. Some of the kids who had bikes rode down to the finish line, while others stayed at the starting line.

I was riding my little R.T. Frazier saddle with the nickel silver horn, had my new chaps on and was ready to race. We got lined up. Somebody yelled "go" and the race was on! Betty and I jumped out to a quick lead and were really splitting the breeze, as we stayed out ahead of the bicycle. Some of the kids were running along behind us, yelling and hollering, as we raced down the road.

As we were approaching the crossroad that Mom and Betty had been turning on every day, I was standing up in my stirrups, looking back over my shoulder to see how far ahead of the bicycle we were. Guess I had forgotten to explain the whole plan to Betty 'cause when we got to the crossroad, at a dead run, she turned left, but I didn't!

I kept going straight and, as I fell off, the three leather thongs across the front of my chaps hung over the saddle horn, turning me upside down and hanging down on Betty's side as she turned and kept running.

My nice stout three thongs across the front wouldn't break and drop me off. I just kept hanging there, as Betty really got spooked at this trick riding I was doing and started trying to buck me off. The chap leg began to rip and, as it did, it would lower me toward the ground. Soon my head was hitting the ground, and as the chap leg kept ripping down, my shoulders and back were bouncing along, rolling rocks and dirt clods off the road.

Betty was really scared and was trying to kick this thing hanging down under her. She would kick me and I would swing out and then swing back under her, as she ran in a panic down the road. Her hind feet flying by my bouncing head and shoulders was getting a little scary! Finally the chap leg ripped all the way down and dropped me off in the road. Betty ran on up the road toward the neighbor's place, glad to get out of there.

Dad was out in the yard at our house. He had heard all the kids yelling and hollering, as the race began and progressed down the road.

Suddenly it got awful quiet. Dad looked down the road to see why everyone was so quiet all at once. All the kids were running down the road to where the wreck had happened. He could see Betty running down the road, but couldn't see me on her! He jumped in his car and drove down to where I had crashed.

I was lying along side the road crying my head off, more scared than hurt. I was sure glad to see him .

"Oh Daddy! I'm dead, I'm dead!" I bawled, as Dad checked me over.

Dad assured me I wasn't dead: didn't look like I had anything broke that he could tell. He wrapped his handkerchief around my head where it was bleeding quite a bit.

My new chaps hadn't fared so well! One leg was ripped all the way down.

"How did that lacing get back in these chaps!" Dad demanded as he picked up the pieces! I had no idea!

If I hadn't been pretty banged up I would probably have got a licking over that deal! I got a pretty good talking to about racing bicycles, leather thongs across my chaps, etc.

Dad put me in the car and drove on up the road to where Betty had finally stopped. She was grazing along side the road, not near as upset as I was!

"Do you want to ride Betty home, or shall I lead her?" Dad asked me.

"I'll ride her," I said.

I was glad to get back on Betty and ride home nice and slow and let Mom patch me up. I had lost a lot of hide off my back and shoulders, and had a pretty big knot and some hair and skin missing off the back of my head. The race was indefinitely postponed, but I was ahead at the cross road!!

◆　　◆　　◆

There was a large dairy farm down the road from our place, about a mile away. They milked 50-60 head of Holstein cows twice a day. The cows were kept up in corrals and fed hay.

Spring came and green grass was coming up all around the dairy. It sure must have looked good to those old cows after a winter of eating dry hay. The cows had rubbed a gate down and gotten out of the corrals, grazing on this fresh green grass.

Another farmer had put in a new alfalfa patch about quarter mile from the dairy. Didn't take the dairy cows long to find this fresh green alfalfa either!

I was out by the corrals at our place with Dad and Uncle Bob when we saw a pickup flying low, headed up the road to our house, a big cloud of dust rolling up behind it. One of the men who worked at the dairy had the old pickup running as fast as it could go as he slid into our drive way.

"Where's the fire, Jim?" Uncle Bob asked, as Jim jumped out of the pickup.

"Ain't no fire !" Jim hollered. "We need help quick! All our cows got in that new alfalfa field and most of them are bloated and dying!"

Dad ran in the house and grabbed a couple butcher knives and rushed over to his car as Uncle Bob got in.

"Saddle Betty and come on down to the alfalfa field!" Dad hollered out the car window, as he and Uncle Bob sped off after Jim.

I caught Betty and headed down to see this big calamity. It didn't take me long to get there, and what a sight I rode up on! An old Holstein cow when she is bloated is about the size of a semi-truck, and the field was full of bloated cows laying all around.

Dad and Uncle Bob, along with Jim and the dairy farmer, were rushing from one cow to the next, wielding their long knives. They would push the knife blade in those old cows sides about four inches down from the back bone and four inches in front of the hip bone. As they slowly twisted the blade to open the puncture hole, the gas would blow out of those cows like a whale blowing when it comes to the surface! As I rode up to the field there must have been 25-30 of the bloated cows down. Betty was snorting and sure not wanting too get to close to the oversized cows! The smell of the escaping gas was sure strong and seemed to hang in the air over the field.

To my surprise, once the gas was released, most of these old cows would get up! Some of them were pretty wobbly, but seemed okay as they staggered off to join the other survivors. Dad told me to gather up all the cows that were up and walking and get them out of the alfalfa. I gathered up all the cows that could still walk and drove them across the road a short distance away from the alfalfa field.

After all the cows were up that were going to get up, the dairy owner asked Dad and me if I would like a job, day herding the dairy cows. School was out for the summer and I was quick to say "Yes," and Dad figured I could probably do the job, so I got my first cow punching job!

Every morning after milking they would turn the cows out to graze. My job was to stay with them all day and make sure they didn't find any more alfalfa fields! I had to keep them off the dirt road and out of the few homeowners' yards around and have them back at the dairy by 4:00 P.M. for evening milking.

After my wreck at the horse and bicycle race, Dad decided the best thing for me, being alone most of the day, was to ride bareback. This posed a problem at times, since there wasn't always a rock or log to stand on, for me to get on Betty.

Betty and I worked out a pretty good system. I would lead her to a nice clump of grass and when she reached her head down to graze I would quickly throw my leg over her neck, sit on the back of her head and when she raised her head I would slide down her neck, roll over on my belly and straddle her, ready to go. I was seven that summer, and Betty and I sure had a good time!

Mom would pack me a lunch. I had an old Army canteen of Dad's for a little water, so I made it just fine. The dairy cows were real gentle and I didn't have any problems with them. The dairy farmer would usually drive out to where I was with the cows and tell me when to start drifting them toward the dairy for evening milking. I made fifty cents a day: but heck, if I'd had the money I would have paid him to get to do this job!

This job lasted through the summer, and when school started I had to give it up. It was sure a good taste of punching cows and I even got paid! Boy you couldn't beat a deal like this!

◊   ◊   ◊

Winter came with its cold weather and snow. The school bus picked me up each morning so I wasn't getting to ride Betty much except on weekends. The stockyards were sure getting sloppy with all the snow and mud in them. Dad decided to take Betty into the stockyards to ride, as walking through all the pens inspecting cattle was getting pretty difficult and wearing him out. I got to go with him on Saturdays and ride Betty in the big stockyards, which was fun and a change for me.

A couple blocks up above the sprawling Denver stockyards set the big horse and mule barns. These huge structures covered most of a city block and consisted of various sized corrals, pens, and box stalls. A big hay loft covered most of the box stalls and smaller pens where the horses were kept. This was home to several hundred head of horses used in the stockyards, as well as the Denver Police Department that kept a contingent of their horses there as well.

Monthly horse and mule sales were held here and just before sale days the number of horses and mules would grow to well over a thousand head. I sure enjoyed the chance to go up to these big barns to see all the horses and always tried to get Dad to take me to the big sales.

One cold January night, after Mom, Dad and I had gone to bed, Dad got a phone call confirming our worst nightmare.

"Damn! I'll be right there!" I heard Dad exclaim.

"What is it Lyle?" Mom asked, in a frightened voice.

"The horse and mule barns are on fire!" I heard Dad answer.

I jumped out of my warm bed and rushed into Mom and Dad's room as he was buttoning his shirt and Mom was scrambling out of bed.

"Is Betty all right?" I cried, as Dad was quickly pulling on his boots.

"I don't know. Get dressed, let's go see if we can find her."

As we ran outside to Dad's car, we could see the glow of a big fire on the horizon toward the stockyards. Mom got in beside Dad as I jumped in the back seat and slammed the rear door shut. We left there like we were in the Indy 500! Boy, I didn't know Dad could drive so fast! It was several miles from our place to the stockyards, and we were sure getting there in a hurry.

As we got closer, the flames soon became more visible. Fanned by a strong west wind, the blaze was roaring high in the cold night sky. Huge clouds of black smoke were billowing up as high as you could see.

We were sure scared, as we finally turned down the street leading up to the horse barns. The police and fire department had the street blocked off to vehicles a couple blocks from the fire. Dad parked his old car, and we jumped out, running around the barricades and rushing toward the raging inferno.

We were surrounded by the sounds of the loud scream of the fire and police sirens, the flashing lights. Big white fire hoses lay all over the street. Firemen with their big hats and rain coats were struggling with the big nozzles, as huge streams of water shot out toward the blazing horse barns and corrals. Thick clouds of smoke rolling out of the barns cut our visibility down to just a short distance. We could feel the intense heat from the fire a block away.

As we got closer we could see the street ahead of us was full of panic stricken, milling horses and mules. About two blocks down, the end of the street was blocked off with police cars, forming a big holding area for the horses and mules lucky enough to have gotten out of the burning barns.

Some men had been able to rush through, opening stall doors and corral gates to free some of the horses and mules before the fire became too intense to stay inside. They were unable to get to all the horse and mule pens, and many were trapped in this blazing inferno. A big horse and mule sale was scheduled a couple days from then, so the barns and corrals were pretty full. The cold night air was filled with the smell of burning hair, the panic stricken neighs and screams of terror, as many horses and mules were trapped inside and burned to death.

I was sure in a panic myself, fearing for Betty. Some horses were so frightened that, even though they were out of the fire, they would rush back in looking for the security of their stalls, perishing in the raging fire.

There were so many horses and mules in the street, all running and milling in total confusion and so frightened, that it was impossible to get down the street among them to try and find Betty. The smoke was so thick you couldn't see very far, and Dad wouldn't let me go looking for Betty. Mom and Dad tried to console me as I was bawling my head off, with all this terror and helplessness we were all feeling.

Dad saw one of the yard men he knew real well, up by one of the big fire trucks that was spraying water up on the blazing barns. The man knew

Betty and told Dad he was pretty sure he had seen her running out of the blazing barn. We just hoped and prayed he was right!

The loose horses and mules that were out in the street had bunched up at the far end of the barricaded street, as far away from the fire as they could get. The smoke was so thick we couldn't see into the milling horses and mules very well. The wind was whipping the flames high and the heat from the huge fire was pretty intense, even back where we were huddled together. I never have felt such helplessness as on that night, trying to find Betty in the smoke filled street with the milling, nickering horses.

Eventually the smoke began to lift a little out of the street, and Dad held my hand as we moved closer to the horses. There were so many horses and mules milling around in this mass confusion we couldn't get very close to them.

Then I saw Betty! I pulled away from Dad and ran up the street calling her name and running toward her. She must have recognized me, 'cause she left the bunch of horses and mules and trotted right up to me! Boy, you talk about a happy kid!

Dad took his belt off and buckled it around Betty's neck. He gave me a little boost up, and I hugged her neck, as I rode her down the street to where Mom was waiting. We were sure happy and thankful, as we hurried down the street away from the fire and confusion that cold January night! Betty's mane and tail were singed pretty good, but she didn't appear to be badly burned.

I don't recall how many horses and mules perished that night in the fire. I know it was an alarming number. Dad found a friend there who had a horse trailer and he agreed to bring Betty out to our place that night.

Betty seemed as happy as we all were to be home. She hadn't suffered any serious injuries, only a lot of singed hair and a couple light burns on her back. We were a mighty thankful family that night!

The horse and mule barns were rebuilt, but Betty never saw them! We all agreed she needed to be home with us!

Bob Knox on his first horse, Betty, taken 1935

Bob Knox on Betty giving friend a ride, 1936

Bob Knox on Betty 1937

Dad checking brand

Dad getting ready to rope cow to check brand

Uncle Bob and Dad, Denver 1937

6

Summer with Dayton and Grandma

Things had sure gotten slow for me the year I turned eight. Uncle Bob had left to go off cowboying and left me behind. Dad had sold the milk cows we had, and the dairy didn't need me to herd their cows. I had gotten tired of running up and down the big boardwalk at the stockyards, while Dad was busy checking brands on the cattle.

Uncle Dayton and Baby Grandma had bought a little ranch over on the western slope of Colorado between Hotchkiss and Paonia, and when they asked me to come over and spend the summer I was ready to go! Especially when Dayton said to be sure and bring Betty! Mom and Dad said, "Okay." So Betty and I were headed for new adventures with Dayton and Grandma.

Dayton had several milk cows on his place, so I didn't get away from milking. Grandma had an old cream separator like Mom's. Dayton and Grandma sold milk and cream. There was an irrigation ditch that ran by the front of the house, next to the dirt road. The ditch always had running water in it. After the milk and cream were separated into big milk and cream cans, Dayton would carry the cans up to the ditch, set them down in the water, cover them with an old tarp for shade, and the milk truck would come by every other day, picking up the milk and cream.

Grandma had an old wringer-type washing machine. She used a little stick to push the wet clothes into the wringer and told me to stay away from the wringer, as it was a good finger smasher. The washing machine was green and ran off a little gas engine with a long exhaust pipe running from the motor out about ten feet. The little engine made a real loud popping noise when it was running. The "pop pop pop" could be heard a long ways off, and you couldn't hear anyone talking to you if you were very close! Guess it burned a little oil because with each loud "pop" a perfect little smoke ring would puff out the end of the exhaust pipe. I would try to catch these rings in a sack but never did get a whole one! I would take a stick and try and stack the rings on the stick, but that didn't work either.

Grandma had a bunch of chickens, guinea hens, and a flock of geese. She sold eggs, and one of my jobs was gathering them. Some of those old hens were pretty cranky. They would sure peck you, and I hated having to reach under a hen setting on her nest in search of an egg! There was a little Bantam rooster and four or five Bantam hens in this bunch, with the little rooster being pretty cocky, acting like he ruled the place.

Dayton told me the bantam rooster wasn't so tough. He would show me how to fix him. Dayton took a couple hands full of corn, soaked it in whiskey for a couple days. When Grandma was busy in the house, he threw several kernels of this high powered, spiked corn out in front of the little rooster.

The rooster gobbled up every kernel Dayton gave him. Dayton kinda grinned and said just wait a few minutes. We watched as the rooster scurried about in search of a kernel he may have missed. Pretty quick he got to walking sideways, staggering, loosing his balance and falling over. He would quickly jump back up, look around kinda puzzled, and Dayton and I were sure getting a laugh out of the rooster's antics. But when the rooster reared back and started to crow, landing on his butt, with a feeble little half hearted crow, flopping over on his side kicking like crazy, and flopping his wings, Dayton and I really busted out laughing! Grandma came out of the house to see what we were up to that was so funny. She picked her little rooster up out of the dirt and brushed him off. The rooster sobered up a while later and Grandma informed us in no uncertain terms not to be getting her pet rooster drunk again!

◊　　◊　　◊

Dayton had made me a little catch rope that I was sure proud of. It was a little lighter than his rope, but just right for me. With a lot of practice I was getting so I could rope any post, or rock on the place. I was ready for a little more action!

I was practicing with my rope down by the hay stack, when what should come strutting by, but Grandma's flock of geese. I had always given them a pretty wide berth, as the big gander that ruled this bunch of geese was one mean, cranky, old bird! If I got very close to them, this old gander would take after me, hissing and flopping his wings, and snapping his bill at me.

Since I had gotten so handy with my catch rope, I figured I would just rope that old gander and show him how a cowboy handled wild stock! I hid behind the hay until he was within roping distance. I busted out from behind that hay stack and charged this herd of geese. They all squawked and took off running away from me with their wings spread. I zeroed in on the old gander and roped him around the neck, slick as you please! Well, that was the wrong thing to do, I found out real sudden like. I jerked my slack and took off running, jerking the startled gander down in the dirt. He was flopping around on the ground, squawking his head off. I was afraid I might choke him to death so I gave him some slack. I started going down my rope to take it off his neck and to my surprise, he jumped up, and came to meet me! Boy, he was mad! I took off running but he caught me and knocked me down, pinching me on the back of my legs and my butt with his long bill and beating on me with his wings. I was hollering and kicking at him, trying to get him off of me. Scared the heck out of me!!

He started running off, dragging my rope, and I jumped up and grabbed my rope! Boy, a cowboy sure couldn't let a darned old goose get off with his rope! I jerked him down again but I couldn't get to him to get my rope off without him chasing me. He could sure pinch with his long bill. Well, all of his harem saw his predicament, so they joined in on the squawking part. Boy that was some racket!

Grandma heard the loud commotion and came down to see what had the geese so stirred up. The gander and I were at a standoff by then. He was all bowed up and hissing at me, and I was wondering how the heck I was going to get my rope back; ready to run if he charged me again!

Grandma grabbed my rope, and in spite of the gander's loud squawking and beating wings, she pulled old gander up to her and got my rope off him.

The old gander gathered up his harem, and they took off out of the hay lot. Grandma eared me down across a pile of hay and proceeded to warm the seat of my pants with my good catch rope! I decided right then, posts and rocks weren't so bad to rope after all. At least they didn't chase you, knock you down and pinch the heck out of you like some things did!

◊   ◊   ◊

Of Uncle Dayton and Grandmas several milk cows, I had one cow that I had to milk morning and night. Uncle Dayton would milk several cows, while I managed to get my one cow milked. He enjoyed telling me cowboy stories, while we were milking, and I sure liked hearing his wild tales.

He told me about working for the big Dodge Brothers outfit in southeastern Colorado, at the turn of the century. The Dodge ranch was one of the largest in that part of Colorado then, covering several hundred sections of grazing land. They ran several thousand cows, and had one of the largest horse herds in that part of Colorado.

Mr. Dodge had sold several hundred horses to an outfit in Oklahoma, and Dayton was on the round-up crew that gathered and took this bunch of horses to Oklahoma. They were pretty wild horses, and as they drifted east out of Colorado, across the corner of Kansas, they started encountering barbed wire fences. These fences were something new to these wild horses. Many of them were badly cut and even killed from running through them. Dayton's account of how these badly cut horses were left behind always haunted me as a kid.

◊　　◊　　◊

Mr. Dodge had received a letter from a rancher up near Lamar, Colorado, informing him that they had picked up a couple cows and calves with the Dodge brand on them. The cows were at their headquarters if he wanted to pick them up. Lamar was a good fifty miles from the Dodge headquarters where Dayton was working. Mr. Dodge asked Dayton to go up and bring these strays back to the ranch. Dayton left the ranch early one morning and rode up to Lamar to get the Dodge cows, arriving there that same evening. Next morning, he let the cows and calves out of the corrals and headed back to the Dodge outfit with them. He said he was glad they were a little wild, 'cause they sure lined out pretty fast. He penned the cows and calves at Dodge headquarters and was in time for supper that same night! Over a hundred miles; fifty or more of these miles, following these cows. I guess cowboys and horses were pretty tough in those days!

While Dayton was working out of the Dodge ranch headquarters, he got to know a well-known outlaw who worked there occasionally. (I can't recall the outlaw's last name. His first name was Sam.) Mr. Dodge liked Sam, as he was a pretty good hand and Mr. Dodge tried to help him when he could. Sam asked Mr. Dodge if he did his banking business in Lamar. Mr. Dodge said no, he banked in Springfield. Sam and his gang had planned on robbing the Springfield bank, but with this new information, they went to Lamar and robbed the bank there, not wanting to steal Mr. Dodge's money!

Sam and his gang got out of Lamar after robbing the bank and headed for the Dodge ranch. They rode into the ranch pretty fast, well after dark. Hearing the riders come in, Dayton and a couple other cowboys had stepped out of the bunkhouse near the main house to see who had ridden in so fast. Sam was standing on the front porch, talking to Mr. Dodge. The light from the old kerosene lantern in the house cast its weak light across the open doorway.

The rest of the gang had dismounted and were standing in the yard, giving their horses a chance to catch their wind. Dayton could hear Sam asking Mr. Dodge if he would let them have some fresh horses.

Hearing riders approaching out of the darkness, Sam told his men to hide the horses behind the barn right quick. Sam and three of his men hid in the shrubbery along side of the ranch house. Mr. Dodge stepped back in the house and closed the door, leaving the yard in darkness. Dayton and the cowboys stood there peering into the darkness to see who was coming.

The sheriff and six men in his posse rode up to the house. The darkness concealed Sam and his men, hiding just a few feet from the posse. Mr. Dodge came out on the porch, silhouetted against the lantern light from inside the house.

"Howdy, Mr. Dodge. Sorry to barge in on you this late. The bank in Lamar was robbed today and we were following the outlaws trail until dark and then lost the trail. Was wondering if you might have seen any riders go by?" the sheriff asked.

"No, Sheriff, I haven't seen any riders going by," Mr. Dodge replied.

"We were thinking we might stay here tonight and start looking again in the morning," the sheriff said.

"You know, sheriff, it's only a couple miles over to Horse Creek, and I'd bet those outlaws would camp there tonight. Maybe you could spot their camp fire if you rode on over there!" Mr. Dodge replied.

The sheriff thought a minute, looking at Mr. Dodge. Something wasn't quite right here and he could tell. Mr. Dodge was famous for his hospitality and he sure wasn't showing any tonight.

"You know, Mr. Dodge, you are probably right. We will ride on. We might come up on them if they stop and camp," the sheriff said as he turned and walked back to his horse. "Come on boys, let's go."

They turned and rode out of the yard into the dark. The sheriff knew he was probably riding away from an ambush. He didn't want anyone killed, if it was avoidable.

Sam and his men came out of hiding, holstering their guns.

"Thank you Mr. Dodge," Sam said. "I'll do my best to get your horses back to you soon as I can."

Catching some fresh mounts out of Mr. Dodge's corrals, Sam and his gang saddled up and rode off into the darkness, going the opposite direction from where the posse was headed.

Dayton's father (my Grandad) was deputy sheriff in Springfield at the time this happened and he knew the sheriff from Lamar who had ridden into the Dodge Ranch that night after Sam. The Lamar sheriff told Grandad he knew something was wrong, when Mr. Dodge didn't invite them to get down and spend the night. The sheriff figured Sam was probably looking down a gun barrel at him and knew Mr. Dodge was right. He didn't want a gun fight when the deck was stacked against him!

Dayton's stories sure fueled my imagination, and many a night I would dream of riding with Sam and his gang! Don't know why I always dreamed of being one of the outlaws instead of the sheriff!

◊　　◊　　◊

Uncle Dayton had a pasture, of about a section, where his saddle horses and the milk cows were turned out to graze during the day. If the cows didn't come in on their own at milking time in the afternoon, someone had to saddle a horse and go get them. I was more than willing to saddle Betty and go get the milk cows every afternoon.

Over the course of many years a real deep gully had been washed out down through this pasture. The gully was about ten or twelve foot deep with sides so steep there was no trail across. Dayton had improvised a log and pole bridge across the gully, where it was about twenty feet wide.

Several long poles laid side by side across the gully with short pieces of planks, boards, and anything he could find to make a bridge across the poles. This makeshift bridge was covered with dirt, and made a passable bridge about four feet wide. If given a little time, cows or horses would go single file over the bridge. With the rain, wind, and stock using it, the bridge developed some dangerous holes between the poles along the outer edge. Dayton always cautioned me to approach the bridge with the cattle real slow and let them take their own time to cross.

I was practicing heeling the milk cows on the way to the bridge, one afternoon. They were strung out single file, walking over the bridge. I saw a good opportunity to get a good throw at the last cows heels and rode up close to her. Guess she didn't want to get heeled! She tried to pass the cow in front of her in a no passing zone! Trying to get away from that deadly heel trap I had thrown, she forced the other cow over the side of the bridge. As the cow fell over the side, her hind leg went through a hole between the poles.

Well there she was! Hanging off the bridge by her leg.

I knew it must be broke, as the cow struggled to get her leg free and get up. All she could do was flop around and I sure got shook up in a hurry! I knew I couldn't pick her up and put her back on the bridge!

I eased by her on Betty and took off fast as we could go for the house hollering for Uncle Dayton. He heard me coming and met me at the corral. He listened to me try and explain how for no reason at all, this dumb old cow just took off running and stuck her leg in that hole! I explained the cow couldn't get her leg out of the hole!

He told me to go to the wood pile and get the ax, while he caught up a team of horses. THE AX! NO,NO!, Dayton please not the AX! For some reason, all I could imagine the ax for was to cut the old cows leg off. I was bawling my head off, as I went to the wood pile and got the dreaded ax!

Uncle Dayton drove the team of horses up to a big hay sled, hooked them up to the sled and told me to get on. I was sure shook up, riding on the sled with Dayton, down to the bridge hoping the old cow would be up and all right. Uncle Dayton was pretty quiet as he drove the team at a brisk trot out through the pasture toward the bridge.

As we got close to the gully, we met the milk cows that had crossed the bridge. They were grazing along, headed toward the corrals. A quick count showed we were one cow short. I counted them several times, still hoping the cow had gotten her leg out of that hole and was with the other cows!

As we approached the bridge, there she was, hanging by that leg. Dayton unhooked the team from the sled and turned them around and backed them up close to the cow. He had a long chain and managed to get it hooked securely around her front feet. Hooking the other end to the double trees, he handed me the lines to the team.

"Okay, start them forward and keep them going," Dayton said as he raised the ax over his head.

Oh man, there goes the old cows leg I thought as I started the team forward. I couldn't bear to look. As the chain came tight the cow rolled over and up on to the bank of the gully. Dayton quickly cut the pole in two, freeing the cow. The team dragged her away from the gully. I stopped the team and looked back to see where Dayton had chopped her leg off. It was still there! Sticking out at an odd angle, but not chopped off! Boy was I relieved. I had never thought about chopping the pole in two!

We got the cow loaded and tied down on the sled, and took her to the corrals.

"Now, tell me again how the hell she got her leg in that hole!" Dayton asked.

"I'm sorry, Uncle Dayton. I was trying to rope a cow and she pushed this one off the bridge. I won't rope them anymore," I said. Dayton made a splint and a cast for her leg, and we hung her in a sling from the cross beam in the shed. I hauled water and hay to her every day, while the leg slowly mended. I sure felt bad for causing this old cow so much grief! I managed to slip her a little extra feed, trying to make up to her.

It wasn't long before Dayton let her down out of the sling, and she could limp around on her crooked leg. She was a little slower than the other cows, but she could manage to get around well enough to graze and go out to the big pasture. Just took her a little longer, but at least she didn't get her leg cut off as I had imagined!

Dayton made me leave my rope at the house, after that, when I went to get the milk cows. That was all right with me, 'cause I sure didn't want another deal like that to happen! I hadn't got a licking over this deal, but I had sure learned a lesson.

After getting whipped by the old gander and causing the milk cow to get a broken leg, I decided I might have to stick to roping posts, and rocks, as my experiences with livestock weren't working out very well!

7

A Taste of Haying

I had sure enjoyed my summer with Grandma and Dayton and hated to see summer end. Mom and Dad came over with their horse trailer and loaded Betty and me up, and we went back to Denver. Back to school. Life was pretty dull for a while.

As soon as school was out the next spring, I was ready to head back over to the ranch and spend the summer with Dayton and Grandma. Dayton was helping several neighbors put up hay that summer, and I got a pretty good taste of haying, confirming my earlier resolution to be a cowboy and not a hay farmer!

All the mowing, raking, windrowing, hauling, and stacking was done with horses since no one around there had a tractor. All the hay was put up loose, since no one had a baler then, either. I never got to drive a team of horses on the mower. That could get dangerous in a hurry, if you should happen to fall off the mower in front of the sickle blades.

I could run the buck rake, though, and that was scary enough for me. Sitting up high on the little seat of the big rake above the long curved steel rake tines, driving a team hopefully in a straight line, the tines of the rake would gather the loose hay. When the rake tines were full, there was a foot lever you pushed down with one foot, causing the rake tines to raise up in the air, dropping the accumulated hay in a pile. Then the tines would drop back to the ground and start raking more hay.

The trick here was to dump each rake full so that it was in line with the pile of hay you had raked and piled on your previous pass, forming a long wind row. After all the field was raked into long wind rows, you would drive down the wind row, one horse on each side, and rake the hay into large piles. This took a little doing, because I could barely reach the foot lever and push it down, while trying to stay in the old slick iron seat!

Dayton had a pretty good team of horses, gentle and they knew what they were doing, so I got along pretty well with them. The job I liked to do best was drive the team pulling a slip. A slip was like a big sled, consisting of two twelve-or fourteen-foot long poles, laying on the ground.

The front ends of the poles were beveled, so they would slide over the ground easily. Across the poles were nailed two-by-six planks to make a solid platform. A big rope net (like a cargo net) was laid on the platform. Two men, one on each side, would walk along beside the slip with pitch forks and throw the hay on the slip as it came sliding along between the piles of hay. The load would get as high as a man could pitch the hay. I would sit on the front of the slip as the men loaded it with hay. The hay would get higher and higher around me and I had to keep scooting around trying to keep from getting covered up. Looked like I was setting in the mouth of a big cave.

When the slip was loaded, I would drive to the stacker, where the hay was being stacked or put up in a hay barn. The stacker looked like a real tall windmill tower without a wheel on it. Sticking out at a forty- five degree angle from near the top was a long, stout pole, which swiveled around, with a pulley attached to the end. Through this pulley one end of a cable extended to the ground and the other end of the cable went back to main platform, then to the ground.

I would drive the team under this stacker arm, where the cable was hanging down. A couple of men would bring the ends of the rope net that was under the hay up over the load of hay, hooking them to the cable. There was a quick release attachment on the end of the net with a long rope hanging down. The other end of the cable went out the other side of the stacker and was hooked to another team of horses. The man driving them would ease them forward, and the cable would lift the load of hay off my slip.

As the load of hay started up in the air, a couple of men would get the long rope hanging from the end of the swivel pole and swing the sling load of hay over the stack.

The team pulling this load up would hold it steady, while the men on the stack would position the sling load of hay above where they wanted it dumped. Pulling the release rope, the sling would open, dropping the load of hay onto the stack. With their pitch forks, the stackers would spread the hay out to form a large, even hay stack. It took a lot of man power and good horses to get all this done.

Dayton was sharecropping a small farm for a widow lady named Mrs. Austin. She had a nice little place about a mile west of Dayton's. Mrs. Austin had a daughter a year or two older than me. Her name was Wanda. When Dayton and I were at the Austin farm, Wanda always tagged along.

Uncle Ray had a rodeo string of bucking horses and bulls. He had two big, stout saddle broncs he called Pat and Blondie and he had asked Dayton to break them to work. Pat was a big bay and Blondie was a sorrel with a flax mane and tail. They were big horses, and Ray figured if he could get Dayton to break them to work, he might be able to sell them as a working team. They were halter broke and fairly gentle to handle. Just don't try to ride them! Dayton had them coming along pretty good.

Mrs. Austin had a field of oats, and Dayton and I were going over to get a load of bundled oats out of the field. Dayton figured this would be a good trip for Pat and Blondie, so he had them hitched up to a hay wagon. The wagon had a real high front and back, with no side boards. The plank floor was slicker than slick, from all the hay having been hauled on it. You couldn't hardly stand up on it when the wagon was moving without holding onto the front or back.

Pat and Blondie were doing pretty good on the road as we headed down to Austin's. Wanda came running out as soon as she saw us and wanted to go. Dayton pulled Pat and Blondie to a stop, and Wanda scrambled up on the wagon, standing next to Dayton on his left side, as we started out to the field. I was standing out on the right-hand side, close to the edge of the wagon, as we entered the field. That field had dried out and was as hard as a brick road. Starting across the field to the rows of stacked oat bundles, the wagon got to bouncing and rattling, making a heck of a racket.

Guess that's what spooked Pat and Blondie, 'cause all at once they started snorting and trying to look back at what was making all the noise. The floor was so slick Dayton could hardly keep his feet under him, and couldn't get any leverage to pull much on the lines. Pat and Blondie couldn't see what was after them, but it sure didn't sound very good. The best thing they could think of was getting out of there fast.

Snorting and looking back, Blondie broke into a short lope. Pat was in a fast trot. Dayton's feet were doing a fancy jig as he tried to keep the lines tight. Pat saw that Blondie was getting a little ahead of him and he broke into a lope. Whatever it was after them sounded louder and closer! They both broke into a run and the race was on! We were really trucking! The ground went by pretty fast as Pat and Blondie tried to out run that rattling thing chasing them.

Dayton hollered, "You kids jump off! Were going to tip over!"

Wanda hollered back, "What!?"

Dayton yelled, "Jump, damn it. Were going to turn over!"

We looked at the ground flying by, and Wanda hollered, "No Way!"

Dayton hollered again, as he reached over and gave her a hard push, "Jump, damn it. You might get hurt if we turn over!"

Poor Wanda. She missed the pile of oats we were flying by and hit the hard ground, bouncing and rolling, really plowing up that field!

Then Dayton yelled at me again "Jump, damn it!"

I just shook my head "no," hanging on for dear life. He couldn't reach me to give me a lifesaving push. Boy we were flat out trucking around that field! Kinda like Ben Hur and the chariot races, only our chariot was a slick-floored, rattling, bouncing, old hay wagon!

We made a couple fast circles around that field, knocking down the piles of bundled oats, bouncing over a small irrigation ditch and occasionally catching a glimpse of Wanda lying on the ground.

I thought for sure we were going to get killed in this deal. Pat and Blondie started getting a little winded, and Dayton finally got them into a tight circle, pulled up and stopped.

I jumped off and ran over to help get Wanda up. She didn't seem to have anything broken! Man, she was crying, all skinned up and madder than hell, 'cause Dayton pushed her off the wagon.

"I'm sorry Wanda," Dayton kept saying, as she sobbed. "I was afraid you would get hurt if we turned over!"

"You damned near killed me!" Wanda hollered at him. "Then you didn't even turn over!"

If the wagon had turned over, Wanda would probably have felt better, but we came through the runaway in good shape. But she was sure skinned up!

I don't think Dayton ever did convince her that he was trying to keep her from getting hurt!

8

Delta

When the news came that Dad was going to be transferred to Delta, Colorado, I was sure tickled, because Delta was pretty close to Grandma and Dayton's place up by Paonia. I realized later that Dad was being used as a trouble shooter by the Brand Board. When an outbreak of cattle rustling started up, or a brand Inspection district was having trouble, they would send Dad in to get things straightened out. He had been instrumental in breaking up several rustling rings, while we lived in Springfield, and had gotten the Denver stockyards running pretty smoothly.

There was a large livestock auction in Delta, where a lot of stolen cattle were being sold, so Dad was sent in to enforce the state brand laws. It soon became apparent to rustlers that you better have proof of ownership, if you were going to try and sell any livestock where Dad was working! He caught several cattle thieves and Delta got the reputation of not being a very good place to try to sell stolen cattle.

We had a real nice place three miles east of Delta on Orchard Mesa. A small acreage, but real good for Betty and me. There were lots of trees around the house, and one of my favorite tricks to pull on Betty was to be riding at a high lope underneath these trees, reach up and grab a low hanging limb and pull myself up as Betty ran under it. Soon as she felt me leave her back, she would stop immediately, look back on the ground on both sides for me. She would seem so bewildered, 'cause I wasn't there.

I had outgrown my little kid's saddle, so I rode bareback all the time. Got to where I could sure ride that little mare. She seemed to know what I expected, and we would tear up the countryside.

From our place near Delta it was around twenty miles up to Grandma's and Dayton's. Mom would pack up a little lunch, I would get some water, and Betty and I would go up and visit Grandma and Dayton to stay a few days, every chance we got.

I sure liked Dayton, and we had grown to be good pards. He was real handy with a pocket knife, and when I got to wanting a bow and some arrows, he whittled out some real fine arrows. He took an old metal hoop from around an old wooden barrel and cut a piece with a hacksaw in the shape of a small triangle. Then on the anvil, he would hammer and bend this triangle of steel around the end of my arrow making a pretty nice arrow point. He would select a nicely curved piece of cedar and whittle and shape it into a real nice bow, I had a pretty good hunting outfit!

Grandma wasn't too pleased with my bow and arrows and told me in no uncertain terms that she better not find any chickens or geese with an arrow in them! I would ride Betty up and down by the hay stack, shooting my arrows into imaginary buffalo, elephants and whatever else I could dream up. I would have liked to have shot the old gander that was still mad at me for roping him, but I feared Grandma's wrath if I did, so I let him escape.

Dayton liked to tell tall tales, and really fired up my imagination with stories of seeing buffalo on the range when he was a kid. Boy, would I liked to have had a chance to go hunt a real buffalo with my bow and arrows!

When it came time for me to go back home, I had my new bow and arrows slung across my back. I didn't see any buffalo on the way, but it wasn't because I wasn't looking for them!

We had a milk cow that was kinda Mom's pet cow. She grazed out in a little pasture near the house. There was an irrigation ditch around the edge of this pasture, and weeds had grown up pretty high along the ditch banks. Betty and Mom's cow shared this pasture, along with a couple steers Dad was fattening up to butcher.

With my new bow and arrows I went out prowling around looking for something to shoot. I got down in the weed-covered ditch and started hunting buffalo. I crept along, hiding in the ditch and weeds. I peeked out through the weeds and was sure there was a big bull buffalo grazing right up to where I was hidden! He didn't see me as I raised up and let fly with my steel pointed arrow.

First good shot I ever made! Socko! Right in his side, my arrow stuck. I jumped up out of the ditch and weeds. Sure enough my arrow had gone true, sticking in his side! But upon closer observation, I saw that the big buffalo bull had suddenly turned into Mom's pet milk cow! Oh crap!

To my dismay, the cow let out a strange bawling sound. I had scared the stuff out of her, and she took off running for the house. I suddenly realized she wasn't the big buffalo bull I had shot at! The buffalo was nowhere in sight, Mom's cow was still bawling like crazy, making a beeline to the back door of our house with my arrow sticking in her side!

Well, things got kinda bad there for a little while. Mom came running out the back door to see what the commotion was. The darn cow was still bawling and running like the devil was about to get her! Worst of all was when the cow stopped right at the back door in front of Mom! The evidence was still sticking in the cow's side. Mom grabbed my arrow and gave it a good pull and it came out of the cow. With the arrow in her hand and fire in her eyes, she came to greet her little hunter!

I sure got a good licking over that hunting trip. When Mom finally settled down a little, my bow and all the arrows were broken, mostly across my rear end. The arrow hadn't hurt the cow, just sticking through her hide and hadn't penetrated very deep.

I remember overhearing Dayton and Mom talking later and Dayton saying, "Hell, Ann, I never thought about him shooting your milk cow with those steel pointed arrows!"

Mom must have made a pretty good impression on me because I never did become a bow hunter after that!

◊   ◊   ◊

Uncle Ray came by to visit and eat some of Mom's good cooking. During supper, Mom mentioned she would like to put in a big garden, if she could get someone to plow the garden plot for her. Ray said he had a real good team of work horses that Dayton had been breaking to work and he could sure do this little plowing job for her.

Well, the team he had in mind was Pat and Blondie! I remembered them well from the wild ride they had given Dayton, Wanda and me in the oat field! I commented that it sure wouldn't take long to plow up a garden as fast as those two traveled. Ray didn't think that was funny, and assured Mom that Pat and Blondie were well broke and working good.

A few days later, Ray came riding in on a bronc he was breaking, leading Pat and Blondie. The jingle and rattle of the harness on these two, as they trotted up the road to our house along behind Ray, sounded kinda like sleigh bells.

There was an old plow out behind the barn, and Ray hooked Pat and Blondie to it. Ray eased the horses along, dragging the plow on its side down to the garden plot. They were kinda spooked and acting like they would enjoy a good race, but Ray kept a tight hold on them and got to where he wanted to start plowing.

Ray stood the plow up so that the plowing end was starting into the ground. He eased his team forward. When they felt the tugs tighten and some resistance to their pulling, they got kinda scared. Not knowing what else to do, they decided to run off! Ray didn't want to run off, so he jammed the point of the plow in the ground as deep as he could and that sure put a stop to the running off for a minute. Pat and Blondie stopped with the plow as deep in the ground as it would go, they couldn't pull it. Ray pulled back on the plow, pushing down on the handles. This tilted the digging point of the plow up to the top of the ground so the team could pull it again. Pat and Blondie weren't used to this heavy pulling. Pat would lunge forward, Blondie would set back, and the plow would veer off to the left. Then Blondie would lunge forward, while Pat was setting back, and the plow would veer off to the right!

Ray was pretty busy, trying to adjust the depth of the plow as they veered off, first to the left and then to the right. The horses would start moving out a little too fast, and Ray would jab the plow point down real deep. That sure worked as a good break. He managed to keep them from running off. The rows were sure crooked. Some of the ground was plowed over two foot deep and, at other places the top of the ground was barely scratched.

It was sure funny watching Ray zigzag around Mom's garden plot, stumbling along behind Pat and Blondie, trying to keep the plow in the ground and in a straight line! Mom was satisfied with Ray's job and assured him the rows didn't have to be straight! I was disappointed though, 'cause I knew how Pat and Blondie could run, and they didn't get away from Ray!

Next morning Ray saddled the bronc he was riding and harnessed Pat and Blondie, ready to go back up to Dayton's. I figured there might be a little bronc riding that morning and I didn't want to miss it! Dayton had told me this bronc Ray was riding could sure buck and was pretty tough to ride. I wasn't disappointed!

Mom had a clothesline out in the backyard. It wasn't quite as long as she wanted, so Dad had strung two strands of barbed wire from the back of the old outhouse over to a big cottonwood tree nearby. This gave Mom a little extra space to hang laundry on.

Ray led his bronc out of the corral and stepped up on him. Before he got all the way on, the bronc blew up, bucking and bawling, really getting with it. Ray was pulling everything he could get a hold of trying to stay with the bronc. He was doing a fair job of riding him. They were sure digging up the ground, as the bronc bucked toward the outhouse and the barbed wire clothesline. The bronc was getting high in the air and Ray sure had his hands full trying to stay with him.

The bronc was headed between the outhouse and the big cottonwood. Ray could see the barbed wire clothes line approaching pretty fast. He hollered "wup,wup,WUP!" and had to bail out as the bronc bucked under the barb wire. He hit the ground hard, just as his saddle horn hooked one strand of the clothes line. The wire broke. The loose end of the wire caught around the saddle horn and the front of Ray's saddle, chewing most of the leather off the horn and cutting the front of his saddle up pretty bad.

The bronc bucked on down to the corner of the small pasture around the house and stopped. Ray caught him, kicked him in the belly a couple times and stepped back on. The bronc blew up again, bucking and bawling, really making Ray bare-down. But he got him rode. The bronc finally quit bucking and Ray came riding back up to the house, commenting rather strongly about barbed wire clotheslines!

Ray picked up the lead rope on Pat and Blondie, and they headed at a long trot, back up to Dayton's place. I was glad I didn't have to ride his horse, nor plow with Pat and Blondie!

◊   ◊   ◊

A couple of weeks later, Uncle Ray came by and was pleased to see his plowing efforts had worked out so well. A few plants were showing along the crooked rows.

"I traded for around twenty head of those wild horses that were caught out west of Delta," Ray was telling Dad. "I'm going to get them in the stockyards in a couple days and could sure use some help branding and castrating some of the studs. Dayton's coming down to do the castrating. Think you can rope them for us?"

"I can give you a hand next Saturday," Dad replied.

"Can I go!?" I exclaimed.

This was the most exciting news I had heard in a long time!

"I doubt that I could get away without you!" Dad laughed.

I had a hard time sleeping that night with the thoughts of roping and branding this bunch of wild horses running through my mind. Seemed like Saturday would never come.

On Saturday morning, I was up well before daylight, wondering why Dad was so late! Mom came into the kitchen and was sure surprised to see me setting at the table with my hat on and my rope in my hand. She laughed as she started the coffee and got out the bacon and eggs.

"I wonder if you would get up this early for school if they had a class on horse branding?" Mom asked me.

Dad came in a few minutes later and he, too, was surprised to see me up and ready to go. He gave Mom a questioning look.

"He was here when I came in! I think he might want to go with you today!" Mom laughed as she poured Dad a cup of coffee.

"Sorry son, but you better leave your rope at home today. These horses are pretty wild and I don't think you are quite ready for one of them yet," Dad said, as Mom fixed us some breakfast.

We finished our bacon and eggs and jumped in Dad's car and headed down the road toward the stockyards, out west of Delta. I didn't much want to leave my rope, but at least I got to go! I was sure excited as I fired one question after another at Dad about branding horses.

As we approached the stockyards, I could see a cloud of dust coming up out of the corrals and I knew the horses must already be in the corrals.

Ray was gathering up some wood for a fire to heat the branding irons. Dayton was squatted down, leaning up against the corral fence, sharpening his pocket knife. I knew what that was for!

The bunch of wild horses were milling around the corrals, snorting and stirring up a lot of dust. They were sure watching us. First time a lot of them had ever been in a corral and they weren't liking it much. A big bay mare, blind in one eye seemed to be the leader. There were several studs of various ages in the bunch. Eight mares with colts at their sides and some young two-and three-year old mares. About twenty head total and all wilder than seven hundred dollars!

The branding-iron fire in the middle of the corral was burning well, and the irons were hot. Dad picked up his rope, shook out a loop, and I got an education on the fine art of fore-footing a wild running horse.

Standing with his back toward the horses, Dad held his loop in his right hand, coils in his left. Holding the loop about shoulder height with his arm across his chest, the loop stood open on his left side.

Dad stood about fifteen feet from the corral fence, so that the running horse had room to run between him and the fence. Dayton and Ray ran the horse by Dad. As the horse ran by, Dad timed it just right, so that when he rolled the open loop across the front of his body, the loop would stand up right in front of the running horse's front feet. The top of the loop was about shoulder high on the horse with the bottom just clearing the ground.

The loop caught the horse by his front feet every time. Dad jerked the slack out of the loop, holding the rope across his hips as the horse ran by. When the loop tightened around the horse's front feet, Dad jerked his feet out from under him, and down the horse would go.

When the horse hit the dirt, Dayton and Ray were on him right quick. Ray grabbed his head, and twisted it around, holding him down. Dayton and Dad quickly tied his feet together, so the horse couldn't get up. It was sure pretty to see Dad, who weighed about 115 pounds soaking wet, roll that forefoot loop out there and catch a running horse by the front feet, jerk his slack, set back on that rope, and flatten this wild, running horse slicker than slick!

I really wanted in on some of this action, but everybody kept telling me to get back out of the way. And some less complimentary things. I saw an extra rope laying there on the ground. Everyone was busy working on a horse they had down. I knew a good opportunity when I saw one! At least I thought I did!

I picked up the rope, shook me out a big loop, and started sneaking up on a horse to rope.

A bunch of horses was crowded up on the other side of the corral. The big one-eyed mare was watching the men and the horse they were working on. Her blind side was toward me offering me just the chance I was looking for. I slipped around and managed to get up pretty close to her.

She didn't see me sneaking up on her. I knew I couldn't forefoot this old, wild mare, but I figured I would rope her around the neck.

I sailed my loop up and it settled around her head real pretty like. Well, that was my big mistake of the day! When that rope touched her, she snorted and left this world, kinda like a rocket headed for the moon with me hanging on for dear life! I wanted to hold on, but when that rope went to sizzling thru my hands I sure wanted to turn loose. I couldn't get the rope out of my hands.

I got jerked down and, still holding onto the rope, the mare dragged me halfway across the big corral before the rope finally smoked on out of my hands. Boy, you talk about hot! The rope had burned all the skin off my clenched hands. Dad helped me out of the dirt as I howled with pain, shaking my hands.

"What did I just get through telling you about roping these horses!?" Dad said as he looked at my still smoking hands.

"Well, he did make a pretty good catch, Lyle!" Uncle Dayton offered.

Uncle Ray just laughed, as Dad wrapped a couple of handkerchiefs around my hands and told me to sit on the fence and not to pick up another rope. He didn't have to tell me that! I'd had enough roping for a while, and my hands were burned so deep I couldn't even hold a rope!

When the branding was finished, Dad took me home. Mom was a little more sympathetic. She doctored me with bacon grease and salve. I couldn't open my hands for a week or so. They were burned into a half closed position! After that, I wasn't too anxious to rope another one-eyed mare!

As my hands slowly healed, I had time to reflect on my roping exploits. So far they hadn't been too good! The darned old goose had whipped me and pinched the heck out of me. I had caused Uncle Dayton's cow to get her leg broke and now this wild mare had about ruined my hands. I began to wonder if I was meant to be a roper or not!

Heck, I was just getting started!!

9

Summer on the Muddy

I was ten the summer Uncle Ray was taking care of a bunch of cows up above Somerset, Colorado, on a Forest Service allotment on the Muddy River. There were several thousand acres in this allotment. A group of ranchers and farmers from around Paonia, Hotchkiss, and Bowie had gone together to run cattle on the Muddy allotment for the summer. Each rancher had put a varying number of cows and calves, and a few bulls in the herd. The total herd was around three hundred and fifty to four hundred head.

The group of ranchers had hired Uncle Ray to care for the cattle during the summer, and he said he would be glad for me and Betty to come along. Boy, was I excited to get to punch cows with him in that high country. I hadn't looked forward to another summer in those hot hay fields with Uncle Dayton.

There was an old dirt road that climbed and wound around through the mountains above Somerset and went on up to Carbondale. The road went within about six miles of where we were going to camp for the summer. A pretty good trail turned off from the road and followed a good- sized stream up through the mountains. The trail wound around through aspen, pine and big fir trees and big open meadows with lots of grass.

An old dilapidated cabin and a set of corrals that were in bad need of repair were setting on the edge of a big meadow with the stream running nearby. Home for the summer! Sure looked good to me, even though there was no stove in the cabin. We did our cooking over a campfire and I thought that was pretty slick!

Uncle Ray had several saddle horses, and a couple were gentle enough for me to ride. So I could give Betty a rest once in a while. We sure covered a lot of country every day, checking the cattle and keeping them on the allotment. There weren't any fences, so we stayed busy keeping track of the cattle. Saw lots of deer and elk everyday, which made it nice as Uncle Ray sure did like elk and deer meat! We never ran out of fresh meat. It didn't take long for me to get toughened up to all the riding, and I was sure enjoying riding this high country. I got pretty tired and saddle sore, but, when thinking about the hay fields, I figured I was pretty lucky.

We needed a few groceries after a few weeks, so Ray and I rode down to Somerset. Ray called one of the ranchers we were riding for and made arrangements for a widow named Mrs. Green to come up to our camp and cook for us. Only problem was, Mrs. Green was one of those picky women who wanted a stove to cook on! Somehow Ray got an old stove delivered by pickup to the trail that went up to our camp. The stove was a full-sized, wood-burning, kitchen range. "Home Comfort" in big letters across the oven door promised a chance of oven-baked biscuits and maybe a cake!

We had to figure a way to get this big stove up to our camp. The six miles of horseback trail seemed pretty long, as we looked the stove over. Part of the trail went up along a hillside well above the stream. The trail got pretty narrow along this hillside for about a hundred yards or so.

Uncle Ray cut a couple poles about eight-or-ten foot long, about six inches in diameter at the big end. He spaced the poles about two feet apart at the small end and tied a stout piece of rope between the poles. With a pole on each side of our pack horse, he looped the rope between the poles around the front cross piece of the pack saddle. The poles extending out behind the pack horse were spaced so they didn't rub the horse, and they were tied so they couldn't spread apart. This rig was like a travois, used by the plains Indians. Bet they didn't haul many big "Home Comfort" kitchen stoves on them! We took the lids and grates out of the stove and tipped the stove over on these poles behind the pack horse. The poles bowed down but didn't break, so we tied our stove to this makeshift sled.

We headed up the canyon along the trail with our stove in tow, everything sliding along pretty well. The pack horse was pretty gentle and didn't mind this contraption dragging along behind him. The canyon narrowed down, and the trail left the bottom of the canyon, climbing along the steep hillside. The trail along the hillside was real narrow; not wide enough for our load to pass by without the chance of falling off the hillside into the stream below. It was forty or fifty feet nearly straight off down to the stream.

We took our stove off the sled, and I got one end and Ray got the other. Boy, that sucker was heavy! I couldn't carry one end hardly, and Ray got mad and told me to get the h— out of the way. He would carry it himself! He took a piece of rope, and made a kinda harness with the rope. He crossed it behind his neck, under his arms, across his back and then around the front of the stove.

Leaning back and lifting the stove off the ground, Ray started along this narrow trail. He had to walk sideways to keep from hitting his shins on the stove. He was quite a sight, with that monster stove tied around his neck and shoulders. Red-faced, huffing, puffing, and cussing about women that had to have stoves to cook on, he side-stepped along the trail. He had to stop and rest a couple of times and hollered for me to come and help steady the stove, as he eased it down to touch the ground so he could catch his breath. Seemed like it was a mile or two to me, but this narrow trail was only about a hundred yards. It was sure a relief when the trail came off the hillside and we could get the stove back on our sled. We made it into camp with old "Home Comfort," without any more trouble, and wrestled it into the kitchen.

Ray had made arrangements with the guy who hauled the stove up to the trail to bring Mrs. Green up the next day. So we took a pack horse and a saddle horse for her to ride and met them at the road. Mrs. Green was sure a nice lady. We packed her stuff on the pack horse along with the lids and grates and two or three joints of stove pipe for our new stove, and headed out to camp. Mrs. Green could ride pretty well. She climbed up on the saddle horse we had brought for her and followed us back up to camp.

We got the stove all set up, while Mrs. Green was getting settled. That night, she cooked up a pretty good supper on old "Home Comfort." She was a good cook and, sure enough, lots of biscuits and several cakes came out of that old oven that summer. Ray even thought packing the stove in was worthwhile, after he got a taste of Mrs. Green's cakes!

Mrs. Green made up a long grocery list of things she needed, so Ray sent me down to Uncle Dayton's to pick up the stuff. It was around thirty miles down to Dayton's place, so I left pretty early. Leading our pack horse, I got to Dayton's late in the evening and was sure glad to eat some of Grandma's good cooking and sleep on the big feather mattress I always got to sleep on while at Grandma's.

Dayton decided to ride back with me to our camp on the Muddy. He saddled his best horse, "Bob", a big bay. Sure a good horse. Bob was a little snorty, but didn't have any buck to him; just spooky, always looking for boogers.

Dayton and I picked up all the groceries we needed in Paonia and loaded our pack horse. I was riding Betty, leading the pack horse as we rode through the small community of Bowie, a few miles east of Paonia. The dirt road went along parallel to the railroad tracks. A big black engine was sitting on the siding beside the road, as we approached. Smoke was slowly rolling out of the big smoke stack.

Bob was watching this scary-looking thing. Looked like a big, black, smoking booger ready to jump out and grab him. With both ears cocked at the engine, and snorting loud, Bob was really zeroed in on this big spooky-looking thing. Being on the other side of Bob, away from the engine, Betty wasn't shying as much as Bob was, but she was sure watching it, too.

Just as we got along side of the engine, the engineer let off a big stream of steam, shooting it right out at us. Bob tried to climb right straight up and out of this world. Dayton managed to grab the saddle horn, as Bob's rocket boosters kicked in and he went over Betty and me!

They were both suddenly on the other side of Betty and me. Betty didn't know what had got Bob, but she wasn't staying around to find out. She bolted after him. The pack horse jerked back and I lost the lead rope as we all stampeded out of there!

We finally got pulled up, and I caught the pack horse. Dayton was sure one mad cowboy. Cussing a blue streak, he stepped off Bob and handed me Bob's reins. Stomping across the dirt road, heading for the engineer, Dayton began telling him what he was fixing to do to him, referring regularly to the engineer's family tree!

The brakeman from the train jumped down out of the engine. He tried to slow Dayton down a little. Dodging Dayton's good roundhouse right, the guy finally got him stopped before he climbed up in the engine.

Dayton gave the engineer about as good a cussing as anybody ever got. He got the scared engineer's apology and a promise not to blow steam at horseback riders. Dayton usually wore his pistol when riding, but fortunately for the engineer, he didn't have it with him this day. No doubt Dayton would have shot the engineer!

We made it on up to our camp without further incident. Dayton was still cussing the train engineer, mad at himself for not having his pistol with him!

We started gathering the cattle off the Muddy around the end of August. Dayton and several cowboys came up and helped with the roundup. This was sure fun for me, getting to ride with them and seeing how they worked and rode. One of the ranchers brought his boy with him, Rusty Gordon, about a year older than me. Rusty was a red-headed kid; face liberally covered with freckles. He was a good rider, and we sure hit it off pretty good. He liked to rope about as much as I did, and we were always getting hollered at to "put them damned ropes up!"

The round up went well. The herd of cattle was brought down off the Muddy, and we penned them at the big stockyards in Bowie. The owners separated their cattle, and most of them drove their small bunches to their respective ranches.

Dayton, and a couple ranchers who had places near Dayton's, had about 100 head of cows and calves. They decided to leave them in the stockyards overnight at Bowie and move them on down the next morning.

Rusty and I were elected to stay overnight with the cattle at the stock-yards, because they didn't want to leave the cattle there unattended overnight.

Rusty and I weren't overly excited about this deal. But they assured us we would be just fine. They told us to gather up some firewood and keep a fire burning, not to worry, and they would be up early next morning to help us bring the cattle down. Dayton, Ray and the other two men turned their saddle horses loose in one of the corrals, threw their saddles in the back of their old pickup, and headed for Dayton's place, leaving Rusty and me on guard.

As darkness started creeping in on us, Rusty and I threw more wood on our fire. We shared a can of tomatoes, a couple biscuits and a few strips of bacon we had brought with us from breakfast that morning.

Sitting around our campfire we started telling each other ghost stories. Rusty knew a couple really spooky ones, and we sat a little closer to the fire. I don't know what time it was when we realized we were about out of fire-wood. Neither of us wanted to go out in the dark and look for more wood.

"How far is it to your Uncle Dayton's place?" Rusty asked me.

"Not very far," I answered, "I rode down there awhile back, and it didn't seem very far."

"Think we could take these cows by ourselves?" Rusty asked, as he peered out into the darkness around us.

"Heck yes! We have a road to follow all the way and there is a little moonlight. Better than sitting here freezing to death!" I replied.

Neither one of us mentioned that it was sure scary in those stockyards in the dark!

We put our dying fire out, saddled up and turned the herd out, heading them down the road.

A ten-and an eleven-year-old kid, middle of the night with around a hundred head of cows and calves, six loose saddle horses, two small towns to go through and about twenty miles to Dayton's! Guess the good Lord takes care of drunks and kids!

The loose saddle horses sure knew the way home, as did most of the cows, and they strung out down the dirt road. With Rusty in the lead to hold the loose horses back from getting too far ahead of us and me bringing up the rear, away we went!

The road went thru the little town of Bowie. Bet there were some surprised people in town the next morning, when they found their yards and flower gardens full of cow tracks and a little fresh fertilizer our cow herd had left as we passed by in the middle of the night!

There wasn't much vehicle traffic that late at night. Some of the road was fenced, but most of the way was open range. Those old cows lined out pretty good, and we didn't have too much trouble keeping them together. The loose horses soon settled down to a running walk, so Rusty could come back on the sides and help me when the cattle got to spreading out too much. We soon warmed up, and it was kinda fun riding along in the dark, hollering at each other.

The next town was Paonia, quite a bit bigger than Bowie, with lots more yards, flower gardens, etc. for us to ride across. Funny how much those old cows enjoyed eating the pretty flowers. They picked the full blooms off and ate them like they had found something really tasty! They thought the mailboxes were put up for them to rub on, and they sure knocked a bunch of them over!

We met a few surprised motorist's in town, but they pulled over and only gave us questioning looks as we rode by. We gave them a big wave and smile and acted like we knew what we were doing!

Somehow we got out of town without the police coming after us and continued on down the old country road.

Rusty and I both sure got sleepy as we rode on through the dark, cold night. Nearly fell off a time or two, as we dozed off. Kinda wished we had another town to go through! Riding through peoples' yards, dodging tree limbs and mailboxes kept us awake.

We traveled all night, and were only a mile or so from Dayton's place as it was beginning to get light in the east. We could see the headlights of an oncoming vehicle, as it pulled over and stopped. We drove the herd past the stopped vehicle. As we rode up to the vehicle we saw it was Dayton, Ray and the other men in their old pickup.

"What the hell are you two kids doing out here with these cattle and horses in the dark!!?" That was kinda the drift of the conversation there at first. We tried to explain that we had gotten hungry and cold. Never mentioned we were a little scared, too.

These reasons didn't seem to satisfy them and they were talking about kicking our rear-ends, but good. Things didn't look too favorable for us. They turned the old truck around and went down the road a short distance to the gate going into Dayton's place.

They got a good count on the cattle as Rusty and I drove them thru the gate. To Dayton and the other men's surprise, we had them all!

First they started bragging on us. Then, they gave us hell for doing such a fool thing! Then, they would brag on us again! They were glad the cattle were there, but they weren't very happy with us for being out on the road at night alone with all their cattle.

Well, it didn't seem like such a big deal to Rusty and me. We had fun going through the towns, checking out all the nice yards! We had stayed fairly warm riding, and it wasn't near as spooky as those old stockyards in the dark!

10

The Gunnison River

Dad was transferred to Colorado Springs, and we had moved into a house in Manitou Springs, where I started school. I had left Betty over at Uncle Dayton's, and I wasn't real happy living in town. When school was out that spring, I was packed and ready to go to Uncle Dayton's the next day. Mom loaded me up, and we headed out for Delta and a few more adventures.

Uncle Dayton and Grandma had sold their place up near Paonia. Grandma was staying with my aunt Tina in Grand Junction. Dayton had bought a little house on about ten acres on the edge of Delta. The house didn't have electricity or water, but Dayton was happy batching there. He and Ray would usually winter there, leasing some grazing country in the summers. Mom took me to Dayton's place in Delta. Betty was there waiting for me, and it was a great reunion, riding her again. Mom went back to Manitou Springs, and I was happy being there with Uncle Dayton and Betty.

The next morning we saddled up, loaded our pack horse, and set out for my new home for the summer. I was as happy as though I had good sense!

Dayton and Ray had leased a place about fifteen miles west of Delta, on the Gunnison river. The camp was on the south side of the river. It was a small three room shack, with the barn and corrals mostly fallen down. It was pretty barren old country; dry, without much feed for livestock. This country was sure a big change from the pretty, high mountain country up on the Muddy.

The river was about fifty yards from the camp and was pretty wide and deep. It would swim a horse about any place you chose to cross it, all the way up to Delta, and was pretty dangerous in lots of places. There was a real strong undercurrent, with lots of big, dangerous whirlpools in it that would sure get a rider in trouble if he got into one of those big whirlpools.

We had several places where we could cross the river. They had good gravel bottoms, so the livestock had good footing going in and coming out. All the crossings were pretty deep, forcing a horse to swim, but safe enough.

On the north side of the river was BLM land. We didn't have a permit to run any livestock on the BLM land; however, with a little encouragement from the three of us, Dayton and Ray's horses and cattle would swim the river and enjoy the BLM grass until one of the BLM men came raising hell about our stock being on BLM land. Then we acted surprised and bring them back for a while.

Dayton and Ray had a good-sized string of horses then, around thirty to forty head. There were several mares and colts, but mostly bucking horses. They furnished stock for several rodeos around that area each summer. They had around forty to fifty cows and several pretty good bucking Brahma bulls. The BLM men really got excited when they found this bunch grazing where they weren't supposed to be.

◊   ◊   ◊

One weekend we had made a trip into Delta and were following the trail from Delta along the Gunnison river, back to camp. Ray was riding a bronc and Dayton was mounted on his good horse, Old Bob. I was riding Betty. Ray and Dayton didn't have a vehicle, so we traveled horseback with a pack horse or two.

Ray saw some of their stock over on the north side of the river, on the BLM land. They decided they would swim their horses across the river and check the stock on the other side, on the way down to camp. I was to stay on the south side with the pack horses and go on to camp. The river was running pretty high and swift. Dayton thought it looked pretty dangerous and said they should ride on down a couples miles to a known crossing. Ray argued they could cross right there. Said he'd crossed there all the time; it wasn't very deep. Dayton argued that it was too swift and deep with no place to get down to the water without jumping off a three-or-four foot bank.

Ray said the magic words then, "Hell, are you afraid!?"

"Afraid, hell! Come on!" Dayton said to Ray, as he spit a big stream of tobacco juice in Ray's general direction.

Dayton wasn't afraid of the devil himself! With his left foot, he reached up, and spurred Bob in the shoulder, and turned him off that bank, into the river. Old Bob tried to jump the river! They hit the water in a big splash, about ten feet from the bank, and both he and Dayton went under and out of sight. I got scared when I couldn't see them because I knew Dayton couldn't swim a lick! Lots of bubbles showed where they had gone under the swift, muddy water.

Old Bob's head finally popped up above the water, and he started swimming. Dayton's hat floated a little ways, then slowly disappeared under the rushing water. Suddenly, behind Old Bob, Dayton appeared. Spitting, choking and flailing his arms, he grabbed for anything around. Luckily, Old Bob's tail came within Dayton's frantic reach. Dayton grabbed that tail and hung on for dear life. Old Bob kinda looked the situation over and started swimming down stream and back to the south side, towing Dayton along behind.

I couldn't believe Ray. He got so tickled at Dayton's predicament, he liked to fell off his horse laughing. I was scared to death for Dayton, but seeing him hanging onto Bob's tail, it looked like he was going to be all right. Guess it was kinda funny, with all the spitting, yelling and cussing going on, but it sure wasn't funny for a while.

Dayton was yelling some pretty unkind threats at Ray, telling him all the different ways he was going to kill him! Ray, being of near average intelligence, decided to get out of there while he could. He just turned and rode back up the trail toward town.

"I'll see you later!" he said as he rode off, still laughing.

Old Bob had to swim quite a ways downstream before the bank sloped to the water enough to where he could get out of the river. I hurried along the trail watching Old Bob still dragging a wet, cussing, mad, Uncle Dayton.

Old Bob finally found a place he could come ashore! Shaking himself like a dog, his nostrils flared as he looked back at the river. He snorted right loud at Dayton, who was on his hands and knees at the water's edge, still spitting, coughing and cussing. Not necessarily in that order!

"Where the hell's my hat?" he demanded.

"It sunk," I said, trying to keep a straight face.

This bit of news sure didn't do much to improve his disposition.

"Where the hell's Ray!"

"He had to go back to town."

"What for?"

"He didn't say."

"I'm going after him and I'm going to kill him!"

He was ready to take off up the trail after Ray, but I finally talked him into going on down to camp.

We got into camp and got a fire going. Dayton dried out and fixed supper. He was still madder than hell and couldn't eat. Dayton figured Ray had lied to him about the river not being very deep. He had damned near drowned and he blamed Ray.

He got his old .45 pistol out of his bedroll and strapped it on. He paced the floor between the door and the window looking out for Ray. He kept saying Ray had to come back sooner or later, and when he did he was going to shoot him on sight! He stayed up all night waiting for Ray. I was too scared to sleep much for fear Ray would come in and Dayton would shoot him.

That summer, Dayton and I had a lot of fence work to do, and quite a bit of riding needed to be done. We were needing a little help. Ray finally showed up about four, or five days after the river incident, carrying a new hat for Dayton.

Dayton was glad to get him back to help us so he didn't shoot him; but he gave Ray one of his famous cussings. He figured it was Ray's fault that he had nearly drowned! The new hat helped soothe his wet feathers, though!

◊   ◊   ◊

My friend Rusty Gordon came out to spend a week with us, while we were at the Gunnison river camp. I hadn't seen Rusty since the summer before when we were up on the Muddy. We had a good time riding together and, being kids, we sure had fun swimming.

About a half mile above camp, where we usually crossed the river, was a place where the river had cut back in the bank, making a nice big, swimming hole. The strong river current didn't hit this hole with much force, so it provided a nice place to swim. We would pull the saddles off our horses and leave them, along with our clothes, on the bank. We would ride out into the big pool to where the water came up on the sides of our horses, dive off our horses, and swim back, climb on, and jump off again.

I had Betty to ride and Rusty had an old horse about the same temperament as Betty. They would stand out in the water, and wait patiently for us to climb on and jump off. This was sure a lot of fun for us.

◊　　　◊　　　◊

We had helped Dayton and Ray gather around forty head of horses that were on the BLM land. We were going to bring this bunch of horses into the corral at our camp and had bunched them about a mile from the river. Being short a few, Ray rode off looking for them. Dayton sent Rusty and me on to the river, so we could be in position to turn the horses when they came across.

This bunch of horses was a little wild, led by the old one-eyed bay mare I had met before. Soon as "Old One-Eye" would cross the river, she would turn east with the herd following her, away from the corrals and camp. If someone wasn't there ahead of her to turn them, they would get away. Then, they were pretty hard to catch and bring back.

Well, it was along in August, really hot. After riding all morning the river sure was inviting to Rusty and me. We figured it would take Ray quite a while to find the other horses. We were really hot, and our swimming hole was pretty close to the crossing. Heck, we could see them when they came off the hillside down to the river, so why not? We swam our horses across the river and rode down to our swimming hole. We could see the far side clearly, so we pulled our saddles, shucked our clothes, and hit the water!

Boy, that old cool, muddy water sure felt good after a long, hot ride that morning. We laughed and had a good time. We kept a watchful eye on the hillside where the trail came down, expecting the bunch of horses to show up at a walk or slow trot. But all at once this bunch of horses came flying off the hill, heading for the river at a full run! "Old One Eye" was in the lead, really leaving the country.

The horses hit the river at a run and started swimming across. Man, we didn't have time for anything! We knew we had to be above them when they came out of the river to turn them west on down the river toward the corrals.

There we went, two naked kids, riding bareback as fast as we could go. The old one-eyed mare saw us coming and she was swimming hard, trying to get out of the river before we could get above her and the band of horses. The deep water slowed her enough so that we beat her and, when she came out of the river, she kinda threw her head up and down at us, like she was saying okay, you won this time. Or maybe laughing at us?

Dayton and Ray came riding up out of the river. Dayton was really laughing. Said that was the first time he had seen two cowboys, naked as jay birds, riding as fast as they could go, and riding bareback! Ray didn't think it a bit funny. He explained in no uncertain terms what he would have done to our bare butts with his quirt if the old one-eyed mare had beaten us and gotten away.

We rode back to our swimming hole and quickly got dressed. We saddled up again and caught up with Dayton and Ray as they were nearing the corrals with the horses. Dayton was still laughing. I think he would liked to have joined us at our swimming hole, but he never did. Guess he had enough swimming when he took his dive in the river on Old Bob.

◊　　◊　　◊

Later that summer, Dayton and I rode into Delta and were spending the night at his little house there. Someone had left a few True Detective magazines at the house, and I got to reading these spooky, gruesome stories, really scaring myself. Reading by the light from the old kerosene lamp, I imagined all sorts of things. The lamp sure cast some spooky shadows!

I had just finished reading about this crazy guy somewhere in Utah who went around to sheepherder camps and killed sheepherders. The story gave a lot of detail about the kind of knife the killer used and how he snuck up in the night and killed sheepherders.

Sitting up close to the old kerosene lamp, I finished the story, but to my surprise, the story said the killer had escaped from jail and was on the loose! Wow! You know it's not very far from Delta to Utah!! When you are about ten or eleven your imagination can get pretty wild and real!

I had to go to the toilet pretty bad, but I figured it was about a mile to the outhouse! Well, maybe fifty yards! Still, a long ways in the dark with sheepherder killers running around loose! Boy, it was dark out there. Maybe

I could wait until morning. Nope, this little matter needed immediate attention!

We didn't have a flashlight. Dayton would laugh at me if I tried to take the lamp! Our old lantern was busted, after I had dropped it one night, and we never had got a new globe for it. Gathering up all my courage, I bravely headed for the outhouse.

I made it inside the outhouse and quickly latched the door, peering out through the crack in the door to see if anything was after me. As I sat there, I got to thinking; maybe the reason they hadn't caught this guy who killed the sheepherders in Utah was that he had gotten away and come into Delta! Naw, I'm just scaring myself, I thought, as I tried to see out thru the crack in the outhouse door.

Then I heard him! I bumped my head up against the door, trying to see out. Something moved! Oh boy! It must be the killer! I think I saw the knife!! I figured he was probably waiting just outside the outhouse for me! He probably didn't know I wasn't a sheepherder. Maybe he didn't care! I felt my throat, thinking of that big knife.

I yanked my pants up, trying to be real quiet, and tried to find another crack in the boards that I could see out of. Man, it was dark out there. I couldn't see anything, but I thought I heard him moving around. I peeked thru the cracks in the door again and sure enough I thought I spotted him! The crack in the door wasn't very big and I couldn't see much to the side, but I figured he was sneaking up on the side of the outhouse. He didn't think I could hear him, and I almost couldn't with the loud pounding my heart was doing. But no doubt about it, he was right outside! I could hear him breathing and moving around.

Maybe he didn't know I was inside the outhouse? No, he knew! That's why he was there! I thought about screaming for Dayton to come and get me. He probably couldn't hear me anyway, but that seemed kinda like a bad idea cause the killer might get Dayton too! I had my eye pressed up to the crack in the door, but couldn't see him.

Real quietly, I unlatched the door. Peering out thru the crack, I couldn't see him. Maybe he had gone around to the back! Mustering up all my courage, I busted out of there at a dead run, and headed for the house.

I ran smack into the side of one of our grazing saddle horses! Scared the crap out of the horse (bet he thought that killer had him), I damn near died of a heart attack! It's a wonder the horse didn't kick the stuffing out of me, as I yelled bloody murder, falling over backward. The horse was as scared as I was and stampeded off into the darkness.

I jumped up and took off for the house. Dayton came running to the back door, peering out into the dark hollering, "What the hell's going on out there?" Well soon as I realized the killer hadn't gotten me, that it had only been one of our saddle horses, I quit yelling.

I was stammering and mumbling that nothing was wrong. Just thought there was a killer out there. Dayton started laughing and said I better quit reading those spooky stories. Guarantee! I made sure all my out house business was taken care of "before" dark after that! I never was sure where that killer was, or if he ever got caught!

11

Nucla Rodeo

Ray furnished stock for several small rodeos in the area around Delta, and I got to go with him for the rodeo at Nucla, Colorado. Nucla is about 50-60 miles from Delta, and Ray had no way of getting the stock there except to drive them.

We packed our beds, cooking gear and a few groceries on a bronc Ray wanted to break. The bronc didn't lead very well, so Ray turned him loose with the other horses. He bucked around with the pack, but stayed with the horse herd. We had around twenty bucking horses, ten or twelve Brahma bulls, and about fifteen cows, and roping calves. Ray took the lead. With me bringing up the drags, we headed for Nucla.

That was sure a fun trip for me; seeing new country, camping out every night, and making sure the bronc with our beds and groceries didn't lay down and roll, especially in a creek! The horse herd stayed together pretty well, following Ray, with the cows, calves and bulls following them.

We had several days to make the trip so we didn't hurry the stock much, letting them graze a little as we moved along. Wondering where we would spend the night always gave me something to look forward to. The first few nights out we tried to find a pen or trap to hold the stock. Most of the country was open range land and corrals weren't too plentiful. The stock stayed fairly close to our camp. Lots of grass and water around. After traveling all day, they wouldn't drift much at night; as they were pretty tired and content to fill up, lay down, and rest. Two of the broncs had bells around their necks, which helped locate them when they did drift off.

Ray would rope our pack horse, get our beds and camp gear un-loaded, and hobble the pack horse along with our saddle horses.

We would build a campfire, cook a little salt pork bacon, fry some potatoes, and eat lots of canned tomatoes and crackers! We would roll our beds out on the ground, and try not to think about a soft bed! Boy, I thought I was in heaven! Didn't get much better than this! One evening we stopped at an old rancher's place, and he invited us in for supper, and a cot in the bunkhouse to roll our beds out on. I was sure glad to have a bed to sleep in and a table to eat at. The old rancher was glad to have a little company. He cooked up some big steaks, potatoes and gravy, and had a big pot of beans on, too. He even made biscuits. Ray and I ate everything in sight! Sure beat salt pork bacon and tomatoes!

After we had cleaned up all the food he put out, and washed up the dishes, he and Ray started swapping stories. I sure enjoyed hearing the old man tell about the old days. One tale I remember well went like this:

The old timer and another cowboy were out riding when they jumped a mountain lion. They took off after the lion, and one of them roped him just as the lion was jumping up into a tree. He had caught the lion around the neck with one front leg through the loop. The lion climbed out on a limb, watching them and biting at the rope. Then the lion jumped out of the tree to run, but he jumped off the other side of the limb.

The other end of the rope was tied to the cowboy's saddle horn, and the rope wasn't long enough for the lion to reach the ground, so the lion was hanging above the ground on the end of this cowboy's rope. The lion's front leg through the loop kept him from choking as he swung there above the ground. The other cowboy managed to get the lion's feet tied together and a big stick tied in his mouth. One of them put the lion across the front of his saddle, and brought him into camp. Not knowing what to do with him, they laid the lion out on the horse feed in the small feed room and latched the door.

Cowboys traveling through that part of the country knew the old rancher's place was always a good stop. He always welcomed them for a meal or two and had some horse feed for a man's saddle horse. That night after dark, a cowboy came by to spend the night. Having been there before, he figured he would take care of his horse before going up to the house. In the dark, he unsaddled. Knowing where the grain room was, he went to get some feed for his saddle horse.

The mountain lion was laying in the grain room and, even though his feet were tied together and he still had the big stick tied in his mouth, he had gotten his feet well bunched under him and was laying facing the door. When the cowboy opened the grain bin door, the lion roared, made a mighty leap and hit the poor, unsuspecting cowboy full in the chest.

The old man said they couldn't figure out where the saddle came from they found laying in the barn the next morning, nor how their mountain lion had gotten out and was gone! It was quite a while later when the cowboy came back to claim his saddle! He explained how he had thought the devil had him that night, when the lion had hit him in the chest, and that he had left there in a big rush, riding bareback!

We rode into Nucla on our sixth day of traveling. I was sure excited, driving our rodeo stock down main street to the rodeo grounds. Lots of people and kids stopped to watch us pass with the rodeo stock.

We penned the stock at the rodeo grounds early in the afternoon. The stock was all on feed and water, so Ray suggested we take a stroll up through town. The rodeo started the next day so we had some time to kill.

As we passed a barbershop advertising a haircut for fifty cents and a bath for a quarter, Ray said we could probably stand to get both. I hadn't had a haircut all summer and I was getting a little shaggy. Hadn't had a bath since leaving the old, muddy river, where we had started, so we waltzed right into this city barbershop.

Ray got his hair cut first and went on in to get his bath. Mom had always cut my hair. I hadn't been to a real barber before so I was a little spooky when the barber whipped that big, old sheet over me with just my head sticking out, and pinned it tight behind my neck.

I guess the barber recognized a pretty good opportunity when he saw one, because he started asking me if I wanted stuff I had never heard of, like a shampoo, and a massage. It all sounded like Greek to me.

I said, "I want a haircut!"

"Sure," he said, "but usually a feller gets all these other things along with it."

I was pretty bashful and scared, so I just kept saying "Okay, I guess so."

He just kept squirting stuff out of a green bottle, then some red stuff, then washed it out and squirted some more on my head. He really gave me the works!

Heck, I didn't know what was going on. I knew it sure did smell different! Ray came in to see what was taking so long and found out I had run up a bill of about four dollars getting a fifty cent hair cut! He was one mad hombre! He cussed the barber good for taking advantage of a dumb old kid, but he still had to pay for my fancy haircut!

Then I went to the shower. We had brought a change of clothes with us. I could hear Ray outside the door still arguing with the barber. He was pretty mad. I hurried in the shower and washed the sweet smelling stuff out of my hair and started getting dressed. The shower room was real small, and they had little thin towels. Since the room was full of steam, it was hard to get very dry. My boots were pretty tight fitting and with my feet half wet so I had a hard time getting my boots on.

Ray kept hollering for me to hurry up. He was still fuming over that high-priced hair cut, but I couldn't get my darned boots on! Ray came barging into the steam room to see what was taking me so long, and I told him I couldn't get my boots on!

"Give me that damned boot!" he hollered, taking his pocket knife out. "I'll fix them where you can get them on!" Boy, I pulled so hard I nearly took the hide off my foot, but I got those boots on before he could work on them with his knife!

We got to eat a hamburger in a cafe. I figured that was the best hamburger I had ever had in my whole life! Might of got a piece of pie, but Ray got to thinking about my haircut, so we just went back to the rodeo grounds. We rolled our beds out behind the bucking chutes, and I sure had a hard time sleeping, thinking of the big rodeo the next day.

Ray had a mare in the bunch of bucking horses called "Hesitation". She was a real good-looking mare, bright bay colored, and showed some pretty good breeding. She bucked twice in the bareback, as well as saddle bronc riding, and put her riders down real quick. When the chute gate would open, she would make a big high jump out, kinda hesitate, then leave the world! Guess that's how she got her name.

She would sure get high in the air, heading east, turn her belly up to the sun and hit the ground going west. After the rodeo, Ray bet fifty dollars no one there could ride her. The cowboys picked the best rider there to try to ride her. Ray didn't have to pay off. Hesitation did her thing and the cowboy hit the ground right quick.

That night after the rodeo, I got to bragging on Hesitation, saying I didn't think anybody in the world could ride her.

Ray says, "Oh, she ain't so tough. I can ride her!"

"Ha, I've seen you ride, and Hesitation would throw you so quick you wouldn't know what happened" I replied.

Ray says, "I'll bet you fifteen dollars that I can ride her all day."

I was supposed to get fifteen dollars for my work for the summer and I hated to risk it, but I knew he couldn't ride Hesitation! So I called his bet. I just knew that he couldn't ride her. That mare could buck!

As we cooked breakfast the next morning, I was sure anxious to see Ray get on Hesitation, imagining how high she was going to throw him!

Ray roped Hesitation out of the bunch of broncs, led her over to his saddle, brushed her off, and saddled her up. She was a little snorty, not real bad, and I was sure looking forward to seeing Ray hit the dirt. He untracked her, turned her around a couple times and eased up on her. Well, you can imagine my dismay, when she just turned and walked off, not even a hump in her back.

Ray grinned all over and said, "Thanks for the fifteen dollars!" I couldn't believe that darned mare didn't even try to buck! There went my summer wages! Maybe she was just hesitating a little longer than usual. But that wasn't the case. She never bucked all day.

Ray roped the young bronc that we had packed our beds and stuff on coming over, for me to ride back. I saddled him and rode him around one of the corrals a little. He bucked around the corral a couple times, but I managed to stay on top, and Ray said he was just fine. He said to just follow the cattle as he turned the stock out and we headed back home.

I had my hands full trying to keep my bronc headed in the right direction. Sometimes we would be up in the middle of the bucking horses, then back on the drags, but after awhile I got so I could handle him a little. At least he kept my mind off Hesitation and how she had cost me my whole summer's wages. She never offered to buck all that day, and Ray rode her a couple times more on the trip back, and always with the same results; no buck.

We stopped and spent the night with our old rancher friend that we had stayed with coming to Nucla. Gave him a full report on the rodeo and, of course, how Hesitation had cost me $15.00. He got a kick out of that, and he and Ray traded winks. I got the feeling there was something I didn't know about Hesitation!

We made it back to the old camp on the Gunnison, after being gone nearly two weeks. Dayton was sure glad to see us as we came riding up. I was still really down in the dumps, feeling sorry for myself, mad at Ray and Hesitation, and Dayton wanted to know what was rubbing me the wrong way. I had to tell him about my bet with Ray and how Hesitation didn't even hump up!

Dayton laughed, "Hell no! She won't buck if you don't put a flank strap on her! Ray knew that, that's why he bet you. He knows good and well he couldn't ride her if he flanked her!"

Boy, I'd been taken big time! First the barber, then Ray! I was getting a lot of education, Ray said. Dayton tried to get Ray to give me my wages, since Ray knew Hesitation wouldn't buck, but he wouldn't. I think he was still sore about my high priced haircut! Anyway my trip to the big Nucla rodeo was quite an adventure and learning experience! I didn't make any money that summer, but I sure got a little more education. I wasn't so quick to jump on a bet for a while.

◊   ◊   ◊

Dayton had been to town and picked up our mail. I had a letter from Mom saying she was coming over to get me and take me home to start school. The date she planned to arrive was just a few days away, so we swept the floor!

No running water or electricity made our camp a little rustic. We had a big water bucket and would simply go down to the river behind the camp and dip a bucket full out of the river. The bucket needed to set still for a few minutes after you got it in the house. This gave the vitamins and minerals time to settle to the bottom of the bucket, along with a considerable amount of mud. A big community dipper hung off the side of the bucket and, when you wanted a drink or water out of the bucket, you just dipped it off the top. You tried not to dip very deep, so as not to stir up all those vitamins and minerals.

We had a big tea kettle that always set on the stove to heat water. We would use this hot water to rinse our dishes after they were washed. Water would be added to the tea kettle as needed, never letting it get empty.

A big family of mice had homesteaded under our cabin and visited our groceries every night. This afforded great sport for me! After supper dishes were done, Dayton would place the old lantern on the kitchen floor. We would toss a few pieces of biscuit out on the floor and sit back and wait. Ray would mutter something about those "damned kids" and go off to his bedroll.

Dayton had on old twenty-two single shot rifle. Shot twenty-two shorts. He had taught me to shoot at Paonia, and I got to be a pretty good shot. Didn't take long for a mouse to appear to get a chunk of biscuit.

"Get him!" Dayton would whisper.

Bang! I seldom missed, and every one I shot brought a big cheer from Dayton! He sure got a kick out of our mouse hunting together. He never did shoot, but kept me in ammunition, and we sure had fun!

The day of Mom's arrival came, and we stayed around pretty close to camp so we would be there when she got in. Late in the evening I was getting a little concerned as Mom hadn't shown up. Looking down the old washed-out road I thought I could see some one walking. I jumped on Betty and took off down the road. Sure enough, it was a slightly ruffled Mom walking up the road to our camp. I wondered why she didn't bring her car!

I rode up to her and jumped off Betty, and gave Mom a big hug. We were sure glad to see each other. We started walking up the road together as I led Betty. She mentioned the damned car was stuck in the mud! She had been walking about two miles and was glad to see me, but that was about all she was glad about right then!

When we got to camp, Mom sat down and had a cup of coffee and rested a little and seemed to get in a better humor. Since Dayton, Ray nor I knew how to drive, Mom had to go back to the car and drive it to camp. If we could get it out of the mud hole, that is! I let Mom ride Betty and I rode one of Dayton's horses. Dayton and I rode back with Mom to the stuck car.

Dayton carried a shovel on his shoulder as we rode along the river bank where the road got dangerously close to the water. The rear-end of the car had slipped off the edge of the road and was sitting in the edge of the water. Dayton dug some mud out from in front of the hind wheels. We put some flat rocks in the trench he had dug. Tying our saddle ropes to the front bumper and our saddle horns and with Mom gunning the heck out of the old car it came out of the mud. She darned near ran over us as the car got traction on dry ground!

As Dayton and I rode back to camp through the dust that Mom's car had kicked up, I was anticipating her good cooking for supper.

"What's in the bottom of the water bucket!?" Mom exclaimed as she looked at the thick layer of vitamins and minerals.

"It's all right if you let it settle and don't stir it up," I assured her.

"Go get some clean water!" she said as she emptied the half full bucket of water out in the yard.

Picky women! There wasn't nothing wrong with the water she had thrown out, but I went to the river to get some more just like that she had thrown out.

"Be sure you let it settle," I said as I set the full bucket on the water stand.

"Have you been drinking this water!!" Mom sounded a little excited.

"Yes, it's good if you let it settle, Mom," I assured her.

"Oh good heavens!" she said, looking up to the ceiling.

"Have you got a pan to boil some potatoes in?" Mom asked as she looked around the kitchen.

"We just boil them in the tea kettle!" I proudly replied.

"This?" she asked, as she lifted the lid on the tea kettle and looked inside.

There were about two inches of mud in the bottom of the tea kettle.

I can't remember just exactly what she said then. I do remember Dayton and Ray suddenly found something urgent to attend to down at the corrals. I was kept busy packing water from the river as Mom had a big fire going in the old stove and everything in camp that would hold water was on the stove boiling water!

She started acting funny around me, feeling my brow, and asking me if I felt all right. Using her finger and thumb she would pry my eye lids wide open and peer into my eyes. Making me stick my tongue out as far as it would go, she would examine it like it was a foreign object. Then she asked me all kinds of embarrassing questions, like when I went to the bathroom and stuff like that! I was sure glad Dayton and Ray weren't there to hear me getting this quiz!

She finally got everything boiled and we had a good supper. Dayton and Ray got a pretty good lecture on boiling the water and keeping things clean, etc., etc.!

That evening, after supper, I thought I would cheer Mom up a little when I said, "Want to shoot some mice, Mom?"

Her reaction to this suggestion met with about as much enthusiasm as my suggesting she boil the potatoes in the tea kettle!

Next morning as Ray and I were packing water up to the cabin, Ray said something like, "Your Mom's damn near as picky as Mrs. Green was about that damned stove!"

I loaded what few clothes I had and gave Betty a big tearful good- bye, and we headed back to civilization. Dayton had promised to take good care of Betty. And I could come back next summer. We got by the mud hole and made it home in good shape. I was glad to see Dad, and slowly re-adjusted to town living. I missed the good, vitamin enriched, muddy water to drink and adjusted to the town water without getting sick! Mom said it took about four baths before I finally came clean again.

12

Baby Grandma

The next summer, the day school was out, I was packed and ready to go back and see Betty, Dayton and Ray. Mom loaded me up again and we headed for Delta. She sure seemed to drive slow when I was in such a hurry!

Uncle Ray had a place leased that summer up in Escalante Canyon, about 25-30 miles west of Delta. He had assured Mom there was a good spring at the camp and we wouldn't be using river water. This seemed to make her feel a little better about me going up there for a while.

Uncle Dayton was staying at his small place in Delta, because Ray didn't have much livestock on the Escalante and didn't need much help.

Grandma was living in Grand Junction with my Aunt Tina and Uncle Frank. Ray asked Grandma if she would like to come up to the camp and cook for us a while that summer. Ray told her we would have to go into the camp horseback and she said, "good"; she hadn't got to ride for awhile and was looking forward to riding again. She'd be glad to come up and cook for us. She was always willing to help out where she were needed. Tina and Frank brought her down to Delta and we met her at Uncle Daytons place.

Grandma always wore real long dresses that brushed the floor as she walked, and buttoned up right under her chin. They all had long sleeves that buttoned tight around her wrists. When she was outside she wore a little bonnet kinda deal on her head, with her hair braided in a little bun.

On the morning after Grandma arrived, we saddled up, loaded a couple pack horses with our groceries and Grandma's stuff. Ray had a good gentle horse saddled for Grandma. Ray picked her up and set her up on the horse. Had a regular stock saddle on him, but Grandma insisted on riding side saddle. She hooked her right leg over the saddle horn, and her left foot in the stirrup. She picked up her bridle reins, turned her horse toward the gate, and said, "Let's go!"

We headed for the Escalante, following the trail along the Gunnison river, past the place where Dayton and Old Bob had taken their plunge into the river. While passing the old swimming hole Rusty and I had so much fun in, I started to ask Ray if we could stop and take a little swim, but thought better of that idea; we kept riding.

The old camp we had lived in the previous summer was still there, empty and looking like it might fall down any minute. It brought back a flood of memories and I would have liked to stop, but Ray kept riding.

Escalante Canyon turned south, away from the Gunnison river, about ten miles past the old camp we had lived in the summer before. Ray's camp was about six miles up the Escalante.

Ray was riding in front, leading one pack horse, then Grandma. I brought up the rear, leading the other pack horse. This wasn't a big deal until you realize that this little lady was 79 years old and Ray didn't ride along at a walk!

We hit a long trot and held it unless the trail along the river got too rough, then we slowed down to a walk. Following the river trail from Delta to the Escalante Camp was around 25-30 miles. Grandma stayed right up with Ray all the way.

We got into camp in late afternoon. We hadn't stopped on the way, and Grandma was getting kinda stiff. Ray lifted her down off her horse.

She said, "I must be getting soft, to be stiff from a little ride like that!"

She soon limbered up, and sent me down to the spring for a bucket of water. She had a fire going in the cook stove right quick. She swept the kitchen floor and was busy putting away the groceries we had brought with us, while the stove was warming up. I flopped on my bed roll, plumb tired out! Grandma had dinner ready in nothing flat.

I helped dry the dishes as she washed them. Then she busied herself cleaning the kitchen and putting stuff away. It got dark and I soon hit the sack, one tired kid. Grandma was still piddling around in the kitchen. I don't know when this little miracle lady rested, 'cause she had breakfast cooking when Ray rolled me out the next morning!

Ray and I were riding every day, and it was sure nice having supper ready when we got into camp. Grandma was sure a good cook and she really enjoyed seeing us eat everything she prepared. I thought Mrs. Green had been a good cook while we were up on the Muddy, but Grandma had her beat!

Grandma stayed with us about a month and, when we took her back to Delta, she sure seemed to have enjoyed her stay with us. We sure enjoyed her good cooking!

◊   ◊   ◊

Aunt Tina and Uncle Frank brought Grandma to our house in Manitou Springs for Christmas, 1943. They stayed with us a couple weeks, and I really enjoyed having her with us, always laughing and sharing our good times.

The night of January 7, 1944, Grandma kissed everyone good night and went to her room to bed. No sign of feeling bad or being sick.

She just went to sleep and went on to Heaven that night. My Baby Grandma was sure a true little pioneer woman. They didn't come any tougher, or more tender. She was 83 when she went to be with the Lord.

13

Manitou Springs

World War was in full swing. Gas was rationed and car tires were near impossible to buy. Dad had enough gas coupons issued to him to keep up with his job. Living in Manitou Springs, the long trip over to Uncle Dayton's was out for awhile, so I had to stay home that summer. I wasn't very happy with this situation, as I figured Dayton sure needed my help!

Manitou Springs and the area around Colorado Springs were real popular place for tourists to visit during the summer. Many natural attractions around the area brought lots of people there. Frank Snell had a big fleet of touring cars and busses to haul tourist's around. The gas and tire shortage pretty well brought his business to a halt.

Being the enterprising fellow that he was, Frank bought an old brewery building in Manitou Springs and converted it into a huge horse barn. He bought around twenty five teams of various sized work horses and every imaginable kind of wagon, buggy, surrey and stagecoach that he could find. He started hauling tourists around in these horse-drawn vehicles. Boy, he really knocked a home run with this deal, as the people really took to this means of transportation.

I was drawn to this big horse barn like a bear to a bucket of honey! I got to know all the drivers and pitched in helping clean stalls, feeding horses, and harnessing the teams.

I wasn't old enough to get a job as a driver, but most of the driver's would let me go with them and sit up on the drivers seat. Occasionally they would let me drive the two-and four-horse hitches.

We would take these tourists up through Williams Canyon to the Cave of the Winds and then down Serpentine Drive. The hairpin curves and steepness of this road sure made a driver sit up and pay attention. Traveling out through the Garden of the Gods, with all the big red rock formations, was a nice trip and real popular with the tourists. It was a long trip from Manitou out through the Broadmoor and up to Seven Falls then up the winding road to Cheyenne Mountain Zoo. These were sure fun trips for me.

The big stagecoach was my favorite. They had one old timer that drove the six-horse hitch on the stagecoach and I always tried to get a ride with him. Sitting away up on top of the swaying stagecoach looking down on the six horse hitch was a real thrill. I sure wanted to learn to drive the six horses and he showed me how to keep the lines separated and how to give and take on individual lines. He would let me drive for short distances and told me to watch his hands, how they handled the lines.

◊　　◊　　◊

There was a candy making business there in Manitou Springs that specialized in salt water taffy. They had a big taffy pulling machine sitting in the front window of the candy shop, mixing and pulling the taffy. The taffy candy was sure sweet and good, but awful sticky. I had a couple of pieces of this taffy in my pocket one day when I got to ride on the big stagecoach with the six-horse hitch. As we were swinging and swaying down the road going through the Garden of the Gods, I remembered my taffy and offered the old timer a piece. I unwrapped it for him and put it in his mouth, as both his hands were pretty busy handling the lines on the horses.

"Boy this is sure good stuff!" he exclaimed, as we traveled along.

Pretty quick he started trying to cuss. But his false teeth were stuck together and he couldn't say a whole lot that I could understand!

Finally, in desperation, he handed me the lines to the six horses! Boy, was I excited as I took over the driving. He took his teeth out and started peeling the sticky taffy off his false teeth.

"Damned stuff!" he said, as he got his teeth back in. He let me drive for a while and then took the lines back.

After that, I always made sure I had a supply of taffy in my pocket when I climbed up on the stagecoach! He couldn't resist the taffy and I got a lot of practice and experience driving the six-horse hitch! He figured me out pretty quick on this taffy deal and, when he saw that I could handle the driving pretty well, he would let me drive more each time I went out with him. He finally got to where he would just take his teeth out, put them in his pocket. Gumming the heck out of that taffy, he'd sit back and let me drive! We were both pretty happy with this deal!

I am always amazed at the Western movies where you see the horses hitched to a stagecoach running wide open with the Indians or robbers chasing them. I'll tell you for sure, those drivers had to darn sure know their business, 'cause they sure had their hands full! The old stagecoaches they had there at Manitou Springs would sure rock and roll if you got the horses into a long trot or a short lope, and you sure had to hang on!

◊　　◊　　◊

Mom and Dad sold their house in Manitou Springs and bought a small acreage between Manitou Springs and Colorado Springs. This was a great move for me, as I had left Betty over at Uncle Dayton's. Now we had a place to keep her. Dad made arrangements to have her hauled over to Colorado Springs, and I was sure glad to have her back where I could ride her again.

The place they bought was out on the edge of town, next to the Garden of the Gods. This area offered lots of trails winding through the foothills and rock formations. It was a fun place to ride and explore.

◊　　◊　　◊

There was a big weekly livestock sale out on Knob Hill, a mile or so east of Colorado Springs. The sale was usually held on Saturday. I would go out with Dad as he inspected all the livestock going through the sale. If an animal had a brand that Dad couldn't read pretty plain, he would rope the animal, snub it up to a post in the corral, and with a pair of hand shears, clip the hair away from the brand so he could see what it was.

Dad had turned the roping over to me. I was sure glad to get this opportunity to rope, and got pretty good at catching and snubbing anything he wanted caught. This wasn't as much fun as roping horseback, but at least I was roping!

I was out at the Nob Hill sale one Saturday, and Dad gave me a quarter to go get a hamburger and Coke. The cafe was just past the sale ring, and as I was going through to get my hamburger, they ran several little kid goats into the ring to sell. Boy, they were cute as could be; real small, not near old enough to wean. The auctioneer was calling for a bid on one or all of these little goats. I stepped up to the ring and bid a quarter. The auctioneer took my bid and sold me my choice of one of the goats. I picked a little black, stocking legged, white-faced billy goat.

When I carried Billy out to show him to Dad, he wasn't overly excited about my purchase! Instead of buying a hamburger and a Coke, I had bought a billy goat!

We had to stop and buy some milk and nipples on the way home to feed my new friend. Mom filled a Coke bottle with warm milk and put one of the new nipples on it. Billy took to it like an old hand. Dad said later the damn goat kept us broke buying milk and nipples for him!

Billy and I had lots of fun together. As he got older and stronger, he would follow me on horseback, just like a dog. After following me for several miles, Billy would get tired. I would pick him up, set him in front of me in the saddle. He acted like he was king of the hill!

He was pretty tough and would keep up with me, following my horse all through the Garden of the Gods. He was sure fun to travel with, always inquisitive, stopping to check things out, then bouncing along to catch up like a little deer. He liked to climb up on rocks and there were plenty places for him to run and climb.

As he got bigger, he got tougher, and I didn't give him a ride very often. His horns were growing and there just wasn't room for both of us in that saddle!

Billy got to where he would get out of the corral anytime he wanted, so I had to keep him on a stake rope most of the time. He was on his stake rope one day, sound asleep in the grass. Mom drove by him in the car, scaring him and he jumped up, and started to run. The rope had wrapped around his hind leg and when he hit the end of the rope, it broke his leg.

Dad made a splint and set the broken leg, wrapping it up tight around the splint. Before long, the leg healed. Billy had a bump on his leg and it was a little crooked, but he got around as good as ever.

I got to wrestling with him. As he grew, so did his horns. He got to be a handful when he would lower his head, shake those horns at you, and charge! He would chase me all around the yard and got big enough that he would nearly knock me down when he lowered his head and butted me.

He got loose one day and went up the road to a neighbor lady's, about a block away. She had a nice flower garden in front of her house. Billy enjoyed sampling the many different varieties of flowers she had grown for him to eat. At least he thought she had grown the flowers for him!

She tried to run Billy off, but he did the running, chasing her into the house in short order. Well, not to be out done by a billy goat, the lady got a pan of water, and thinking that Billy would scare away if hit through the screen door with this water, she threw it at him. Big mistake! Billy didn't like that game one little bit and busted through the screen door to tell the lady he didn't like water thrown in his face. Out the door she came, screaming bloody murder, heading for our house as fast as her short, plump legs would carry her. Billy thought that this was kinda like chasing me, so he would run up behind her and give her a little bump to keep her going. Unfortunately, she lost her balance a time or two and, by the time she reached our house, her knees and elbows were sure skinned up! Might have been more skinned up than I knew about.

Billy was in a heap of trouble right quick. I caught him and tied him up, while Mom tried to console the nearly hysterical, mad lady. She finally calmed down, and Mom assured her we would do something with Billy.

Dad got a little tickled when Mom was telling him about Billy's latest venture. Mom got after Dad about it not being very funny, and he agreed with her. Billy would have to go.

Dad was firm about Billy having to go back to the sale ring. I couldn't talk him out of selling Billy, so the next Saturday I had to take him back to the sale. I sure hated to let him go, but guess it was better than having Dad get sued or something!

◊　　◊　　◊

Knob Hill Auction Co. held a big horse sale once a month. I thought I needed another horse and I had been saving up my money. I had about $50.00 to buy a horse. Dad didn't figure I could buy much of a horse for that, but I was sitting in the auction watching the horses sell and hoping I could pick up a good horse with all this money I had!

Several horses came through the ring that I had looked over and liked out in the corrals. But they all sold for more than my bank account would stand.

A real good looking black horse came in the ring. He seemed well broke and sure did handle well. I wondered why I hadn't seen this horse out in the pens before the sale and just figured I had missed seeing him. A guy was riding him, with a great big, oversized saddle. Boy, that horse was really handling good. I kinda liked his looks. He was only four or five. I wished Dad was there, but I knew I had to bid now or forget it. I never had bought a horse in a sale ring before, just one billy goat! All the racket from the auctioneer, the ring men, and the crowd had me pretty nervous.

Looked like he would bring more than I could afford, but when the auctioneer was calling for a starting bid of forty dollars, I nodded at the ring man and got the bid at forty.

Someone else bid forty-five. The ring man was pointing at me, hollering fifty?, Give me fifty?

I hollered, "Fifty dollars!"

"SOLD!" cried the auctioneer, pointing at me, to my surprise.

The auctioneer didn't even try for fifty-five. I felt something was haywire here or I was sure getting lucky! I had been to enough horse sales to know that the rider would get off and unsaddle the horse while the bidding was going on, so the bidders could see the horse's back.

The rider stepped off the horse and uncinched his saddle. As he pulled it off, a murmur went through the crowd as the horse's back was exposed. Boy, you talk about sway backed! I mean sway backed like you never seen! I wasn't as lucky as I had thought!

I jumped up and hollered, "No sale! I didn't see his back."

"You can see it now! He's your horse!" the guy who had been riding him said, as he opened the gate and the horse ran out of the ring down to the outside catch pens.

Laughing, the auctioneer started calling for bids on another horse that came into the ring, not paying any attention to me, hollering, "NO SALE!" "NO SALE!"

I rushed out of the sale ring and went down to the pen where my new horse was. I sure felt bad for the horse. His back was the worst deformed I had ever seen. No wonder they had that huge saddle on him, as a regular saddle would have never fit, unless you stood it on end!

Well, I was pretty upset by this little deal and went out in the stock yards and found Dad. He went with me to look at my new horse, as I explained how the big saddle had sure covered up his sway back. When I told him that the auctioneer had dropped the bid on me before they unsaddled the horse, he was getting a little hot under the collar. Then when he checked his papers to see who had consigned the horse, he really got hot.

The guy who had consigned the horse into the sale was the same guy that was riding the horse in the ring. He and the auctioneer were pretty good partners, working sales in a large area, buying and selling. Their reputation as being a little crooked seemed well-founded. Dad knew them both well, and said, "That damned Bud! I'll educate him."

Dad was five foot four, weighed one hundred and fifteen pounds when wet and mad. He wasn't wet, but he was damn sure mad when he went looking for Bud.

Bud was a big stout horse trader, stood about six three, and weighed over two hundred. Bud was out in the alley, between corrals, when Dad caught up with him. Reaching up over his head, Dad started poking Bud in the chest and in a pretty loud voice let Bud and the whole world know what he thought of a man that would try and pull that kind of a deal on a kid. Bud was backing up as fast as he could walk, and Dad stayed right in his face, poking Bud in the chest and really telling him how things were and how they were going to be!

"Hell Lyle, I didn't know it was your kid! He don't have to pay for the horse!" Bud kept saying as he backed up from Dad's jabbing him in the chest.

Dad told him it didn't matter whose kid it was. Bud knew a buyer should have a chance to see a horse's back before the sale was final and he agreed whole heartedly! Bud kept apologizing, as Dad backed him all the way down to the end of the alley.

Dad finally left Bud and headed in to have a little chat with the auctioneer. The auctioneer got the same lecture from Dad about dumping their junk unfairly, and on kids. Looked like the auctioneer was going to get to eat his microphone. But after another sincere apology from him, Dad cooled down.

Well, I didn't pay for old sway back, and Bud didn't try to drop off any more of his junk at Knob Hill while Dad was the brand inspector there.

I kinda took another look at my Dad too! He wasn't very big to look at, but I think Bud and the auctioneer thought he was a pretty damned big, little man. I know I sure did!

14

Tommy and Schoolboy

Tommy Webb was a kid about my age, who lived on a ranch out east of Colorado Springs. Tommy liked to ride about as much as I did and, when he had to come into Colorado Springs to go to school one year, he was sure missing his horse, School Boy.

Dad made arrangements with Tommy's dad to keep School Boy at our place. Tommy was going to school in Colorado Springs, while I was in school at Manitou Springs. He would come out every weekend and we would ride together. Tommy was a wiry kind of guy, not near as tall as I was, but tougher than a boot. He was sure a good rider and we had lots of good times riding through the Garden of the Gods.

One of our bright ideas was to ride out through the Garden of the Gods after dark, ride up beside parked cars at the numerous lover's lanes, and shine a flashlight in the parked car windows! I won't go into too much detail about these adventures except to say that when a guy jumped out of his car, shooting his pistol, we disappeared into the dark and decided maybe we better find something else to do, not quite as exciting! He scared the crap out of us!

School Boy was a bright bay, good looking horse that couldn't stand much prosperity. He would darn sure buck if you didn't keep him rode pretty regularly.

Spring came with its abundance of green grass, and School Boy got to feeling real good. Tommy came out one Friday night and spent the night with me, and we were down at the corrals early Saturday morning saddling up School Boy and a black, stocking-legged horse I had bought called Socks.

School Boy was sure humpy, and when Tommy got on him he blew up, and bucked Tommy off. I caught School Boy and led him back to Tommy. He led him around a little, rubbing his shoulder and hip where he had landed. Getting on School Boy again, Tommy really got with it this time and was bearing down on him, but School Boy quickly sent Tommy up to join the bird gang! Tommy hit the ground pretty hard this time. I loped out to catch School Boy. He was really turning the crank. The stirrups of Tommy's saddle were popping together over the seat of his empty saddle. Tommy was still sitting on the ground as I led School Boy back to him.

"You all right?" I asked as he got up and took his bridle reins from me.

"Yea. You want to ride him?" Tommy asked me.

"Not very bad!" I replied.

"Try him. I'll bet you can ride him," Tommy said offering me his bridle reins.

"I don't think so! That S.O.B. can darn sure buck!" I answered, not liking where this conversation was heading.

"I think he's getting tired now and I'm sure hurting. Try him for me!" Tommy said.

I knew better, but sometimes you just gotta do something you know ain't going to work too good. I pulled my saddle off Socks as Tommy unsaddled School Boy. I threw my saddle on School Boy and cinched him up. I led him around a little as Tommy gave me first hand instructions on how to get him rode. His instructions hadn't worked for him but maybe they would help me?

I eased up on School Boy as he exploded. I had ridden a few of Ray's and Dayton's horses that had bucked with me, but this little booger had his act together and he flattened me out pretty darn quick. Tommy took on my job of catching School Boy and brought him back to me. I wasn't hurt and was more determined than ever to ride this sucker.

I pulled my hat down and climbed on again. I thought for a little bit that I might get him rode, as I stayed with him a little longer than I had my first trip, but he sent me off into the wild blue yonder, and I made a rather ungraceful landing on my head.

"I wish Bill was here. Bet he could ride him," Tommy said, as he led School Boy back to where I was getting up out of the dirt.

Bill Williams was a cowboy who was riding colts for Emil Clark at the Garden of the God's saddle stable. Bill was a tall, slim cowboy who had drifted into the area. Tommy and I rode over to the saddle stable pretty regularly and had gotten to know Bill and had seen him ride some pretty waspy colts. He could sure ride a bucking horse. Bill always had a big smile on his face and we sure admired him and his bronc-riding skills.

"Let's take School Boy over to the stables and see if Bill will ride him for us!" I said, not wanting to try him again!

I pulled my saddle off School Boy and threw it back on Socks and let Tommy ride Betty. Leading School Boy, we rode off to find our hero and figured we would sure see a good bronc ride! We were both a little sore from our forced landings and were eagerly anticipating watching Bill knock the sass out of Mr. School Boy!

Bill was at the stables as we rode up leading School Boy.

"You are a heck of a pair, letting this old broke horse bluff you out!" Bill chided us, as he heard our tale of woe.

"He don't look like an outlaw to me!" Bill said, as he threw his saddle on him.

Tommy and I exchanged grins, figuring Bill was about to find out whether he was an outlaw or not!

Bill cinched his saddle down on School Boy, turned him around and stepped on, wheeled him around and kicked him out into a lope. That dirty little bugger didn't even offer to buck! Bill loped him back to where we were standing, and slid him to a stop. We were looking kinda amazed, not believing what we were seeing.

"Pretty bad ain't he boys!" Bill laughed, as he whirled him around and loped off again.

This seemed like a rerun of Uncle Ray and Hesitation!

Loping back to us and sliding School Boy to stop, Bill laughed and stepped off.

Bill pulled his saddle and Tommy threw his saddle on School Boy. Tommy eased up on him, and to his relief, School Boy moved out like an old broke horse!

We never did figure out Bill's secret. Tommy made sure he rode School Boy every day after that and got along with him pretty good. School Boy still liked to buck, and every once in awhile, he would flatten Tommy out, just to show him he could if he wanted to!

I had told Tommy about my summer up on the Muddy. Being raised on the flat country out east of Colorado Springs, Tommy had never been in the mountains and was eager to ride some high country.

We decided we would go on an overnight pack trip up in the mountains near Cheyenne Mountain. I had an extra horse we could pack. We put our camp outfit together, a small tent and some cooking gear, bedrolls, and enough food for an army. Dad helped us get everything together and packed on Smoky. I rode Socks and Tommy was riding School Boy Saturday morning as we headed off into the high country several miles from our house.

We picked up a Forest Service trail and climbed higher into the mountains. Tommy was sure enjoying seeing this kind of country and I sure liked it too. That afternoon, as we rode by tall trees, lots of grass and a little creek, we came to a big meadow that looked like a good place to camp. Lots of grass to stake our horses on, water, and we were set!

We unsaddled and staked our horses. As evening settled in over the meadow we pitched our little tent, and got a fire going. Peeling some potatoes and getting supper started, we were having a good time.

"What's that!" Tommy yelled, pointing out in the meadow.

"It's a damn bear!" I exclaimed.

The biggest bear either one of us had ever seen was walking across the meadow! He had to be the biggest we had ever seen because he was the first one we had ever seen!

The big black bear stopped and looked us over. Our horses were snorting and were all on the end of their stake ropes, as far away from the bear as the ropes would allow. We all stood there staring at each other. The bear continued walking on across the meadow and disappeared into the timber.

"Where did he go? Will he come back?" Tommy asked, more than a little concerned.

"He's probably circling around behind us!" I answered looking all around.

"Let's get the hell out of here!" Tommy nervously said.

It sure didn't take us long to put out our fire. We quickly took our tent down, repacked everything and kept looking all around for the bear. We saddled up and hit the trail out of there! Riding in the dark, we high-tailed it down off that mountain and headed for the lights of Colorado Springs sparkling down below us.

Next morning early, Dad looked out the kitchen window and to his surprise there in the corral were our horses! Wondering what was going on, he came down to the corral. The little tent was pitched right next to the barn and when he opened the front flap on the tent there was a couple rugged mountain men, sound asleep in their bed rolls!

He sure got a good laugh out of us when we started telling him how big that bear was! We had got bluffed out of our wilderness camping trip, but Mom sure made a good breakfast!

◊   ◊   ◊

By the time I was thirteen, I had kinda out grown my little mare, Betty, and had bought a couple other horses to ride. We had some good friends that had a couple small kids, who sure wanted a small horse. They had a nice place to keep a horse, and we felt they would give Betty a good home. It was sure tough selling Betty to them, but I got to see her often and she had a good home and was making a couple of little kids as happy as she had me.

They took good care of her and kept her until she went on to join the big remuda at the ripe old age of twenty-five.

Tommy Webb on School Boy, Bob on Socks,
leaving on pack trip, Colorado Springs, 1944

Lyle Knox the brand inspector,
mighty big small man

Bob with Lyle, 1945, the long and
short of the Knoxes

Bob feeding pet goat, Billy,
Colorado Springs

Bob on Socks, Colorado Springs, 1944

15

Summer in Manitou

When school was out for the summer of 1944, I got a job riding colts and taking dudes on guided horseback trips through the Garden of the Gods, working for Emil Clark at his saddle stable. My friend Bill Williams had moved on and I was riding several colts he had started. This was quite an experience, herding dudes instead of cows!

Emil had sixty-five saddle horses at this stable and kept them all busy during the summer. He rented horses out by the hour and had two scheduled guided horseback rides every day. Two nights a week, there was a big chuck wagon dinner and Western entertainment out at the Kissing Camel Rock formation in the Garden of the Gods. We would take riders out to this dinner which was popular with the tourists. Don't know if it was the smell of saddle leather, or the horses, but the good looking tourist girls sure flocked around this saddle stable! I was about the right age to start thinking about girls instead of cows anyway, so it was a pretty good job for the summer!

Bud Geising ran the stable for Emil. Bud was about six foot tall, weighed around 180 pounds, and was about the toughest guy that size I ever ran into. He never wore a hat over his dark curly hair. The friendly grin on his face all the time was sure misleading. He would rather fight than eat. He had a punch about like a mule kicking you and he was sure quick.

The big military bases, Fort Carson and Peterson Field, were both located on the outskirts of Colorado Springs. The personnel from these two bases gave us a lot of horseback riders.

Some of the dudes wanted a guide and others preferred to go by themselves. We had strict rules about running and over-heating or abusing the horses. Some of the military people abused our rules and mistreated some of the horses. Bud was tough enough to pretty well enforce the rules! I've seen him jerk more than one smart aleck off a sweated-up horse and kick the guy's butt pretty handily.

There was one other kid, a few years older than me, working there. We called him Tuffy and he lived up to his name pretty well! He was like Bud, he liked to fight. I wasn't too much of a fighter. I was busy romancing the girls and left most of the fighting to Bud and Tuffy.

Emil had a pasture a couple miles from the stable where the horses were turned out at night. Our job was to bring the horses into the stable each morning pretty early. Tuffy and I would meet Bud at the stable, get our bridles, and Bud would take us out to the pasture in his car where we would catch a horse and ride bareback bringing the other horses into the stable. Each horse had his stall and his particular saddle and bridle. We would feed, brush and saddle the horses and get ready for the day's business.

When we turned the horses out at night, Tuffy and I would drive the big bunch of horse out to the pasture. Bud would come out in his car and pick us up at the pasture gate.

One night when Tuffy and I were taking the horses out to pasture after dark, the horses were in a hurry and traveling at a high lope. I needed to get around them and get the gate open before they got there. Riding bareback, I kicked my horse out in a pretty good run, going around the right side of the herd, trying to beat them to the gate.

The horses were fed a lot of baled hay and the baling wire had always been hauled over by a big tree and dumped out in a big pile. As I raced by this pile of baling wire, somehow a loop of baling wire caught the button on my right spur as I went charging by. The other end of the looped baling wire was tangled in the wire pile pretty solid. Well, things came to a sudden and not very pleasant stop! That loop of baling wire jerked me off my horse so sudden I didn't know what had me. I smacked face down in the dirt. I felt like I was just about split in two! Guess that's why I'm kinda long-legged! Needless to say, the horses beat me to the gate!

I had just bought a new pair of aluminum spurs and the baling wire loop had caught the outside button of my new spur, nearly twisting it off. I wasn't hurt much, but I sure gave that pile of baling wire a wide berth when I rode by it after that!

◊   ◊   ◊

Emil had a small ranch east of Fountain, Colorado, about twenty miles east of Colorado Springs. He raised some hay and a few horses and a little bunch of cows. He had me go down to the ranch and start riding five three-year-old colts. He had a good round pen there to start these colts in, and I was glad to get out of town for a while. I got along well with the colts and had them going good. In no time, I had them ready to go to the stable for me and Tuffy to ride, guiding dudes.

Emil had a guy come in, cut, and bale his hay. When the baled hay was still in the field, Emil asked me if I knew anyone who would come down and help get the hay into the barn. I had a buddy from school, Ray Cutting, who needed a job, so I got Ray and another guy to come down to the ranch and haul hay for a few days.

Emil had a big, fat team of horses that he used on the hay wagon. He cautioned me about his team, warning me to never let them get out of a walk because they were prone to run away without much provocation.

I assured him I was an old hand at driving a team. (Guess I was a little cocky).

"Never mind the bull stuff" he said. "Don't let them get away from you! Don't let them get out of a walk!!"

Ray and this other kid didn't know anything about horses, so I appointed myself the designated driver. They threw the hay bales on the wagon as I drove the wagon. Not a bad deal at all!

We had hauled hay for a couple days without incident. The team had been pretty fresh when we started, but I had kept a pretty tight hold on them sure to keep them checked, and in a walk. Ray and his loading partner were sure getting a workout, and I was enjoying my position as driver!

Saturday morning we were finishing up the hay hauling. We had hauled and stacked a full load that morning. We lacked about a third of a load, so we headed out to finish cleaning up the field. When we had the flatbed trailer loaded with about fifteen or twenty bales on it, we headed for the barn. It was hot and we were anxious to shower and get a cold drink. It was a long slow haul to the barn from the far end of the field.

"Come on. Let's go! Hell, we're going to be out here all day. I'm hot and need a drink!" Ray hollered at me.

"I'm hot too, but we'll get there," I replied.

"Hurry up! Can't you go any faster?" Ray's partner chimed in.

"I thought you were such a great team driver. Can't you go any faster?" Ray hollered again.

Well, I did have a pretty good hold on my team. They had been working hard and had the edge taken off them. Sure didn't act like they wanted to run like they had before. I figured a slow trot might shut Ray and his partner up. And it was pretty slow going. It looked like a long way to the barn, so. . . .

"Easy boys. That's it. Just a little slow trot." The wagon sure got to bouncing at a trot. Ray and his partner were sitting on the left side of the wagon, with their feet hanging over the wagon bed. I was standing up in the front of the wagon, with no front rack, just a slick flat bed. I could sure tell how slick the bed was as we trotted along. The wagon bounced a lot, and I tried to keep my feet under me. Of course the designated driver had to wear his leather-soled cowboy boots! The footing became more precarious by the minute!

Ray and his partner hollered, "Yea, that's more like it ! Let's go get a cold beer!"

It didn't take but a minute for my team of horses to get right into the spirit of things! As I struggled to keep my feet under me, the team got a little faster, and the wagon got to bouncing even more!

When the horse on the left broke into a lope, I knew I was in trouble. I couldn't check them. Then the other horse broke into a faster lope, and the race was on. Boy, did we start scattering bales of hay! The bales were bouncing off that wagon like rats leaving a sinking ship. Ray and his partner had pulled their hats down and were hanging on for dear life as the wagon really got to doing the hoochy goochy!

I had pretty well lost all control, and all I could do was try to keep from falling off the wagon. We had bounced off our little jag of hay, and the team left the road, heading off across the alfalfa field. Boy, that was rough, and I could hardly stay on that old wagon. I saw a deep irrigation ditch coming up fast in front of us. Since this wasn't a ship, I saw no reason for the captain to go down with it, so I baled out over the side!

"Ditch! Jump!" I yelled, as Ray and his partner looked up and saw me hit the dirt. They both jumped, plowing up the field along with me, as the team jumped the ditch.

The wagon just wasn't designed for ditch jumping! The front wheels of the wagon went into the ditch. The tongue broke off, freeing the team, and the wagon did a nice flip in the air, landing half in the ditch upside down. The wheels were sure spinning fast as the dust settled around us and the wagon.

I jumped up, thinking I hadn't broke anything. I was banged up from rolling across that hard, dry alfalfa field. Ray and his partner were moaning and groaning. None of us were hurt bad and we stood there and watched, with mixed emotions, as the team raced in panic to the barns and corrals.

Going into the big corral next to the barn was a fourteen-foot wooden gate standing half-way open. Racing toward the barn, the team started into the corral. The horse on the left shied to the right, forcing the other horse to go on the other side of the gate standing half-way open. This brought the runaway to a sudden crashing stop. The gate was splintered, harness torn up, horses skinned up, and the haying crew came hobbling in about as skinned up as the team.

Later, after we had doctored the horses, taken a shower and made it into Fountain for a cold beer, I asked Ray and his partner, "Was that fast enough!?"

Well, Emil wasn't too happy with this little deal. I got a pretty good butt chewing. He didn't fire me, but I made sure I was on my good behavior for awhile!

16

Getting a good Taste

In the spring of 1947, I was a Junior in high school in Manitou Springs. Uncle Bob was cowboying for the CS ranch at Cimarron, New Mexico. I hadn't seen Bob in a long time. He had written often, telling me about the different cow outfits he was working for. I sure wanted to go cowboy with him, so when he called to see if I could get out of school for a week to come down and help with the branding, I was sure excited. I managed to get out of school for the week, and talked Mom into taking me down to the CS Headquarters.

I rolled out my bed on an empty bunk in the bunkhouse with Bob and a few other cowboys working there at that time. It was great being there and listening to them swap stories.

One evening, while we were waiting for the cook to ring the dinner bell, the chore boy came by the bunkhouse on his way to do the evening milking. The milk cow shed was near the bunkhouse. I saw a couple of these cowboys kinda grinning at each other, so I figured they were up to something.

The chore boy had an old crossbred milk cow that was a little ornery to milk. He had to hobble her and take his chances trying to get a little milk. These two cowboys slipped out of the bunkhouse, and I followed to see what they were up to. There was an old bucket half full of rocks up against the milk cow shed. One of them picked it up and tossed it up onto the tin roof of the milk cow shed. Boy, what a racket that made as the bucket and rocks rattled down that old tin roof!

The cowboys ran back in the bunkhouse, and I followed right quick. We were all sitting around the table, looking as innocent as a bunch of choir boys, when a damn mad chore boy came storming in. He was pretty well covered with a nice mixture of fresh cow manure and warm milk. He was one mad hombre, offering to whip the S.O.B. who had spooked his milk cow and caused the wreck! Of course, no one knew what he was talking about, and he finally left, vowing to get revenge on all the no good cowboys in the world. Cowboy humor was a little hard on chore boys at times!

Joe McLaughlin was cow boss at the CS then, a sure enough tough old cow puncher. Joe mounted me on a good horse, a little humpy in the morning, but I got along with him pretty good. It was a pleasure to ride with this crew gathering the day's branding into the corrals every morning at daylight. I paired up with a pretty good hand, and we sure earned our beans and biscuits, flanking calves when we started branding.

We had only one roper dragging calves. I can't remember his name, (I think it was Joe Cook), but he was riding a big, brown horse named Irene. I can remember the horse's name but not the ropers!

We branded four or five days, and he was the only roper, working two sets of flankers. We sure didn't wait around for another calf! I don't think he ever missed a loop; double heels every time, and he was riding up to the fire with another calf as soon as we turned one loose. He would ride a fresh horse every morning to gather on, but old Irene was waiting at the pens to drag calves on every day. Sure was a pretty sight watching those two work together.

◊　　◊　　◊

On Saturday night Uncle Bob asked me if I'd like to check out the bright lights of Cimarron. I was all for it, of course. Bob had an old pickup that was broke down, so we saddled our horses and rode the six or seven miles to town. The old dirt road came around behind a big hill, coming into the main part of town along the Cimarron river. There was a big rock house on the corner that looked kinda like somebody's idea of a castle. On the corner was the Blue Eagle Bar and across the street from the Blue Eagle was Faustine Samora's grocery store and gas station. On up Coco Street was a little cafe. Chris's barber shop was next to West's Grocery store, and across the street was the El Dorado Bar.

Little kids were playing in the dirt street, and dogs were barking at our horses as we rode down Coco Street. A few chickens ran for cover as we rode by. Several horses were tied to the long hitching rack in front of the El Dorado. We tied up and went in for my first taste of Cimarron's night life.

Bob warned me to keep a low profile, since it was pretty easy for a cowboy to get into a fight in there. We bellied up to the bar and ordered a couple beers, kinda looking the place over. I was pleased the bartender didn't ask me for any I.D.

There was a big poker game going on in the middle of the room. One of the players, was the town marshal, Chili. We were enjoying our beer, watching the poker game, and casting a glance at some girls over at a nearby table. From where we were standing, Chili had his back to us, and we were looking over his shoulder at the game and the girls.

Suddenly, we heard what sounded like a muffled gun shot. Chili started to jump up, then he grabbed his chest and fell over on the card table, knocking drinks, chips, ash trays and money in every direction!

Bob hollered, "Damn, somebody shot the marshal. Let's get the hell out of here." We joined the others in a mad dash for the door.

We scrambled over the over-turned chairs, spilled beer, scattered ash trays, and money. Chili was lying on the floor, kinda moaning and rolling back and forth, rubbing his face. I didn't see any blood and wondered where he had been shot. As we stepped around the moaning Chili, we got a good dose of tear gas, nearly blinding us as we rushed outside.

Well, nobody had shot Chili! He had bought a new-fangled tear gas gun that looked like a fountain pen. Carried in his shirt pocket, somehow the tear-gas pen had gone off! When the pen fired, it sounded like a muffled shot, and when the tear gas hit Chili, it just wiped him out.

We all had a good laugh over the "marshal shooting." Chili was all right after he got his eyes and face washed. We went back into the El Dorado as the players tried to sort out the money and chips scattered all over the floor. We finished the night without any more excitement. My first night in Cimarron! Boy, I thought this was some great place! I could hardly wait to get out of school and get back down to this cowboy country!

17

In and Out of Texas

I graduated from Manitou Springs High School in May, 1948. I had enjoyed a good four years of playing football, basketball and running track. I turned down a couple scholarship offers to play college basketball because the cowboy bug had me hooked and I sure wasn't interested in any more schooling. I didn't figure I had to be too well educated to cowboy, and that's all I wanted to do!

I had got pretty serious about a young lady named Mary Alice Dulmage. The first of August, we kinda rushed off into a hasty marriage. Shortly after, we both realized it was a mistake. The marriage was annulled and we went our separate ways.

◊　　◊　　◊

Dad served the State of Colorado as brand inspector for nearly thirty years. While he was working El Paso County, Mom had to go to Phoenix for some medical tests. Dad requested a two week leave of absence. He was refused. He requested two weeks vacation. Again, he was refused. He went to the main office in Denver and explained his request, pointing out that in thirty years he had taken only one two-week vacation. An emergency sick leave was also refused.

Dad explained that he didn't have much choice; he had to take Mom to Phoenix. He had an experienced deputy inspector working with him, so he loaded up Mom and they went to the specialist in Phoenix, leaving his brand inspection duties in the capable hands of his deputy. He was gone ten days and when he returned home he got a notice in the mail he was fired, losing all his retirement benefits, insurance, and any recognition of thirty years of dedicated service. This was pretty hard for Dad to take. It really set him back for a long time.

I had worked a couple years as a deputy inspector for Dad. I had passed the state exam and had thought of being a brand inspector as my Grandad and Dad had been. But after the way Dad had been treated, I wanted no part of Colorado's Livestock Brand Board, and Dad agreed. Guess that's part of the reason I've never wanted to live in Colorado.

Dad was never bitter though, always having something good to say about everyone and everything. I guess I carried a grudge more than he did.

With Dad getting fired and coming out of an unpleasant marriage, I was glad to hear from Uncle Bob. He had left the Cimarron country and was working for the Hayhook Ranch out of Pampa, Texas. Bob called and told me I had a job there with him if I wanted to come down and work with him through the winter. I had an old car, so I loaded my saddle and bedroll and headed for Texas.

I was glad to get out of that cold, snow-covered Colorado Springs. Heck, I didn't know what cold was until I got to the Texas Panhandle with the wind blowing ninety miles an hour. The only windbreak between me and the North Star was a cedar fence post.

Winfrey Maddox was the foreman for the Hayhook Ranch and he was glad to see me, as I drove into the ranch just after noon. He was needing to go into town that afternoon and pick up a "little jag" of cake and, since he had a bad back and couldn't lift anything heavier than a coffee cup, he was right glad to have me start work right then and there! Uncle Bob was over at one of the cow camps and wouldn't be back until late that night.

Winfrey and I climbed into an old Dodge power wagon, 4x4, and headed out for the feed store in Pampa. A fellow working there started wheeling out the 100-pound sacks of cake. I had been lazing around town, not doing anything worthwhile, except finding out that I couldn't drink all the beer in town, so these 100-pound sacks of cake got to be a hand full after a short while! I got twenty sacks loaded on the old power wagon while the boss drank coffee. Then we headed out to the ranch.

The twenty-five miles was all on a narrow dirt road. The road was pretty muddy and slick, with a single set of tracks down the middle of the road. Winfrey was trying to stay in those tracks while talking with both hands. Well, Winfrey was busy telling me some big windy and slid off the road into the ditch. Even in four-wheel drive, he couldn't get back up on the road.

The only thing to do, he said, in his infinite wisdom, was to unload that cake. Then he could pull out of the ditch. So, I unloaded the 125-pound bags of cake (I'm sure they weighed that much by then!), but he told me to be careful and not get any sacks in the mud. Each sack had to be carried up the bank and stacked neatly in the semi-dry tracks in the middle of the road. Well, I had nearly all of the cake up on the road when here comes an old man and lady chugging down the road in an old, beat up pickup.

Naturally, they were in a big hurry. They couldn't get by the double row of cake sacks I had stacked in the road without them maybe slipping off the road, too. The old feller also had one of those bad back problems, and of course couldn't help move those 135-pound bags of cake.

"No problem," Winfrey says, "Bob here will just move them all over to the side of the road so you can get by!" And to me he said, "Be sure and stack them sacks as high as you can, so we don't get them any wetter than we have to!"

The wind had got up and was blowing pretty hard, sure getting cold. It was almost dark. Winfrey and the old couple kept the window rolled up and the heater going and didn't get too cold while I moved all the 145-pound sacks of cake over to the edge of the road. The old couple waved and smiled as they drove off. (I wanted to go with them!)

Winfrey got the old power wagon out of the ditch and backed up to the long stack of 150-pound sacks of cake. Somehow I got them all back on the old power wagon, and we headed on out to the ranch.

We pulled into the ranch pretty late. I was plumb wore out and hungry as an old bear, as I had skipped lunch and breakfast had been a cup of coffee on the road somewhere up the line.

Winfrey says, "Looks like the cook's done turned in, so I guess you won't get any supper, but I bet you have a good appetite in the morning!" Great sense of humor, old Winfrey.

"There's no one here to help you unload this cake, but I sure need the power wagon real early in the morning. So if you don't mind, go ahead and unload the cake tonight. Stack it in the cake house. The bunkhouse is over there. Just roll your bed out anywhere in there, and I'll see you in the morning," Winfrey said, as he went up to his house.

So I unloaded and stacked those 200-pound sacks of cake that night. I found an empty bunk in the bunk house and collapsed on it. I was too tired to think about being hungry and finally went to sleep, wondering what the hell I was doing in Texas!

Uncle Bob had been over at the camp on the river that night so he missed out on moving the cake. But he got a good laugh out of my initiation to the Hayhook!

◊   ◊   ◊

Soon afterward, Bob had a load of hay on the old power wagon and was headed for the river camp. Winfrey had changed his plans and decided to send me over to the river camp, too. I had missed getting a ride with Bob, so Winfrey sent me in a fairly new pickup. It wasn't long before I caught up with Bob and the big load of hay going down the road. I thought I'd have a little fun. Bob had no idea I was anywhere around. The road to the river camp was real hilly. The power wagon didn't have any rear view mirrors, so every thing was just right!

Bob would get to really going downhill, then have to shift two or three times to get up the next hill, then get to rolling going down hill again. The pickup I was driving had a big pipe front bumper and grill guard, so when I eased up to the power wagon and started pushing it with the pickup, everything fit pretty good. Bob couldn't figure out what was getting into that old power wagon! It would just take off running like the devil. He would slam on the brakes, trying to get things under control. I would drop back a little and let him get to shifting gears again, then ease up to the back of the power wagon and give him a good fast push! Away we would go, then he would slam on his brakes again!

I kept this up for a mile or so, then dropped back and stopped. I waited a little while before driving down to the camp. When I drove up, Bob rushed up to the pickup and started telling me all this wild B.S. about how the damned old power wagon wasn't safe to drive! It would just run off with you, and you couldn't hardly stop it! It was several years later before I ever told Bob what I'd done. He laughed then, but I don't think he would have that day the power wagon ran off with him!

◊   ◊   ◊

Spring branding on the Hayhook was something I was sure looking forward to. The owners of the ranch had another ranch in Kansas, and the crew from the Kansas ranch had came down to help us through the spring works. They had a couple older hands and one kid my age, and we hit it off pretty good. The morning of the first branding, we were on the back side of the pasture before daylight, ready to start gathering the cows and calves in toward the corrals.

The road from town to the ranch was nearby and we could see an awful lot of headlights shinning in the dark, headed for the branding corrals. When we got close to the corrals, we were met by more "cowboys?" than I had ever seen. With all this extra help joining us, the cattle were pretty well surrounded. All the riders from town had their ropes down, hoping something would break back. They were ready to rope anything that even thought about breaking back.

We got started branding, with me and the young guy from Kansas flanking calves, along with another team of flankers from the Kansas ranch. The guys from town sure weren't much help. They all came to rope, seemed like, and sure didn't offer to do anything else! But boy, they would have put the Marlboro Man to shame, with their big hats, pants stuffed down in those real fancy, tall top boots, silver spurs, and all wearing big wild rags, and fancy shirts! They sure looked the part, but doing anything was something else. They never got off their horses, just waited their turn to rope and drag calves. No one offered to flank a calf, pick up a branding iron, or anything else. . . . Oh well!

The next river camp branding, Bob and a couple ranch cowboys let Winfrey know they really didn't need all these town punchers. They didn't show up, and we got through branding without a hitch, even though we didn't look very pretty.

◊   ◊   ◊

Bob had a double rank horse in his string, and one morning he bucked Bob off. Winfrey happened to be there and told Bob to go ahead and ride this horse several days in a row to see if the horse would get the bucking out of his mind. The saddle horses usually got a two or three day rest between rides.

Well this horse blew up and sure bucked every day for four or five days, and Bob kept riding him. This was a pretty good match, as this old horse could sure buck and didn't show any sign of quitting Bob was putting some good rides on him.

One morning, after about a week of this bronc riding match had been going on, I jingled the saddle horses in and fed everything as usual. I had saddled my horse and was waiting at the corrals for Bob and Winfrey. It was unusual for them to not be there when I brought the saddle horses in. I figured they were probably talking business at Winfrey's house, so I just waited. After about an hour I was getting pretty antsy, so I rode up toward Winfrey's house.

I saw Bob over at the cabin where he and his wife were. When I rode up, I saw that they were busy packing up all their stuff.

"What's going on?" I asked Bob as he came out of the cabin carrying a box of pots and pans.

"Hell, we got fired! We're leaving here! Didn't Winfrey tell you?"

Fired! I couldn't believe it! Who? Why? When? How? Boy, was I shook up. I never had been fired and I didn't like the sound of it.

"Winfrey fired me for riding that damned old bucking horse too much," Bob said. "He told me to ride him, and then fired me for riding him too much!"

"But how about me?" I complained, "I didn't ride him!" (Heck I couldn't have rode him!)

"Winfrey said you were out too," Bob said.

I stormed up to Winfrey's house.

"Yes, I figured you would probably want to go with your uncle," Winfrey said.

I told him I sure didn't like the idea of getting fired over something I didn't do. But he was right, I was going with Bob!

We loaded up and headed back to the Cimarron country. Best thing that ever happened! I didn't mind leaving the cold, constant wind and fancy would-be cowboys. Since then I have had the privilege of knowing and working with some sure enough good hands that came out of the Texas Panhandle! They sure weren't like that crew from town that kinda gave me a sour taste for a while!

18

Punching Cows on the WS

After we left Pampa, Texas, I wanted to try my luck around Cimarron. I got a job on the WS/Vermejo Park Ranch, working for Sandy Valdez, who was the cow boss for the Cimarron branch of that big ranch. He put me at the Boxcar Bremmer camp. The camp was just like its name implies, an old railroad boxcar in the Pinon trees at the mouth of Van Bremmer Canyon. The camp had a cook stove and table in one end and room for a cot or two at the other end. No electricity or running water, but it was dry and fairly warm.

There were two good cowboys not very far from my camp. Bill Johnson was at the Van Bremmer camp, about six or seven miles west, and Slim Burmiester was camped at the Carrizozo, about five miles to the south. They were both sure good hands. Several years later, Slim took on the job of cow boss for the WS until he retired.

Joe, a young guy from Mexico, was camped at the Carrizozo with Slim. He wasn't a cowboy; his job was driving the feed wagon. Joe would drive his team of mules pulling the feed wagon and come over to my country every other day. I would throw a big circle around the pasture, pushing the cattle into the feed ground where Joe and his mules would be waiting to scatter a little cake or hay, whichever we were feeding at the time. Joe's team of mules had run off with him and the wagon a time or two. He was pretty spooked about these runaways, so he kept a pretty good hold on them.

I was riding a colt one day, gathering cattle in toward the feed ground where Joe was circling and throwing off hay. I was riding close to the wagon, and he threw a bale of hay under the colt. This caused quite a commotion, what with the colt trying to buck and kick the hay bale and run off all at the same time. I managed to ride out the storm, cussing Joe and threatening revenge!

Joe really got a big laugh out of this little episode. About a week later, we had finished feeding and I invited Joe up to my camp for lunch. He was real glad to accept my offer, so I told him I would lope on into camp and get a fire going to cook up a little dinner.

I had found an old dried cow hide in the shed down at the corrals and drug it down the road a ways from the camp. The road to the camp wound around through the pinons and cedars and through an occasional clearing. I had stashed the old dry cow hide about a quarter mile from the camp, in a place where I could hide from sight. I was hid on the west side of the road. On the east side was a long, open draw headed back out to the open prairie country.

Joe had the mules strung out in a long, ground covering trot, just short of a lope, their heads up high, long ears working back and forth and looking for boogers. Joe was reared back, really singing a pretty lively little Mexican ditty. Just as the mules were almost even with me, from my hiding place, I slid the old cow hide out into the road, right at the nearest mule's feet!

Wow! That mule jumped so high I could see daylight between that mule's belly and the other mule's back! That sucker could sure jump and kick! Well, I guarantee the race was on! The mule on the other side didn't know what the hell had his spooked partner and he wasn't fixing to hang around and find out. They blew out of there like a shot out of a cannon!

For some reason, Joe suddenly quit singing. I could hear him yelling "Whoa! Whoa!, you S.O.B's" and a few other choice words pertaining to the situation, as they disappeared down the draw in a cloud of dust. I learned a few dandy words of Spanish before they got out of earshot!

I picked up my trusty old cow hide and hurried back to camp. I hid the cow hide in the shed and was busy cooking up a little bite to eat when Joe showed up.

He came driving his mules into camp at a slow walk, coming in from the opposite direction from where they had been shortly before! He was pretty excited and in his broken english was trying to tell me what had happened. Only problem was, he didn't know what happened! Something had sure spooked his mules, though! He was pretty sure I had had something to do with his runaway, and he never did throw anything under my horse again!

Along in December we had a pretty good snow. Sandy told us to feed a little more hay than we had been feeding. Joe really loaded up from the hay stack at Carrizozo, stacking the bales six high on his old wagon. The lines down to the mules were just barely long enough for him to hold from his high perch up on top of this load.

There was a pretty fair wagon road from Carrizozo over to Boxcar Bremmer, and with the mules going along at a walk, the load was riding pretty well. Joe didn't have the hay tied down, and sitting out on the front tier of bales, his perch was a little precarious. Joe had made it all right all the way to camp, until he turned off the road to go down to the feed ground.

There was a small ditch that he had to cross just before getting to the feed grounds. He had crossed it on every other trip so he didn't pay much attention to it. The only thing was, he had never had that much hay stacked so high! As the front wheels dropped down into the crossing, the front row of bales peeled off, falling on top of the mules. Joe went right along with the falling hay, landing between the mules. When those bales started falling on those mules, I guess they thought they were under attack from something! Anyway, the race was on again! You talk about unloading hay in a hurry! Those mules did a bang up job!

The wagon passed over Joe without a wheel hitting him, and he wasn't hurt in the wreck. Joe jumped up and started running after his runaway hay wagon. I managed to get up in front of the mules and got them stopped before the wagon turned over. One thing about it, we didn't have to unload any hay. The mules had taken care of that little job for us! Joe drove the mules back up to where the wreck started, and we cut wires off the bales that weren't broke open and scattered the hay best we could. Joe didn't stack the hay quite so high after that!

◊   ◊   ◊

Around the first of the year, Uncle Ray had came over to Cimarron and gone to work for Sandy at the WS Ranch headquarters. I was calving out a bunch of cows and had a good number of calves that were big enough to start moving across the highway to another pasture. Sandy sent Ray up to help me move these pairs, so he was camped with me at the Boxcar Bremmer.

We had put a bunch of pairs across the highway and were riding back toward camp one evening, when we came upon an old wild cow that had retained afterbirth. She sure needed a little cowboy doctoring. Ray didn't like to rope very much, and we were pretty close to the corrals, so we tried easing her in toward the nearby corrals at camp. We had an old chute and figured to put her in there to work on her. She was pretty wild and was sure wanting to get away from us, but we got her into the big holding pen adjoining the corrals.

This big pen had an old shed built across the west side. Made a pretty good wind break. It was all open on the east side facing the pen, with solid walls across the back and sides. Pole rafters about six feet high and about four feet apart ran from the front to the back of the shed, bracing the shed, below the roof.

The cow was sure getting on the fight, and made a run at Ray's horse, butting him pretty good. She didn't have any horns and didn't hurt the horse any as she ran by him headed toward the open gate we had just brought her through. I had my rope down, tied hard and fast to my saddle horn, and I roped her just before she made it to the gate. I turned her back and started across the pen with her. Ray rode up and caught both hind feet and we stretched her out. So much for the chute!

I got down and took care of the business at hand on the cow. She was sure getting mad and bellering her indignation as loud as she could. I got back on my horse and rode up, giving her some slack in the rope around her neck.

Ray had a good loop on her hind feet and, in spite of her struggling and bellering threats at us, she couldn't get up with her hind feet held securely in Ray's heel rope. I got off my horse and walked back to the ungrateful patient and slipped my rope off her head, trusting that Ray's heel loop would hold her down until I could get back on my horse. Wrong!!

As I started back to my horse, Ray turned his horse around and rode up toward the mad old cow, hollering at her and pitching her all the slack in his rope! Madder than hell, she quickly got to her feet and came up looking for trouble, ready to whip the world.

I saw what was coming and started running toward my horse. Of course, my running at him spooked him, and away he went. I didn't have time to plant a tree and wait for it to grow, so I could climb it, and I was afoot in the middle of the big pen with one mad, old momma looking for something to take her rage out on. I was in trouble aplenty right quick!

The closest thing I could see was the old shed on the west end of the pen. It wasn't very close, but I took off for it as fast as I could go, with old, mad momma gaining on me pretty fast. Her bellering and hot breath on my hip pockets gave me lots of encouragement, as I tried to set a new world record for the 100 yard dash in chaps and spurs!

As I ran under the shed, I managed to jump and grab one of the pole rafters overhead, as the mad cow's head hit me just above the knees, lifting me up in the air. I managed to hang on to the rafter as the cow ran under me, then she whirled and charged again. I was able to pull my legs up and got to swinging enough to reach the next pole over with my feet. There I hung, holding on to one pole with both hands, and my spurs hooked over the next pole, with my rear end hanging down for old, mad momma to vent her rage on!

She was standing under me, bellering real loud and slinging her head up at the swinging target I presented to her. I would pull myself up as far as I could, so she couldn't quite reach my rear. I was glad she didn't have teeth to bite with, 'cause she was mad enough to eat me!

There I hung, kinda like an old floppy hammock. I was hollering for Ray to get this damned cow out of there. He was sitting on his horse laughing so hard and enjoying the show he didn't seem in much hurry to ride up and help me out.

When my arms began to play out and I started sagging in the middle, a reassuring bump in the rear-end from the old mad cow gave me incentive, and I pulled my rear up again. Her nose was nice and clean from wiping it on the seat of my pants!

Ray was sure getting a big laugh out of my predicament. Same laugh I had heard when Uncle Dayton and Old Bob had jumped off into the river! He finally tired of watching all this and rode up toward us, and the mad momma took after his horse. The mad, ungrateful, old gal left the pen at a run, and I was sure glad to see her leave!

I gave Ray hell for letting her get up before I could get to my horse. He laughed and bragged about my running and acrobatic skills, and I finally had to laugh, too. Guess it was a funny sight. After that, I wasn't too quick to head those old cows for Ray. I kinda liked the heeling end! Let the header take the rope off!!

Bob with Uncle Bob at Boxcar Bremmer Cow
Camp, WS Ranch, Cimarron 1949

Lyle and Bob at Boxcar Bremmer, Uncle Dayton in background

Knox brothers, Ray, Dayton, Bob, Lyle at Boxcar Bremmer, WS Ranch, Cimarron New Mexico, 1949

Dad with Uncle Bob, Aunt Tina, Uncle Ray and Uncle Dayton 1970

Knox brothers, Bob, Ray, Lyle, Dayton at Moreno Ranch, Eagle Nest, New Mexico, 1970

19

Jesse and The Bat Wing Chaps

Uncle Bob came by the Boxcar Bremmer camp one evening and told me he had contracted to build a new boundary fence between the Philmont Scout Ranch, Ute Creek Ranch, and Atmores Ranch. All the way across to Vermejo Park, close to twenty-five miles, it sure was some rough country. Bob needed some help, and I was always eager to work with him, so I gave Sandy my notice that I was leaving.

Bob had an old, rattle-trap pickup, not a four-wheel drive like we have today. All the posts and wire had to be packed in, and he wanted me to take on the packing job.

We started this job in Cimarron Canyon and headed north. There was an old, abandoned stagecoach stop about a mile west of where the present Forest Service buildings are. We camped there when we first started building this fence. There was a good spring near the camp. We fenced off a little trap for our saddle horses and pack burros, and fixed up the old adobe building enough to camp in for a while.

Bob had borrowed a couple of big stout burros from Philmont, and these were my pack string. Turner Welding Shop in Cimarron built a couple sets of metal-framed pack racks that fit a burro pack saddle. I could get about fifteen to twenty cedar posts on each burro. The pack frames were well built so the posts didn't rub the burro. With a full load of posts on him, about all of the burro you could see was his head sticking out one end and his legs poking out the bottom of the post pile!

Bob had two or three guys from a little south of the border digging post holes. We didn't use any steel posts on this job, so there sure were a lot of holes to dig. I did all the packing of barbed wire, posts, digging bars, post hole diggers, staples and anything else needed on the job.

After the men had dug the post holes, my job was to drop a post in each hole. Then the crew would come along to set the posts and tamp them in. My burros soon learned what we were doing and would follow the line of dug holes, while I rode along beside them, reaching over and taking a post off the load, standing it up in the hole; I didn't even have to get off my horse. Those burros were sure smart and nice to work with. I tried to gage my packing so that I was always busy and didn't have to help dig too many holes!

On this job, Bob rode a big buckskin, bald-faced, stocking-legged gelding named Billy Sunday. About as good a horse as I was ever around. Bob used Billy Sunday to string all the barbed wire. We put a steel digging bar through the center of a full reel of barbed wire. Then we wired the ends of the digging bar between two trees with the roll of wire suspended about three or four feet off the ground so it could spin as the wire was pulled off the reel. The reels of wire had a quarter mile of wire on each.

Bob took an old piece of rope and tied one end to the strand of wire coming off the reel. The other end he dallied around his saddle horn and headed Billy Sunday north! This got to be a pretty hard pull, as the fence line went through a lot of trees and brush. A narrow trail had been cleared along the new fence line, but going up and downhill this quarter mile of barbed wire sure got heavy and hard to pull. Billy Sunday laid into the rope and pulled like a big locomotive. He kept going with it until they reached the end. Bert Phipps was working with us and he would watch the wire and keep it feeding off the reel. Bob and Billy Sunday were too far from Bert to hear him holler when they were getting to the end of the wire reel. Bert had a .38 caliber pistol and fired a shot to let them know when to stop. There were several pretty good sized trees that got cut down from the strand of wire being dragged against them! Billy Sunday never failed to pull a full quarter mile of wire every time.

From our camp we had about a mile of open country to cross to get to the trail that followed the fence line into the timber, leaving Cimarron Canyon and climbing up the mountain. Bob had borrowed some gentle dude horses from Philmont for his crew to ride to the job. He mounted me on a big sorrel horse called Jesse he had gotten from Uncle Dayton. Jesse was kinda cowboy broke. It didn't take much provocation to touch him off, and he could darn sure do a good job of bucking a feller off.

I had gotten along pretty well with Jesse, sweet talking him a little and not giving him any excuse to blow up. We had saddled up pretty early one morning, and I was sure fretting about how the wind was blowing, coming down Cimarron Canyon well above all the posted speed limits! It was really whistling across the flat country we had to cross. I put my big bat wing chaps on, pulled my hat down as far as I could, eased up on Jesse, and headed out on Jesse toward the trail.

Jesse was sure humped up, looking back, first to one side then the other, really grabbing his ass, and I was sitting pretty tight. The wind caught the bat wing on the right chap leg, slapping it around toward Jesse's shoulder, and he blew up like big time! I rode him three or four jumps before I joined the bird gang and came crashing down. Jesse bucked on out a ways and Bob ran up on him and caught him and led him back to me.

"Try him again, I don't think you were ready!" he said, as he handed me my bridle reins.

Well I didn't know how I could have been more ready, but I took my reins from Bob and stepped back on Jesse.

He was sure boogered and was really watching for that thing to jump out and try to get him again. I was sitting tight as I could get. I had a choke hold on the saddle horn when the wind caught the left bat wing chap leg, flopping it out, and slapping Jesse on the other side!

I was damn sure ready this time and rode him about two jumps further than the first time! I hit the ground pretty hard, leaving a nice set of spur tracks across the seat of my saddle with my spur rowel. I came up with a hand full of dirt and grass.

Bob caught Jesse and brought him back to me again.

He kinda grinned and said, "I think you about got him figured out!! Bet you can ride him this time!"

I sure wasn't sharing Bob's confidence, but we were getting closer to the timber, and I knew the wind would not be so bad on those bat wings once we got there. Bob rode up in front of Jesse as I got on again. Bert rode up on the other side of me, and I managed to get Jesse rode to the safety of the trees.

That night in camp I was cussing those bat wing chaps. I was sore and bruised from hitting the ground a little hard that morning.

Bob said, "How would you like to have a pair of shotgun chaps made out of them?"

I was all for it! Bob got his pocket knife out and proceeded to cut those big bat wings down to long fringe that the wind wouldn't catch. He cut the snaps and rings out of them and took a thong and laced the legs up the back, making a pretty nice pair of fringed shotguns.

This change sure did improve my relationship with Jesse on a windy day! He never did buck me off again, and I kinda got partial to shotgun chaps after that!

20

Starting at Philmont

Around the first of May, 1949, the fencing job with Uncle Bob was nearing completion when I got a job working for John Stokes, horse foreman, at the Philmont Scout Ranch. It wasn't a cow punching job, but it paid a $135.00 a month. Sure beat the $85.00 a month the WS was paying cowboys! So figured to give it a try. I was nineteen the spring I started at Philmont.

I met John Stokes at the Philmont horse barns. He showed me the bunk house, where I dropped off my stuff, and we went up to the corrals. There stood a big thin sorrel horse with a strange look about him.

John said, "Saddle him and ride down to the polo barns. Couple guys working there and you can go help them today."

After telling me how to find the polo barns John got in his pickup and drove off. I caught the big horse. He sure acted strange, as I saddled him up. He blew up and bucked around the corral with my saddle on him, and I was wondering what I had got into. Finally he quit bucking, and I caught him and eased up on him. He blew up again, but wasn't very hard to ride and I warmed him up pretty good in the corral.

This knot head was sure seeing lots of buggers as we headed down the road to the polo barns. He went along pretty well for a little ways, then spook real bad and want to buck again. I wasn't real happy with my first mount at this outfit, but I made it to the polo barns on him.

As I rode up to the long barn across the front of the corrals, I could hear some laughing coming from around in back. So I rode around the end of the barn to see if the guys I was supposed to help were back there.

I rode up on two sure surprised cowboys, Lawrence "Boss" Sanchez and Melvin Hall, heading and heeling burros! I told them who I was and that I was supposed to start work with them. They were mighty glad it wasn't Stokes who had come up on their roping practice, as he kinda frowned on this activity! They invited me to join them, but all I could get my old goofy mount to do was try to buck. I didn't have much luck trying to rope off him.

"How come you're riding that loco S.O.B.?" Melvin asked.

"Stokes told me to ride him, so I did," I replied.

He laughed and said, "Guess he was trying you out! That horse locoed a while back and no one's ridden him since he got on the "goofy grass!"

The old horse was seeing spooks everywhere, I was just glad he couldn't buck very hard. The next morning, Stokes asked how I got along with the horse. I told him how he was, and he cut him out of the saddle horse string and I didn't have to ride him anymore. Eventually, the old horse went to the sale ring, and I was glad to see him go.

Boss and Melvin were sure fun to ride with. Melvin was always eager to rope anything that would run. He was a good roper, winning several calf ropings at local rodeos. Boss was a good horseman, and I learned a lot working with him over the next twenty-five years. We became close friends, and still are today.

◊　　◊　　◊

We started gathering horses, getting ready for the summer season when the ranch filled up with boy scouts. Since we didn't have the luxury of horse trailers and trucks, there were some long rides.

The summer wranglers started coming in to go to work along toward the end of May. I wasn't quite prepared for these young fellows, expecting some cowboys to show up. Boy, was I in for a surprise! Two guys who came to work had some horse experience, but about ten were as green as gourds.

They were around my age, mostly college kids, wanting to be cowboys. Most of them didn't know how to saddle a horse, let alone ride one! Shoeing a horse was as foreign to them as flying an airplane. Boss was a good teacher, though, and got this crew started pretty well.

Seemed like there was a wreck of some kind happening all the time. The new wranglers had to learn to shoe a horse, and this was pretty dangerous, both for the horse, and the wranglers! Wranglers got kicked, horses got a nail driven into their foot wrong and being "quicked". Horses jerked their feet away from a would-be horseshoer, with the sharp end of a horseshoe nail protruding, just looking for a leg or hand to rip open. Horses set back, broke halters, and jumped over and onto wranglers! Things got a little western at times!!

Philmont had what they called the Health Lodge. This was an over grown first-aid station, staffed by a doctor and a nurse or two, to care for the boy scouts visiting the ranch. They stayed pretty busy patching up the wounded wranglers. And Boss Sanchez stayed busy doctoring crippled and rope-burned horses.

All the dude horses had been turned out for nearly nine months and were pretty fresh when we got them in to shoe and ride out, a little before the boy scouts started coming in. Each horse had to be ridden and, how they acted determined how much riding we had to put on them to have them ready for the kids. Philmont had a remuda of around 200 head of horses at that time, so we got a good workout getting them all shod and ridden!

I figured if that bunch of wranglers could ride them, those horses sure had to be gentle! Boy, the health lodge really got busy when we started riding this bunch of horses! Bucking off, just plain falling off, runaways, you name it, and it was fixing to happen! I felt sorry for some of those guys. They got toughened up quick. A few rolled up their beds and went home, replaced by another eager "wanta be."

A broken arm or collar bone was about the most serious injury we had. Most of the new wranglers caught on and those who survived the first two weeks went on to be fair help as we rolled into the summer and the scouts started coming.

The older, more experienced hands were horsemen and assigned a camp or cavalcade. Each horseman had two wranglers, and each camp had around 40-45 head of horses. There were horse strings at Ponil, Carson Maxwell, and Cimarroncito. As the visiting campers came through these camps, each with a horse string in it, they would get a two-hour horseback ride. The horseman and wranglers had to have the horses gathered and brought into the corrals, brushed, fed, saddled and ready for the morning ride at 8:00 AM and ready for another ride at 1:00 PM.

I had some experience packing horses so Stokes gave me a job as horseman taking out cavalcades. I had one wrangler to help me, and our job was to take twenty-five to thirty-five boy scouts on a ten day horseback trip around Philmont. Each boy scout was assigned a saddle horse, his to ride, feed, groom and care for, for the ten days. All the scouts' personal gear, food, cooking utensils, sleeping bag, etc. was packed on two or three pack horses. When put in one big pile all this gear would make even the stoutest pack horse tremble at the sight! It took a little figuring to get all this stuff on the pack horse.

Every day, we would ride six to ten miles to a different camp where we would spend the night. There were two lay-over camps, where the scouts participated in program activities for a day.

A typical cavalcade left the horse barns at headquarters on the first day, riding up past the Stockade, Lovers Leap, and over Stone Wall Pass. Following the trail along the side of Urraca Mesa, we would stop at Toothache Springs to eat the sack lunches the headquarters dining hall had prepared for us. Afterward, we would ride down the side of the mesa to Carson Maxwell base camp to spend the night. Melvin Hall was horseman at Carson Maxwell and Buddy Maldonado was one of his wranglers. They had a nice bunkhouse to stay in, and my wrangler and I rolled our beds out there. We ate in the big dining hall there along with the campers. We got fed a pretty good meal that first night out.

The cavalcade laid over there the second day so the campers got to tour the Kit Carson Museum and watch the black-smith work.

There was a small arena at Carson Maxwell where we let the scouts try their hand at riding Philmont's several longhorn steers. This was always fun, but due to the number of health lodge cases coming in from the steer riders, it was discontinued after a couple summers! Buddy Maldonado got a lot of practice on these longhorn steers and sure got to be a good rider; good enough that he went on to win the saddle bronc riding and the All Around Cowboy title at the Cimarron rodeo a few years later!

Third day out for the cavalcade was a short ride of two or three miles to Olympia. This camp offered gun safety and small bore rifle shooting. We stopped here and let the campers try their skills at target shooting. After lunch, we rode on up the five miles or so to Abreu camp for the night.

Our scouts would have to set up camp, cook supper and breakfast. The did the cooking over an open camp fire and slept in tents. My wrangler and I ate with them and usually slept in the saddle room at the corrals. We had a big rough horse pasture here and it was pretty tricky getting all our horses found and corralled early in the morning.

The fourth day was sure a pretty ride going along the Rayado River up the bottom of Rayado Canyon. The trail crossed the river thirty some times as it wound up through this deep canyon. The big rock formations were pretty impressive, towering several hundred feet above the canyon floor. The roar of the river as it cascaded down over huge boulders and big rainbow trout darting out of the way as our horses crossed the river made this an interesting and fun ride.

The trail followed the river through the canyon most of the seven miles to Fish Camp. About four miles above Abreu, the canyon became very narrow, the river turning into churning white water, and the trail climbed several hundred feet above the canyon floor.

This trail was one of Waite Phillips' favorite horseback rides when he was active on the ranch. Waite Phillips was the donor who gave the Philmont Ranch to the Boy Scouts of America in 1941.

As the trail climbed steadily higher above the river below, it went around a sharp outcropping of rock. The trail here had been dynamited out and was just wide enough for a loaded pack horse. Looking up, it was nearly solid rock, and looking down we could see the swift, white water rushing down the canyon. The roar of the river was pretty loud, even this high above it. Kinda made a guy pay attention there for a little while! The trail had a little retainer wall about ten inches high, made out of rock and concrete along the outside edge to keep the trail from washing out. As we rode around the face of this near sheer cliff, we couldn't see ahead because of the sharp curve in the trail. I always hoped I wouldn't meet a bear on that curve, as I led a pack horse and the cavalcade around this hairy part. When the trail dropped back down to the canyon bottom, after going around that high curve, everyone relaxed a little.

The canyon began widening as the trail approached Fish Camp. As we rode out of the timber, we came into a series of large, open grass covered meadows. The Rayado River couldn't make up its mind which way it wanted to go, as it wound around through these pretty meadows.

Setting just above the junction where the Rayado River was joined by the slightly smaller Aqua Fria creek, was the main lodge of Fish Camp. It was a long, log building with four or five bedrooms, a large living room and dining room. Each room had a big rock fireplace. The kitchen and pantry were on the south end, near the Agua Fria. Across the creek was a series of three other slightly smaller log buildings. All of these buildings were remarkably built and well cared for. There were no roads into Fish Camp then, and it always amazed me to think that all the logs and material used in this construction came right from this area.

The main lodge and all the other buildings were completely furnished with beds, couches, chairs, dressers, tables, both large and small, kitchen cabinets, etc., all hand-crafted there at Fish Camp. Some of the finest woodwork I have ever seen, and all made without the luxury of electricity! Waite Phillips had these log buildings built and he didn't cut any corners. He was pretty picky, so all the work had to be first rate.

The cavalcade laid over at Fish Camp, on the fifth day out, and the scouts had the option of a horseback ride up to Lost Cabin and the far western boundary of Philmont to view the huge meadows of the Agua Fria country of the UU Bar ranch, or a day of rest, learning how to tie fishing flies, and to try and catch some fish. The trout were plentiful, but catching them wasn't so easy! This gave my wrangler and me the opportunity to shoe any horses that may have lost a shoe, and fish a little too!

The sixth day, we made the long, steep climb out of Rayado Canyon, watching Fish Camp and Rayado River get smaller and smaller, as we topped out over Webster Pass. As we rode down toward Bonita Canyon we could see the wreckage of a B-52 bomber that had crashed during World War II up near the top of Trail Peak. The trail went off the pass down across Bonita Canyon, up again over Fowler Pass, then dropped down to Crater Lake.

This was a pretty long ride for the scouts, and Crater Lake was a welcome stop. The camp sat high up on the east side of the mountain, just above a small natural lake, hence the name Crater Lake. From the front of the Crater Lake lodge, we had a view of the foothills and plains spreading east toward Oklahoma and the Texas Panhandle. Crater Lake had been a hunting camp built for Waite Phillips, and consisted of two rock and log buildings. They were pretty nice, but didn't compare with the workmanship at Fish Camp.

Uncle Bob was staying at Crater Lake, running the pack string from there to the outlying camps. I sure enjoyed this stop, staying up most of the night playing poker and swapping stories. I rolled my bed out in the cabin with Bob and some of the other staff. My wrangler, Truman, slept in a tent along with the scout leaders, directly behind the cabins.

On one trip, I got up early and went out to the tent and hollered at Truman to roll out. We needed to jingle the horses while the scouts were getting up and getting breakfast. I went back in the cabin, drank coffee with Bob, and complained about Truman being hard to roll out early in the morning.

"I'll show you how to break him of staying in bed!" Bob told me. "Take a bucket of cold spring water and dump it in his sleeping bag and he will damn sure get up!"

Seemed like a good idea to me. I got a bucket of cold water.

The sun hadn't quite made it up yet as I eased up to the tent.

Looking in the dark tent, I could make out the forms of several sleeping bags. I spotted what I thought was Truman's sleeping bag. Creeping up to the sleeping form, I had the bucket in one hand as I jerked the sleeping bag down and dumped the cold water on the unsuspecting sleeper.

Great plan! Only it wasn't Truman! A very surprised scout leader jumped out of that sleeping bag, madder than hell, yelling his head off! Truman was in the sleeping bag next to him, laughing like a hyena! Boy, you talk about doing some back pedaling and sweet talking! I rushed into the cabin, grabbed a towel and a cup of coffee, and went back to the wet scout leader, apologizing as fast as I could! I brought him into the cabin and got him dried off, and he soon saw the humor and didn't stay mad. I was ready to kill that damned Truman!

Seventh day was an even longer ride, going from Crater Lake down through Miner's Park, then dropping off to the bottom of Urraca Canyon. Crossing the small creek, the trail climbed up and over Shaeffers Pass, down by Clark's Fork, and finally reaching Cimarroncito. We put some miles on the scouts on this ride, and they were a tired bunch when we unsaddled at the corrals just below the Cimarroncito camp.

Scouts as well as the horses got a deserved rest on the eighth day, as we laid over at Cimarroncito. The campers had the opportunity to try their skills at rock climbing.

It was a welcome break after several days in the saddle. There was a horse string here, like Melvin had at Carson Maxwell, so my wrangler and I had some story trading to do with the horseman and wranglers.

The ninth day out was the fun day for the scouts. Nearly all the riding had been single file trail riding, without much chance of getting to ride at a lope. Except the occasional runaway! All the scouts wanted to try out their newly acquired horsemanship skills, so we took them for a short trail ride up through Cathedral Rocks above Cimarroncito Lake, into Hidden Valley.

Hidden Valley was a small, open, grassy little area completely surrounded by high rock formations, with only one small opening coming into it. We let the scouts have a few horse races, imaginary barrel races, and just plain fun trying out their new riding skills. Quite a few managed to fall off, but they sure enjoyed themselves. My wrangler and I stayed near where the trail came in, to block any horse really running off. We could keep them in this kinda natural enclosure!

The last day out, we would leave Cimarroncito, winding down through the foot hills, around the Tooth of Time ridge and into Headquarters. Saddle sore, but mostly happy, the scouts would head back home with some pretty wild tales of riding on Philmont!

With a little luck, me and my wrangler would get a day off before getting a new Cavalcade, and start another trip.

There was usually two cavalcades on the trail at the same time. One would follow the itinerary I have just described and the other one would ride the same trails only in reverse order. Each trip had its share of wrecks and runaways. There was some mighty poor meals as the kids did their own cooking. Sure made me think of the simple life of punching cows!

Camping season closed at the end of August. All the scouts and summer staff headed back to their homes with some good stories about Philmont. Mostly good, anyway!

Bob Knox having Cavalcade lunch, spam covered with peanut butter, 1949

21

Packing Salt and Deer/Dean Cow Hilton

Stokes kept me working, along with Boss Sanchez and Melvin Hall, after the summer season ended. All the horseshoes that had been so laboriously put on had to be pulled off before the horses were turned out for the winter. We were doing a lot of riding, moving horses out to fall and winter pasture, along with doing a lot of fence fixing, packing salt, and checking waters. All the dude saddles, bridles and miscellaneous gear was given a good cleaning and oiled, and checked for any repairs that might be needed.

We had put a bunch of horses in Harlan and up on Deer Lake Mesa and needed to put some salt out for them. Stokes decided to take one of his rare horseback rides and go with me to put salt out.

We packed three horses with salt and headed out from Headquarters for Cimarron Canyon, dropping off a couple blocks of salt at different salt licks along the Cimarron River. Climbing up out of Cimarron Canyon, we went up to the Harlan Camp, past the Vaca Pond, and climbed to the top of Deer Lake Mesa.

Walter was one of our pack horses. He was a big black horse that Stokes kept bragging about, telling me how well he would follow us with out being led. On this trip, we had unloaded most of Walter's salt at Deer Lake. There were still two blocks of salt on him, one in each panniered.

As we headed for Devils Wash Basin, Stokes said, "Just tie Walter's lead rope to the pack saddle and turn him loose. He will follow us."

"I don't mind leading him. He's no problem," I replied.

"No, tie his lead rope up and turn him loose. I want to show you how good he follows," Stokes said.

Well, I didn't really care how good he followed, but at Stokes' insistence I stopped and tied Walter's lead rope to the sawbuck pack saddle, and he was loose. Stokes seemed happy, and so was Walter, since Walter had the freedom to stop and grab a mouthful of grass as we followed the trail to Devil's Wash Basin.

"See what I told you?" Stokes bragged, as Walter followed along.

Walter seemed to like his new-found freedom, stopping to sample the tall grass, then following along behind us as I led one pack horse and Stokes led the other one.

Walter's stops to graze grew frequent, lasting a little longer at each stop, but he trotted up and caught up with us. I kept watching over my shoulder for Walter, and he kept coming.

At one point I guess Walter was overcome by a sudden urge to see the horse barns, 'cause after stopping to grab a couple mouthfuls of grass, he threw his old head up and headed south at a long trot!

Stokes hollered, "Where the hell are you going Walter?"

Walter didn't seem to hear and didn't pay any attention to Stokes. He just trotted a little faster toward the rim rock on the edge of the Mesa.

"Hell, he never done that before!" Stokes exclaimed. "I don't think he can get off the rim but you better go catch him! We need that salt!"

I handed Stokes the lead rope to the pack horse I was leading and took off after Walter.

Walter saw me coming after him and broke into a run, beating me to the rim. He didn't seem to hesitate as he baled off, down a break in the rim that would test a mountain goat. I didn't see how I could ride off of that rim, but Stokes was hollering at me real encouraging, something like, "Catch that old S.O.B. Don't let him get away!"

I was riding Rusty, a sure, good horse. We finally got down off the rim and I could see Walter headed for points south at a pretty good clip. He was looking back to see if I had made it down off the rim okay. I cinched up pretty tight, and shook out a loop and took off after good old Walter.

Looking back, Walter saw us coming and decided we were in a hurry to get to the barns, too. He sure didn't want to come in second! He really hooked up and the race was on. With Stokes perched up on top of the rim yelling instructions and cussing Walter, Rusty and I ducked and dodged trees and rocks. We were sure having a horse race.

Finally we hit a long clearing, and Rusty closed the gap on Walter. I let fly with my loop trying to rope this old black sucker that followed so good. My loop sailed out just right. Well, almost just right. It hit up on

Walter's neck right behind his ears, then flipped over and settled around the cross bucks on the pack saddle pretty as you please! Really not the best place to catch a running horse!

I was tied on hard and fast to the saddle horn so there was no turning loose. Rusty started trying to stop when I threw my loop, and Walter thought it was a signal to speed up, so things got kinda tricky there for a little bit. When Walter hit the end of my rope, Rusty got jerked down on his knees, and Walter got set back on his haunches. Neither one went plumb down, but it was close! Rusty scrambled up and got his feet under him so when Walter tried another run we had him slowed down. Walter dragged us down the hillside a little ways, but soon got tired of that and stopped.

I got the lead rope down from the pack saddle. Walter had blown his chance to show me how good he followed. Leading Walter, I started back up the way we had come. Stokes was still sitting high up on the rim and hollered down for me to work on around the mesa and pick up the trail from Ute Gulch to Devil's Wash Basin, and he would wait for me there. We finally got up on top, put out the last of the salt, and headed into headquarters and I'll guarantee Walter got led all the way! I had seen enough of how good he followed. Stokes claimed it was the first time he had ever done that, and that something must have spooked him, but I sure kept hold of him anyway!

◊   ◊   ◊

We stayed pretty busy through September and October. Toward the end of October, Stokes told me he needed someone to camp at Dean Canyon Cow Camp and pack deer during the upcoming hunting season. He asked me if I had any hunting experience and ever packed out a deer.

I had been with Uncle Bob when we had gotten some camp meat and I knew how to field dress a deer. We had packed our poached deer to camp, so I told him I could sure handle that little job! I didn't know what I was getting into!

Stokes told me to take a couple pack horses, get enough groceries from the commissary to last a couple weeks, some grain for my saddle horse and pack horses, and to set up camp at Dean Cow Camp. It was around twenty miles up to there. I had been by once, gathering horses, but I didn't remember much about it.

We got a pretty good snow the night before I was to move up to the camp. With several inches of snow already on the ground, it was snowing hard as I got packed and left headquarters pretty early in the morning. I rode in through Cimarron, out to Ponil Canyon and rode up past the Chase Ranch, and headed for the Dean Canyon turnoff. By then, the snow was really coming down hard.

I knew the old road to Dean Canyon was a little hard to see, and as the snow got deeper, I knew it wouldn't be easy finding the road. I got up past the Chase Ranch and started watching for a road leading out of Ponil Canyon going south. Snow was about ten inches deep by then and no sign of a road. I knew I was on track when I came up on a little boy scout sign, "Dean Canyon", with an arrow pointing south. It was snowing so hard visibility was down to about 50 yards, and I knew Dean Canyon was still about three or four miles south. The snow had hidden any road, trail, or any clue as to how the hell to get to Dean Canyon!

Boy, that was some rough old canyon this sign was pointing to, but I turned off and headed into it. I figured I would pick up the road any minute. The further I went, the rougher it got. Jumping rocks, I picked my way through the thick brush. Seemed like it was snowing harder and getting deeper the further I went. Visibility was about as far as my horse's ears, and it just got rougher and steeper the further I went.

I soon gave up the hope of finding the road. I knew I must have missed it somewhere. Just getting out of that deep canyon was my main priority for awhile! I finally made it to the top of the ridge between Dean and Ponil. It was sure a welcome relief when I finally topped out! I headed off the side of the mountain and as I got to the bottom of a big canyon I found the road and knew I must have blundered into Dean Canyon!

I rode east, down the canyon, snow a good foot deep by now. A couple miles down the canyon, I rode up on the Hilton Hotel of Dean Canyon! A windmill set below the cabin, a set of small corrals, and a little shed were about a fifty yards south of the camp.

I unloaded my pack horses and left them in the corrals while I made a quick check on the fence around the small horse trap. The fence was in pretty good shape, so I grained my horses and gave them a little hay that had been hauled in earlier, and turned them out in the trap, while I went down to register at the Dean Canyon Hilton!

This Hilton was a little on the rustic side, you might say. It was a one-room board cabin, missing a board on the north wall. The floor had a couple boards broke through, but it made it handy to sweep that way. If I'd had a broom. One window was brokeout, and had an old gunny sack nailed over it. It looked like the security system on the door was good though. The piece of baling wire holding the door shut looked fairly new!

A little half-size cook stove, a table, a three-legged chair were at one end of the room. These and an old broken-down metal cot with a worn out mattress were the extent of the furnishings. The view looking out from inside the cabin wasn't hampered much by the gunny sack over the window, as the cracks between the boards on the wall were wide enough you could see out in most places!

I picked up the axe left leaning against the wall near the stove and went out and found a suspicious pile of snow. Kicking around in it I found some fire wood and got a fire going. Home Sweet Home!

I found a water bucket in the cabin and went down to the windmill. No wind blowing, so it wasn't pumping any water. I broke the ice on the tank and got a little water. I fried a little meat and a potato, made some coffee, and laid back to enjoy all this luxury.

I didn't have any overshoes, and my boots were soaking wet, so I decided to put them in the oven of the stove to try and dry them out.

Did I mention the stove was kinda small? Small I guess! Only one boot would fit in the oven at a time, and my feet aren't that big! Anyway, I don't think my boots ever dried out for two weeks.

Wind got up pretty strong during the night, and the open space where the board was missing allowed for ample ventilation. Next morning there were little snow drifts all across my bed and the floor. It felt good to jump out of bed, try to get a fire going, break the ice on my water bucket, and try and get those frozen boots on! Boy howdy, this was one romantic S.O.B.! How could a guy get so lucky?

I went out to feed my horses and saw the snow was about eighteen inches deep. I got the axe from the wood pile and chopped a hole in the ice at the windmill tank for the horses to get a drink. When I went to get some grain from the sacks I had packed in, I noticed that there was a big pile of sticks and cow chips stacked on top of the sacks. I thought that was kinda strange, but being in a hurry to get saddled and on my way, I didn't think too much about it.

The hunters hunted afoot mostly, driving up Ponil and North Ponil canyons in their vehicles and hiking up the side canyons and ridges hunting deer. Big mule deer were sure plentiful in this area at this time. There wasn't any 4x4 vehicle hunting then. The hunters were instructed on how to mark the location of their downed game, and a packer from Indian Writings would pack out their game for them. There wasn't a building at Indian Writings then, just an open cook shelter with a bulletin board nailed to a post where you could leave a note.

My instructions from Stokes were to take my pack horses and ride up North Ponil to Indian Writings Camp each morning. There, the deer hunters could find me if they needed help getting a deer out to the road.

Leaving the Hilton just about sunup, I had to go back up Dean Canyon to Chandler Pass, over it to Ponil Canyon, down a mile to North Ponil and then up North Ponil Canyon six or seven miles to Indian Writings. Well, luckily the snow had blown and drifted enough that the road up Chandler was visible when I got there and I didn't have to go back the way I had came in!

As I was riding up the road near the top of Chandler Pass, I heard gun shots, and soon came upon a hunter with a big buck down. He was sure glad to see me as it was a couple miles down to his truck.

I loaded his deer on Walter, my big black pack horse, and packed it down to the hunter's truck. Stokes had told me the fee for packing a deer was $2.00, so when the hunter asked what he owed me, I told him $2.00.

"Hell kid", he said, "don't pack a deer out for $2.00! It's worth at least $5.00 to pack a deer out!"

So he gave me $5.00! Well, I being a pretty good business man, I put $2.00 for Stokes in one pocket and $3.00 for me in the other pocket! Seemed like a good deal to me! Easy Money!

I rode on up to Indian Writings where a couple of hunters were waiting for me and I stayed busy packing deer at the new rate of $5.00 each!

I got quite a bit of packing business right quick, as there were lots of deer and hunters. I was kept busy, and the packing fee at $5.00 was adding up pretty good! I got back to the Dean Canyon Hilton after dark and enjoyed another night in the cool, romantic luxury, thanking Stokes for being so considerate to offer me this great opportunity!

Next morning, when I went out to feed and saddle up, I discovered the big piles of wood chips, small sticks, cow chips, and a flattened tin can piled neatly on top of the feed sacks. Now who the heck is messing around here, I wondered. No tracks, just all this stuff on the feed sacks. I wondered if Melvin, who was camped over in Cimarron Canyon, was trying to pull a trick on me. I didn't figure he would ride twenty miles just to do this, but he was the closest person around that I knew of.

This went on every morning while I was there at Dean Canyon Cow Camp, and I was beginning to get kinda spooked! I would throw all the stuff off the feed sacks, scatter it out in the corral, and next morning here it all was again, stacked on top of the feed sacks!

This was my first encounter with pack rats! I learned later that they would always leave something in return for what they took. But up there at the cow camp I was sure getting jumpy, trying to figure out what was messing around at night!

The packing business was pretty good, and my cut on the packing fee was adding up. I had been making my daily jaunt up to Indian Writings every morning for a week, when I ran into Doc Loomis, who was the ranger living up at Ponil Camp.

He knew what the Dean Cow camp was like, so when he found out I was camped there, he invited me to move up to Ponil and stay there with him and his wife for the remainder of the hunt. I thought about giving up the luxury of the Dean Cow Hilton! Sure took me a long time to decide if I wanted to take him up on his offer. Thinking of a warm cabin and his wife's cooking, I said, "I'll be there tonight!" before he got through asking me! The move meant riding a few extra miles every day, but I sure didn't mind that. I was kinda glad to get away from that spook that was messing with my feed sacks!

Mrs. Loomis was glad to have me stay with them a few days, and it sure made the last of the hunting season better for me. She was a good cook, and I enjoyed visiting with her and Doc. Riding in every night after dark with a hot meal waiting for me in a warm house and pleasant company kinda helped me get over leaving the luxury of Dean Cow Hilton!

I got back to headquarters to find a very irate Stokes waiting for me!

Seems he had gotten word of my business venture, and frowned deeply at the $2.00/$3.00 split and fired me! Boy, was I ticked off! I offered to give the ranch the extra $3.00, but he refused it. So I rolled my bed.

Melvin, while camped at Harlan Cow camp, packing deer in that area, had gotten paid $5.00 a day from the Game Dept. for helping them patrol Cimarron Canyon for poachers! He was only charging $2.00 to pack a deer, but making an extra $5.00 from the Game Dept. Guess Stokes couldn't handle our extra business activities, so he fired Melvin too!

Melvin and I moved into Cimarron. I got a job with a survey crew preparing to pave the road up Cimarron Canyon. This was a pretty easy job, just holding that long stick up in the air while a guy tried to see it looking through his little telescope. If you ever wondered why the road to Eagle Nest was so crooked, now you know! I helped do the survey work.

My survey job lasted about three months. I rented a room above the old Post Office in Cimarron and was eating in the local cafe. Not a bad way to pass the winter. I didn't even miss the luxury of the Dean Cow Hilton!

Stokes came to me and Melvin the first of March and asked us to come back to work for him. I had had enough town living and so had Melvin, so we went back to work for Stokes.

22

The High Dive

Stokes had sent a cowboy, Bud, and me up to Ponil to gather some burros. We camped in the bunkhouse there; sure a lot better than the Hilton over in Dean Canyon! Bud had stopped and bought a new pair of Levis in Cimarron on our way through town. Next morning Bud pulled the tags off, and pulled on his new, stiff Levis.

We rode up to the boundary fence at the old Stern's Ranch, several miles above Ponil. As we approached the creek crossing, Bud was complaining about his new Levis not feeling very comfortable. He hadn't put his chaps on that morning, and I soon saw why. He pulled up at the edge of the creek, got off his horse and handed me his bridle reins.

"Gonna fix these damn, stiff Levis," Bud said.

He sat down on a big rock, unbuckled his spurs and pulled off his boots. Giving me a big grin, he waded out into the cold creek and sat down! The water was a little above his waist when he sat down, colder than cold! He sat there for a few minutes, grinning like he had good sense and got his new Levis soaked up real good. He got up out of the creek, sat back down on the rock, and dried his feet best he could with his shirt sleeves. He pulled his boots on, got back on his horse and we went on hunting burros! Think that was the only time those Levis ever got in any water, except when we got caught in the rain. They sure shaped up to fit him! Sure broke them in right! I never tried that process, but it worked good for Bud!

I was riding a big, good looking sorrel horse called Slingshot that day. He was a new horse Stokes had picked up at a horse sale. He was a tall thoroughbred-looking horse with a nice small head. He just didn't have much inside that good looking head! Slingshot had been pretty humpy the couple of times I had ridden him, but I had managed to keep him pulled up and kept from going for a bronc ride.

I spotted some burros way up near the rim rock, and being that they were on my side of the canyon, I turned Slingshot up the side of the mountain to ride up and bring them down. Slingshot had been pretty humpy that morning, sure wanting to buck and grabbing his butt as we rode up the Ponil Canyon. I figured climbing up that steep, mountain side would help his attitude.

It sure got steep right quick. The higher we went, the steeper the mountain side became. I had to switch back and forth at an angle, as we climbed higher and higher through the rocks, brush, and scattered Pinon and Cedar trees. I got a lot higher than I wanted to be on this horse. The burros saw me coming and they headed up a little higher.

Finally, they got to the rim rock, as high as they could go, and stood there watching me try to climb up to their high perch. I finally got up to the rim and the burros saw they couldn't get any higher, so they turned and started working their way down. Slingshot was sweating and blowing pretty hard by then, and I figured the hard ride up there had taken the buck out of him. WRONG!

Every time I tried to turn him downhill he grabbed his ass and tried to buck. As long as we were going parallel or uphill he seemed all right, but as soon as I turned downhill just a little, he sure acted like he was going to blow up. I tried him several times with the same results, so I got off and checked the hobble on my flank cinch. It was okay.

I got back on him and tried to ease him downhill. Same thing; grab his ass and try to buck. I turned him uphill and he traveled out fine. I pulled my saddle and checked my saddle blanket for something that might be pinching him, but everything seemed okay.

I got back on him and turned him downhill, with the same results. He was all swelled up like a big bull frog, sure wanting to buck. I guess I probably had more guts than sense. I figured if he was crazy enough to try to buck up there, I was crazy enough to just ride him anyway! WRONG AGAIN! I had ridden him up there and I damn sure wasn't going to walk and lead him down! I turned him downhill, figuring I'd call his bluff.

That first jump was a dandy! He just wheeled and blew away, making a big jump straight out and nearly straight down. None of that switch backing stuff for him. We went a long ways before he hit the ground. On the second jump, we really got high, and with the mountain side being so steep, I kinda lost track of where the ground was. When his head and neck disappeared, I figured I might be in a little trouble.

We were turning a perfect somersault, and I saw it wasn't going to be his feet that hit the ground first when we got back down to earth, but probably me, so I tried to bale out. As he continued his somersault, I went out over the side, and his rump hit me and drove me head first into the rocks and brush. Slingshot landed right beside me, on his back and glanced off of me without really landing on top of me.

He bounced and rolled on down the steep mountain side, hitting and rolling, through rocks and brush, not able to get his footing. I raised up and watched him roll and bounce, his feet kicking wildly in the air. He bounced high in the air and as he came down the seat of my saddle slammed into a big Pinon tree, stopping his fall.

I couldn't get up very well, and I just sat there taking inventory to see if all my working parts were still functioning.

"You all right?" I could hear Bud hollering.

"Yea, I think so," I hollered back.

I was having a little trouble getting my breath. I looked around and spotted my hat, emptied the rocks and dirt out of it, and got it back on.

"That was the wildest ride I ever saw!" Bud exclaimed as he rode up to where I was taking a little siesta.

"I figured I would just bring a shovel and cover you up after that somersault!" he said as he sat down next to me. "I think your horse is dead. Looks like he broke his neck when he hit that tree."

"I sure as hell hope he's dead!" I replied. "I thought I was gonna be dead when he turned upside down!"

"I didn't think he would buck off this steep S.O.B. It's nearly like going off a cliff!"

"I didn't either!" I grinned.

"Why the hell did you try to ride him!"

"I guess I didn't want to walk?" I answered.

I completed my inventory. My ankle was banged up a little and some ribs didn't seem to be in the right place. Bud helped me up and with me leaning on him we managed to get on down to where Slingshot lay crumpled up under the big Pinon.

We couldn't see his head. It was bent back under his shoulder. He wasn't kicking or moving, and looked like he was dead all right.

Bud got hold of one of my bridle reins and pulled right hard and managed to get Slingshot's head out from under him. To our surprise, he raised his head up and looked around kinda dizzy like, blinked his eyes a few times and went to struggling to get up! I didn't know whether to be mad or glad. I had hoped he was dead, 'cause I thought I was for a little while!

Slingshot struggled around and got back on his feet. Boy, was he one peeled up old horse! He had lost hide from the top of his head to the bottom of his hind feet. One eye was swollen nearly shut, and he was kinda dragging one hind leg. He was bleeding, seemed like all over. My saddle looked like it had been to war, but the tree seemed all right in it.

Bud led him on down to level ground, and I hobbled along behind them.

"Want me to ride him into camp?" he asked, as I came up to them.

"Hell no," I replied, "I still think I can ride him."

I got back on him and was glad to see he didn't have any buck left in him. He was stiff and limping a lot as we rode the few miles down to Ponil camp and penned the burros that had caused all this.

Next morning, Slingshot was so stiff he couldn't walk to water. Looked like he came out second in a fight with a bear! He had several big knots on his ribs from where they were broke. He had lost a lot of hide, and was skinned up from one end to the other. One eye stayed swollen shut for nearly a week. I wasn't much better off, but could get around enough to pack water and feed to this knot head!

Slingshot finally healed up and I started riding him again. The wreck at Ponil hadn't done much to change his attitude. He was still pretty humpy and would darn sure blow the plug if you had to ride him down much of a hill.

◊　　◊　　◊

I had healed up pretty well from my episode with Slingshot, when Stokes sent me, along with Alex Alexander, back to Ponil to gather horses. Alex, a tall, lanky feller from down around Portales, and I had become pretty good friends in the short time he had been working with us.

We were the same height, 6'4", but his legs were a good four inches longer than mine! I couldn't reach his stirrups when I got on his saddle. To see him riding, he looked like a small guy from the saddle up, but his feet hung down under most horses' bellies.

He was a lot of fun to work with and had a great sense of humor. Alex and I made the rounds in Cimarron on Saturday nights. He really loved to play his fiddle and he could sure do a job playing "The Orange Blossom Special!" He won the New Mexico State Fiddle Playing Championship the year he worked with us, and it was sure a treat to listen to him play.

He was about as good at drinking Jack Daniels whiskey as he was at playing a fiddle!

We had around fifty or sixty horses gathered up and in the Ponil horse pasture on a Friday evening. Saturday morning we decided we probably ought to take them on in to headquarters, since there was going to be a dance at the Ranch Bar Saturday night, and we didn't want to miss that!

We gathered the horse's, got a good count, and headed them for Cimarron and headquarters. On the way, Alex kept pointing out the bad things about drinking beer, which I was kinda prone to do on Saturday night at the Cimarron dances. He explained how beer would rust your innerards and overwork your bladder. He just had a lot of good information about the harm of beer drinking. At the same time, he was promoting Jack Daniels. He kept explaining how much better it was for you than beer, and by the time we got to Cimarron, he had me about half way believing him.

As we rode through Cimarron and were passing the Don Diego Hotel and Bar, now called The St. James Hotel, Alex rode up to the entrance. "Hold my horse a minute. I'll be right back," he said.

He stepped off and handed me his bridle reins. I glanced up and down the street hoping Stokes or somebody from Philmont wouldn't be coming by. Alex was back out in short order, grinning like he had pulled a good one.

As we loped up to catch the horse herd we were driving, Alex handed me a half-pint of Jack Daniels. He had bought two, one for each of us.

"Here, I'll show you what I was talking about." He said giving me a big grin. Not wanting to hurt Alex's feelings, I took the handy, little bottle, and took a pretty good drink.

"Not bad," I finally managed to say, after I quit choking and caught my breath! He laughed and said I would never drink beer again after this.

We had around six miles to go with our bunch of horses, so we started making toasts to the horses, the country, the weather, the good life, different ladies we had met and hoped to meet, Stokes, payday, and just about anything to have another little toast!

As we turned the horses off the road and headed up toward the corrals at headquarters, my bottle was empty and so was Alex's. We tossed the empty bottles in an irrigation ditch along side the road, penned the horses without incident, and rode up to the saddle room and bunk-house.

I stepped off my horse in front of the saddle room, and to my surprise, the ground jumped up and smacked me right in the seat of the pants. I kinda banged into the saddle room wall, knocked my hat off and there I sat with a silly grin on my face, trying to focus on the fast spinning corral!

Stokes walked out of the saddle room and looked down kinda surprised to see me sprawled out on the ground trying to prop myself up against the bunkhouse wall.

"What the hell's the matter with him?" he said.

Alex quickly stepped up and said, "I don't know Mr. Stokes. Think it was something he ate. He hasn't been feeling too good. I think he just needs to lie down awhile."

Alex and another guy dragged and carried me into the bunkhouse, rolled me out on a cot, and threw an old pack horse tarp over me.

Stokes was pretty suspicious, "You guys been drinking?" he asked Alex.

"Hell no!" Alex replied. "He must have got sick from something he ate." Alex could be pretty convincing when he wanted to be.

Alex couldn't revive me, so he went to the dance without me. The next morning Alex swore up and down it had to have been something I ate that affected me like that, 'cause he never heard of Jack Daniels doing that to a feller!

"Hell," I argued "I hadn't had anything to eat since breakfast!"

Anyway, I didn't try and drink a half-pint of Jack Daniels on an empty stomach again!

23

If It Runs, Rope It

One morning, just after daylight, I had one of the wranglers with me, jingling the saddle horses out of the Stockade pasture. I was on the upper end of the pasture, coming down through some pretty thick oak brush when I jumped a pretty good sized bear. I scared him and he took off running so I just took out after him, wanting to get a better look at him. The bear ran out of the oak brush into the open and it was some distance to anymore brush.

The bear was running across the open pasture. I was riding Slingshot. He didn't seem scared of the bear, and since the bear was running, I jerked my rope down and built to him. Still not showing any fear of the bear, Slingshot ran right up on him, giving me a good throw. I missed my first loop, but Slingshot stayed right on him. I built another quick loop and roped the bear around the neck. I jerked my slack. Slingshot set down like a good calf-roping horse, and jerked the bear over backwards.

The bear jumped up, tried to run again, but we had him stopped. The bear rolled over on his back and quickly pulled my rope off his head. He jumped up and gave us a loud "Wuf! Wuf!," snapping his teeth and giving us a big growl. Well, when he started toward Slingshot and me, we hauled ass out of there, muy pronto. The bear turned off and headed for the brush again.

He was still running away from us, so I took out after him again. Slingshot wasn't quite as anxious to run to him this time. Guess it was something the bear had said. Got up close enough for another loop and caught the bear again. We jerked him down, but the bear rolled over and pulled the rope off his head again. The bear jumped up, a little madder than before, and showed more fight as he popped his teeth at us, growling and "Wuf Wuffing" pretty loud. I didn't have to turn Slingshot! He was out of there! I got him pulled up, as the bear quit chasing us, and took off for the brush again.

Well, this time when he turned for the brush, I figured I'd have to do something different to make this work. Slingshot didn't much want to do this anymore! The bear was running as fast as he could go, nearing the brush. Slingshot ran to him again and I managed to rope him around the head and got one front leg thru the loop. The bear hit the end of the rope and we jerked him down again. He quickly rolled over on his back and tried to pull the loop over his head again, but the rope didn't slip off his head this time, as I turned off and started dragging him. I had roped my first bear!

I didn't know what the hell I was going to do with him, but I had him roped! The bear grabbed my rope in his mouth and started chewing on it, so I turned Slingshot around and drug the bear a little ways. With his front leg through the loop, I wasn't afraid of choking him, and he quit chewing my rope. When I stopped dragging him, he got up, a little mad about all this fun, and took after me again.

Slingshot was getting a little boogered at all this teeth popping and growling and didn't need much encouragement to get the heck out of there. I turned Slingshot and took off. The bear stopped chasing us and headed for the nearby oak brush. When the bear hit the end of the rope, we jerked him down, and dragged him again, and he quit trying to chase me.

Slingshot was facing the bear, getting pretty nervous, snorting, and getting hard to hold. As long as the bear was running away from us, he didn't seem scared of the bear, but the bear wasn't running away now, and Slingshot was wanting out of there. The bear was getting hot and was kinda sulled-up, laying there watching us, growling and snapping his teeth. I didn't know what the heck I was going to do now! I thought about trying to get my rope off of Grandma's old goose! That hadn't worked out very well and this little deal looked like it might get pretty interesting!

I was sure glad when the wrangler who was helping me gather horses came loping up. He got all excited about seeing his first bear. I told him he was going to have to heel the bear and he finally managed to get one hind foot of the bear roped. We stretched him out and I got down and got a big stick in the bears mouth, and got his mouth tied shut around the stick. Slingshot was sure working that rope, watching us pretty close and snorting right loud. Got the bear's feet tied together, and we had us a bear captured. The wrangler and I were both pretty excited and then we got to wondering what we were going to do with our bear! I told the wrangler to lope in to headquarters and tell Stokes we had a bear ready to load if he would bring his pickup.

A cloud of dust heading toward me told me Stokes was on the way. He had several wranglers in the pickup, and they all jumped out to see this unusual sight.

"Well I'll be damned!" Stokes exclaimed, "What the hell got into you to rope a bear!"

"Well he ran, so I roped him!" I replied, thinking this sounded pretty logical.

There was a small enclosed pen at camping headquarters that housed an occasional raccoon or porcupine for the scouts to see, so we decided to take the bear and put him in this little pen. The pen wasn't designed for bears, and this bear about filled the little pen! He weighed a little over two hundred pounds. He was about a three year old, not fully grown, but big enough to make it all exciting.

It was a real hot day, and I think with all the chasing and running the bear got, it was just too much for him. He'd gotten overheated and he died that afternoon. I really felt bad, 'cause I never intended to kill him. Just wanted to rope him! Anyway, I got turned in to the State Game & Fish Department for killing a bear out of season.

The local game warden came out, and I finally convinced him I wasn't hunting and sure hadn't meant to kill the bear. The bear was running and it seemed like the thing to do at the time. Just rope him! The officer finally agreed not to give me a citation if I agreed not to rope any more bears, so we struck a deal! The Game & Fish Department let us keep the hide and head from the bear, and George Bullock, director of camping at that time, had the head mounted and it hung on the wall at camping headquarters for many years after that.

Stokes gave Slingshot to Buddy Maldonado to ride shortly after I had roped the bear on him. I told Buddy that Slingshot was pretty good to rope bear on, but sure a dirty bugger to ride off anything very steep! Sure enough, Buddy was riding him, coming off the side of a steep hill when Slingshot pulled the same trick with Buddy that he had with me, gathering burros. Buddy didn't try and ride him through his high dive, though! He baled out before it got too western. Poco smart Hombre!

◊   ◊   ◊

Stokes's nephew, Truman, was working as my wrangler, and Stokes told us to throw our saddles and bridles in his pickup one morning after breakfast. Said he wanted us to ride some new horses he might be buying. Truman and I loaded up with Stokes, and he drove out the road through Cimarron, headed toward Raton.

About thirty miles from the ranch, he turned off the main road at Hoxie and headed east toward a set of corrals on the old Crews ranch. There was an older rancher there with a pickup and some feed he had used to coax the horses into the corrals.

"You boys get your saddles and bridles, and let's see how these horses ride," Stokes said to Truman and me.

Ten or twelve head of horses in the corrals watched Truman and me carry our saddles into the corral. We started catching and riding these horses, as Stokes watched and argued the asking price with the rancher.

There was a pretty good looking bay horse in the bunch, sure snorty acting and not letting us get close to him, as we caught the others and rode them in a big corral. Most of them were riding out pretty good. A couple had crow-hopped a little, but nothing had really tried to buck, and all of them handled pretty well. I had a feeling the bay horse might change all of this and I was right.

"Bob, you ride that bay horse," Stokes said.

"He might be a little fresh," the Crews ranch man said.

The understatement of the day! The bay wasn't about to let us catch him, so I took my rope off my saddle and roped him. He did a lot of snorting and jumping around as I bridled him and eased my saddle on him. Looked like there was a water-melon under my saddle the way it was setting!

I turned him around a couple times and stepped up on him. He blew up like I figured he was going to, but I managed to stay with him. The north side of the corral was in the shade and was pretty wet and slick from some recent rain.

As the bay bucked across this slick place, his feet went out from under him and he landed flat on his side. I fell away from him, into the board corral fence. I hit the fence with my back as I went down landing in a sitting position, with my back against the fence. Old bay had fallen away from the fence and was kicking and struggling to get up, with his hind feet in my lap. He was sure knocking the dust out of my shirt with his hind feet as he struggled to get up. I couldn't get away from him, and he was using me like a punching bag. Sure was mashing up my cigarettes! I managed to roll a little to the side when he finally got up, leaving me in the mud.

I felt like every rib I had was broken! I couldn't get enough air in me to answer Stokes as he ran up asking me if I was all right. I finally managed to get a little air back in me and got to my feet.

Stokes bought all the horses. I was hoping he would pass on the bay! He asked me if I could ride, and I told him I guessed so. I would try it anyway. He told Truman and me to go ahead and start driving the horses to Philmont, and he would go get another wrangler to take my place.

"Looks like the bay horse needs a little riding, Bob. Go ahead and ride him since your saddle's on him!" Stokes said as he climbed into his pickup.

Truman and I started driving the horses. Boy, I was sure hurting as we headed them down the road toward Cimarron. Old bay seemed to have gotten the buck out of his system and traveled out real nice.

The further we went, the more I got to hurting, and I was sure looking down the road hoping to see Stokes coming back with someone to take my place. We were crossing the bridge at the Ponil, coming into Cimarron, when Stokes came driving down the road with my relief. We had only ridden twenty-five miles! Stokes said he hadn't been able to find anyone and was sorry it had taken him so long to get back to us. I think he just forgot!

Alex took me into Raton that night and I had some Xrays done on my chest. I had three broken ribs and about three inches of the bottom rib on my left side was broken off, floating around on its own. The doc at the hospital said he could operate on me and take this broken piece out, or just let it float around, and it would dissolve in time. Would probably be all right if it didn't puncture a lung or something else! The doc wrapped me up in a tight girdle and tape and I got along fine.

I sure didn't want anything to do with an operation. Alex and I figured a little Jack Daniels would be pretty good medicine for something like this, so we went out and doctored me a little that night. Made a few toasts to the "Floating Rib." Alex kept assuring me that Jack Daniels was the best thing to take to help dissolve chunks of floating ribs, and other foreign objects. I could tell it was working, because I started feeling a little less pain pretty quick!

155

24

Some Rank Mules

Uncle Bob had gone to work for Stokes, running a pack horse string from Crater Lake to Fish Camp and Porcupine Camp. These were two of the main camps used in the back country then. No roads went this far into the mountains and all the supplies and equipment needed in the back country had to go in by pack horse or burro. Both Fish Camp and Porcupine were staffed by Philmont staff members, serving several hundred scouts daily. Scouts would pick up provisions at one of these two camps as they hiked through this part of the back country. It took a lot of groceries and miscellaneous items to keep all the scouts supplied.

Stokes bought seven head of four-and-five year old mules that had never been handled. They weren't halter broke and were all wilder than seven hundred dollars. One small mule in the bunch weighed around nine hundred. The rest of them were bigger, weighing a thousand or better.

Uncle Bob got Stokes to let me help him get this bunch of mules started. Boy were they rank and wild! They had never been caught before and they thought a cowboy was something to kick, bite, paw, run over, or just destroy the best way they could, and they sure tried it all on us.

There was a long horse chute down at the polo barns that opened out into a big high-fenced corral. We ran these mules into the chute and managed to get big stout halters on them. We had seven pretty good sized cottonwood logs and we dragged one of these logs up fairly close to the front of the chute. After we got a stout halter on a mule, we tied an end of a long stake rope to one of the logs and the other end into the mule's halter, and turned him out!

The education process started real fast, as each mule bolted out of the chute as fast as he could run when the chute gate opened. For forty or fifty feet they would sure run hard. Then stop just about as hard! The mule would be flying low, then usually turn a nice flip in the air and land flat on his side as he hit the end of the stake rope. The rope and log gave enough to keep them from breaking their necks, but darn sure put a "Whoa!" on them. Some of them jumped up and tried to run again, but after a couple hard stops they stood and faced their log, trembling and snorting.

The mules were pretty smart and didn't fight the stake rope, so after a couple days of this staking, we ran them back through the chute, tying a good stout lead rope into each halter. Bob had his big stout saddle horse, Billy Sunday. Riding up to the front of the chute, I would hand him the lead rope from the mule in the chute. Bob would dally up pretty short and I would turn the mule out.

Billy Sunday could sure hold him if the mule tried to run. Most of them were scared to death of the horse being so close and would sure try to get away. Billy Sunday would drag this fighting mule around the big corral as the mule would pull back, then try to jump over the top of him. Some of the mules would set back and tried to paw Bob or Billy Sunday, then jump forward and try to take a big bite out of whatever they could bite! Bob sure had his hands full, but before long the mule would quit fighting and start thinking about leading.

I had a good stout horse, Rusty, and after the mules' first session out with Bob, Rusty and I would snub one of the mules to my saddle horn and take our turn getting these mules to lead. After a few days of this, most of the mules were leading fairly well, at least they stopped trying to jump over the top of us.

Stokes had bought some new mule pack saddles, and with the mule in the chute, we saddled each one, getting each saddle adjusted so it fit the mule. When the mules came out of the chute wearing their new pack saddles, they put on a good show, bucking and braying, pretty upset about all this.

We had them leading pretty good, and wearing their new pack saddles. They had gentled down a little and we tried to saddle them without putting them in the chute. By tying up a hind foot, we could get a pack saddle on them. A couple of them had to be hobbled and blindfolded. They were sure bad when you were on the ground around them, kicking quicker than anything I ever saw! Some of them would sure paw us, or bite if they had half a chance. We would have a mule blindfolded, hobbled, a hind foot tied up, and the sucker would still nail us if we weren't careful! After a lot of messing around with them, we were ready for their first trip out as a bonafide pack string! That was sure funny to see; seven bronc mules, all sporting new pack saddles and halters, each one tied to the back of the saddle of the mule in front of him. With Uncle Bob up in the lead, riding old Billy Sunday, the parade was ready to start.

Well, I guess we forgot to tell all these mules what the plan was, or they got the instructions cross wired, 'cause the lead mule set back and wouldn't lead. The second mule thought it was a race and tried to run off. The third mule thought it was a rodeo and started bucking. The fourth mule wanted to do right and was hustling right along trying to keep up with his bucking friend. The fifth mule wanted timeout and to just sit down, causing some sudden stops up ahead. The sixth mule tried to jump the one sitting down and landed upside down on top of him. Of course all this scared number seven, who tried to run off, but didn't make it far! It took several trips like that to finally get those mules where Bob could take them to Crater Lake. Some of them stayed pretty snorty, and Bob would have to tie a foot up to pack or unpack. Bob said it sure made life interesting, as there was usually a wreck of some kind every day!

Bob had a little dukes mixture bred dog that sure did make a hand helping Bob with the mules. If a mule ever pulled back in the pack string, the little dog would slip in and heel the mule, then duck right quick as the mule would try to kick him. He was pretty quick and never got kicked hard. But he sure made the mule lead up and kept things pretty well in line. Several of these mules never did get to where you could saddle or pack them without tying up a foot. A couple of them would sure bite, or paw you if the opportunity was there. Most of them though, got pretty gentle and sure made a good pack string.

Uncle Bob and the mule pack string were getting along pretty well, making regular pack trips to Fish Camp and Porcupine. The mules were doing good, major wrecks becoming less frequent. Packing some pretty strange items in to the camps caused a little concern at times! Wash tubs, ironing boards, whatever the staff could think of, Bob would pack it in to them.

The camp director at Fish Camp was complaining to Bob about one of his staff members. Seems the boy kept faking being sick, and wouldn't do any of the work around camp he was supposed to do. Mornings were his worst time. He couldn't get out of his bed and laid around until after lunch.

Then he started feeling well enough to go fishing.

Bob thought he might have a cure for the boy, so he told the camp director which day he would be back into Fish Camp with the pack string, and to be sure and keep the sick guy in bed.

Bob asked me to go over with him and help bring the pack string back. Bob and I arrived at Fish Camp on his regular schedule. The camp director told us the phony was sick and hadn't gotten up yet. Bob went into the cabin, looked the young man over, and took his temperature. In the best professional manner he could come up with, Bob diagnosed him as sure being very sick and needing plenty of bed rest. Bob suggested they carry him out to the open front porch, where he could get a little fresh air. This sounded good to the patient, lots of bed rest!

The guy was in his sleeping bag, and Bob got the guy's arms tucked in at his sides, and zipped the sleeping bag up as far as the zipper went. Not wanting the guy to get chilled, Bob had the other staff members wrap an old army blanket around him. Wrapped him up pretty tight so he couldn't move much.

Bob and the camp director then brought in a body carrier, made of wire mesh. The top opened up to lay the body in and latched shut on the sides. It had three reinforcement bars running the length of it, so it wouldn't sag.

With our patient wrapped tight in the army blanket we hoisted him into this carrier, and latched the cover down over him. He was captured, no way of getting out!

We carried him out to the front porch and laid the body carrier down, while Bob went to get the ambulance, which happened to be the biggest pack mule in the string! Not necessarily the gentlest, but the biggest.

Our sick staff member suddenly figured this little deal out and went to yelling bloody murder, trying to get out of the body carrier. He couldn't get out and was sure raising a ruckus, getting more suspicious as to what was about to happen to him.

With a good-fitting blindfold on the mule, and a hind leg jacked up and firmly tied, we proceeded to load our hollering, struggling patient up on the back of this trembling mule. This carrier was designed to fit and tie onto a pack saddle, with the body lying parallel to the mule's back, the head sticking well up front of the pack saddle, and the feet out over the mules rump.

Bob threw a good diamond hitch over this little load. He got on Billy Sunday and dallied up pretty close, as I let the mule's foot down, and I eased the blindfold off.

Things might have got off to a little better start if the patient had been still, but he started yelling and struggling to get off, and the mule, who agreed with him, started trying to buck. Bob had him dallied up pretty close, but he still managed to buck around in a tight circle, causing the patient to holler all the louder!

After a couple of quick circles snubbed up tight, the mule quit trying to buck. The patient was hollering bloody murder, still trying to get out of his cage, but he couldn't do anything but holler and kinda flop up and down. He was wrapped pretty good!

Bob explained to the patient the ride would be much more comfortable and less bumpy if he would shut up, quit kicking, and lay still 'cause he damn sure wasn't getting out of that carrier until they got to Crater Lake, and could get him the proper medical attention. After all, it was only seven or eight miles to Crater Lake, going up over Webster Pass, down through Bonita Canyon, then up over Fowler Pass and down to Crater Lake! It was nearly all steep up hill or steep down hill.

Bob turned Billy Sunday toward the trail, the mule following, with a wary eye cast back at his strange pack. When the patient would flop around, the mule would jump right hard, and the patient would lay still.

I followed, leading the rest of the pack string as we started the long climb up Webster Pass. The patient finally gave up his struggling, but sure didn't give up his hollering! Cussing, pleading, threatening, begging, demanding, and you name it; he tried it all. Bob would look back occasionally, with a big grin on his face!

As we topped out going over Webster Pass, the trail was all down hill for a mile or so. Bob moved Billy Sunday out to a little jog trot and the patient got a whole new perspective on the situation as the "ambulance" trotted right up with Billy Sunday! You talk about getting shook up! This guy was getting a shaking like you wouldn't believe!

Riding along behind, I couldn't help but feel sorry for the patient, 'cause I could see that if he hadn't needed a doctor before this trip, he would need one pretty soon!

We crossed Bonita Canyon and slowed back to a walk, as we started up the trail to Fowler Pass. Bob stopped at the gate on top of Fowler Pass and lit a cigarette. He got off Billy Sunday and walked back to check the patient.

After a little talk with the patient about doing his share of the work at Fish Camp, and the perils of laying around in bed most of the day, the patient made a remarkable recovery! Seems he was feeling much better, was sure he could do his share of camp work, and promised to be the first one up every morning! In fact, if we would get him off this @#$%$# mule, he would walk back to Fish Camp and go to work!

We got him down off the pack mule and he took off back down the trail to Fish Camp, slightly banged up, sore and about half scared to death, probably in worse shape than before he got his ambulance ride!

The camp director told us later the kid sure had made a remarkable recovery. He was the first one up every morning and turned into a good staff member. Kinda strange though, he always seemed to disappear when the pack string arrived at Fish Camp! Bob had a knack for giving kids like that some valuable education.

Uncle Bob packing mule at Crater Lake, 1951

25

Bettye

While living in Cimarron and working with the survey crew, I had started going to the high school basketball games. Having played basketball while I was in high school, I enjoyed watching the local boys' games. I particularly liked seeing one of the good looking cheerleaders! Found out her name was Bettye Maldonado, older sister of Buddy, whom I worked with at Philmont.

She was a good looking gal, sure a ball of fire, jumping and yelling, and really getting into that cheer leading. I was pretty busy making the barroom scene in Cimarron and this good looking cheerleader wasn't in the circle I was making, so I didn't get to meet her.

Working with Uncle Bob and the mule pack string had put me at the polo barns every day and that's just where the Maldonados were living then. I would catch a glimpse of her once in a while as I rode by her house, but I just didn't know quite how to approach her.

Buddy and I had became pretty good friends. He was sure making a good hand. Bronc riding little booger, he won the saddle bronc riding at the Cimarron Rodeo the next year! As he and I were riding by the Maldonado house one hot afternoon I got a bright idea!

"Buddy, I'm so thirsty I don't think I can ride much further with out a drink!" I croaked, as we approached her house.

"I guess we could stop at my house and see if Bettye could give us a drink," he answered kinda surprised at my sudden need for water.

"I sure would appreciate it," old sneaky me replied.

We rode up to the house and got down. I held the horses as Buddy went in to see if he could get Bettye to help save my life!

Wow! There she was, even better looking up close than out on the basketball court, and smiling right at me! Buddy introduced me to her and no wonder I liked her, her name was Bettye! Same name as my first horse, so she had to be all right! She seemed all to glad to offer us some water. I drank so darn much water I could hardly get back on my horse!

Bettye and I seemed to hit it off pretty good. Somehow I got the courage to ask her if she would like to go to a movie in Springer. She said yes and we went to a pretty heavy duty Bette Davis movie that made her cry! I had to put my arm around her and comfort her, so it worked out pretty good!

◊   ◊   ◊

I got the horse string at Cimarroncito that summer instead of the Cavalcade. Taking scouts on horseback rides every day out of Cimarroncito was kinda calm after the two summers I had spent on the trail with cavalcades. I started pursuing Bettye pretty regularly, and being camped at Cimarroncito made it a lot better than being on the trail all the time.

I had an old car. Staff couldn't take personal vehicles to camp, but this was no problem. It was only about ten miles from Cimarroncito to headquarters. After all the chores were done in the evening, I would just saddle a good horse, ride down to my car at headquarters, and drop by to see Bettye.

There was a lady in town that did laundry, and I would take her my dirty clothes to get them cleaned up a little. I would go by and see if by any chance Bettye would like to go in with me to pick up my laundry. Her dad would say I was either the dirtiest or the cleanest cowboy he ever saw! Never had seen anyone with that much laundry!

She was glad to go with me, but her mom or dad would say, "No, you can't go until all the dishes are washed!" Well I made a darn good hand at doing dishes! I could sure handle that dish towel and Bettye and I had those dishes done in nothing flat!

Bettye's mom kinda liked me, but her dad, Fred, wasn't too pleased with his daughter's choice of boyfriends. Guess he had seen me in action down on Coco Street on Saturday nights, and he wasn't too keen on our going out together. He wasn't too crazy about her going out with a cowboy anyway.

Bettye's mom, Priscilla, was cooking for the staff at Cimarroncito that summer and we sure ate good! Bettye stayed at their home at the polo barns at headquarters taking care of her younger brothers and sisters. Her youngest brother, Billy, stayed with his mother at Cito occasionally. When he was there, he got to hanging around the horse barns wanting to go on the horseback rides. He was a nice little kid, and I put up with him because of his sister. I told Billy he would have to help me and the wranglers if he wanted to ride every day. His job would be to put a gallon of grain in the feed bags twice a day for the dude string. We were feeding about forty horses twice a day. He wasn't big enough to saddle a horse then, so I figured the feed bag job ought to suit him pretty well.

Billy filled the feed bags for a few days. Then the newness wore off the job and he didn't want to do that any more. Billy was a little spoiled, and I told him if he didn't do his share of the work, he couldn't ride. He came dragging in one morning, as we were getting ready to leave the corrals with the riders.

"Where's my horse!" he demanded.

"I turned him out," I answered. "You didn't show up to fill the feed bags. No work, no ride!"

Boy was he mad!

"You have to let me ride! I'm going to tell my mom!" he yelled at me, as he stomped off to tell his mom.

"I'm going to tell Bettye not to go out with you anymore, too!" he hollered.

Bettye and I were a pretty steady item, and Billy's objection didn't seem to phase her. Her two younger brothers, Billy and Bobby, were pretty small then, and kept asking me how I got to be so tall. I told them it was from eating so much peanut butter. They believed me and Priscilla told me later that she couldn't keep enough peanut butter on hand 'cause those two ate it up as fast as she brought it home! Buddy didn't believe me. Bobby and Billy both grew to six foot three or so but Buddy..... See what happens to you if you are a non-believer!? 5'5"?

Bettye's brother Bobby didn't have much interest in riding then and when he asked to go with me one day, I agreed to take him. He was pretty young and green, but a likeable little kid, and I was trying to get on the good side of the family.

A couple of my horses had gotten out of the horse pasture and I figured they were probably down in the Brush pasture. I thought this might be a nice little ride to take Bobby on. When we jumped these two horses, they took off like a couple wild mustangs!

"Hang on and stay with me!" I hollered at Bobby as I lit out after these two renegades.

We were popping brush and rolling rocks, in hot pursuit. Looking back, I couldn't see Bobby anywhere. I hated to let the horses go, but this kid might be my future brother in law, so I pulled up and rode back the way I had come. Pretty soon I found him, crying up a storm, mad, scared and wanting to go home. Well, so much for the horse chasing that day. I got him home and he never wanted to ride with me any more. A few years later, Bobby was cowboying for the UU Bar ranch and went on to a rodeo career, where he excelled in both bull and bronc riding! A far cry from the little scared kid I had with me that day in the Brush pasture. Bobby punched cows for a lot of big outfits and sure made a top hand.

I finally got around to asking Bettye to marry me and she said "Yes!" Her Mother was happy, but Fred threw a fit. He wasn't about to let his daughter marry a %$#&@^ cowboy! Well it took most of the evening with Bettye, her mom and me all working on Fred to finally get him calmed down and to agree to letting us get married. We agreed to wait until Bettye graduated from high school.

I had joined the Naval Reserve while in high school at Manitou Springs, dropping out of it when I left home. I had nearly forgotten about it, but I sure got a quick reminder when I got my papers in the mail ordering me to active duty! I had to report to Great Lakes Naval Training Center and go into the Navy for at least two years.

Bettye and I had to decide whether to get married and have me go in the Navy or wait until I got out and came home. This was not a good time! Against nearly everyone's advice we decided to go ahead and get married.

We were married on July 16, 1951, and I had to go into the Navy, August 1! Fred, Priscilla, Mom, Bettye and I went to Judge Federrici in Raton, where he married us there in his office. Wasn't a very fancy deal, but Judge Federrici sure knew how to tie the knot, because it has held for fifty years!

I've always been thankful for Bettye. She has stuck with me through some rough old times. The old knot has been tried a few times over the years, but it has held tight.

We had sixteen days before I had to leave for the Navy. We went to Cheyenne to the Frontier Days Rodeo for our honeymoon. It was pretty tough for both of us when I had to pull out and trade my Levis for a little white hat and a set of Navy blues!

Bettye was a senior in high school when we got married and she went ahead and finished her senior year and graduated while I was in the Navy. Nine months after we got married, we were blessed with a big baby boy! He was a dandy. We named him Robert Charles, and everyone called him Little Bob.

◊　　◊　　◊

I was sent to Great Lakes Naval Training Center up by Chicago. This was about three months after my wreck with the bay horse at Hoxie and I still had some big bumps on my ribs. The examining medics noticed the knots on my ribs and sent me in for some Xrays. The doc called me into his office where he was looking at my Xrays, and my reserve service record.

"What the hell do you guys eat out there in New Mexico?" the Doc asked me as he stared at my Xrays.

"Whatever we can find!" I answered.

"You sure have something floating around in you that shouldn't be there!" he said. "I never have seen anything like this!"

I explained this strange phenomenon to him, and that I was a poor risk. I'd probably die any minute and the best thing they could do would be to send me back home. I sure didn't want to be in the Navy right then. I thought maybe my floating chunk of rib would get me out of there.

"I guess if you can ride them damned horses, you can ride one of our ships!" he said as he sent me back to the line to get some more shots!

Boot Camp was a little difficult. I was not a happy camper and seemed to get into one scrape after another, resulting in lots of extra duty. I was the only guy there from New Mexico. Nearly all the other recruits had come from Chicago or the surrounding area. A cowboy was about as foreign as a Martian!

The Navy asked us recruits what our interests were, and what kind of schooling we were interested in while in the Navy. I didn't see anything that looked like a cowboy job on the long list of opportunities offered, so I said

I would like to go into the Seabees and learn to operate heavy equipment. Figured I could learn to run a bull dozer. The Navy gave us a GTC or some kind of test, to see what we qualified for.

The test results came back, and I got sent to storekeepers school in Newport, Rhode Island. The heaviest equipment I got to run was a typewriter! From there, I was assigned to the U.S.S. Darby DE 218, a small destroyer escort. That was good duty; a small ship, pretty relaxed and I had Bettye send me my Levis. I got away with wearing them most of the time aboard ship. I would mess up occasionally and my superior, the ship's supply officer, would holler at me, "Knox, get rid of them damned cowboy pants!"

There were a few times when the seas really got rough and it looked like our little ship was going to capsize sure as hell! Reminded me of riding old Slingshot off the side of the mountain, only in slow motion! Got a little western a few times, but the wilder it got, the better I liked it. We made a cruise to Norway and Scotland and visited Havana, Cuba several times. I had good duty aboard ship and it wasn't bad, except for missing Bettye and cowboying.

My ship was sent to Key West, Florida, for the winter and Bettye and Mom brought Little Bob out there to visit. My ship came into port every night and I got to spend the nights with them.

I was scheduled to stay in Key West for a couple more months. Mom headed back home to Colorado, Bettye and Little Bob got a duplex in Key West, and the Navy duty got a lot better right quick! I had to spend one night a week aboard ship, so on those nights, Bettye and Little Bob could come aboard and watch a movie with me. Little Bob took his first steps aboard my ship. Thought he ought to make a good sailor, but he never showed much interest, and I was glad of that!

After three months, my ship got sent back to Norfolk, Virginia, where I got my discharge from the Navy. Bettye's cousin, Jimmy and his wife lived there. Jimmy was in the Navy, too, stationed at Norfolk, so Bettye went to Norfolk and stayed with Jimmy and his family until I was finally discharged. We caught the train out of Norfolk and headed back to the Cimarron country.

26

Cowboying at The Ring Place

After I got out of the Navy, Bettye, Little Bob and I got a place to live in Colorado Springs. I went to work for a guy who owned a lumber company and a ranch located up by Castle Rock. He promised me a job on the ranch in about a month and put me to work in the lumber yard. The ranch job never materialized. After getting burned a little by him, we left Colorado Springs and went back to Cimarron.

Judd Knight gave me a job with Vermejo Park, gathering cattle for the fall works, riding out of the Ring Place. He didn't have a camp open then for a married man, but assured me there would be a camp job open soon where I could move my family. So I went up to the Ring Place and had to leave Bettye and Little Bob again. They stayed with Bettye's folks, who were still working at Philmont. This sure wasn't a good situation, having been away from them in the Navy and now out in a cow camp, maybe getting to be with them on Saturday night and going back to camp Sunday night!

I was sure wanting to get horseback, and Judd didn't disappoint me there! He was from the old school, believed in leaving early, riding hard, and getting in after dark. You just as well traded your bedroll in for a lantern cause you didn't spend much time in bed, but a lot of time in the dark!

There were four or five cowboys riding out of the Ring when I joined the crew. Being I was the new man there, I got the glorious chore of jingling the remuda each morning. We had around forty-five to fifty head of horses at the Ring Place. The remuda was brought in each morning. The day's mounts for the cowboys were caught and the rest of the remuda was turned out until the next morning.

In the remuda, there were a couple pack horses we kept bells strapped around their necks. The remuda was turned out in a several section pasture, and the sounds of the bells on those horses sure helped in locating them as the pasture was pretty rough with a lot of trees and brush in it, and they were usually gathered before daylight.

Judd's wife, Ethel, was cooking for the crew that fall. She got up each morning about three-thirty and rolled the horse wrangler out so he would have time to have all the horses in the corral before five. Breakfast was ready around four-thirty or five. The cowboys ate and were at the corrals to get their horses for the morning circle around five-thirty. The horse wrangler got to eat, too, IF he found all the horses in the dark and had them penned before five!

Here's the fun part! We kept up in the corral this little brown mule, and his sole job was to find those horses that were hiding from him out there in the dark. Boy he was good at his job! Too bad someone had to be on him when he did his job! He wasn't very big. I almost had to tie a knot in my cinch. He had no withers, could hardly keep a saddle on him. The only good thing about him was, he didn't try to buck me off! He was content to just run away with me! I had better have my hat pulled down and a good hold when I got on cause he would leave the corral at a dead run.

Didn't make any difference what kinda bridle I put on him. There wasn't anything that was going to slow him down, 'cause he had a job to do and he was going to do it. It would be pitch dark and away we would go, just hoping he could see better than I could! There was a small hill about a quarter mile out in the horse pasture and he would fly up to the top of it and stop just as quick as he had left the corrals. He would cock his head first one direction then another. His long ears worked back and forth, trying to pick up the sound of one of those belled horses. Soon as he heard the faint tinkle of a bell, away we would go, off out into the dark, in the direction of the bell, hard as he could run. I just had to hope I didn't get drug off by a tree limb, or bang my knee on a tree as he flew along like a heat-seeking missile!

He could sure find those horses, and when we came charging down on them at a dead run, they would immediately stampede. The saddle horses would head for the corrals as fast as they could go with me and the little mule in hot pursuit. Some mornings we got in, in plenty of time to go up to the cookhouse and get a bite of breakfast with the rest of the crew. But sometimes when I was a little late, I just had time to run up to the kitchen and grab a biscuit, a chunk of bacon, and stick it in my chap pocket for later.

Harvey was the only cowboy Judd would let rope the horses out of the remuda. A cowboy would tell Harvey the horse's name he wanted, and

Harvey would sail a nice hoolihan loop out and it would settle just right over the horses head. The saddle horses were all broke to be roped and as soon as they felt the loop around their neck they would turn and face the roper. The cowboy would go down the rope with his bridle, put it on his mount, slip the rope off the horse and lead him out of the roping corral to his saddle, then saddle up.

I got to know my saddle horses pretty quick, so I could tell Harvey which one to catch for me. I had about ten head in my string, including two green colts that Donald Webb had started.

They were sure started right and didn't have any bad habits like some of the older horses. Some of the older horses I sure didn't want Harvey to catch. But Judd made sure we rode all of them in our string regularly. Those first-time meetings were pretty wild at times.

Whenever I noticed the other cowboys grin at each other as Judd called out a certain horse for me, I knew I was fixing to put on a little entertainment! There was an older cowboy, Allen, in the crew, who was a good friend of Uncle Bob's and he kinda helped me out. He would come by where I was saddling up and offer a little advice, like "Watch him, he is hard to get on" or "Take a deep seat. He will sure buck" or "He's okay" There just weren't very many "He's okay"!

I got bucked off a couple times and managed to get a couple rode that blew up with me, so all in all it wasn't too bad. We left the corrals in the dark, with Judd out in the lead at a long trot. After riding several miles, Judd started dropping cowboys off with instructions on where to ride to start the days gather. We drifted whatever we found down to a central point where we threw everything together and headed them out and down toward the Van Bremmer.

We had a pretty good-sized bunch of cows and calves gathered, and it seemed like we had been driving them for days. They were getting tired and hot and so were the cowboys. There was a cowboy called Nick in the crew, and as we passed an old abandoned windmill and rusted out tank, Nick spotted an old rusty bucket.

"I'll show you boys how to get these S.O.B.'s to moving," Nick said as he rode up to the bucket.

He got off his horse, picked up this old bucket and put a couple hand fulls of small rocks in it. Then set the bucket on an old tree stump near by.

Getting back on his horse, he rode by the stump, picking up the bucket.

"Watch this boys," he hollered.

He spurred his horse into a lope and charged the slow moving bunch of cows. He leaned out over his old horse's neck, yelled like an Apache on the war path, rattling this bucket of rocks.

Nick's horse didn't know what the hell was happening, with this blood curdling yell and the rocks rattling in the bucket right out over his head, so he just bogs his head and pitches Nick head first out over the cows that are trying to get out of the way! Nick landed in a heap, scattering his rocks all around. The cows stopped to look at this new turn of events, and we all got a pretty good laugh out of Nick's idea. He didn't have much to say when one of the cowboys caught his horse and led him back to Nick. He got back on, but left his bucket and scattered rocks where they lay.

We kept pushing those old cows until it got plumb dark, and I was wondering if we were going to drive them all night. Suddenly, out of the dark, a set of pickup lights appeared. I guess Judd had told Ethyl where to come in the pickup to get us, and she was a welcome sight.

Judd says, "OK, boys, unsaddle and throw your saddles in the truck. Turn your horses loose. We'll get them later. Lets go to supper!"

Heck, it was ten thirty when we got to the Ring Place, and I was too tired to eat! And it wasn't going to be long until I got to jingle horses again! We got picked up like that several times while I was there, and I never saw the horse I was riding that day again! I'm sure they were picked up some-time later but I always felt kinda funny about just turning them loose out there in the dark and going off and leaving them. They had plenty of grass and water and got a pretty good vacation! There were plenty of horses at the Ring so we never ran out of mounts.

On one of the rare evenings when we got back to the Ring Place before dark, Judd asked me to go with him in his old pickup. As I got in, I noticed a thirty-thirty rifle in the seat of the pickup.

"We're getting a little low on camp meat, maybe we can get a little venison," Judd said as he drove away from camp.

A short distance down the canyon, we spotted a bunch of deer brows-ing along the hill side.

"There's a nice fat buck," Judd said, stopping the pickup.

Taking a good bead on the buck, he fired the thirty-thirty, and the buck dropped in his tracks. Looked like a good clean shot.

"Got him!" he said, as he laid the thirty-thirty down in the seat.

I hurried up the hillside to the downed deer, Judd right behind me. As I reached down and took hold of his horns to pull his head around so Judd could cut his throat, the son-of-a-gun came to life and tried to jump up! Judd's shot had stunned the buck, knocking him down, but he was sure coming to in a hurry!

Judd kinda stuttered when he got a little excited, and he reached the stuttering stage in a hurry.

"Wh,Wh,Wh,What the hell!" Judd stammered. "Ga,Ga,Ga,Grab him! He's going to ge,ge,ge,get up!"

The buck was nearly on his feet. I grabbed his horns and bulldogged him to the ground. I managed to push his horns into the ground, twisting his head around, but barely able to hold him down. That sucker was kicking up over his head, knocking the stuff out of me as I tried to dodge his flailing feet. Judd had his long bladed hunting knife in his hand, ready to cut the buck's throat. He went to stabbing at the buck, hollering for me to "ho,ho, hold him still!"

I didn't know whether to be more concerned with the buck's flailing feet or Judd's wild thrusts with the hunting knife! It looked like if one didn't get me the other one would! My shirt was nearly torn off, and I was sure getting skinned up! The buck managed to land a solid kick to Judd's knife-wielding hand, sending the knife flying off into the brush.

"Ho,ho,ho hold him! I'll b,b,b,be right ba,ba,ba,back!" Judd said as he crawled around on his hands and knees into the brush, searching for the knife.

Finding the knife, Judd jumped right back in the middle of the fracas, stabbing and cussing as best he could. He finally managed to get the best of the buck and got his throat cut.

I got up and retrieved my hat. It was the only thing about me that wasn't bloody! Judd and I looked like we had been separating fighting wild-cats! With plenty of our blood mixed in with the ample supply from the deer, we were quite a sight when we got back to camp. We were greeted by a variety of comments, like,"Why didn't you take a gun?" "Run out of shells?" "What did the other guy look like?"

This was getting pretty old after three months and only getting to see

Bettye and Little Bob on Saturday nights and half a day on Sundays! Judd said the ranch was cutting back on help, and he didn't know if he could keep me on through the winter.

Getting a camp where I could move Bettye and Little Bob to didn't look very promising. So after nearly three months at the Ring Place, with the crew getting ready to move to another camp, I rolled my bed and pulled out.

27

Arizona

I quit cowboying when I left Judd and Vermejo Park, and we moved to Arizona. It seemed like I had got to see Bettye more before we had gotten married than after we were married! I needed a job where we could start living like real people, instead of going out to sea on a ship or going off to a cow camp and leaving her in town.

Jobs were pretty hard to come by in Phoenix, not much demand for cowboys. I finally landed a job with the Arizona Public Service Company as a groundman. This wasn't a very prestigious job, but it paid the bills. I had some experience digging post holes, but the holes we had to dig for the line poles were something else! Six foot deep and at least two foot in diameter! Seemed to me it was like digging a well! A lot of the work was out in the desert and the sand was a little tricky while digging these big holes, as they would keep caving in as we dug.

After a year, I got promoted to driving a line truck. This was sure a good job and brought with it a substantial pay increase.

We were blessed with a little girl while in Phoenix, Myrna Ann; a little blonde gal, cute as a bug!

I transferred down to Yuma, with another good pay increase, and we were doing well. But living in town sure was getting old. Three years in Phoenix and Yuma working for Arizona Public Service and I still had the cowboy bug pretty bad. Easy job, good pay, living in town, and all I was getting was ulcers!

Bettye and I loaded our kids up and took a vacation. We went up to visit her folks who were still living on Philmont. Getting back in the mountains again, seeing old friends and horses and cattle, I really had a bad attack of the cowboy blues!

Bill Littrell was ranch superintendent at Philmont then, and I managed to go by and ask him for a job while we were vacationing. He told me to fill out an application, and they might call me if a job came open.

I had heard that old line before, so I wasn't too excited about my prospects. We loaded up and headed back to Yuma. Bettye and I both hated to leave.

We had been back in Yuma about a month or so, and I had given up on hearing from Littrell. In mid-August, I got a letter from Littrell, offering me a cowboy job, starting September,15th. The cowboy job paid $160.00 per month. Heck, I was making more than that a week at Arizona Public Service!

It took a little worrying and figuring, but Bettye and I decided to go for it. So I gave my two weeks notice. We packed up what little stuff we had in a little rental trailer and headed home!

◊   ◊   ◊

We moved into cattle headquarters at Philmont, September 15,1956, and I went to work for Bill Littrell as a cowboy in the cattle department.

The horse and cattle departments were separate entities then. I knew from having worked there for Stokes, we never got to help the cattle department and the cowboys working cattle never came around the horse department. The horse department was included in the camping department, while the cattle department was part of the ranching department. The horse department, being a big part of the camping operation, was funded quite generously. The cattle department had to make its own way, with very little funding from the Boy Scouts of America, and it was kinda touch and go at times. Littrell was always in a sweat over money and really kept a tight rein on the operation.

John Stokes had left the ranch. Lawrence Sanchez was still a horseman, along with a good hand, Leo Martinez.

Shorty Martinez was the only cowboy working in the cattle department. He was kinda like an old landmark that had been around a long time. Having started there when he was a kid, he had worked for Phillips before the Boy Scouts got the ranch. He was probably up in his fifties when I went to work with him.

If Shorty stood on tip toe, he might have stretched out to about five three or four. Weighed in at a whopping 120 pounds. What he lacked in size, he made up for in his hat! He always wore a big black hat with a five inch brim that he could hardly see out from under. In the summer he would get the widest brim straw hat he could find.

No matter what we had to do, how tough or disagreeable the chore might be, Shorty could always find something humorous about it.

Shorty was a good cowboy, and sure a lot of fun to work with. He sure liked his liquor and always had a bottle hidden away some place. He would sure take a little sip when the opportunity presented itself. Shorty had come up with a little black, one-inch-brim round top derby, like Charlie Chapman wore. This was his "get drunk and be somebody hat". When we saw Shorty wearing his derby we knew he was going on a bender!

It was sure good to be back in the old Cimarron country again. Kinda like coming home, and I was ready to let the games begin!

◊   ◊   ◊

Most of Philmont's cattle were still in the high country, when I came back to work. As soon as I got the family half-way settled in our house at cattle headquarters, Littrell told me to go with Shorty and Johnny Casias to Bonita Cow Camp to start gathering cattle.

Johnny Casias was the heavy equipment operator for Philmont. He did all the bulldozer work and helped out when an extra cowboy was needed. He was a pretty good hand horseback, sure knew the country, and was a real pleasure to be around.

We packed a couple of mules with our beds, some grub and a little grain for our saddle horses, and headed out to Bonita. Shorty rode out in the lead with our extra saddle horses following him, as Johnny and I followed up with the pack mules.

After about fifteen miles, of winding up into the mountains, we topped out over Fowler Pass and rode down into Bonita canyon. We followed the little stream up the canyon about three miles. Bonita camp was sure a pretty sight when it came into view. Setting back up a little draw from the main canyon, nestled in among the tall aspen and huge fir and spruce trees, it was sure a pretty location.

The fall roundup out of the high country of Philmont was sure a treat to me. After being away from the mountains, horses and cattle for three years in Arizona, I was sure having a good time.

Bonita was a nice little two-room camp with an additional bedroom built on by Johnny and Shorty a year or so before I got there. They were sure proud of there handiwork. It was a nice job, all log walls with a pretty good roof. The only problem was Shorty and Johnny were both about five foot three and they couldn't reach very high, so the ceiling in the new room was about five foot five high! Had a nice little fireplace in it and couple small windows. It was pretty comfortable. I just had to get used to not standing up straight!

Shorty was a good cook, and he liked to cook, which suited Johnny and me just fine. Johnny and I kept the wood box full, plenty of fresh water carried in from the nearby spring, and the dishes washed up so it worked pretty good.

We were gathering cattle back around Fish Camp, Apache, and Porcupine camps where the Aqua Fria and Rayado creeks were running, and the trout fishing was good, so we had a fresh batch of trout pretty regularly. Shorty could sure do a job frying trout and making sourdough biscuits.

Johnny had an old pair of shot gun chaps that didn't get used much and were real stiff. Shorty kidded Johnny about his stiff chaps, saying they looked like two chimneys. They were so stiff that Johnny could barely walk in them, and had a heck of a time bending his leg to get his foot up to his stirrup to get on his horse.

We pulled out pretty early one morning from Bonita. Johnny was riding a young horse called Rodeo. Rodeo would sure live up to his name when he got a good chance and could do a pretty decent job of bucking. Johnny managed to get on Rodeo in the round corral that was just below the cabin. Rodeo was a little humpy, but after a few circles around the round corral, he seemed to relax, and Johnny was ready to go out on him.

We took the trail down through the big horse pasture. Rodeo was trotting right along like an old broke saddle horse. The trail went down a little embankment and crossed Bonita creek, then went through a pretty boggy place.

Johnny was feeling pretty good about the way Rodeo was moving out and trotted up in front of me and Shorty as we started down to the creek crossing. Maybe Rodeo didn't like getting his feet wet? Cold water splashed him on the belly? Maybe it was just time!

Whatever the reason, when Rodeo crossed that creek, he blew up big time! Johnny was hanging on for dear life as Rodeo bucked across the top of the bog. About five jumps and Johnny joined the bird gang. Boy, he did go up high, really a spectacular dismount, keeping his legs straight, and tucking his head for a nice, full somersault. His landing was a perfect, one point crash, right on his head, and in the soft bog. I loped out and caught Rodeo as he bucked on down the canyon a little ways. Shorty jumped off and was busy digging Johnny out of the muddy bog.

"Johnny, it's a damn good thing you had them chaps on. They was sticking straight up out of the mud, like two chimneys, and I knew right where to dig to find you!" Shorty said as he helped Johnny dig the mud out of his ears and eyes.

"Go to Hell," Johnny grumbled as he spit mud out of his mouth.

Johnny got back on Rodeo and made the day on him without any more trouble, but he sure kept him pulled up pretty tight! Johnny was sitting on Rodeo pretty steady and hadn't got planted in the mud anymore. Fall had made its colorful appearance with the aspen and oak brush taking on their golden and various shades of red. Mornings were getting pretty fresh, with a little skim of ice appearing on the water bucket.

Shorty, Johnny, and I had around 250 cows with their calves in the Bonita horse pasture, ready to go down the mountain. Early one morning we turned them out and headed them down Bonita canyon. About two miles down the canyon the old stock drive turned east out of the main canyon.

The stock drive wasn't fenced, just a series of interwoven cow trails winding up through the thick timber. Most of the brush and small trees had been cleared out of the stock drive, leaving quite a few large trees that the cow trails wound around. The stock drive varied in cleared width from fifty to a hundred and fifty feet.

The cows were ready to get out of the high country, strung out and headed down the canyon with their big, summer fat, calves following them. Shorty was riding point as the leaders approached the turnoff to the stock drive. Johnny and I were keeping any stragglers pushed up and kinda working the sides as needed. These old cows didn't need much pushing as they knew where they were going, so we were just along for the ride.

Shorty turned the leaders out of the canyon bottom, and the old cows headed up the stock drive as the main herd followed the lead cows.

As the lead cows moved up the stock drive, Shorty rode back down to help me turn the main bunch of cows out of the canyon. They were starting up the stock drive when suddenly the lead cows came running back down the stock drive, scattering the main bunch of cows and calves down the canyon. Johnny came loping up to give us a hand, and we got the cows stopped and headed back to the stock drive. The lead cows didn't seem very anxious to go back up, but we got after them and got them started up again. We were riding pretty rapidly, trying to get the leaders started up and to keep the main bunch of cows from getting on down Bonita Canyon. We were getting a little short-handed all at once!

Seemed like we had them finally going our way, when here came the leaders, really coming down the stock drive at a run, putting a scatter on the main herd big time! Cows and calves were going every direction there for a little while. We couldn't figure out what was wrong. Finally we got everything thrown back together and held up at the foot of the stock drive.

Shorty and I trotted up the stock drive a little ways to see what was scaring the cows back. There stood our problem, growling, and snapping her teeth at us, as we rode up. A big sow bear stood under a large tree, right in the middle of the stock drive. Perched out on a limb above the sow sat two little cubs, peering down at us. Well, we backed off right quick, seeing why the cows had came back down so fast!

I guess the sow and her cubs had been crossing the stock drive about the time the lead cows got there and probably scared the cubs up the tree. Every time the cows got near the tree where the cubs were, the sow ran the cows away from her cubs.

Shorty said he figured the cubs had climbed the tree to watch the parade of cows go by. Could have been, I guess. They sure had a good viewing seat!

Shorty and I rode back to the herd and told Johnny we had a temporary closure of the stock drive. We held the cows at the bottom of the stock drive for a few minutes, giving the sow a little time to convince the cubs that the parade wasn't coming by. After about ten minutes, I eased up the stock drive to where I could see the cubs' bleacher seats, and they had moved on.

We started the cows up again, the lead cows a little leery as they approached the bears' viewing stand, but with the sow gone, the cows headed on up the trail, and we got the herd over Fowler Pass.

Bonita Cow Camp, Philmont Scout Ranch

Bonita with horse corrals in foreground

28

Bull in the Window

The fall roundup was over and I was settled in our new home at cattle headquarters. Late one night I got a phone call from Littrell. I sleepily mumbled, "Hello." I looked over at the alarm clock sitting by the phone,10:30. Heck, I'd been asleep an hour and a half!

"Bob, I just remembered that Rudolph Schwartz from the UU Bar ranch called and said they had one of our bulls in the corral at Uracca Camp," Littrell said.

"Okay, Bill," I said trying to sound wide awake, "I'll get Shorty first thing in the morning and go get him."

"Rudolph called me yesterday, and I forgot to tell you guys, so you better go get him tonight," Bill replied.

"Well it's pretty late and dark. Reckon he will be all right until morning?" I said, sure not wanting to get up in the middle of the night and go off looking for a bull!

"Hell, he has been in the corral without feed or water for two days!" Bill replied. "You guys better go get him now!"

From the tone of his voice I knew I'd better not try arguing.

"Okay, Bill, I'll get Shorty and we are on our way!" I tried to sound enthused.

I didn't know where Uracca was and didn't much want to go wandering around in the middle of the night by myself trying to find it, so I went down and rolled Shorty out. Shorty lived in a small house down by the corrals at cattle headquarters, and after I nearly beat the door down, he finally opened the door.

"What the hell's going on?" he mumbled, rubbing the sleep from his eyes, as he stood there in his long handles.

I explained Littrell's phone call. I better not write here exactly what Shorty had to say, but the drift of it wasn't too complimentary about our boss!

We had an old US Army surplus pickup, with a set of stock racks on it, and we fired it up and headed out for Uracca.

Shorty said the best way to get to Uracca was through Cimarron, out about five miles, to Miami Lane, and turn south. Several miles down Miami Lane, we found the turn off to Uracca. Our lights picked up the corrals.

A big horned Hereford bull looked out through the corral boards as we drove up. He looked like a greyhound ready for a race! It was obvious he had been off feed and water quite awhile. I backed up to the loading chute and he loaded right up in our old pickup.

"Reckon we ought to tie his head to the stock racks?" I asked Shorty. "Naw", he replied "he ain't going no place." So we headed back toward the ranch.

Cimarron was pretty well shut down for the night. As we crossed Cimarron River, we could see the lights still on at the Don Diego Hotel and Bar, now the St. James.

Shorty says "What'ya think about a beer?"

"Well you know what Littrell said about us going to town or drinking in this company pickup!" I replied. "We would get fired right quick!"

"Hell, he's done gone to bed," Shorty replied, "and I would be too if it weren't for him calling us out in the middle of the night!"

"Yea, but somebody might see our pickup at the bar and tell him sure as hell," I answered, not liking this idea very much.

"Just pull in the alley behind the Don Diego," Shorty said, "Nobody can see our pickup there. I hide my car back there all the time!"

Well, he seemed to know his way around, so I pulled around behind the Don Diego, and pulled up right next to the old hotel. We slipped in the back door.

We ordered a couple beers, and started visiting with Vera, the lady who owned and ran the bar. I was a little nervous about this deal, but after a beer things seemed better.

Vera rented rooms in the old hotel. The rooms had real high ceilings with old two-pane windows about four feet high and around three feet wide. The bottom halves of the windows had shades or curtains over them, but the top halves of the windows, being up so high, didn't have shades or anything over them.

I was starting to relax a little, thinking Shorty was one pretty smart hombre, knowing where to hide our pickup and bull the way he had.

Suddenly there came an awful screaming and yelling from down the hallway that led to the guest rooms. We rushed out into the lobby of the hotel with Vera to see what all the commotion was about.

Well, here comes this lady running and screaming down the hall into the lobby. Vera managed to get her stopped and tried to get her calmed down enough to tell us what was wrong.

"There is a huge monster trying to come in my room through the window," she yelled. "It's great big and has big horns!" Shorty and I liked to tore the door down, as we both hit it at the same time trying to get the hell outa there. We ran around the corner of the hotel into the alley where our pickup and bull were.

There was our bull, hanging out over the top of the stock racks, with his head about a foot from the ladies upper window! He had gotten tired of waiting and tried to jump out, getting his front legs and shoulders up on top of the stock racks. When he tried to lunge forward, his head got almost to the upper window. He just couldn't get enough footing with his hind feet to push himself up and over. If he had managed to jump out, he most likely would have fallen right through that window!

We jumped up on the side of the pickup and got a rope on his horns and managed to pull him back in and tied to the stock racks so he couldn't try jumping out again. We sure got out of town in one big hurry! "Oh hell, I didn't finish my beer!" Shorty exclaimed, as I slid the pickup around the corner headed for the ranch.

"The hell with your beer! What if that bull had landed in that lady's bedroom?!" I answered as I watched the rear view mirror for the police.

No one seemed to be after us as I blew the coggs out of our old pickup, as fast as it would run, and headed for Philmont. We finally relaxed a little and started laughing about it, figuring just how we would have explained to Littrell how we happened to be driving down the alley and the bull jumped right into that lady's bedroom!

Luckily, we didn't have to explain it to anyone but Vera and she kinda laughed about it later. Actually, it was quite a while later before she laughed about it!

29

K-21

Philmont had a good herd of Hereford cows, around five hundred, including around 125 registered Herefords, back in the fifties and sixties. This meant a little more work for the cowboys as we had to keep accurate records on each registered cow. Each cow was tattooed in both ears with an identification number, with a letter indicating the year of her birth, and with a number following the letter. As the registered heifers came into the cow herd, their tattoo number was branded on their horns for easier identification, without having to catch her and look in her ear for her number.

Each cow had a complete record kept on her, showing when she had a calf, what sex, weaning weight of each calf, etc. Shorty and I would watch these cows pretty closely when they were calving and catch their calves when they were just a few days old. We tattooed them and put little ear tags in the calves ear. It was a lot easier to tattoo the calves when they were pretty small and staying pretty close to their mothers. We sure had to be sure we got the right calf for each cow.

Hank Gordon was the cow foreman, working with Shorty when the registered cow, K21, started building her reputation. K21, along with several other first-calf heifers, were brought into a big lot behind the corrals at cattle headquarters to have their first calves. Since these heifers were going into the registered herd, they were given extra care at calving time.

This big lot had a shed across the west side and a long feed rack and hay manger along the north side. This feed rack was around 150 feet long. It was built along the solid board fence of the corral with a frame about four feet wide across the top. Small poles, about five feet long and six inches apart, were nailed to the top of the frame and the poles sloped down to the back and bottom of the manger. The manger was solid boards across the front about three feet high. It extended to the board fence under the sloping poles. The manger served to catch the loose hay cows would pull out from between the sloping poles above the manger.

Hank and Shorty had saddled up around seven one morning, getting ready for the day's work. Shorty was headed up to the Webster and Upper Heck pastures to check the cattle there.

Hank was going down to the Chicosa and Weaning pastures to check the cattle there. Hank said he was going to catch the new calf in the back lot and tattoo it before he left.

"Need any help?" Shorty asked as he was finishing saddling his horse.

"No, there is only one new calf back there and I can get him," Hank replied, as he picked up the old boot top made into a carrying pouch for the tattoo outfit.

Shorty mounted up and said, "I'll see you this evening," and headed out. Hank left his horse tied in the stall, saddled and ready to go, as he headed to the back lot to tattoo this new arrival.

The little calf was laying right up next to the hay manger, sound asleep, enjoying the morning sunshine, as Hank walked into the corral. The calf's mother was across the corral at the water tank. Hank slipped up on this little sleeping calf, grabbed him and took his pigging string out of his belt and started to tie the calf down. Big mistake!

This little sleeping beauty woke up to find this guy holding him down and he started bawling bloody murder for his mother! K21 made her grand entry, charging Hank and hitting him in the rear end, as he tried to dodge her. The impact of her head on Hank's rear end knocked him over into the manger. His hat fell off, outside the manger, right next to the calf.

Hank was lying down flat in the bottom of the manger and K21 couldn't get her horns down to him. She could reach him with her nose and mouth, and she proceeded to use his shirt for a Kleenex. She gave Hank a good pushing around with her nose. Checking her baby to make sure he was all right, K21 spotted Hank's hat laying there on the ground and she promptly fertilized it, wetting it down good so it would grow.

Hank crawled on his belly to the other end of the manger and peeked up over the edge. K21 was watching for just such a move and over she came! Bellering her rage, she gave Hank a good nose pushing again, getting his shirt a little wetter with all her slobbering and nose wiping. Hank lay real still for a while and peeked out again. Here she came again! K21 stood guard over that hay manger all day! Hank crawled from one end to the other, but every time he raised his head up to the top of the manger, K21 rushed up to give him another nose massage and wet him down.

Shorty came riding back in to headquarters around five that evening and was surprised to see Hank's horse still standing in the stall where he had been that morning. From the amount of manure behind the horse, it was obvious he had been there all day.

Shorty figured Hank must have gone some place with someone and just left his horse tied in the stall all day. He unsaddled and fed his horse. When Shorty led his horse out to the corral to turn him out. Hank heard the gate open and went to hollering for help. Shorty went around the end of the shed and saw K21 standing guard over the hay manger.

"Hank, are you out here?" Shorty hollered.

"Over here in this damned manger!" a strained voice answered.

Hank's head appeared over the edge of the manger and K21 quickly put it back down out of sight.

"What the hell are you doing in the hay manger?" Shorty hollered.

"Get this "%$#%#@$%" cow out of here!" Hank hollered back.

Shorty went outside of the corral to a gate opening out into the pasture and swung it open. K21 got her baby and they left there in one big hurry. Hank peeked over the edge of the manger again and started crawling out as he saw K21 and her calf running out into the pasture.

"That "$#@%$#@" has had me penned in that "$%#@$" manger all day long!" Hank exclaimed as he tried to get the hay brushed out of his clothes.

He was pretty well soaked down from all the slobbering K21 had given him during the day.

"Where the hell's my hat?" Hank asked, as he was trying to get straightened up.

"I think this is it," Shorty said, as he kicked at a pile of fresh cow manure that vaguely resembled a cowboy hat!

"Did you get the calf tattooed?" Shorty asked.

"Hell no! I been in that damned manger all day long!" Hank said.

Since Hank was the boss, Shorty didn't laugh too much right then. Hank wasn't seeing very much humor in the situation. But Shorty sure got a lot of mileage out of Hank's story, when Hank wasn't around!

From then on, K21 was a cow to be reckoned with anytime you got around her. I never did check her pedigree, but I'll bet there was a little grizzly bear and water buffalo cross back in her ancestors because she had a disposition fitting that kind of breeding!

I started my first calving season with Shorty and soon got my first taste of K21. She was with the registered cow herd and we were calving them in the Upper Heck pasture.

We rode through the cows every day a-horseback and would catch calves that needed tattooing, as we checked the cows. We were feeding these cows every other day out of our old pickup, and when the opportunity offered, we would catch a calf on the feed ground and tattoo it, if we were sure who the mother was. We spotted K21 and her new baby one morning while feeding.

"Keep an eye on her calf," Shorty said, "We can drive up close to the calf and grab it and tattoo it while K21 is eating."

I drove in a big circle while Shorty scattered the cake out on the ground for the cows. K21 ran in to the chow line with the other cows, and I drove up close to her calf. I jumped out of the pick up and grabbed the calf by the hind leg. The calf started bawling as loud as it could as Shorty came running up with the tattoo outfit. I flanked the calf and knelt down over it. That's as close as we got to tattooing that little booger that day!

"Look out!" Shorty yelled, as he took off running toward the pickup.

I barely made it to the pickup before K21 roared onto the scene. She made a run at the pickup as I jumped in, slammed the door and rolled up the window. K21 stood there peering in the window, shaking her head, blowing snot on the window, and bellering some unprintable obscenities at me!

Not to be out done by this hot-tempered cow, Shorty and I plotted a new strategy.

"We just need to get the calf in the back of the pickup," I reasoned with a little cowboy logic.

We had a set of stock racks on our old pickup. We had taken the back gate off of the racks and stood it up inside, wiring it to the side, out of the way while feeding out of the pickup. We dropped down the regular tail gate while pouring out cake.

A few days later, I was driving while Shorty was pouring out the cake. I had K21's calf spotted, and when Shorty hollered he had all the cake fed,

I drove over to where our little, unsuspecting calf was watching the milling, pushing cows. I eased the door open, jumped out, grabbed the calf by the hind leg, and drug her to the back of the pickup. Shorty reached down and grabbed the calf by the ear as I boosted her up into the pickup. Boy were we smart or what! Another big mistake!

Of course as soon as I grabbed the calf's hind leg she went to bawling like a bear had her. I think that was a trait of K21's bloodline. All of her calves could bawl louder than anything I ever heard.

"We gotcha, you little bawling S.O.B.," Shorty said as he knelt down over the squirming, bawling calf. "Your momma can't help you this time!" Wrong again.

K21 came charging up to the pickup and made a quick circle around the truck searching for her little one. The calf kept bawling like she was getting eaten alive, and K21 finally zeroed in on where we were with her baby. She stuck her head in the back of the pickup and bellered her rage.

I had just gotten the numbers lined up on the tattoo machine when all hell broke loose. K21 jumped up in the back of our pickup like a big cow dog! I'll tell you what, there isn't much room in the back of a little half ton shortbed pickup for two cowboys, a little calf and one, damn mad momma! You think a quail or pheasant can take flight quick, you should have seen Shorty and me bail out over the top of those stock racks! We both fell to the ground. The fall damned near killed us both, but we managed to scramble into the cab, roll up the windows, and lock the doors!

K21 took her baby, untattooed, and they jumped out the back and took off. Of course she fertilized everything in the back before leaving.

"That was a hell of an idea you had!" Shorty grinned, as we both lit up a smoke and tried to calm our frazzled nerves. "Got any more?"

The next idea took a little more planning, and some sweet talking to Shorty. This time we wouldn't fail! Shorty didn't like to drive the pickup, but I was a good driver!? The plan was for us to feed in the circle as usual. I would drive around to where I could kidnap K21's calf. Shorty would stay in the back of the pickup and I would throw the calf into him and then jump back in the front and get the hell out of there, with Shorty holding the calf down. The plan was, I would drive away to a hidden place where she couldn't find us, do our tattooing, bring the calf back and dump it off as we drove by.

"What if she catches us?" Shorty asked, not too excited about my plan since he was going to be in the back of the pickup.

"Hell, she can't catch us, and she won't know where her calf is if I drive off," I explained.

Shorty wasn't sold on this plan, but I assured him I was taking all the risk in the deal, as I had to get the calf to the pickup. All he had to do was help me load it and hold it down, while I drove away.

The kidnapping started off as planned. The cows were all crowding along the line of cake Shorty had poured out. I drove up pretty close to K21's calf. I could see the suspicious mother watching us some distance away. I jumped out and made the grab on the calf's hind leg. True to her breeding she let out this ear piercing bawl. Shorty reached down and grabbed the calf's ear, as I boosted the victim up into the back of the truck with Shorty.

"Hurry up!" Shorty yelled in a near panic, "Here she comes!"

I jumped in the cab and peeled out as K21 came blowing up to the pickup. She knew this time right where her baby was and she made a run at the back of the pickup.

"Faster, faster!" Shorty yelled, "Here she comes!"

I peeled out. Shifted gears, and we were moving right out, bouncing and dodging rocks and brush. Looking in the rear view mirror, I saw we hadn't fooled her yet. She was running and bawling in hot pursuit!

I stuck my head out the window and hollered to Shorty, "Go ahead and tattoo the calf. She's still coming!"

The calf was kicking and struggling, and Shorty was having a heck of a time just trying to stay in the back of the speeding pickup, holding the victim down. I drove off quite a ways, leaving K21 in the cloud of dust.

I kept driving and figured we had this little deal well in hand. I drove around behind a big stand of oak brush and stopped, jumped out, and started to the back of the pickup to give Shorty a hand. Shorty had just about finished tying the calf's feet together, when out of the brush came a roaring tornado in the disguise of a Hereford cow!

I made a mad dash back to the open door of the pick up as I heard Shorty yelling, "Look out! Here she comes!"

I popped the clutch and peeled out again. This sudden start threw Shorty off balance. He fell over, and the calf jumped up and baled out the back end with Shorty's pigging string around her front foot. Retrieving her baby, K21 stood in the dust bellering her defiance and shaking her head and just daring us to come back. But she had given up the chase. I stopped again a couple miles from there and Shorty got back in the front with me.

"To hell with her calf!" Shorty exclaimed. "I could have got killed! I damn near fell out when you took off back there! I wonder where my pigging string is?"

"I'll take you back to the calf if you want to get it," I offered.

Shorty gave me a look and said something about where I could go and it wasn't back to the cow and calf!

"I'll make you another one," I offered, trying to sooth his ruffled feathers.

Another one of K21's calves didn't get tattooed until we branded! We plotted and figured, but never did come up with a good plan to catch her calf out in the pasture! We could always identify her calf at branding time as it was the only calf without an ear tag or a tattoo!

When we were moving the registered cows, we always kept an eye out for K21, because she would sure charge a horse. Her horns had been horn weighted when she was young, and they had turned down, and curled in, just below her eyes. This kept her from being able to gore a horse, but served like a bumper on a diesel truck. She could sure knock the stuffing out of an old pony if she got a shot at him.

Shorty was riding a little black horse he called Papoose as we were moving the registered cows from Upper Heck over to Nash Draw. K21 was staying up in the lead of the herd as we drifted the cows by Webster Lake. They were all wanting a drink and were crowding around the edge of the water trying to get to the water. Shorty was on the side next to the lake as he rode along the edge of the water, pushing the cows on. Suddenly, this big, mad, water buffalo came roaring out of the water.

Well, we thought it was a water buffalo, but it was really only K21! She had lost her place up in the lead and suddenly found herself confronted by Papoose and Shorty. She charged Papoose, hitting him broadside as Shorty tried to rein Papoose away from her. Shorty's flank cinch was pretty loose and as K21 hit Papoose in the belly, her curved horn hooked in the loose flank cinch. Papoose blew up, trying to buck and get away from this battering ram! As he made a big jump, K21's horn jerked the flank cinch and yanked Papoose back to her head where she promptly rammed him again!

Shorty was yelling, and cussing, and kicking at her head, as she butted Papoose, then jerk him back with her horn, and butted him again. Papoose jumped and tried to run, but K21 had a good hold on that flank cinch and yanked him right back for another good belly massage! Looked like she was using a punching bag, as she had a pretty good rhythm going there for a little while until the flank cinch finally broke, freeing Papoose. He proceeded to really blow up and buck, but Shorty made one of his better bronc rides as K21 finally gave up the punching bag workout and went back to the herd.

"Nice ride!" I commented, as Shorty finally got Papoose pulled up.

"Hell, I didn't have no choice," Shorty answered, all out of breath. "What if I'd 'a got bucked off!"

K21 produced a top heifer calf every year. Every calf she had made it into the replacement heifers. At least none of them had her disposition. I cut her to sell every year, but Bill Littrell would look at her record and cut her back to keep. Figured a cow this good was probably worth three or four cowboys like Shorty and me!

We finally shipped old K21 when she was about fifteen years old. She sure had left her mark on Philmont cowboys!

30

Choking his Foot/Inky's Bronc Ride

Shorty had a pair of shotgun chaps that laced down the back and fit him like a glove. They were sure hard to put on, as they fit so tight his pant leg would get pulled up when he pulled on his chaps. To remedy this little problem, Shorty had a leather thong, like a long leather shoe lace, that he would tie real tight around his pants leg, just about boot-top high. With the thong tied tight around his pants leg, he could pull one leg of his chaps on, untie the thong, and tie it around the other leg, and pull that chap leg on. He carried this thong half-hitched around the string across the front of his chaps.

We were prowling a bunch of cows and calves in the Harlan country. Shorty was riding the Cimarron River bottom country, and I went on up around the Bench. We were going to meet at the Vaca Pond and go on up Deer Lake Mesa.

I got to the Vaca Pond ahead of Shorty and was laid back under a tree waiting for him. Before long I saw him riding up. He looked kinda peculiar, the way he was riding, kinda off center with his right foot out of the stirrup.

"What's a matter, Shorty?" I asked as he pulled up and started to get down. "Hurt your leg?"

"Damn," he said, "I don't know. My foot got sleepy. It's numb and my leg hurts like hell," he complained.

He got down on the ground and couldn't hardly walk, so he sat down and started moaning, and groaning, and voicing a few choice words about his predicament.

"Did you bump your knee on a tree? Twist your leg?" I asked.

"Hell NO! I didn't do nothing to it! It just got numb and sleepy," he moaned.

Shorty got up off the ground, and tried to walk a little. That didn't seem to help.

"Why don't you take your boot off, maybe your sock's twisted, or maybe you got something in your boot," I offered, trying to be helpful.

"Help me pull my boot off," he asked, cussing and moaning.

When I pushed the bottom of his chaps up so I could get a hold of his boot to pull it off, I spotted the trouble! There tied as tight as he could get it was his trusty leather thong around his leg right at his boot top. I started laughing.

"Here's your trouble, Shorty," I said as I untied the thong and handed it to him.

"Well I'll be damned" he kinda grinned, "Thought I took that damned thing off! I been choking my foot! Good thing you found that damn thong. My foot might have just fell off!"

He had been riding five or six hours with that thong tied around his leg, cutting his circulation down to about zero! He soon recovered, and we went on about our business.

◊   ◊   ◊

Shorty's wife, Mrs. Martinez, had a small black dog, kinda cross between some kinda terrier and a Chihuahua. He was black with a little white strip in his face. They called him Inky, and he seldom went out of the house except to ride in the car if Mrs. Martinez was going someplace. He was always in her lap; a sure enough house dog!

Mrs. Martinez was going to Albuquerque to spend a couple of weeks with her daughter. Seems where their daughter lived, they couldn't have dogs, so Shorty had to baby sit old Inky while Mrs. Martinez was gone.

Only problem with this was Shorty and I had to go to Bonita, and transporting Inky up there was somewhat of a challenge to our packing skills. We didn't have a pickup at that time and everything we took up to camp went by pack mule.

We had a small, bronky, little mule we called Black Jack to pack our groceries and stuff on. Black Jack was sure known to blow up pretty regular. Seems he got most of his life's little pleasures out of trying to scatter our stuff over as much country as he could.

Well, Inky drew old Black Jack as his means of transportation to Bonita! We balanced our panniers out pretty even weight-wise; Inky weighed about as much as a dozen eggs. We fixed him a little corner in the pannier to ride in. We left him a little air hole on top, not big enough for him to climb out of. We tied Black Jack's hind foot up so we could get our panniers on him, threw our bed rolls over them and a diamond hitch over our pack.

Shorty snubbed Black Jack up pretty close. Surprisingly, when I let Black Jack's foot down, he didn't throw his usual fit, trying to buck everything off. Trembling and whining a little, Inky settled into his little compartment pretty nice and quiet, and we headed to Bonita.

Shorty and I were real pleased with Black Jack's attitude, leading right along like a good pack mule. Inky hadn't made a sound, and the trip was uneventful as we rode past Crater Lake and up the stock drive to the top of Fowler Pass.

I stepped off to open the gate at Fowler Pass, as Shorty led Black Jack through. As Shorty stopped to wait for me to close the gate, he laid Black Jack's lead rope loosely over his saddle horn, reaching in his shirt pocket for a smoke.

"How ya doing, Inky?" he called out as he struck a match to light up.

Well, Inky had been doing fine until he heard Shorty call his name, then he came alive big time! He went to barking and scratching on that canvas pannier, trying to dig his way out of there! Just barely got his head out of the little air hole we had left him.

This sudden commotion, scratching and barking coming out of that pannier was more than Black Jack could stand. He had been on his good behavior too long anyway. He jerked away from Shorty, the lead rope sizzling off the saddle horn. Black Jack bogged his head and really went to bucking, braying, and stampeded off down the side of the mountain. He left the stock drive and headed straight off the mountain side, through the rocks, trees, and brush.

Shorty hollered something about Black Jack's breeding and ancestors, jerked his rope down, and spurred his horse off down the side of the mountain in hot pursuit of the barking, scratching Inky, and the bucking, braying mule!

"Hang on Inky. I'm coming, I'm coming. Hang on Inky!" he yelled as he tore off down the side of the mountain, in hot pursuit.

I got the gate shut, jumped back on my horse, and joined the procession that was sure moving fast. With all the tree limbs breaking, brush rattling, rocks rolling, dog barking, mule braying, and Shorty hollering "Hang on Inky," it wasn't very hard to follow them!

When they got to the bottom of Bonita Canyon, Shorty finally got

Black Jack roped. Inky had made a hell of a bronc ride, and came out of the pannier in better shape than the dozen eggs did in the other pannier!

Inky of course slept in the cabin with us, being the house pet that he was. One morning, around 4:30 A.M., he woke Shorty up, needing to go out side to the bathroom. Shorty got up and let him out and climbed back in his bedroll, not quite ready to get up.

In just a few minutes Inky like to tore the door down trying to get back in! His frantic barking and scratching was like it had been riding Black Jack! Shorty jumped back out of his bed and rushed to the door to see what Inky was so upset about. There on the porch was a big wild turkey hen, a pecking and flogging Inky with her wings. She was sure getting after the little dog and when Shorty got the door open Inky nearly knocked him down trying to get away from the mad, turkey hen.

Guess it was a good thing Inky couldn't talk, 'cause he would have sure had some wild tales to tell Mrs. Martinez about his cowboying adventures when he finally got to go home to her. And Shorty would sure have been in trouble!

◊   ◊   ◊

Philmont had a summer program for scouts who couldn't afford the regular camping fee. It allowed them to come to the ranch and work with the ranch department for a week and get two week's free camping in return.

These were older scouts, and they worked at putting up hay, fixing fence or whatever little jobs they could do. One program was for them to come up to Bonita and ride with the cowboys for a few days.

They would stay at Bonita three or four days, just enough time to get really saddle sore. Most of them were pretty green and were in the way most of the time. We would get two or three of these groups during the summer. Shorty called it our babysitting duties.

A new group had hiked in one morning as Shorty and I were leaving camp. They wanted to go with us, so we ran in the dude horses and gave them a quick instruction on riding, and let them follow along on their first day with us. We were going to gather some cows and calves in Bonita Canyon and separate some steer and heifer pairs, and figured these kids could maybe help hold the herd.

That idea soon proved wrong when we got to trying to cut out pairs. These helpers were causing more trouble than help! They seemed to have a knack for riding the wrong way and turning the cuts back to the herd. Shorty and I were getting a little flustered!

We had the small herd up against the horse pasture fence, and could see the Bonita camp from where we were working the cows. Shorty and I held a little pow wow and decided to send our helpers to camp. Told them to unsaddle and turn their horses out in the corral. Go up to the cabin, chop some wood and build a fire in the cook stove, and get some water from the spring. We assured them we would be along pretty quick and cook supper. They hadn't been in the cabin yet, having just hiked in that morning, but they could see the cabin from where we were, and we could see them, so we figured they could handle that on their own.

Shorty and I were doing fine. The cattle settled down and were working out real good. A little while later, we heard a bunch of yelling and hollering. We looked up at the camp. Here were all these kids standing out in front of the cabin, yelling "Fire! Fire!" Black smoke was rolling out the front door like a bunch of old tires were burning!

"Those damn kids set our cabin on fire!" Shorty hollered over at me. We just dropped the cows and took off as fast as we could to Bonita. We loped up to the smoking cabin. Kids were all jumping up and down yelling, "Fire, Fire!" Well, what we had to say to them right then is best not put in print! Didn't see any fire any place, just all this black smoke coming out the door and even out the cracks in the walls!

We rushed up on the front porch, but couldn't see any fire. The black smoke was so thick coming out the open door that we couldn't see into the kitchen. I ran around to the back of the cabin and looked in the window. Seemed like the smoke was coming out of the oven in our cook stove. We finally managed to get inside to see what was burning. The fire seemed to be in the oven, and I grabbed the full water bucket and dumped it in the oven. That put out the fire.

We had two wood boxes in the kitchen. One we kept our regular fire wood in. In the other one we had some pure, pitch pine we used to start a fire with. This pitch pine was so rich with pitch, it only took one or two small pieces to start a fire.

Our dandy little helpers had gotten into the box of pitch pine, put a bunch of it in the oven, and lit the fire!

These kids had never seen a wood burning stove, didn't know anything about where the fire box was, what the oven was for, or what pitch pine was! But, I'll guarantee they got a good education on the subject that night!

The damned, black pitchy suet, was hanging in long black strings down about a foot long from the ceiling. Everything in the cabin was black and suet-covered. Boy, you talk about a mess. Our little helpers spent most of the night heating water and scrubbing everything in the camp. We let them scrub away, while we built us a campfire outside and cooked supper. Finally, we weakened and let them eat a little too! Just lucky the old camp didn't catch fire and burn down. They all got to spend the next day at camp, trying to clean up the suet!

Shorty was sure good at catching trout out of the Rayado and Aqua Fria creeks. We always carried a piece of fishing line and a fly or two in our chap pocket, and would catch a nice batch of trout anytime we were riding that part of the summer country. Grasshoppers were plentiful, and they sure made good bait to catch these elusive trout.

Crossing the creeks horseback you could see some nice eight or ten-inch trout darting out of the way. Our summer helpers knew about as much about catching trout as they did about building fires in a cook stove, so they didn't have much luck at fishing.

One of Shorty's favorite tricks for these kids, was to pull some long hairs out of his horses tail. Braiding these horse hairs into an old safety pin, Shorty would proudly show off his fishing tackle. The kids would laugh at his make shift fishing line, and it was usually pretty easy to get a bet with them whether he could catch any fish.

Shorty would bet a six pack of beer that he could catch enough trout for supper. The kids would take this bet every time.

Shorty would explain that he had to be alone while he fished, so I would offer to take the kids back to camp and leave Shorty alone. Soon as we left, Shorty would throw away the horse hair and put his safety pin away for the next time. Taking out his fishing line and flies from his chap pocket, it wouldn't take him long to have a nice mess of trout rolled up in his slicker. Kids never figured him out and thought he was one heck of a fisherman! Shorty made them shell out enough money to buy himself a six pack.

31

Cowboy Dramatics

We usually had our calves branded and worked around the first part of May and had the cattle ready for the long drive up to the summer country by the first part of June. Seemed there were always four or five calves that got missed in the spring branding and a few that were too small to work, so we would brand and work them during the summer at Bonita.

Shorty and I had a little bunch of cows and calves penned at the old pole corrals at Bonita. All the calves needed to be branded and worked. We had our fire burning good, heating up the branding irons and were about ready to start on these calves, when a couple of groups of boy scouts came hiking along the trail that went by the corrals. We kinda stalled around a little, hoping they would go on, but they all dropped their backpacks and got their cameras out, so we decided to go on with our business. We got the cows and calves separated, with all the calves in a small crowding pen. Not enough room for a horse, so we were going to catch these calves afoot. There was a big bull calf in the bunch that was pretty wild and was keeping everything stirred up, so we decided we would tackle him first and get him out of the pen.

I roped him around the neck and Shorty went down the rope to flank him. Well, he was a little juicy and came a running to Shorty, bellering and jumping pretty high. He banged into Shorty, knocking him down, ran over him, and kicked him where a guy hadn't ought to never get kicked as he went by.

Shorty started talking to this big bull calf in some language some of these boy scouts may not have heard before. We ganged up on this bellering little bovine and got him thrown down and hog-tied after a pretty good wrestling match! Well, Shorty was pretty upset with this calf, having made him look kinda bad in front of those boy scouts. He decided to put on a little show of his own.

Shorty whipped out his pocket knife, stropped it a few licks on the leg of his chaps, and said, "You little S.O.B., you kicked me there so I'm just going to cut yours off!"

He proceeded to castrate the calf amidst the cries of astonishment and protest coming from our audience! I just fell right in with Shorty, telling the calf in a loud voice that since he had butted me with his little horns, I was just going to cut them off, and proceeded to dehorn him. Of course, the blood squirted up in the air, adding a little to our show. I shook the can of blood stopper on the calf's head and got the bleeding stopped.

Shorty then made a big production of ear-marking him, then tells the calf he's going to burn his ass good for giving us so much trouble, and branded him.

Well, that was about all these boy scouts could handle. They grabbed up their packs and headed on up the trail to Beaubien. Shorty and I got a big laugh out of this little exhibition we had put on and went ahead and finished our working and branded the rest of the calves without an audience.

We rode by Beaubien the next day and were kinda surprised when we got a message that had come on the two-way radio from Littrell, telling us to get down to headquarters and come to his office immediately!!! We finished prowling that day, and early next morning saddled up and headed down the mountain, wondering what Littrell had cooking for us.

We were a little surprised when we went into his office and found a mad Littrell, upset Jack Rhea, director of camping, and a very hostile Ray Bryan, general ranch manager! Boy, we were suddenly in with the sure enough big shots! Only trouble, they all seemed pretty well pissed off at Shorty and me! We quickly decided they hadn't called this meeting to give us a raise in pay! Needless to say, we were a little shook up, wondering what we had done.

Seems the two leaders from the two groups of boy scouts that had taken in our little branding exhibition had gotten on the radio to Jack Rhea, telling him about the barbarians at Bonita and how we were torturing poor, helpless, little calves. They had accused us of all sorts of cruelty to animals, mutilation, torture, you name it we had done it! They had demanded that we be reported to the Humane Society and fired immediately.

Boy, it sure took a lot of explaining and sweet talking to get out of that deal, since Jack Rhea and Ray Bryan had no idea of what a branding was all about.

I think Littrell kinda wanted to laugh, but he didn't dare, as we tried to explain to these big shots what we were doing. He finally saved our butts by explaining to Bryan and Rhea it was just a little cowboy humor Easterners may not appreciate! Littrell sure didn't approve of our antics, but he assured Jack Rhea and Ray Bryan that castrating, ear marking, dehorning, and branding was all a legitimate part of ranching.

They finally agreed not to fire us, but made it pretty damned clear we better watch what we did around scouts in the future if we wanted to work at Philmont! After that we kinda cooled our dramatics around boy scouts.

◊　　◊　　◊

Prowling our cattle in the high country at Philmont during the summer was always interesting. The high country was full of scouts. We could always be sure that when we had a bunch of cows strung out moving them along a trail, we would always run into a bunch of scouts coming down the same trail, scattering cows everywhere. Made life interesting and scared the hell out of a lot of kids as we would go crashing through the brush and trees to turn the cows back, yelling and cussing as we went!

Shorty and I would always make it a point to just happen to be near a staffed camp at lunch time. We were always welcomed, made a lot of friends, and spread a little cowboy wisdom amongst the boy scouts. Taught a lot of the staff the finer points of playing penny ante poker, and answered questions like we really knew what we were talking about, no matter what the subject.

We fixed it up with several camp directors at these back country camps, to leave a little canned stuff at the close of season so when we were gathering cattle after the scouts had left, we could still get a little bite to eat at their camps. Most of them would leave a jar of peanut butter, a box of crackers or canned spam, all kinds of stuff, and it was pretty nice to drop by and get a bite. We didn't carry a lunch with us and we could usually find something left for us.

Once, when Shorty and I were gathering cattle out of the Apache Country, Shorty dropped off at Lost Cabin and went down the Aqua Fria, through Fish Camp, going to meet me below Porcupine. He said he would get something for us to eat at Fish Camp. The camp director who had been at Fish Camp told us he would leave some food for us.

I had a little bunch of cows and calves and was holding them at the junction of Rayado and Apache Canyon when I saw Shorty riding up the trail, grinning from ear to ear. I wondered what he had been up to 'cause he was sure happy about something.

"Boy, wait till you see what I got us to eat," he hollered as he rode up.

That was sure good news cause I was getting hungry.

"Great, what did you come up with?" I answered, expecting a can of pears, or some peanut butter and crackers.

"Fried chicken!" he exclaimed.

"Where the hell did you get any fried chicken up here?" I asked, really surprised at this good news.

I knew there wasn't anyone at any camp around. Then I thought maybe somebody was at Fish Camp we didn't know about who had given Shorty some fried chicken.

"Was someone down at Fish Camp?" I asked, as he was getting down. "No," he said, "Those boy scouts left us a can of fried chicken!"

He was untying his slicker from behind his saddle and he sure enough had something wrapped up in it. He rolled his slicker out on the ground, took out a big can and proudly showed me a three pound can of Crisco with a big picture of fried chicken on the label!

"Hell Shorty, you got a can of lard!" I exclaimed.

"Lard? Hell, it ain't lard! Look at that picture. This is fried chicken!" he answered, kinda put out that I didn't know fried chicken from lard.

"Hell, that ain't fried chicken! That picture is what the chicken looks like if you fry it in that lard!" I exclaimed.

He sat there on his slicker, holding his prized can of Crisco, looking in disbelief at the picture of golden, brown, fried chicken.

"I'll be damned. I was sure ready for some fried chicken. Are you sure?" he said, "Let's open it cause it might be chicken!"

Nothing would do until he got the can of lard open. He probed around in the lard with a stick, not finding any golden, fried chicken. Throwing the can of lard off in the brush, Shorty got back on his horse and mumbled and cussed, as we headed the cows and calves up the trail. We skipped lunch that day.

◊   ◊   ◊

Shorty and I had finished our day of prowling through the cattle and turned our horses out at Bonita. Throwing our saddles in our old pickup we headed up to Beaubien Camp for a cup of coffee and a little poker game. It had started raining around noon and we were looking for a place to dry out and warm up.

There were several groups of scouts camping around Beaubien for the night. Shorty and I were enjoying the coffee and relaxing and teaching some of the staff a little about seven card stud. The staff had a good fire going in the fireplace, a fresh pot of coffee on, and we were drying out and pretty relaxed. We had some eager-to-learn pupils in the poker game and things were looking up!

This peaceful scene was suddenly interrupted by a loud scream, and a lot of yelling, like someone had gotten scalped or something. All the poker players jumped up and ran to the door, not knowing if Apaches were attacking the camp or if it was Poncho Villa on a raid!

There were a couple burros staked out in the meadow in front of the camp. One of the burros was at the end of his stake rope, ears up, looking at a guy laying on the ground yelling like he was getting killed. Seems this guy making all the racket was an advisor with one of the groups of scouts in camp for the night. He had decided to jump on and ride this burro that was on the stake rope. The burro would put up with just so much nonsense, and getting rode while on his time off wasn't something the burro was going to put up with!

The burro promptly bucked the guy off and took off running. Only one, small thing wrong with this deal; the guy who got bucked off had somehow gotten his leg tangled up in the stake rope.

When the burro hit the end of the rope, which was tied solid to the stake, he was going pretty fast. The would-be burro rider got caught in the middle, and when the rope came tight, it broke this guys leg slicker than slick!

He was yelling bloody murder, as some of the staff rolled him onto a stretcher and carried him up to the cabin. The camp director got on the two-way radio and called the health lodge, informing them of the accident. The good doctor at the health lodge informed the camp director that they would have an ambulance leave headquarters immediately to come up and get this guy. I told the camp director to tell the doctor that I was at the scene and would be glad to bring the guy in for them. The doctor asked about the type of vehicle we had, and when he was told that it was a cattle department pickup, he let us know he didn't think the back of our pickup quite met their sanitary requirements! I assured him that we could shovel some of the manure and old hay out of the pickup, spread some tarps down and make the patient fairly comfortable.

The doc said, "No, wait for the ambulance!"

Well, that didn't make sense to me to wait over an hour for the ambulance to come all the way up there when I was already there, but I didn't argue. The cards were falling pretty good anyway, so I got back in the poker game.

It had started raining again. Soon it really got serious and it really poured down. The guy with the broken leg wasn't taking it very well, hollering and cussing, and smoking up all of Shorty's and my cigarettes. About an hour and a half later, the ambulance came slipping and sliding into camp, and we got the burro rider loaded up in their nice sanitary, muddy ambulance, wished him well, and returned to our poker game.

The rain just kept pouring down. Our pupils were out of money, so Shorty and I headed back to headquarters. The ambulance had about an hour's head start on us.

The road was sure slick and tricky coming down off that mountain. We were sliding along pretty slow, taking it easy and trying to stay on the road. We had just passed Miners Park and drove up to the normally dry creek crossing. Well, it sure wasn't dry now. It was up and running big time!

Down the creek about a hundred feet sat the ambulance, washed up in a pile of rocks and debris. It was pointed down stream, with the water splashing up against the back doors. The water was up on the sides about four feet. The driver and his helper were sitting up on top of the ambulance, yelling and waving their arms like they had been stranded on this island a long time! Their radio was dead, and they hollered for us to call the health lodge.

We had a tow chain in the pickup, but I couldn't get the pickup down the creek far enough to reach the ambulance. I called in on our radio to the doctor at the health lodge and informed him of his ambulance's plight. I told him that we couldn't pull the ambulance out of the creek with our pickup. Looked like a job for the wrecker.

He questioned our sanitary conditions again. I told him the hay and manure was pretty wet now, but we could kick most of it out! He finally agreed to have the poor guy with the broken leg put in the back of our pickup and for us to bring him in.

The two guys with the ambulance waded out to the back of the ambulance and managed to get the doors open. When they got the back doors open, the water flooded the inside of the ambulance. Then the burro rider was really yelling! He was doing a pretty good backstroke, trying to stay afloat while the guys got his stretcher out of there!

I eased our old pickup off into the water and we got across all right. Shorty and I got up in the back and kicked some old hay and manure out. We had an old wornout pack tarp behind the seat and we spread it out in the back of the pickup. The ambulance boys got their stretcher up into the pickup and we made the burro rider as comfortable as possible. Gave him one of our last cigarettes and headed for the health lodge.

The doctor was waiting for us and he looked rather shocked when we opened up the back of the pickup and he saw his patient lying there in not very sanitary conditions! Oh well, so much for cowboy ambulances. The burro rider sure wasn't complaining! The sanitary boys had damn near drowned him!

32

Danny

Hardy Kaufman and Floyd Brannon pulled into cattle headquarters one evening hauling four head of horses. I always enjoyed seeing these two fellas from Stratford, Texas. They were Billie Littrell's uncles, both of them in their fifties. Hardy was a hard-twisted rancher, who always had some good whiskey, wild stories, and always rode good horses. Floyd worked in town and was a little more refined than Hardy. They were going to spend the night with Bill and Billie Littrell before going down to Zastro Cow Camp the next morning on one of their regular bear hunting trips. They were leaving their horses and bear hunting dogs at cattle headquarters for the night. I went down to the corrals to show them where to put their horses and dogs.

As they unloaded their saddle horses a bright bay horse stepped out of the trailer and I was sure looking him over. Boy, he was one good-looking horse. He had a little real fine head, short ears, with a real intelligent look about his face. Stood around fifteen hands and looked like he would weigh around 1150-1200. Muscled up about as good as they make them, he looked like a picture of the perfect quarter horse.

"Sure a good looking bay horse, Hardy," I ventured as he led him over to the corrals.

"This is Danny. Don't let his looks fool you!" Hardy said as he turned Danny loose in the corral. "He will damn sure buck you off and he don't need much excuse to do it!"

Hardy went on to explain that his son, Powder, had been trying to rope calves on this bay horse with various results. I knew Powder as being a pretty darn good calf roper. Seems Danny would either buck Powder off or let him catch a calf them blow up and run off. He would work perfect for a few runs, then pull one of his stunts and cause a big wreck. After bucking Powder off and running off, dragging and killing a calf at the Amarillo rodeo, Powder said he didn't ever want to see that no good S.O.B. again.

"I figure a week or two of riding in these mountains chasing bear is what this dirty bugger needs," Hardy said. "I'm going to camp on him and get that buck out of him."

"Well, he is sure a good looking rascal. If you need some miles put on him, bring him back and I'll sit on him," I jokingly replied.

Next morning early, Hardy and Floyd came by and loaded their horses and dogs and headed out for Zastro.

The old Zastro Cow Camp set on the Rayado River some twelve miles south of headquarters. It was an old, rough two room cabin in a stand of big cotton woods trees with the Rayado River running just a few feet from the back door. You could catch enough trout for supper right out the back door! There was an old barn and a set of corrals close by.

The Zastro sat at the bottom of the stock drive that led up into the high summer country of the Philmont, CS, and UU ranches. The camp was used by all three ranches when they were moving cattle to summer country. The cowboys would put the cattle going up to the high country in the big pasture around the camp. They would spend the night in the old cabin and head the cattle up the stock drive at daylight the next morning. Many thousand head of cattle had passed through Zastro through the years, and many a cowboy had rolled his bed out in the old cabin.

Hardy and Floyd were always welcome to camp here when there weren't any cattle moving through. It was real handy for them, as lots of bear used this part of the country. Hardy and Floyd got to Zastro pretty early that morning and decided to throw a little circle up the Rayado Canyon to see if they could find any bear sign. The dogs were sure keyed up and ready to run. Hardy saddled Danny, and Floyd saddled one of his horses and they headed up the Rayado.

They hadn't gone but about three hundred yards from camp when the dogs opened up with a loud chorus of barking on a fresh bear track in the trail. A couple hundred yards further and the dogs had a bear treed right beside the trail!

"Hell, this ain't no fun!" Hardy exclaimed. "We didn't get a chase at all. I want these dogs to get a little exercise and this damned horse too! I'll get the bear out of the tree and we will give him a head start and tree him again."

Floyd got down off his horse and got all the barking dogs collared together so he could hold them. He led the dogs back away from the tree a little ways and told Hardy he had the dogs held, and to go ahead and get the bear out of the tree.

Well, being the super smart hombre that he was, Hardy rode Danny up under the limb the bear was sitting on, about ten or twelve feet above the ground. Pulling his twenty-two caliber pistol out of his holster, he took careful aim at one of the bear's hind paws that was hanging over the side of the limb. Hardy figured he would shoot the bear in the foot and the bear would jump out of the tree and they would get a good chase out of him before treeing him again.

Like a lot of well-laid plans, this one didn't quite work out as planned! Hardy's shot hit the bear in the foot all right, but instead of jumping out away from Hardy and Danny, the bear jumped out right on top of them. The bear's right front paw caught Danny high up on the neck and clawed him down the neck to his shoulder. His left front paw grabbed at Hardy and ripped his chap leg off down to his boot top.

Danny promptly bucked Hardy off and headed east, running and bucking. The bear hit the ground and took off running west. The dogs jerked loose from Floyd and took off after the bear. Floyd's horse got spooked from all this sudden activity and took off following Danny. Hardy was left sitting in the trail wondering what the hell happened!

Fortunately they were only a few hundred yards from camp and Danny and Floyd's horse stopped at the corrals. Floyd caught his horse, and Hardy unsaddled Danny and doctored the long scratches on his neck and shoulder.

"I ain't riding that S.O.B. again!" Hardy said.

They finally got the dogs gathered up and let the bear go for another day! Hardy's hip was hurting a little by then from where he had hit the ground, and he figured he had had enough for the first day.

I was a little surprised to see Hardy and Floyd driving into cattle headquarters that afternoon, with one horse in their trailer. Hardy unloaded Danny and turned him loose in the corral. I noticed the long cuts down his neck and shoulder, and I asked what happened?

"You said you would like to sit on him for awhile, didn't you?" Hardy asked.

"Yes, I sure would," I replied, wondering what was going on.

"Well get your rig on him! I damn sure don't want to ride him!" Hardy grumbled.

Then he told me about the bear jumping on them and the wreck that had happened. I had to laugh as he told his story.

"Well, I'll try him and see how we get along," I told Hardy as they pulled out to go nurse Hardy's battle wounds.

I saddled Danny the next morning and stepped up on him. I felt as if I had straddled a big keg of dynamite. I just hoped nothing would light his fuse and cause him to blow up! Boy, was he one powerhouse. Never had rode a horse that had such a handle on him as Danny did. I knew then that the expression of turning on a dime and giving you back a nickel in change must have came from someone who had ridden Danny, 'cause he would sure turn back through himself.

I rode Danny several days and we got along real good. He was still pretty spooky for a while, after his bear experience. I had a big, black border collie dog named Bob. Bob liked to keep all the rabbits and squirrels chased out of the way as we rode through the brush. His jumping out of the brush in front of Danny kept things pretty interesting for a while too! Danny finally got used to Bob, but I think Bob reminded Danny of the bear jumping out of the tree on him!

Hardy and Floyd came by about a week later, headed back to Stratford. I hated to see them drive up as I figured they would take Danny home with them.

"Well how many times has that S.O.B. bucked you off?" Hardy asked as he walked into the saddle room.

"Hasn't yet", I answered. "He is sure one good bugger. I really got along with him good".

"I'll be damned," Hardy said. "How many times have you rode him?"

"I've rode him five days, and he just gets better every day!" I answered.

"I'll tell you what," Hardy said. "I damn sure don't ever want to ride him again, and Powder said he didn't ever want to see him again! Since you like him and want to ride him, I'm just going to give the S.O.B. to you! He is your horse!"

Boy, I could hardly believe this! This was the best horse I ever threw a saddle on, and Hardy gave him to me! I told Hardy I would take care of Danny and if he ever wanted him back, he knew where he was. We shook hands on the deal, and I was one tickled cowboy!

Danny had spent most of his life in an arena under a lot of pressure. Outside riding the open country seemed to be pretty good therapy for him, as he really seemed to like whatever we had to do. He was the most willing horse I ever rode. Well, most of the time any way!

I had made several rides on Danny and hadn't had a reason to rope anything on him. I was about ready to see how he was to rope on. Shorty and I were prowling the Brush pasture when we came up on a big, wild horned cow that had a bad eye. She needed doctoring, and I was most willing to oblige!

"Want me to head her?" Shorty asked. "You can heel her on your new horse."

"Naw," I replied, "This is supposed to be a high-powered rope horse. Let's see how he handles this old cow."

We both cinched up pretty tight, and I built me a loop and took to this cow. She had a bad eye but it wasn't slowing her down any! We were moving on, Danny ran right up on her, gave me a nice throw and my loop settled around her horns pretty slick. Only problem was a big stand of oak trees was approaching pretty fast and we didn't have much room to slow down. We needed to stop right quick before we hit the oak brush. I was tied hard and fast to the saddle horn, and Danny stopped as if I had roped a calf. The cow hit the end of the rope really carrying the mail and gave us a pretty hard jerk. This was a little more than Danny wanted right then! He bogged his head and did buck me off quick. He bucked on around the oak brush, and the cow ran into the brush. My old grass rope broke right at the honda. Shorty rode on around the oaks and got Danny stopped and came leading him back as I was getting the dirt and leaves out of my shirt.

"Well your new horse sure runs good; followed that cow and gave you a good throw, but he might need a little more work on his stop! That son of a gun can damn sure buck, can't he?" Shorty said, as he laughed and handed me my bridle reins.

"Yea, I guess he can buck pretty good. I really wasn't on him long enough to tell very much!" I answered.

"Want me to catch her this time?" Shorty said as he continued laughing.

"Hell no!" I answered. "I think that was probably my fault. I had to set him up too quick. Let me try her again."

I tied a new honda in my rope and we found the cow again. I built to her and Danny put me in perfect position again. I roped her, but had a lot of room to slow her down without giving Danny a hard jerk. Shorty rode in and heeled her and we got her doctored without further incident. That's when Danny and I reached an agreement. You don't cause me to get too hard of a jerk and I won't buck you off!

That was the only time Danny ever bucked with me. I roped lots of stock on Danny, from big bulls to little calves and he never did buck again. Of course I tried to keep my end of the agreement!

I would hear from Hardy every once in a while. He always asked about Danny, but never did want him back. Hardy was sure pleased that Danny and I got along so well. I rode Danny many years at Philmont, and finally retired him and he passed on to where the good horses go at the ripe old age of twenty-five.

Danny was real sensitive and if I raised my voice and cussed him out, he acted like he had got a whipping. You never wanted to hit Danny with anything. Bridle rein, rope or even your hand. If you ever hit him he would fall apart and be mad and stay mad for two or three days!

Hardy described shoeing his hind feet pretty good. He said picking up Danny's hind foot was like picking up the corner of the courthouse. He was about that heavy and you knew all the damned bricks were going to fall on you any minute!

Ray Bryan was the general manager at Philmont. He had a daughter in college back East somewhere, and she spent some time in the summer at Philmont. She rode quite a bit, I guess, English style. She happened to see me riding Danny one day and she decided she wanted to ride him. I told her no, he was not a Philmont horse. He belonged to me, and I didn't let anyone ride my horses. The young lady wasn't used to anyone telling her no, especially a cowboy.

She complained to her dad that I wouldn't let her ride this horse and he jumped on Bill Littrell about it. Bill was my immediate boss and he came to me wanting to know why I said no to any request from Bryan's daughter! I told him she wanted to ride Danny, and I wasn't about to let her. He tried to convince me I should let her do whatever she wanted cause Bryan was

"THE MAN!" Well, I wouldn't give in, so Bill finally let it go. I don't know what he told Bryan.

About a week later, Shorty and I were out riding somewhere and when we came in that evening I noticed our saddle horses out in the pasture behind the corrals, and they didn't look quite right. I rode out to get a closer look at them and there stood Danny with a flat, English saddle on him and a bridle with the reins broke off!

I took Danny to the barn and jerked that flat saddle off him, and stormed up to the house madder than hell. I got Bill on the phone and started raising hell about finding Danny with that English saddle on him and I wanted to know what the hell Bryan's daughter had been up to!

"Now calm down," Bill said. "I think Danny took care of the situation by himself!"

Seems Bryan's daughter and her boy friend had come up to cattle headquarters while Shorty and I were gone. Danny and several other horses were loafing around the drinking trough in the back corral. The only horse they could catch was Danny, but that was fine because he was the one they wanted to ride. He let them put that flat saddle on him and their bridle.

The boyfriend got to ride first. Big mistake! Danny stuck this old kid's head in the hard corral right quick, breaking the boy's arm. Danny ran out to the horse pasture and they couldn't catch him to get their saddle and bridle off. They rushed the boy off to the hospital in Raton. They never did ask to ride him again! Guess they didn't like him.

Shorty and I were leaving one morning well before daylight. I had made arrangements with one of the farm workers to come up to cattle headquarters and milk our milk cow. I told him not to try riding any of our horses, just to holler real loud and the cow would come into the milking corral. The cow was out in a small trap and always came in to be milked.

Well, who should be standing there in the corral, looking all tempting, but Danny. This boy couldn't see hollering at this cow when this nice looking horse was right there ready to go get the cow on, and he would get to ride! Danny was real easy to catch, and the boy found a bridle and an extra saddle in the saddle room. He saddled Danny and got on him to go get the milk cow. Another big mistake!

Bettye was at the house getting ready to go to work when this farm hand came limping up to the back door. He was all dirty, a big cut on his head, blood running down his face, and looked like he had been run over by a truck. He was holding his arm which was hanging at a peculiar angle.

"I think I need a doctor!" he said.

Danny had struck again! Bettye took the guy down to the office, and they hauled him off to the hospital. The boy suffered a broken arm and broken collar bone and had a few stitches in his head.

Bettye came back and went down to the corral where Danny and the milk cow were waiting. She unsaddled Danny and turned him out. She spent rest of the morning trying to get the cow milked! Milking cows was not one of her long suits!

I think that's why Danny was so easy to catch. Anyone could catch him anyplace. Catching him was easy, but the riding sometimes posed a problem! He was just waiting for another sucker!

◊　　　◊　　　◊

Boss Sanchez and his son Eddie had bought a pretty good horse from the Bell Ranch. The horse had been raced some and could sure get up and run. Boss and Eddie were getting this Bell horse in shape to run in the cow pony race at the Fourth of July rodeo. They had run him against about all the horses they had in the horse department and hadn't found anything that would give their horse any competition. They were wanting something that would give their horse a better test.

Boss and Eddie came over to cattle headquarters one afternoon. Shorty and I had just gotten in from checking some cattle. They explained what they wanted was something that would make their horse have to run, as they didn't have anything that would give him any competition.

"Heck, we don't have any race horses over here, Boss," I told him.

"We heard that bay horse you got from Texas was supposed to be pretty fast," Eddie said.

"Well, he can catch a cow or a calf, but he ain't no race horse," I replied.

"Come on. We want to show you how fast our horse is. You don't have to feel bad when we beat you. This is the fastest bugger around here and we are going to win that race at the rodeo," Eddie bragged.

I figured we might get outrun, but it wasn't going to be as easy as Eddie seemed to think, so I said okay.

They had a smooth straight course marked off over in the Antelope Pasture across the road from cattle headquarters. Boss and Eddie drove off to go get their racehorse. I rode Danny over to the marked off course, and they drove up with their horse in the trailer. He was a good looking old pony all right. They had a little flat English saddle on him, and Eddie jumped up on him and warmed him up a little. The horse had been out here to this race course enough to know what was fixing to happen. Danny was as unconcerned as could be, just watching this Bell horse and wondering why he was getting all worked up!

The course was a little over two hundred yards and Eddie and I got lined up for the start. I was riding my regular old work saddle, but after noticing the light flat saddle on their horse, I reached around and untied my slicker from the back of my saddle and dropped it on the ground. Figured I didn't need anymore handicap!

Danny jumped out to a quick lead on the Bell horse and flat out ran him all the way. We crossed the finish line a good two lengths ahead. I was a little surprised at how Danny could run and was sure pleased that he had done so well.

Boss and Eddie were surprised too, but relieved when I told them I wasn't going to run Danny in the race at the rodeo. Danny had made a pretty good statement! The Bell horse won the race at the rodeo.

I rode Danny into Cimarron on the fourth of July for the big rodeo. Shorty and I had entered the wild cow milking and I was going to rope on Danny.

Horses and riders were getting lined up in town preparing for the parade that went through town ending at the rodeo grounds. Bettye's younger sister, Josephine, came up to me all bent out of shape because there wasn't a horse around that she could ride in the parade and she sure wanted to be in that parade.

I jacked my stirrups up to where they would fit her and got her up on Danny. She had ridden some but sure wasn't very experienced. She had heard a little about Danny and was just scared enough to pay attention and do what I told her. I adjusted her reins so Danny had enough rein to move out okay and told her to hold her hand right there and don't move it! Don't mess with him, just keep your reins like this, no looser or no tighter. I figured Danny would get in line with the other horses and follow along in the parade.

The parade started off down the street, with Danny moving right out in line with the other horses. Josephine looked like a pretty statue. She had a death grip on the saddle horn with her right hand and her left hand right where I had positioned it. As the parade progressed down the street, Danny kind of got caught up in the parade bit, and started passing the horses in front of him. He figured, heck, I'm a leader, not a follower! He just stepped out at a nice fast walk, nonchalantly passing everything in front of him!

Josephine had her best rodeo queen smile on as she passed the other riders. As the parade started down Coco Street, Josephine was right up in the front of the parade instead of in the back where she had started!

Mike Hope and Cootie Jackson were carrying flags, leading the parade. Danny moved up between them, and then passed them, too.

"Hey, get back in line!" Mike hollered.

"I can't," Josephine answered.

"What do you mean you can't! Pull up on your horse and get back in line!" Cootie hollered.

"Nope," Josephine replied, "Bob told me not to move my hand and not to mess with my reins and I'm not going to!"

Josephine and Danny led the Grand Entry into the rodeo grounds! They sure looked good, even if the flag carriers were a little perturbed. Josephine did just what I had told her. She said she was a little embarrassed at first, but it was kind of neat leading the parade!

33

Shorty

Shorty was camped down at Zastro Cow Camp, looking after a bunch of cows, when Hardy and Floyd came up on one of their annual bear hunts. Shorty always welcomed them camping with him, as he liked their company. But mostly he liked their abundance of drinking whiskey.

I drove down to Zastro one evening to visit with them and to give Hardy a report on Danny's latest conquests. Figured to eat supper with them and maybe sample some of that Texas whiskey before Shorty drank it all!

We were sitting around swapping stories, and Hardy mentioned he had a good 30-30 Winchester rifle he wanted to sell. Shorty was sure interested in this 30-30, so after looking it over pretty good, Shorty said he wanted to see how it shot.

We all went out in front of the cabin, looking around for something to shoot at. We didn't have a target of any kind. The old barn and saddle room was a couple hundred feet from the cabin. The old barn had a bunch of rats and mice in it, so Shorty and I had tied a couple pieces of rope to the ceiling rafters and would hang our saddles from these short pieces of rope so that the rats and mice couldn't get to them. Hardy and Floyd had hung their saddles in the old barn next to Shorty's.

Hardy said, "There is an old tin can lid nailed over a knot hole above the door on that old barn. Shoot at that!"

"Wait a minute," I said, "your saddles are hanging in there".

We went over to the old barn and looked in at where the saddles were hanging and where the tin can lid over the knot hole was. The lid was well above where the saddles were so it sure looked like a good target to try this 30-30 on.

Shorty got a good rest on the corner of the cabin and fired a round from the 30-30. Right through the lid! Second shot, right through the lid!

"Shoots pretty good," Shorty said, "Let me try a couple more." All four shots were close together, right through the middle of the tin can lid.

"You try it," Shorty said, handing me the 30-30.

I put two more rounds through the center of the can lid. Shot good.

We went back in the cabin, Shorty and Hardy made their deal on the 30-30, we had a couple more drinks and a few more stories, and I headed back to cattle headquarters.

Next morning after breakfast they went out to catch their horses and saddle up. Shorty opened the old barn door and Hardy said you could have heard Shorty cussing for miles around! There, laying in the middle of the floor, was Shorty's saddle. All the saddle strings were chewed off, the cinch was chewed into two pieces, and the latigo was chewed about half into.

The rope Shorty had tied his saddle up with told the tale! The six shots from the old 30-30 had punched right through the tin can lid, cutting the rope holding Shorty's saddle, dropping it to the floor for the rats to enjoy all night! Shorty was one mad hombre. Hardy and Floyd had an old cinch and latigo in their tack box and got Shorty rigged up until he could get his rig put back together. Shorty wasn't real proud of his new 30-30 for awhile, even if it did shoot pretty good!

A while later Uncle Bob came by Zastro, and Shorty was telling him about his new 30-30. Bob said he was needing to get a deer, as he was out of camp meat and his rifle was busted. Shorty offered him his 30-30 and a box of shells. Bob said he sure appreciated the loan. Bob took the rifle and took one shell out of the box and handed the box back to Shorty.

"Hell, take the box," Shorty said.

"I only need one shell," Bob said, "I only want one deer!"

Bob put the 30-30 in his scabbard on his saddle and rode off. Shorty was sure shocked as he stood there with the box of shells in his hand.

The next day Bob came by the camp and returned Shorty's 30-30 and a chunk of fresh venison.

"You were right Shorty," he said, "that's a good shooting little rifle!"

◊   ◊   ◊

Maverick Club Rodeo in Cimarron on July 4th was always a big event around Cimarron. The big rodeo was always a time to see all your neighbors and friends, and a good excuse for Shorty to get pretty drunk.

Shorty and I got in the wild cow milking every year and always had a good time, winning second one year, but usually ending up in a big wreck. With eight or ten mounted cowboys roping some old, wild cows and their muggers trying to get hold of the cow so that the guy milking could get a couple squirts of milk in a coke bottle from a wild jumping, kicking cow, all in one big, wild scramble was pretty interesting to say the least!

Shorty always planned on getting in the calf roping, but this event came up in the afternoon and Shorty was always too drunk by then to rope his calf.

We had a big sorrel horse, named Red, in the ranch remuda that was a pretty good rope horse. He was sure aggravating to ride out in the pasture. His homing instinct was locked in on the barn. No matter where you might be out in the pasture, Red always had his head and one ear cocked toward the barn. You had to constantly keep turning him toward where you were headed, 'cause if you gave him his head, you would suddenly be headed back to the barn! Shorty and I seldom rode Red, keeping him for times when we knew there was going to be quite a bit of roping to do, as Red was sure good to rope on.

Shorty was going to ride down to the Weaning pasture, about five miles south of headquarters, to check some cows. They all had calves on them and Shorty figured it might be a good opportunity to tune up his and Red's roping skills.

Shorty had a habit of leaving gates open when he rode through if he was going to be coming back that way later.

Shorty rode down the old dirt road to the gate going into the Weaning pasture, and true to form, threw the gate back, leaving it open. As he was riding through the cows and calves, thoughts of the upcoming rodeo came to mind. There were several nice sized calves just begging to get roped. He cinched Red up a little tighter, shook out a loop and built to a calf.

Red ran right up on the calf, giving Shorty a good throw and Shorty made a good catch, pitched his slack and got down and tied the calf.

Shorty took the rope off the calf and noticed Red looking back toward the barn instead of looking at him and the calf. He picked up the loop end of his rope and flipped the rope at Red, hollering, "Get back!" The rope slapped Red on the neck, and with Shorty flipping the rope at him and hollering "Get back!" Red did just that. He whirled away from Shorty and headed back—to the barn! The rope was tied hard and fast to the saddle horn and Shorty had the other end of the rope. Red had the barn on his mind and he struck a long trot, holding his head off to one side so he didn't step on the bridle reins.

Shorty tried to get in front of Red to stop him, but Red wasn't about to stop then, ignoring Shorty hollering, "Whoa! You old S.O.B., Whoa!" He got to the gate that Shorty had so thoughtfully left open for him and went to the road. Remembering Shorty's command, "Get back", he headed back to headquarters.

I had been riding through some cattle in the Brush pasture, and when I got into headquarters, there stood Red at the barns. Shorty's rope hanging from the saddle horn, had been drug five or six miles and the part of the rope that had been dragging on the ground was pretty well worn out. The grass rope looked like an old gunnysack, frazzled and pretty limp.

Shorty was nowhere around, so I got in the old pickup and headed down to the Weaning pasture, to see if I could find him. Couldn't help but be a little worried about him. Lots of things could have happened and, of course, I thought of a bunch of bad things. Even though Red was pretty gentle, things could happen even on a gentle horse.

I got almost to the Weaning pasture, when I saw something along the edge of the road. As I got closer, I saw that it was Shorty, sitting on a rock beside the road. As I drove up to him he got up with a sheepish grin on his face. I was sure relieved to see he was all right.

"What happened?" I asked as he got in the pickup with me.

"Aw hell," he exclaimed, "that %$#$% Red! I roped a calf and he wasn't paying attention like he should've been, and I popped him with my rope and told him to get back. But hell, I didn't mean for him to get that far back! He left me afoot and there hasn't been a damned car come by all afternoon! Sure glad to see you!"

◊   ◊   ◊

Sometime back, Shorty had lost a couple of his front teeth in an argument at the Ranch Bar. This sure added a little character to his weather beaten face, which looked like a road map of New York City, lines going in all directions.

One morning he came into the saddle room looking a little puny.

"What's the matter with you, Shorty?" I asked as he came draggin in.

"I'm sure feeling bad," he answered as he flopped down on a couple of old saddle blankets. "Feel like a smooooth ran over me."

"Feel like what ran over you?" I asked.

"A smooooth! You know, that big machine they smoooth the road with!" he exclaimed. Shorty's use of English was quite descriptive!

One of his sons, Silo, had come to visit and stay a little while with Shorty and Mrs. Martinez. Shorty and Silo had gone into the old Ranch Bar and were pretty well lubricated as the were driving back out to cattle head-quarters late at night. A deer jumped out on the road in front of them and they ran over it in Shorty's old car. Not about to pass up the opportunity to get a little venison, they jumped out of the car and opened the trunk, picked up the deer off the road, put it in the trunk, and headed home.

"I told Silo we would take the deer home and put him in the bath tub and gut him there. That way we could wash all the blood away and carry the guts and hide off the next day and bury them!" Shorty explained to me the next day.

"I drove up to the front of the house, tossed Silo the keys to the trunk and told him I would go get the light on in the bathroom and tell the wife what was going on. I got the lights on and went back out to help Silo carry in the deer. I couldn't see Silo anywhere."

Shorty hollered, "Hey, Silo! Where did you go?"

"Back here!" Silo hollered from behind the car.

Shorty walked around to the back of the car. There was Silo! Flat on his back, lying in the road!

"What the hell you doing?" Shorty says. "Where is our deer?"

"That S.O.B. ran over me!" Silo said. "When I opened the trunk, he hit me in the belly with his head and took off!"

Shorty said, "I looked down the road and sure enough, there was those little poof, poof, poofs of dust going up off the road as our deer bounced away! So much for getting venison with our car!"

Shorty and Mrs. Martinez would go to Albuquerque every two or three months to visit their daughter there. Shorty would stash his bottle in the trunk of the car. Mrs. Martinez would sure not let him stop anywhere near a bar on the way. Shorty would tell Mrs. Martinez he thought he may have a low tire, so he would have to stop and check. He would get out, slip the trunk open, have a couple big slugs of hooch, walk around and kick the tires. He would have to check the tires several times on the way to Albuquerque. Mrs. Martinez could never figure out why Shorty would always be drunk by the time they got to their daughter's house!

◊   ◊   ◊

The ranch put in a new road up the mountain to Beaubien and on over to Clear Creek, opening up the back country to vehicles. Mrs. Martinez had never been to the back country of Philmont. Shorty decided to take her for a ride up to the high country and let her see how pretty the mountains were, now that this new road was opened. He had bought a used car that had the gear shift on the steering column. Shifting gears was still a challenge to Shorty. He loaded Mrs. Martinez up in his car and they headed for the mountains.

I never did figure what he was thinking about, taking his car up this road! I couldn't ever get him to drive our pickup anywhere! The road was pretty good up to Miners Park, but then it went along the bottom of the canyon and it was sure rough and rocky. The road turned back out of the canyon bottom and started a pretty steep climb up the side of the mountain. The further the road went, of course, the higher it got. Nearing the top of the mountain the road was pretty narrow. The road was carved out of the side of the mountain, nearly straight up on one side and just about straight down on the other! Rocky son of a gun! No place for a passenger car!

A logging outfit was hauling logs down this new road. Coming around a curve, you guessed it, Shorty met a logging truck with a full load of logs and a trailer-full behind it!

Panic time! Shorty slammed on the brakes, killing the motor in his car. The logging truck got stopped and there they sat. Neither driver quite believed what he saw there in the road.

Using a little cowboy logic, Shorty told Mrs. Martinez to jump out and put a rock behind the back tires of his car. He didn't have enough feet to step on the brakes, the clutch and the gas all at the same time, to get the car running again.

Mrs. Martinez was a real small little lady, maybe five foot tall, and around a hundred and ten pounds. She managed to get out and walk behind the car. Being on the passenger side, she hadn't been able to see the sheer drop off on the driver's side of the road. When she got to the back of the car, she looked over the edge and just fainted dead away!

Shorty couldn't see her in the rear vision mirror, and with a death stomp put on the brake pedal, he couldn't turn around enough to see her. He thought maybe she had fallen off the cliff!

The logging truck driver had seen her walk around to the back of Shorty's car, then disappear! He shut his truck down and jumped out, running down the road to see what had happened to the little lady.

Shorty was bouncing up and down in the seat of his car hollering, "Put me a rock! Put me a rock!"

The truck driver found Mrs. Martinez passed out, lying behind Shorty's car. He picked her up and carried her up to the car and placed her back in the seat. She came to and started giving Shorty hell for being in the predicament they were in!

The truck driver managed to scoot Shorty over enough so he could get in and he backed the car down to a wide enough place to pass them.

"Just stay here until I pass you. Then you can go on up," he said.

"To hell with this! We are going home!" Shorty said.

That's all of the high country Mrs. Martinez ever got to see. Shorty said she never did ask to go back!

◊   ◊   ◊

Bettye had a collection of miniature whiskey bottles that she had collected over the years. She had this collection on a corner shelf, and Shorty would always admire these tempting little bottles whenever he came up to the house. Bettye wouldn't let us open any of them. They were all sealed and full. We went on a trip one time and Shorty was going to look after things around the house while we were gone. It was some time after we had gotten back before Bettye noticed the seals had all been broken on the miniature bottles. They were all empty! Shorty had no idea what could have emptied all those bottles. Must have evaporated he figured. With his charming little smile at Bettye, she couldn't stay very mad at him very long.

Shorty sure loved a good poker game, and we would get a good one going out in the bunk house about once a week. We had several regulars who would come over and sure get some good games going. Shorty would win a pot and exclaim, "Blind hog found an acorn!" With his big hat on, dark sun glasses and a cigarette in the corner of his mouth, he was quite a picture. He loved to play Hi-lo, passing you out! If we were short a player, Shorty would ask Bettye to play, then get mad because she always beat him.

◊   ◊   ◊

Shorty got to drinking more and more, coming to work drunk, and I was having a hard time covering for him. I had asked, pleaded, threatened, and done about everything I could think of to get him to quit drinking so much, but he was pretty well hooked on the booze.

Bill Littrell had gone to town to get Shorty out of jail several times and threatened each time to fire him. Bill was kinda like me though, we sure didn't want to fire Shorty!

Shorty was camped up at Bonita and would come down over the weekend. Usually he would ride back up to Bonita early Monday morning. Once in a while he would ride up Sunday evening. I went down to saddle up one Monday morning and noticed Shorty's saddle was gone and figured he had rode up to Bonita. I didn't think any more about it since it wasn't uncommon for me not to see him Monday mornings.

Monday evening Bill called me on the phone.

"Did you see the six o'clock news on channel four?" Bill asked.

"No, I got in a little late and missed the news. Why?" I asked.

"Where in the hell's Shorty?" Bill answered.

"He's at Bonita," I replied. "I didn't see him this morning when I saddled up, but his saddle was gone. Guess he went up yesterday evening."

"Look at the ten o'clock news!" Bill answered, sounding a little out of sorts. "I think that old S.O.B.'s in Albuquerque. Damn sure looked like him, but I didn't get the name of the guy on the news!"

I stayed up past my bed time to watch the news and sure enough, there is Shorty and his son in-law George right there on the T.V.!

Seems the police had arrested these two jokers for being drunk and trying to direct traffic on horseback down on Central Avenue in downtown Albuquerque. The newsman gave Shorty and George's names and reported that Shorty worked for the Phimont Scout Ranch in Cimarron! Showed Shorty and George being handcuffed and put in the paddy wagon, and the police leading their horse off to load in a trailer.

Of course the news person had to go into a lot of detail about Philmont Scout Ranch being a part of the Boy Scouts of America, pointing out again that one of these self-appointed traffic directors was an employee of the B.S.A.!

My telephone rang as soon as that story ended.

"Did you see that!" Bill yelled into the phone. "I thought you said he was in Bonita!"

"Hell, I thought he was!" I replied, trying to hold back my laughter!

"How the hell did he get to Albuquerque? Did you give him some time off? What the hell's he doing down there?" Bill demanded. He was just plumb full of questions!

I didn't know nothing from nothing and that didn't help calm the boss's nerves that night! I could hardly keep from busting out laughing, and Bill wasn't seeing a damn thing funny about this little deal.

This really wasn't the kind of publicity for Philmont that Bill was looking for! The main scout executive in Albuquerque had seen the news and called Bill, wanting to know just how he explained his employee's behavior. He wasn't too happy about the publicity the news people were giving the Boy Scouts of America!

The police took Shorty and George to jail, letting them make their one phone call. George called his wife, Juanita, to come down and bail them out. Juanita showed up at the police station, inquiring about her father, husband and her daughter's horse. The police told her how much the bail was to get Shorty and George out of jail.

"How much for the horse?" she asked.

They told her she could take the horse home but would have to pay the bail on Shorty and George.

"I'll take the horse, you can keep those two guys in jail!" she said.

She loaded her horse and went home leaving George and Shorty to spend the night in jail!

The next morning, Juanita went down and paid the fine, and they let Shorty and George out. Having spent the night in jail, they were a little put out with Juanita. She threatened to run them both off so they loaded up and came back to Cimarron.

Bill was one mad boss when Shorty finally got back to the ranch. He told us how he had hidden his saddle and turned his saddle horse out in another pasture where we weren't likely to see him. He had been drinking with an old buddy and had caught a ride to Albuquerque with him Sunday night.

Shorty had been thrown in jail many times in Cimarron, and Bill had bailed him out but this time Bill was catching a lot of flak from the higher ups in the B.S.A. and had no choice but to fire Shorty. We all really felt bad for Shorty, but he was ready to move on.

He lived out his remaining years in Albuquerque and came by to see me once while I was in Taos. I sure had a lot of good times with Shorty.

Shorty Martinez, Bob Maldonado, Bob Knox on horse, Bill Littrell, Li'l Bob, Unknown, branding on Philmont, 1959

Li'l Bob, Shorty Martinez, branding

Shorty Martinez dragging calf to flankers Johnny Casias and Manuel Cordova, Philmont branding

Philmont cowboys Johnny Casias, Shorty Martinez,
Manuel Cordova

Li'l Bob—this gray horse sure liked to run away with Li'l Bob!

Shorty Martinez and The Tooth of Time, Philmont Scout Ranch. A couple Philmont Landmarks

Bob Knox and Bill Littrell at Cattle Headquarters, Philmont Scout Ranch

Bob Knox and Shorty Martinez, here is a pair to draw to!

Shorty Martinez and it is Party Time!

34

Sonny

Sonny was the best Shetland I ever came across. He was a black and white paint, with a pretty little head, nice conformation and a good disposition to go with it. Sonny belonged to George Russell, Shorty's son in law. George had bought Sonny for his daughter, who was several years older than Li'l Bob and Myrna. George and his family came to visit Shorty over the Fourth of July weekend, bringing Sonny with them. George's daughter had outgrown Sonny, and George had traded for another horse for her.

George told Li'l Bob and Myrna to go ahead and ride Sonny while he was there. He was just their size. They could saddle him, get on and off without any help; just what they needed at that time. I didn't have anything in my string gentle enough for them to ride without me leading them, so they sure liked having something more their size to ride.

When George saw how my kids took to Sonny, he said he would just leave Sonny at the ranch for them to ride a while. George left Sonny with us around three years, and Li'l Bob and Myrna sure enjoyed him and learned a lot from him.

Sonny was gifted with a fast running walk. He could keep right up with a big horse without trotting a little kid to pieces. He was always willing to go wherever they wanted, not a spoiled hair on him. He had a lot of cow savvy and would sure pay attention to what was going on. He really had a handle on him. I had never seen a Shetland broke this well.

Soon after we got Sonny, Li'l Bob and Myrna had him up at the house, saddled up and were taking turns riding around. Guess Li'l Bob was showing off a little to Myrna. Anyway, he got Sonny out on the road that went up a couple hundred yards to the mailbox. Li'l Bob slapped Sonny across the rear with his bridle reins and Sonny took off up the road as fast as he could run. They slid to a stop at the cattle guard at the end of the road, whirled and headed back toward the house as fast as Sonny could run. I managed to get out on the road and flag them down as they came flying down. They slid to a stop. I was a little unhappy with this little deal!

"This little horse can do something besides run up and down this road!" I said.

"He can? Wow, what else can he do?!!" an over eager Li'l Bob asked.

I had to explain he wasn't in the movies and he didn't need to ride everywhere like he was going to a fire!

I would take Li'l Bob with me when I wasn't going too far, and he and Sonny were doing real well. We had been prowling some cattle on top of Uracca Mesa. We had followed the old jeep road to the top of the mesa and were ready to head in for the day. I was sure pleased with the way Li'l Bob and Sonny were getting along. Li'l Bob was about five or six that year.

I decided to save a little time and several miles by taking an old trail that cut down through the rim rock, instead of following the road off the top of the mesa. It was sure steep going this way and, as I picked my way down through the timber, rocks and brush, I was making switch backs instead of riding straight down.

"Daddy! Sonny! DADDY!" the frantic hollering came from back up the mountain side.

"What's the matter?" I hollered as I pulled up and looked back over my shoulder.

I couldn't see Sonny and Li'l Bob. They had dropped back a little way, but I could sure hear Li'l Bob!

"Daddy! Damn it, Sonny, keep your head up! DADDY! DADDY!" the hollering sounded pretty urgent.

I turned my horse and hurried up through the brush and timber to see what was happening. Li'l Bob's hollering was getting pretty desperate. I rode up through the timber a short way and there they were.

Sonny was setting back on his haunches, front legs wide apart, braced to keep from falling on down the steep mountain side. Li'l Bob's saddle had slipped up over Sonny's withers and was well up on his neck. Sonny was holding his head up as high as he could to keep the saddle from slipping off over his head! Li'l Bob was rocking back and forth, trying to keep his balance perched out there on Sonny's neck. Sonny's little ears were about three inches in front of Li'l Bob's saddle horn!

"What's all the hollering about?" I laughed as I rode up to them.

"Daddy, would you just look where Sonny has got his saddle!" Li'l Bob demanded, as I got off to help them out.

Well, they both learned a little about switch-backing that day! They had decided to cut across and go straight down, but it hadn't worked too good for them!

Another time, Li'l Bob and Sonny were helping me gather some year-ling and two year old registered bulls out of the Vega below headquarters. These young bulls were feeling good. They didn't know what to think of this little horse and rider out there with them and were wanting to play, not giving Sonny any respect at all! They weren't trying to fight him, just run-ning around him to see if he would chase them. Li'l Bob and Sonny were sure getting after them, trying to get them to go.

There was a great big willow tree growing there in the Vega, and the bulls sure liked to hang around this big tree. There was a big limb growing out from the tree horizontally, about four feet above the ground. The bulls could go under the limb, which just barely cleared their backs. The limb was too low for a horse to go under, so the bulls were having a good time dodging Sonny, by going back under the limb. Li'l Bob and Sonny would have to go out around the limb, circle the tree and start them out again. Back under the the limb the bulls would go, stand there and watch Li'l Bob and Sonny have to go around.

They had made three or four passes at these bulls when Sonny had gotten about all of this nonsense he could stand. Next time around, Sonny ducked his head and went right under the limb after the bulls. Sonny just barely cleared the limb but Li'l Bob's saddle didn't! The limb hit the front of the saddle, Li'l Bob dropped his reins and grabbed at the limb with both hands before it could drag him off.

Sonny pushed forward about two steps, then the limb pushed him back about two steps! Back and forth they went. Li'l Bob had both hands on that tree limb, trying to keep it from coming over his saddle horn and wiping him out.

"Daddy! Sonny! Daddy!" Li'l Bob yelled as Sonny kept trying to go, and the tree limb kept pushing him back.

The bulls were all standing there watching to see if they were going to have to leave their tree or not. Finally, Sonny backed up enough to get out from under the tree limb. Li'l Bob jumped off and looked around to see where I was.

"What's the matter! Can't you get those bulls out from under that tree?" I kidded him.

Li'l Bob saw he wasn't in much danger then and seeing the bulls standing there watching him really made him mad. All the grief they had caused him fueled his anger and he grabbed up a handful of cow chips and small sticks and took after the bulls, yelling and throwing chips and sticks!

The bulls were sure surprised at this sudden turn of events. This little chip-and-stick throwing, yelling booger really spooked them out from the safety of their tree. They ran out into the open Vega and Li'l Bob got back on Sonny and took after them. The bulls didn't get a chance to get back to the tree, and we went ahead and got them out of the Vega.

On a particularly hot day, Li'l Bob and Sonny were helping Shorty and me gather a bunch of cows and calves out of the Chicosa pasture. As we approached a big dirt tank full of water, the cattle crowded around the edge trying to get a drink as we tried to keep them moving on. We were all hot and dry but had a ways to go yet and didn't want the cattle filling up on water.

Sonny was sure thirsty and walked out into the water to get a drink. I rode around one side of the lake, Shorty on the other side, as we pushed the cattle on. Li'l Bob was sitting there on Sonny looking for frogs in the water, his bridle reins hanging down in the water. Sonny filled up on water and looked up and saw Shorty and me on the other side of the lake. Without hesitating, Sonny started straight across the lake to where we were. By the time Li'l Bob got his bridle reins gathered up he found himself out in the middle of the lake! The water got deeper and Sonny had to start swimming. Li'l Bob forgot about hunting frogs and sure got concerned about where he and Sonny suddenly found themselves. Li'l Bob had never been in any deep water and his eyes were about as big around as his hat as he started yelling.

"Daddy! Sonny! Daddy! Daddy!" he yelled, as the water filled his boots and came up on Sonny's sides.

Shorty and I sat there on the other side and had to laugh as we watched Sonny swim across the lake with his yelling rider getting pretty wet! We thought this was pretty funny, but Li'l Bob sure didn't think it was a bit funny. After that, he sure kept a tight rein on Sonny whenever they went up to a lake, giving him just enough slack to get a drink!

George Russell came back the following Fourth of July for the rodeo in Cimarron. He saw how well Li'l Bob was riding Sonny so he asked Li'l Bob if he would like to ride Sonny in the Shetland pony race at the rodeo. This was right up Li'l Bob's alley. He was always ready for a good race!

We took Sonny in to the rodeo. Kids and horses everywhere! All the kids in and around Cimarron managed to come up with a horse for the big rodeo.

There were five or six kids with Shetland ponies. Among them was Eddie, whose folks ranched out in the Farley country. They raised some good horses and top quality Hereford cattle. Eddie was riding a small bay horse. This little bay was just a bit taller than the other Shetlands, but he was allowed to enter in the Shetland pony race. Eddie claimed this small bay was a Shetland. Another story on the small bay was that his mother was a registered Quarter mare, sire was a pretty good horse, too. His mother died when he was born, he was orphaned and just never did grow. Anyway—

The Shetland pony race was a big event! They were running for some big bucks! First place paid a whopping $5.00, second paid $3.00, and third paid $2.00! Entry fees were $2.00. George, Shorty and I managed to get enough between the three of us to pay the entry fees. Of course, helping with the entry fees entitled the three of us to give a lot of coaching and direction to Li'l Bob!

The six entrants lined up across the race track! The starter's flag was up! A hush fell over the grandstand as the crowd quieted and watched the start of this horse race. You would have thought you were at the Kentucky Derby! The nervous Shetlands and their riders were crowding the starting line! All eyes were on the starting flag.

BANG! The starter's pistol fired, the flag dropped and the race was on! Sonny and Li'l Bob broke on top. The little bay was a neck behind as they left the rest of the field in the dust. The little bay pulled up even and then passed Sonny, about half a length. Li'l Bob whapped Sonny down the hind leg with his bonafide jockey bat, and they pulled up neck and neck with Eddie and the little bay.

Down the track they came, running wide open and neck and neck! The roar from the crowd was deafening. The finish line was right in front of the grand stand. There wasn't any paramutuel betting at this race track but there must have been an awful lot of money bet on this race, as evidenced by the crowd's enthusiasm.

As Sonny and the little bay crossed the finish line, the little bay beat Sonny by a neck. Li'l Bob had sure done a good job riding Sonny in spite of all the last minute instructions he had received from George, Shorty and me! We all celebrated the second place finish and started making plans as to how we would beat Eddie and the little bay next year!

George came back the following year for the Fourth of July rodeo. We were all determined to win the big Shetland pony race. Li'l Bob and Sonny had a year of experience behind them and they were ready for this rematch with the little bay.

The crowd in the grand stand was sure excited, with the talk going around about this rematch between Sonny and the little bay. They were just about even on the betting side. The purse for the winners remained the same as last year.

All eyes were on the race track as the starters pistol cracked and echoed across the arena. The Shetlands broke from the starting line. A roar went up from the grand stand as the Shetlands and their riders thundered down the race track.

The little bay got the jump on Sonny and had about a length on him as they crossed the halfway marker. Sonny and Li'l Bob kept closing the gap on the little bay and Eddie. As they crossed the finish line the little bay beat them by barely a nose. Boy, it was about as close as it could be.

Li'l Bob and Sonny ran against this little bay and Eddie again the next year, getting beat by a nose. Finally Li'l Bob and Eddie got too big for the Shetlands. Sonny just never did beat the little bay, but it sure wasn't because he didn't try!

George came and got Sonny and it was almost like saying goodbye to one of the family when he left. Li'l Bob and Myrna had pretty well out grown Sonny, both riding bigger horses by then. Sonny had sure been good for them and they really learned a lot from him. He was one in a million!

Li'l Bob had got bitten by the same cowboy bug that had bitten me when I was a kid, I guess. He sure wanted to go with me when I left the house and I took him about everywhere I could. We sure went through a lot of horses trying to find one that he could ride and get along with as well as he had with Sonny.

Myrna and Li'l Bob on Sonny 1960

Li'l Bob on Sonny, ready for big horse race, Fourth of July rodeo, Cimarron

Myrna on Sonny at Philmont

Myrna on Sonny, Li'l Bob on Slick, ready to ride

Li'l Bob and Myrna feeding pet fawn at Philmont 1957

Shorty Martinez, Bob and Li'l Bob in Philmont Cattle Department's first four-wheel drive vehicle. Not very fancy but we sure had a lot of fun in it! Shorty named it the "Hoodlum"

Bettye, Myrna and Li'l Bob, four wheeling at Fish Camp on Philmont

Bettye, Myrna and Li'l Bob having fun in the "Hoodlum"

35

Cowboy Antics

Li'l Bob was around five or six, and we had a little bunch of cows and calves penned at cattle headquarters, branding and working the calves. I was roping and dragging calves to the flankers. Bill Littrell, Shorty and three or four farm hands were working the calves at the branding fire.

Li'l Bob wasn't big enough to help, so I had told him to stay on the boardwalk that went along the side of the working chute in the corral where we were branding. He could see all the action from there and not get in the way.

I had an extra rope coiled and laying on the boardwalk where Li'l Bob was watching the branding. He was sure wanting to rope a calf but I had told him to cool it. The boss was there and he had to just stay on the walk, out of the way.

I had a calf heeled and was riding toward the flankers, dragging the calf, when I heard a calf beller behind me. All the calves had crowded up next to the walk where Li'l Bob was standing. Suddenly they all started running to the other side of the corral. Right in the middle of the bunch of calves was a big bull calf with a rope around his neck! On the other end of the rope, dragging along in the dirt and rocks was, guess who?

When the calves all crowded around the boardwalk Li'l Bob was standing on, he couldn't resist the temptation and had dropped a loop over this big bull calf's neck! The calf bellered and took off running. Li'l Bob hung on for dear life and proceeded to plow up the corral as the calf drug him by the flankers!

The rope finally burned through his hands and he slid to a stop, coughing and sputtering, spitting dirt out of his mouth. The ground crew started to laugh, then got real quiet as they looked at Li'l Bob, then at me. I stepped off my horse and went over to this new roper and got him set up and the dirt wiped off his face.

I suddenly had a flash back of a kid roping an old wild, one-eyed mare and getting drug and his hands rope burned. Guess some things are inherited? Li'l Bob was all right, skinned up a little and had some pretty good rope burns. When I saw that he wasn't hurt much and I laughed, the ground crew all rushed around Li'l Bob, laughing and telling him what a nice catch he had made and asking him to do it again so they could watch him dive off the boardwalk! He was one of the crew then and everything was all right.

◊　　◊　　◊

While Shorty was working with me, we had always gotten an old hand-me- down pickup for the cattle department to drive. By the time Shorty and I got them, they were well-used by the US Army from Camp Carson at Colorado Springs. Of course these Army pickups, donated to the Boy Scouts, were always breaking down, and the worn out tires, kept us busy changing flats. Littrell and I had a couple run ins over the maintainance costs of keeping our old pickup running. I told him to trade the damned old pickup off for a good team and wagon, as we could sure get along without the piles of junk he was giving us to drive!

You can imagine Shorty's and my surprise when Littrell called us down to the office one morning and handed us the keys to a brand new Ford 4x4 pickup! New set of stock racks! Boy, we were in tall cotton! We just couldn't believe our good fortune. This went along with about a forty-five minute lecture on taking care of our new pickup. Proper maintenance, speed, tire rotation, etc., etc. We got the whole manual read to us. Brush and tree limb scratches were forbidden, absolutely no dents. Wash jobs were mandatory. We sat through the long lecture, anxious to try out our new wheels.

We left the office, grinning like two kids with a new toy and went up to cattle headquarters and loaded a few sacks of cake to go feed the bulls. I drove out to the bull pasture, going real slow, enjoying the strange new smell of our new pickup. Neither one of us had smelled anything like this in our old junkers!

I stopped and started honking the nice sounding new horn, calling the bulls into feed. Shorty and I were busy checking out all the new gadgets, while the bulls drifted in to the feed ground. Most of the bulls had gathered around, checking out the new 4x4. We were waiting for a couple slow stragglers we could see coming in. For whatever reason, a couple older bulls got to arguing, banging heads and making a big fuss. Suddenly one of the bulls made a hard charge at the other bull, knocking him backward, his rear end slamming into the door on Shorty's side! We both damn near had heart attacks right then and there! Caved in that door big time! Oh crap! What do we do now? Too big a dent to hide from Littrell!

"Bet he fires us both!" Shorty said.

I was inclined to agree. We hadn't had our new pickup an hour yet and we had done got her smashed in!

"Reckon we can straighten the door?" Shorty volunteered.

"How the hell we going to fix that!" I replied, looking at the caved in door.

Carrying my hat in my hands, I went into Littrell's office and laid it out to him. He came as close to having a coronary as Shorty and I had when the bull smashed us! Guess I better not try to write what all the boss had to say.

Our new pickup got sent back to the dealer to get a new door put on it. The motor pool gave us a little half-ton, automatic transmission, pickup to feed with while ours was getting the new door. Two-wheel drive, but it was better than a wheelbarrow!

The next day, I loaded a few sacks of cake in this little pickup and went out to feed. Shorty wasn't with me, having gone horseback.

I noticed this little pickup sure seemed to run faster than the old junker I was used to. No way to gear it down, as the automatic transmission had only two speeds, fast and faster!

I drove out in the big field across from the Villa Philmonte, honking the strange sounding horn and giving my best rendition of a cattle call. The cows came running up. I don't know if it was from being hungry or coming to see what all the racket was. I opened three or four sacks of cake, standing them up against the side of the pickup bed, ready to pour out to the cows. I looked the course ahead of me over pretty close. No big rocks, no brush or trees. An irrigation ditch went along the outside edge of the field, and just past the ditch was the Cimarroncito Creek. The ditch was quite a ways from where I was parked. It looked like I had plenty of room to feed.

It was pretty cold that morning, and I had the windows rolled up and the heater on. I got a good count on the cows, had them all, so I eased the pickup into the lowest gear it had, and jumped out, sitting on the tailgate pouring out cake as we took off. No problem scattering the cake as fast as we were going! I emptied one sack and grabbed another as I looked around the side of the pickup to see where we were headed. That ditch was sure coming on pretty fast! I increased the amount of cake getting poured out, grabbed the third sack, and looked again! To hell with this! The ditch was getting pretty close, and I didn't have time to pour anymore cake.

I jumped off the tail gate, nearly doing a somersault as I hit the ground. Man we were trucking, and the ditch was suddenly right there! I made a frantic run to the door as the pickup bounced into and out of the ditch. I grabbed the door handle. Yea, you guessed it! The damned door was locked. I nearly jerked the door off the pickup trying to get in. Locked! Window rolled up.

As the pickup bounced on by me, I rushed around to the other side. As I ran to catch the pickup before it went off the bank into the creek, I thought to myself; if this door is locked too, I'll just walk home, tell Bettye to pack all our stuff and we will get the kids and slip off into the night and never tell anyone where we went!

I ran as fast as I could, caught up with the runaway pickup. The door wasn't locked! I did a belly-flop across the seat, turned the key off and slammed the brake pedal down with my hand. The pickup jerked to a stop. I probably had ten or fifteen feet to go before going over the bank.

I guess I had pushed the door lock knob down with my elbow when I jumped out to start feeding. Maybe a wheelbarrow was what I needed!

◊   ◊   ◊

The next summer, we had moved the cattle to the high country, and had about eight or ten pairs that had been missed on the drive. The ranch had an old bobtail truck the farm crew used to haul hay on and they had a set of stock racks for it. We borrowed it to haul this little handful of cows to Bonita. Their calves were pretty small, and we didn't figure they would make the long drive up over the mountain.

Manuel Cordova was working with me, and he, Li'l Bob and I loaded the cows in the bobtail and the little calves in my pickup and headed out for the mountain. Li'l Bob sure wanted to ride in the truck with Manuel.

We were trucking right along the winding road, and as we drove up to Crater Lake the road got pretty steep. Manuel had shifted down to second gear. Right at Crater Lake, the road went from steep to really steep, for about fifty yards. Manuel figured he could pull it in second gear.

As he started up this real steep part of the road, Manuel saw that he had to get into a lower gear. Almost stalling out, Manuel stomped down on the clutch, jamming the gears into first with his foot pushing the gas pedal to the floor! Popping the clutch, the little bobtail couldn't handle that sudden power surge, and just reared up and sat down on its hind end!

The front wheels were about four feet off the ground, the back end of the bobtail stuck in the dirt in the road, with the back wheels not quite touching the ground! There they sat, weaving back and forth as Manuel kept his foot jammed down on the gas peddle, shifting gears as fast as he could, with the rear wheels spinning in the air as fast as they would go.

I looked out my rear vision mirror and all I could see was the under carriage of the bobtail! I jumped out and ran back to the not very steady truck, as it weaved back and forth, threatening to tip over any second. Li'l Bob was peering out the side window at the ground far below. His eyes were about as big as his hat as he pondered whether or not to try and jump out. I finally got Manuel to get his foot off the gas pedal, and the truck engine quit screaming.

"Just sit still and don't rock the boat!" I hollered up at Li'l Bob.

"Don't try to jump!"

I ran to the back of the truck, all the cows were in a big pile up against the tailgate. No way to get it open. I ran back to my pickup and backed it down the road to the weaving truck. I had a long logging chain and hooked one end of it to the axle on the truck and the other end on to my trailer hitch on the back bumper of the pickup. Easing forward, I managed to pull the old bobtail off its hind end and got the front wheels on the ground again. As soon as the truck quit bouncing, Li'l Bob jumped out and told Manuel he thought he would just ride with his Dad!

◊　　◊　　◊

Manuel and I were riding in one evening from prowling the Brush pasture. It was pretty chilly and we both had our coats on as we jumped a flock of wild turkeys. The young turkeys in the flock were about half-grown.

"Wish we had a gun! I bet those young turkeys would be good eating," Manuel said as we watched the turkeys scurrying off ahead of us.

"I'll show you how to get one without a gun," I answered.

"Let's charge them and make them fly. Pick one out when they fly and stay after him. They won't fly too far. When your turkey lands, take after him and run him down! They won't fly a second time, and we can rope one!"

Manuel looked at me like I had been smoking something strange. As I took my rope down and took after the turkeys, he jerked his rope down and followed suit.

The turkeys flew right quick as we took after them. I had one picked out and followed him as he flew away. We were out on the flats and keeping the turkey in sight was no problem. The turkey Manuel picked out flew back north across the creek and I lost sight of him as I watched my supper flying south.

Sure enough, the turkey landed and took off running as I closed in on him. I swung my rope and hit the turkey in the neck, knocking him down. I jumped off my horse and I suddenly had supper!

I gathered up my turkey and rode back toward where I had last seen Manuel, hollering at him to see if I could locate him. I heard him answer and pretty quick he came riding across the creek with a grin a mile wide, carrying his turkey. We were pretty proud of ourselves as we laughed and rode on toward home with our suppers! Manuel thought I was a poco smart hombre!

One little problem! We had to ride by camping headquarters and then down the main road a mile to get home! Our turkeys were pretty good sized and a little hard to hide. Since it wasn't turkey hunting season we really didn't want to advertise our conquests! Lots of people around camping headquarters and who knew who we would meet on the main road!

It was getting pretty cold, but we didn't have much choice. Using a little cowboy logic, we got off our horses, took off our coats and wrapped our turkeys in them. We tied our suppers behind our saddles, and bravely rode toward Camping Headquarters. Boy, it was getting colder!

We waved at some of the staff as we rode by, not stopping to visit! We weren't a bit conspicuous, of course, colder than hell, our coats tied behind our saddles with these big bundles wrapped up in them! We hit a long trot, trying to hold our suppers from bouncing around behind our saddles and made it home. No one ever said anything about our riding by so fast and not wearing coats when it was so cold!

Those young turkeys were sure good eating!

36

Corona

In June of 1963, Bill Littrell called me into the office at Philmont and told me about a pretty good sounding job open down around Corona, N.M. He knew the people who had this ranch and they were looking for a manager. Sounded like it might be a pretty good opportunity for a guy to do a little better than just cowboy wages.

Bettye and I went to Albuquerque to meet with the owner of this ranch, J.W. Bates. He was a wealthy oil man from Tulsa, who had around thirty-five thousand acres of Forest Service land leased near Corona. We visited with Mr. Bates and agreed we would like to go down and look his ranch over. It was about an hour and a half drive from Albuquerque.

On the way down to the ranch, Mr. Bates explained he had several small pieces of deeded land, and a long-term lease on the Forest Service land, which made up the major part of the ranch. He had around four hundred mother cows, several top notch saddle horses, a lovely home, etc, etc. He painted a really pretty picture. The wages weren't very good but the promise of a percentage of the ranch profit made it sound good. We were pretty well sold on the deal before we got to the ranch.

It was a nice little ranch, laying at the base of the Gallinas Mountain, some fifteen miles southwest of Corona. Pinon and cedar trees were sure thick, with a good cover of grass. The rolling country looked like it was pretty good cow country.

"I haven't told the man working here that I was going to replace him," Mr. Bates explained, "so we can't go in and see the house you will live in."

Bettye wasn't very happy about that situation, but Mr. Bates assured her she would just love the comfortable little home. Well, it looked okay from the outside as we walked by it going down to the corrals. Mr. Bates's house was about a hundred yards up above the ranchhand's house and the corrals.

We agreed to take the job, packed up and headed south to the Corona country. Bettye's new home wasn't quite like Mr. Bates had described. The back bedroom wall on the west side had pulled away from the floor so you could just sweep the floor right outside without going to all the trouble of sweeping into a dust pan! Pretty handy. A little breezy, though, when the wind blew. Took two, two by four blocks under one side of the kitchen table to keep our coffee from spilling out of our cups. Anything that was spilled or dropped on the floor rolled to the outside wall, making it pretty handy to clean up! Bettye cried for a week or so, then just gritted her teeth and made us a home. She had a lot of grit and a lot of love for us!

Mr. Bates sure had an eye for good horses and the money to buy them with, so we were well mounted. Several of his horses had come from the Vermejo Park Ranch near Cimarron. They were well-bred and good cow horses. We had enough good horses to mount the whole family on, which was sure a good deal, because they were the only help I had! Working this ranch was a good time for our family. It sure drew us close together as we all pitched in and made a pretty darn good team.

◊   ◊   ◊

Most of the cows on this outfit were Hereford with some Brahma crossbred cows. They were a little wild, but mostly just spoiled and smart. They weren't used to being worked horseback, as the guy before me had used a pickup and cake to call the cattle into the corrals anytime they had to be penned, like at branding time and shipping time. If they didn't come in the corrals, they just didn't get branded or shipped! He just hollered to "Let'er go!" They had a pretty good sized bunch of "Let'er go", cows, bulls, yearlings and two and three year olds that had never seen the inside of the corrals! Hell of a deal!

Mr. Bates told me to start gathering these mavericks as he soon saw we weren't pickup cowboys. Just one little hitch, he didn't want his cowboys to carry a rope on their saddle!

Li'l Bob and I had to laugh at this deal. Well, since Mr. Bates was the boss and we had just started working for him, I figured all we could do was to try it his way. Once, anyway.

Mr. Bates saddled up and went with us as we headed out to gather some of these old spoiled cows. The pinons and cedars were thicker than any place we had ever seen, with a generous amount of cholla and other varieties of cactus, and oak brush throwed in for good measure. We jumped a little band of cows and bulls and started riding toward them. As soon as they saw us headed toward them they threw their tails up and headed into the trees at a dead run.

We pulled our hats down and built to them, tree limbs and brush cracking and popping as we tried to keep them in sight. About a half mile of this and I came into a little clearing. I pulled up, letting my horse catch his wind, and took inventory on my extremities.

My shirt pocket was hanging by one corner and the left sleeve of my shirt was torn off and hanging by the cuff. I felt something running down the side of my face, but didn't think I had broke that big a sweat. Wiping my face, my hand was pretty bloody. My chap leg was nailed pretty solid to my leg with a big chunk of cactus.

I had gotten off my horse, trying to get the cactus out of his shoulder and off my leg, when Li'l Bob came busting out of the trees. The front of his shirt was ripped away, one sleeve was torn off, and with his hat pulled down over his ears he looked like he was a tornado survivor! Wiping the blood off his face he grinned at me and wanted to know which way the cows had gone!! Hell, I had no idea!

We rode back the way we had come, laughing at each other and looking for Mr. Bates. We met him easing along through the trees and brush. I guess our adrenalin was still pumping pretty fast and we, in no uncertain terms, informed our boss we damn sure weren't going to try this again without a rope because we didn't much like getting beat up like this and having nothing to show for it!

He relented and we started packing our ropes again. The next time we jumped these wild ones we got a couple roped and tied to a tree. We left them tied to soak awhile, then went back and led them out to where we could get to them with a pickup and trailer. Over the course of time we got the mavericks caught and hauled off to the sale ring.

These old cows were sure pretty smart. If you got to crowding them a little, they would duck off into a thicket and just lay down and try and hide! We had some pretty wild runs. Mr. Bates was sure pleased every time we hauled some off to the sale. He never said anymore about carrying a rope.

The kids were in school and Bettye was helping me pick up a few pairs we were short, getting ready to ship. We jumped six cows and calves and after a short horse race I got around them and had them held up in a little opening. The cows seemed to settle down pretty quick, and I saw we were short one calf. I told Bettye to stay there and hold those cows in this little opening while I throwed a little circle back where we had been to see if I could pick up the calf we were short. I heard a calf bawl back in the trees and brush, so I headed that way to bring him in to his mama.

I found the calf and got around him and headed him toward the opening where Bettye was holding the cows. I followed the calf out into the opening and there sat Bettye, tears of frustration running down her cheeks. Not a cow in sight. In my gentle, quiet way, I hollered, "WHERE THE HELL'S THE COWS!!"

I almost lost my helper right then and there! I calmed down and assured her it was okay, as she tried to explain how the cows all took off at one time in six different directions!! She also mentioned something about if I hollered at her again I could just get somebody else to help me get those *%$#@* cows next time!

We had penned a bunch of cows and I was preg testing them as Bettye, Myrna and Li'l Bob were running them through the chute. We had missed a cow on the gather and she came walking out in the open a little way from the corrals. I told Li'l Bob to go out and bring her in, as we needed to check her with the others. That day I was riding a good bay horse we called "Fiddler". Li'l Bob was always asking me if he could ride Fiddler, but I hadn't let him.

"Can I ride Fiddler?" Li'l Bob asked, as he headed over to where our horses were standing.

"Yea, I guess so," I answered, busy checking a cow in the chute.

My stirrups were about a hole too long for Li'l Bob, but he was in a hurry and didn't take them up, just climbed up on Fiddler and headed out to get around the cow. Fiddler would darn sure get down in the dirt with an old cow. They didn't get by him. You sure had to sit up and ride him. He was quick as a cat and sure liked getting down with a cow.

The cow saw Li'l Bob riding out toward her and headed back to the safety of the trees. Li'l Bob and Fiddler quickly headed her off and started her toward the open gate coming into the corral. The cow saw this wasn't much to her liking and made a break for the trees. They got her turned again and were bringing her along the woven wire trap fence. As the cow got close to the open gate she threw a kink in her tail, ducked back and made a last desperate run for freedom. She was running as fast as she could, just the way Fiddler liked them! He built to the cow in a dead run, ears penned back and fire in his eye as he cut her off. The cow plowed into the fence and came up running the opposite direction, with Fiddler biting her on the butt and really enjoying this. The cow ran in through the open gate into the corral. Fiddler stopped and looked around, kinda puzzled. No Li'l Bob. There he was, back where Fiddler had made his last quick turn, on his hands and knees crawling around in a circle.

I jerked my plastic glove off and climbed over the fence and shut the gate on the cow. I ran down to where Li'l Bob was still crawling around in a circle on his hands and knees.

"You all right?" I asked him, as I knelt beside him.

"I think so Dad, but I lost my memory!" he answered. "What happened?"

"Well I don't think you're going to find it crawling around here on your hands and knees. I don't think it was your memory you lost!" I laughed as I helped him up and he hobbled back to the corral. He wasn't so anxious to ride Fiddler again for awhile!

Myrna hadn't got to ride with me at Philmont near as much as Li'l Bob had and she was really liking the cow punching she was getting to do with us at Corona. She was sure making a good hand. She had a big gray horse we called Blue to ride. He was pretty gentle and a good cow horse.

We were penning a bunch of cows at the shipping corrals one day and Myrna was riding Blue. A big calf broke back on Myrna's side and Blue wheeled and took to the calf. They were moving out pretty fast when Blue got the calf turned. Blue rolled back with the calf, pretty low and fast, and Myrna just kept going! She sailed out over the rocks and cactus, making a perfect one point landing right on her head!

I rode up to her and jumped off, rushing up to her as she was trying to sit up.

"Are you all right?" I asked. Dumb question at a time like this!

"I think so, Daddy," she said trying to hold the tears back.

She seemed to be all right, nothing broken, but her pride was injured. Bettye and Li'l Bob came riding up asking her if she was okay.

"You know what you did wrong?" old wise, comforting Dad asked. "What Daddy?" she asked looking up at me as the tears slipped out of the corners of her eyes.

"Well, when you are way up in the air like that and you start down, flap your arms real fast like a bird and you won't hit so hard!" I consoled.

She jumped up and kicked me in the shin. And what she said then, a little girl like that hadn't ought to say! Anyway, so much for my consoling abilities.

Another day, Myrna was riding another horse and one of the Bates kids was riding Blue. As Myrna rode up behind Blue, he kicked at her horse and caught Myrna right on the knee, breaking her knee cap. She hobbled around in a full leg cast for quite a while after that. From then on, she didn't like old Blue much and I didn't blame her!

Li'l Bob on Cowboy at Corona, New Mexico, 1964

Li'l Bob on Uncle Bob's horse, Zorro, Philmont 1962 with cow dog Bob

37

Roping Bulls and Sheep

While at the Gallinas Ranch near Corona, we became acquainted with a young couple, John and Jane Books, who were on a ranch about eight miles south of us. They had a couple of kids who were a little younger than Myrna and Li'l Bob. We became good friends with them, and John and I traded work. He was running a bunch of registered black Angus cows and had a pretty good-sized herd of sheep until the coyotes cleaned out his sheep herd!

Li'l Bob and I had come into the house to get a little bite of lunch one day, when John Books came roaring up in his big four wheel drive pickup. He always drove like he was headed to a big fire somewhere. He slid to a stop and came rushing up to the house. He appeared a little upset, and I wondered what good news he was bringing.

John was pretty excited as he started telling us his latest tale.

Seems his neighbor, an older Spanish fellow, had a big cross bred bull that had gotten in with some of John's registered Angus heifers. John had saddled his horse and rode down to drive the bull out and put him back on the neighbor's place. But the bull kinda liked it there with the heifers and had run John and his horse out of the pasture. The bull was sure on the fight, and John had decided to rope him, but the bull had nearly knocked John's horse down and John had to cut his rope at the saddle horn to get away from the bull. The bull had gone back to the heifers, dragging Johns rope. John was needing some help as he sure didn't want this long, gangling bull breeding his good registered heifers.

I had a big sorrel horse called Red saddled, and Li'l Bob had his horse Cowboy saddled, too. So we loaded them in our old horse trailer and followed John down to his place to help him get the neighbor's bull. I was glad I had Red to ride on this little adventure because I knew that if I had to rope this bull, Red was the horse I would want to be riding. He was big, fast and about as stout on a rope as any horse I had.

We drove down to where the heifers were and there was the big bull, dragging John's frazzled rope along, and he sure had loving on his mind! John jumped out with his rifle in hand, ready to shoot this Romeo, but I convinced him not to shoot him, we would get the bull out of there. The three of us unloaded our horses and started toward the heifers and the bull. We figured the three of us could start a little bunch of heifers, along with the bull and drive them all to the neighbor's and cut the bull off there. We had just gotten them started when the bull quit the heifers and charged Li'l Bob and Cowboy. Li'l Bob wheeled Cowboy around and tried to get out of the bull's way, but the bull had zeroed in on them and hit Cowboy a glancing lick, almost knocking Cowboy down. Cowboy scrambled around, finally managing to get away from the bull and haul ass out of there.

Seeing Cowboy and Li'l Bob nearly getting knocked down by this sorry bugger sure fired me up! I was instant mad, my adrenalin nearly going thru the top of my hat! I was really scared for Li'l Bob, and I took to this bull like a bulldog after a stray cat!

The bull saw Red coming and took off running toward the bunch of heifers.

That's just what I needed, getting him to run and Red drove up on him, and I roped him clean and throwed a trip over his right hip. I kicked Red into overdrive as we turned off to the left. Standing over in my left stirrup, the trip was perfect and when we hit the end of the rope Red flattened out about a thousand pounds of hamburger. Red laid into the rope, and I got down and got the surprised bull tied before he could get up. Li'l Bob and John rode up and tossed me another piggin string which I used to double tie this son of a gun. I sure didn't want this bugger getting up. I would probably have gone to get John's rifle and shot the sorry son of a gun if he had gotten up! I was still pretty hot under the collar.

Leaving the bull tied down, we all got in John's pickup and drove up to his house where he had a phone, and called his neighbor. The guy was at home and said he would be right over to get his bull.

The neighbor showed up pretty quick, driving an old Ford pickup with a set of two by four stock racks held together with baling wire. How the hell is he going to haul that fighting son of a gun in that old contraption, and how is he going to get him loaded, we wondered aloud as we drove back down to where we had left the bull tied down.

The bull was right where we had left him, laying there banging his head on the ground.

"If that S.O.B. gets up I'm going to shoot him," I said as the old man drove up beside the bull.

We drove over by my pickup and trailer where Red and Cowboy were standing watching the bull bang his head on the ground. I got out and started to tighten up my saddle again, as I figured I would have to try and load the bull with Red.

"No horses, no horses!" the old man hollered at us.

"What do you mean no horses," John said. "How the hell you going to load your bull?"

"No horses, boys! I'll load him. My bull don't like horses!" the old man explained.

Well, we had damn near figured that out by now! The feeling was mutual, as we didn't especially like his bull either!

The old feller gets an old rope halter out of his pickup, walks over and pets his bull on the head, and slips the halter on him, taking what was left of John's rope off. Talking nice and soft in Spanish, I guess he was apologizing for us. He assured the bull everything was fine and proceeded to take my pigging strings off the bulls legs. I looked around at John's pickup figuring how quick I could get to the rifle.

The bull got up, shook himself like a dog climbing out of the water. The old feller led the bull over to the back of his pickup, unwired the tail gate on his stock racks, opened the gate and the damned bull jumped right up in the pickup!

John, Li'l Bob and I stood there looking like we were entered in a fly catching contest, our mouths hanging open with a stunned look on our faces!

The old feller wired shut the tailgate and walks up to me, handing me my piggin strings and what was left of John's frayed rope.

"Thank you, cowboy. Next time just call me. I'll come get him. My bull don't like horses!"

He got in his pickup and drove off. The three of us just stood there for a while. We had each caught about three flies!

We finally got our mouths shut and started laughing. I had sure cowboyed the hell out of the old man's pet bull!

◊   ◊   ◊

Mr. Bates had bought a couple of pretty good colts from the Mora ranch near Wagon Mound. One was a real good looking buckskin that I had started riding. He was sure making a good horse, but he was a little humpy and would sure buck if things didn't go just right.

Li'l Bob had made friends with a boy about his age in school, whose Dad was running a big ranch out east of Corona. They ran several thousand head of sheep, and Li'l Bob had kinda volunteered us to help with the big sheep roundup at shearing time. This was a little different, to say the least, but I figured it would be a good ride to put on my buckskin horse, as he was needing some good, long, hard rides.

We saddled up and loaded our horses well before daylight for the thirty-mile haul down to the ranch for our first big sheep round-up. There were several cowboys there, and I noticed most of them had two or three piggin strings across their chests, and I soon found out why.

We fanned out over a several section pasture looking for sheep. The gather was going well as we had several hundred head drifting down a long draw toward the shearing pens. More sheep than I had ever seen.

As we neared the holding pens, some of the big wild lambs and sheep started breaking back. A cowboy would take to them, roping and tying them down, one by one. A couple of wetbacks in an old pickup pulling a stock trailer were following the herd and, when a cowboy tied down a sheep, they would drive up and load the sheep in the trailer. Boy, there was a lot of sheep roping going on right quick, and I saw the need for all the piggin strings.

I had roped a couple of sheep on Buck and he was doing real good. I figured I probably had me a top notch sheep-roping horse! Just what I needed. A big lamb broke back on my side and headed up a pinon covered hill. Buck and I took to him, rope down and having fun! I roped the sheep and hog tied him and suddenly realized we were up in the trees where the pickup and trailer couldn't get to us.

I picked the sheep up and started to Buck, going to put the sheep up in front of my saddle and carry him down to where the pickup could get to him. Wrong! Buck snorted and went to running backwards as I held on to my reins, trying to get him stopped. I dropped the sheep and got up to Buck, leading him over to a near by tree where I tied him.

I went back and got the sheep and saw a big dead limb sticking out of a nearby tree, about six or seven feet above the ground. I carried the sheep over to this dead limb and hung the hog tied sheep on the limb. Poco smart hombre, no!?

Untying Buck I got on him and rode off in the opposite direction. Buck was snorting and looking back to make sure I hadn't brought that booger with me. I rode around a little and Buck relaxed, so I headed back to my hanging lamb chops. Acting real nonchalant, I rode by the dead limb, reaching out and grabbing the sheep off his perch and holding him in front of me. I figured I had sure fooled Buck! Wrong again!!

The stupid sheep started squirming and flopping his head! Buck didn't even have to think about it. He just blew up big time, and I knew he was about all I could ride under the best conditions and old lamb chops wasn't making the conditions any better! One of us had to go! I pitched the sheep out over the side, as I tried to stay on top of Buck, bucking down off the side of the hill. He bucked down to the bottom of the hill and one of the other cowboys, seeing the little commotion, rode over to me as I got Buck pulled up.

I explained poor old lamb chops' predicament and he laughed as we rode back up to where he had stopped rolling. I picked up lamb chops, and the cowboy held him across the front of his saddle as we rode back down to the herd. Bet old lamb chops thought twice about breaking back the next time! I never did break Buck to packing sheep! Of course the need never came up again, either!

38

Snow Storm and Windmilling

We had a little "mickey mouse" Scout pickup to use on the ranch. I sure didn't think much of this little rig. It would huff and puff trying to pull our old stock trailer and you could haul only about ten or twelve bales of hay on it. Mr. Bates was sure proud of this little toy and he wouldn't agree to buy a good full-sized pickup for the ranch, so we had to do the best we could with this little toy pickup.

The first winter we were at the Bates ranch it started snowing pretty hard one evening in early February. Snowed all night, and by the next morning we had around eighteen inches of snow on the ground. I loaded the little toy pickup with all the hay I could get on it and headed out to try and feed. It was sure snowing hard and I managed to slide off the road in a deep bar ditch. I shoveled, jacked and cussed all morning to no avail, trying to get dug out. I finally had to give up and walk back to the house. I figured the State road grader would be coming up our road before too long and I could get it to pull me out. The road was usually kept open for the school bus that came up to the house to pick up the kids.

It just kept snowing, and the wind kicked up, blowing pretty good. We didn't have a telephone, but hearing the news on the television, we learned the Corona area, along with most of the State was getting hit with a pretty severe winter snow storm. Looking out the window as the snow continued, we could confirm this newsworthy note! Snow was well over two feet deep and still coming down hard and fast, and the wind got worse. We had a big wood pile and kept the old fireplace going, as that was the only heat we had in the house.

It snowed all that day and the next morning it was still snowing! Nearly three feet deep and still coming down, and the wind was really howling. Li'l Bob and I saddled up our horses and headed out into this winter wonderland to see if we could get down to where most of the cattle were. Riding by where I had parked the little Scout we saw that it was completely drifted over, just the top bales of hay in the back were sticking up out of the big snow drift covering the Scout.

The cows had some protection with all the pinon and cedar trees for a wind break and they seemed to be making it pretty good, but they were sure needing some groceries. We were able to drift most of the cows up to where our hay stack was and with our saddle horses pulled out enough hay bales to where we could feed most of the cows. When it finally quit snowing, we measured just over three feet, and then the wind started getting serious! The snow really got to drifting, some drifts over six feet high. We were pretty well snowed in for the duration!

The news and weather reports on the television informed us that all the State and County road-clearing equipment had been stranded on the eastern part of Lincoln County, and they feared there may be some ranches isolated by this storm! Well, no kidding! Here we sat with no help on the way! To help make the situation a little more enjoyable, our water line from the well froze up, and we had no water. Breaking icicles off the roof, and melting them and snow for water wasn't exactly Bettye's idea of romantic ranch living! The kids thought it was fun for a little while, but the fun soon wore off and we weren't exactly a bunch of happy campers.

Dragging hay bales a horseback to the cows kept Li'l Bob and me busy every morning. Bettye and Myrna kept busy sewing and trying to keep the house warm. The only heat we had was the fireplace in the little living room. One afternoon, Bettye noticed a little more smoke than usual in the room. Looking over at the fireplace she saw flames coming out the side heat vents on the rock fireplace! The walls on either side were on fire!

She grabbed some old pictures off the walls and pitched them out the front door on to the porch. Luckily she had a couple buckets of melted snow water in the kitchen and managed to get the fire out before we lost our happy home. Whoever built the fireplace had put wooden heat vents in the rock chimney to let heat out into the room. We just had to much heat coming out and the vents caught on fire. Thanks to her quick thinking we didn't burn the the old house down!

Bettye told me, after about a week of this fun and games, that we could use a few items from the grocery store!

The next morning, Li'l Bob and I saddled up. We had a good pack saddle and a set of panniers which we put on a big, stout, saddle horse and we headed out for town. It was fifteen miles to Corona. The snow was sure deep and the drifts were pretty hard to break through. We took turns breaking a trail through the snow. It was pretty hard on an old horse, bucking this deep snow. We had to give the horses a break now and then. The snow was packed up over the top of our breast collars across our horses' chests. Twelve miles of this and we came to the main highway where the snow had been plowed and the going was a little better. We rode on into town, picked up a horse load of groceries, our mail, and found out the County road clearing equipment was all stuck out east of town!

Riding back to the ranch, the wind got to blowing pretty hard again. The trail we had made going to town was pretty well filled in and it was nearly like breaking a new trail again. As we rode by where I had parked the Scout load of hay, we could see a huge snow drift and figured no one would steal our little Scout because you couldn't even see the damned thing! We made it to the house just before dark. This had been a long day!

We were snowed in twenty-two days before the road crew finally got our road open. They dug through the snow and found a bumper to hook a chain to and pulled the little Scout out of the snow bank. I was even glad to get it out to where I could drive it again! The kids were glad to see the old yellow school bus come chugging up to the house, and I finally got the water lines thawed out and we laughed about our ordeal. I was even able to talk Mr. Bates into buying a full sized four wheel drive pickup!

◊　　◊　　◊

Mr. Bates and his wife lived in Tulsa and came out to the ranch two or three times a year, usually at branding and shipping time. They would stay about a month in the summer. He liked to get horseback and ride around the ranch. They were both up in their seventies and sure kept in good physical shape.

Mr. and Mrs. Bates both loved to swim and had put in a big swimming pool just above the big house they stayed in when at the ranch. The pool was kept full from a mountain spring about two miles up on the side of Gallinas Mountain, with a plastic pipe line running cold spring water into the pool all the time. There was no heating system for the pool, so it was pretty darn cold most of the time. Mr. and Mrs Bates would faithfully jump into this frigid water every morning right at six o'clock, and you could hear the shriek and screams for miles around as they hit the water, each of them swimming about twenty laps!

July rolled around and it was hot and dry. One Sunday when we took a rare day off, Bettye and the kids wanted to go up to the swimming pool and have a family picnic around the pool just like the rich people do. Bates's were gone and we had the pool to ourselves, and with a lot of threatening and persuasion, they talked me into going swimming.

It was sure hot and I figured the water might have warmed up enough that I wouldn't turn blue as soon as I got in. So we all went picnicking and swimming. We had a great time. The water was cold, but bearable.

There was a big reclining, floating chair at the pool. I climbed up in this little bit of luxury and floated around, while Bettye and the kids swam and had a big time in the pool. I fell asleep in this big floating chair and when I woke up I looked like an over-cooked lobster! Boy you talk about sunburned! That was me. From the top of my head all the way down to my bare feet was sunburned big time! I could hardly get on my shirt or Levis and my feet were sunburned so bad I couldn't get my boots on! The kids sure got a good laugh the next day when I had to ride in my slippers!

There sure were a lot of rattle snakes on this place. We killed several over six feet long. It was pretty common to kill two or three every day while riding, most of them prairie rattlers, two to three feet long. Mr. Bates and I were riding one day and came on a rattler about three feet long. I got down to kill it and Mr. Bates said, "Wait, let me show you how to kill a rattle snake."

As he got off his horse he pulled a big, neatly folded handkerchief out of his hip pocket.

Handing me his bridle reins to hold, he unfolded his handkerchief and holding it by the corner, start swinging it back and forth in front of the coiled rattlesnake. About the third pass in front of the snake the rattler struck at the handkerchief. His fangs were hooked into the fabric and Mr. Bates quickly picked the snake up off the ground by the handkerchief. As the snake was hanging by the fangs, Mr. Bates reached down and got a good grip just above the snake's tail and dropped the handkerchief. He started swinging the snake around his head. About three fast swings and Mr. Bates snapped the snake back just like he was popping a bull whip! I still don't know where the hell that snake's head went! It was darn sure gone as Mr. Bates held the headless rattler out to show me how to kill rattlers! I really rather prefer the old method of throwing rocks, sticks and what ever else you can find at them!

We had several six-to-eight hundred foot deep water wells on the ranch. I wasn't much of a windmill man, so I really had to rely on my neighbors to help me change leathers and whatever else seemed to go wrong with these windmills. I was sure gun shy about climbing the big tall windmill towers. John Books was helping me one day and he said I should get a little climbing experience. So he talked me into climbing up to the top of the tower and tying the logging chain around the top of the tower to hook the pulley into, as we prepared to pull the well.

I mustered up all the courage I could come up with and reluctantly draped the ten-foot long logging chain around my neck, and started up the shaky steps. Each step was sure scary, and I just kept getting higher and higher. John was hollering encouraging words of comfort up to me like, "Hell, my grandma could climb faster than that" and "Come on, old man, what the hell's the matter?" Just all kinds of reassuring little things to help me get to the top. I finally did get to the top!

"Hey, John, I got a little problem here!" my quivering voice squeaked out.

"What's the matter, Granny?" he hollered up at me, unable to keep the laughter out of his voice.

"Well, I can't hook this damned chain with my teeth, and I sure as hell ain't turning loose with either hand!!"

I managed to climb back down and John had to go up and hook the chain! I could make a hand on the ground, but I sure wasn't much help at climbing those high towers.

John had an old wooden windmill tower on his place, but it wasn't as high as the steel towers on Bates's, and he came over asking me to come down and help him change the stroke in the windmill head. I had no idea what he was talking about, but he assured me it was real easy, hardly any climbing and not very high. He assured me I could hang on with both hands, so against my better judgment, I agreed to help him. As we drove up to the wooden tower it didn't look too threatening. As I followed John up the wooden ladder on the side of the tower, it wasn't real encouraging when he would stop and tell me to skip the next step as it was pretty rotten! The creaking and cracking sounds coming out of the old wooden tower were real comforting.

We got up to the little miniature platform of half rotten boards at the base of the windmill head. John had set the brake so the wheel couldn't turn, he said, and he climbed in through the spokes of the wheel. Sitting with his arms and legs sticking through the spokes he was facing me as I sat half on the little platform with one leg over the arm of the windmill tail, my knuckles turning white from the death grip I had on the boards I was sitting on.

John reached through the spokes and took the cover off the windmill head, chattering away, trying to get me to relax and quit squeezing the old boards, that I was trying to hang onto!

"Oh crap! You better get a good hold of something!" John said looking out behind me.

I quickly looked over my shoulder and saw what John was talking about. A great big "dust devil" was bearing down on us! This Corona country produced some big whirl winds and this looked like a dandy headed right for our roost. I grabbed the windmill head like it was my long lost brother and hung on for dear life as the wind and dust hit us. It was pretty strong for a minute or so then the wind stopped and everything was quiet. I started spitting dirt out of my mouth and tried to rub some out of my eyes. Finally getting my eyes opened I looked at John. Hell, John was gone! All I could see were his feet. I heard him cussing so I knew he hadn't gone far.

The brake on the windmill had allowed the wheel to turn a half turn when the wind hit it, and it had turned John upside down! He scrambled in and out of the spokes and got back to where he had been before the wind hit us, and we finished the job. He thought that was great fun, but he never could get me to climb another windmill tower!

Mr. Bates decided we should creep feed our calves and try and put some extra pounds on them. He had several big creep feeders on the ranch and we patched them up so we could use them. We put several hundred pounds of small grain pellets in these creep feeders for the calves and they started using the feeders. They were built with a little pen around them with a little opening that the calves could go in to the feed, but a full-grown cow couldn't. Boy, as fast as the feed was disappearing, we thought those calves were sure eating a lot!

Coming out to the ranch one night, well after dark, the headlights of the car flashed on one of the creep feeders close to the road. Looked like a big convention of porcupines was going on over there! I stopped and turned so the lights shown on the feeder, and there must have been eight or ten porcupines in there eating our high priced calf feed!

I told Mr. Bates where all our creep feed was going and we declared war on those porcupines. The next night Mr. Bates drove down to our house in his big Lincoln Continental.

"Get your guns, boys! Let's go hunting!" Mr. Bates said.

Li'l Bob and I got our twenty two rifles and a couple boxes of shells and headed out to the pickup.

"That pickup is too rough riding. Let's go in my car," Mr. Bates said as he got in his big Lincoln.

I couldn't believe we were bouncing around the pastures in that Lincoln, shooting porcupines!

Li'l Bob said, "This is the way to go, Mr. Bates! Now were hunting in style!"

In four nights of hunting we eliminated sixty-five creep feed eating porcupines! Li'l Bob claimed we got so many porcupines because we were in the Lincoln! It was a much better hunting rig than our pickup!

We had a lot of good times at the Bates ranch, some pretty tough times too, but looking back, it was sure a good time for our family. We grew pretty close.

The good deal with Mr. Bates didn't materialize, and when Bill Littrell let me know my old job was open again, I took it and we moved back to Philmont. We were all a little homesick for the Cimarron country, and ready to go back.

39

Cowboying Buffalo

We moved back to Philmont, into the old house at cattle headquarters, and it was like coming home again. We had all missed Philmont, and the country we knew and loved.

This was in the late fall of 1965, just after the major flood that had devastated the area in June. I had heard of the big flood, but couldn't imagine the tremendous amount of damage it had done.

I soon found the impact of the flood, when I started discovering trails, roads and stock drives I had known so well were washed away. The big grass-covered meadows below Fish Camp were turned into sandy, boulder-covered wasteland. One of the original Phillips cabins was washed away, as was the kitchen from the main lodge. The trail was impassable from Abreu to Fish Camp. The grass-covered pasture along the Rayado River at Zastro was like the meadows at Fish Camp; big boulders, sand, and no grass. Big trees that had washed down from the country above littered the once grass covered pastures.

The Rayado River, where we could fish out the back door at Zastro Cow Camp on the north side, was now rechanneled one hundred yards south of the cabin! The water line inside the cow camp was four feet high. Some how the old camp had survived. Part of the corrals were lost to the flood. But the little saddle room and barn were still standing, with a new mud floor. The tin can nailed over the knot hole that Shorty had shot so well, was still in place.

Wherever I went, seems the flood had left its mark. Philmont is a survivor and crews were busy rebuilding roads and trails. The new kitchen at Fish Camp did have a nice big window looking out over the rushing stream and it wasn't near as dark as the old kitchen was! Nothing stays the same. I even thought the Tooth of Time was about three or four inches shorter, but I never got that confirmed!

◊   ◊   ◊

Philmont had a herd of around one hundred twenty five buffalo or bison, if you prefer, when I came back from Corona. They had been under the care and supervision of Philmont's game manager, Bob Lee. Bob was killed in an unfortunate truck accident, and the buffalo became part of the cattle department's responsibility. They didn't take much care; a little feed in the winter, and keeping salt out for them year round.

We kept the herd culled down to this number by keeping only a few of the best heifer calves and one or two of the top bull calves each year. The older cows and excess calves were butchered on the ranch and lots of visiting Boy Scouts got a treat of a genuine "buffalo burger".

A new environmentalist for the Raton area visited our facilities at Philmont and determined that we were not up to State health department standards in our butchering and meat processing facility. He closed the ranch butcher shop to all processing of game or buffalo meat.

None of the custom slaughter houses in Raton, Trinidad, Las Vegas or Taos would take our buffalo to butcher. Finally, we found a place in Tucumcari that had adequate facilities to handle these live buffalo; about a hundred and sixty miles from the ranch.

A small problem suddenly came up. How were we going to get these buffalo to Tucumcari? The buffalo had never been in a corral, besides there weren't any corrals around close anyway!

That's what cowboys are for! We started roping and loading them in our stock trailer and hauling them into the corrals at cattle headquarters. We caught yearlings and some two year-olds. When we had twenty or so in the corrals at cattle headquarters, we hauled them in the bobtail truck to Tucumcari. This was something new and sure fun for awhile.

It took a pretty good horse to catch these young buffalo. They were surprisingly fast and agile. They had a strong smell about them and made a deep grunting sound. Most horses were sure scared of them. I had a big, stout sorrel horse called Bill that sure had the speed to catch a buffalo right quick, and he wasn't afraid of anything. I had roped and tied down a lot of steers on Bill. He sure was a good rope horse, and he took to these buffalo like they were roping steers.

They were harder to rope than horned cattle. Their heads set lower and they don't have much neck, so you had to throw a little different loop. They were pretty wild on the end of a rope and would sure fight a horse. If we caught one near the main herd we would have a mad, fighting cow challenge us. Buffalo didn't bluff one little bit! Things got pretty western at times, trying to get to the trailer with a buffalo on the end of your rope, hoping your partner could keep that mad fighting cow away from you.

The cow buffalo were getting worse about fighting a horse, and we didn't want to get a horse or cowboy hurt, so we figured we might need to change our tactics. We had caught fifty some head, but had that many or more to go.

We got a couple pieces of an axle about three feet long and stuck them down in the holes in the back of our pickup bed side panels. They fit pretty tight, making a good solid saddle horn! Putting our horn loops around the axle, we were ready to catch us another buffalo. As we poured cake in a circle, the buffalo would line up along the row of cake. As we stood at the back of the pickup, we had a shot at catching one when he dropped his head down to get a bite of cake. We sure had to sharpen our skills at throwing the "hoolihan", as much movement, like whirling a loop over our heads, would spook them out of range. Two ropers could rope at a time, as we had two saddle horns. We tied two saddle ropes together to give us a little more range and flexibility. Only thing with this, when you caught one and he was out on the end of your two ropes, he was sure a long ways away!

We had another pickup, pulling the stock trailer, parked nearby and when we caught one, we drove to the pickup and trailer, leading our fighting catch, load him and go back and try for another one. Slow process but a lot easier on horses and cowboys.

Fred Sisneros was working with me, and he was having a little trouble mastering the art of throwing the "hoolihan". He would build a loop big enough to catch a full-sized pickup! I kept telling him to use a smaller loop. He swung his big loop out at a nearby yearling, missing him, but the loop settled nicely over a big full grown cow's head! She grunted right loud, and headed north as fast as she could run.

"Oh *@#&!, Lookout!" he hollered as he pitched his slack at the fast moving cow.

The cow hit the end of the rope at an angle, jerked her down and the pickup kinda scooted around and leaned over like it had been sideswiped by a running buffalo! The saddle horn held, but the side panel split out at the top of the hole. Looked like we might loose a pretty good chunk of pickup!

"Now what the hell are you going to do?" I asked, as we watched the cow fight the rope and rock the pickup.

"That's my new rope! I sure don't want to cut it!" he exclaimed.

"Just go down to her and take it off then!" I suggested.

He didn't know if I was kidding or not. He sure didn't appear anxious to go down the rope and take it off that fighting cow's head!

"Maybe I can heel her, and get her down," I ventured.

Boss Sanchez was driving the pickup with the stock trailer, and I told him to drive to us right quick if we got the cow down, and help us get the head rope off.

Hoping the back panel of the pickup held together, I managed to get around behind the cow, as she fought the rope. When she jumped forward, I managed to rope both hind feet. As I jerked my slack, Fred grabbed the rope with me, and we got the cow's hind feet out from under her, and she went down. We set back on the rope for all we were worth as Boss drove up to her. He jumped out of the pickup and took the rope off her head as we kept the heel rope tight. With the rope off her head, we pitched her slack in our heel rope and ran and jumped in the back of the pickup.

"Let's go, Boss!" I hollered, as the cow scrambled up, looking for trouble!

We made good our escape, leaving the mad cow in the dust, as Boss sped off. I noticed my roping partner started using a smaller loop after that!

This method of culling the herd worked pretty well for a couple of years. Seems there would always be a few buffalo that got wise to our pickup roping, and we would have to catch them horseback. The majority we caught on the feed ground.

We had twenty some yearlings in the corrals at cattle headquarters, letting them get used to a corral before taking them to Tucumcari. They had settled down pretty well and were taking to the feed in good shape.

As Fred and I drove into the corrals one evening, we could hardly believe what we were seeing out in the milk cow pasture. All of the buffalo had gotten out of the corral, into the big pasture. They were all walking back toward the corral, following the well worn cow trail.

Walking along behind them with a little switch in her hand, was Myrna!

She was nine or ten then and acted like she knew just what she was doing. She followed the buffalo into the corral, shutting the gate behind them.

"Hi, Dad! I put the buffalo back for you!" she said, giving us her big pretty smile.

"I'll be damned! Thanks, Honey" I managed to mumble.

"How the hell did you do that!?" Fred exclaimed.

"Do what?" Myrna asked, acting like she just went around driving wild buffalo afoot everyday. "They seemed to know where to go, so I just followed them," she explained.

I didn't know whether to be glad or mad! I was glad they hadn't run over her, and amazed that they had walked back into the corral for her.

This kinda took the wind out of our sails! It was tough for a couple of old buffalo ropers, to get upstaged by a little girl!

We made sure the gates were all tied shut after that!

◊   ◊   ◊

Jim Byrd had come to work for me and had heard us talking about roping buffalo. Jim was sure a good roper and was anxious to get a chance to rope buffalo.

We had roped several on the feed ground, but not on horseback. This method wasn't giving Jim as much action as he wanted.

"Let me rope one out of the back of the pickup. Just drive up on the one you want, and I'll rope him," Jim said.

I figured we might give it a try, so I cut a big two year old bull out of the herd with the pickup and took after him. Jim was perched up in the right hand corner of the pickup bed. He had his horn loop over the pickup saddle horn and was swinging his loop as I tried to get the buffalo lined out and running.

Seemed like the closer I got, the faster he ran! Ducking and dodging. We were really trucking in hot pursuit. Every time Jim would almost have a throw, the buffalo would duck off to the right. I was sure putting down some fancy skid tracks as we chased this buffalo around in big circles.

Jim was hollering, "Faster, closer, faster", as I closed the gap between the buffalo and us. Closing in on him pretty fast, I figured we had him this time as I pulled up closer to him. Then he ducked off to the left instead of

268

the right! He turned right in front of the pickup. I slammed on the brakes as I broad sided him going about forty miles an hour! The heavy duty grill guard protected the grill, but the pickup knocked the buffalo over, and we ran right over the top of him.

It felt like I had hit an oversized speed bump as the pickup bounced up in the air and came to a sliding stop.

As the dust boiled around us, I jumped out to see if I still had my roper in the back. Jim was piled up in the corner, in a pile of feed sacks, an arm and leg sticking out at odd angles. Jim rose up out of the debris looking a little worse for wear.

"Damn, did you run over him?" Jim asked as he struggled to get up.

"I couldn't miss him! He turned right in front of me and I nailed him broadside!" I replied.

"Hell, there he goes!" Jim said, pointing back through the dust at a fast running buffalo, headed to the herd.

"I'll be damned! Do you think that's him?" I answered as I dropped down on my hands and knees, peering under the pickup.

Jim climbed out over the side of the pickup and looked underneath.

"Must be him, cause he sure as hell ain't under here!" Jim laughed.

I checked the front of the pickup for damage. The big heavy grill guard had deflected the buffalo, and I couldn't see anything broken or bent.

We jumped back in the pickup and took off after him again. I noticed we had suddenly developed a bad shimmy in the front end of our pickup. We caught up to the running buffalo as he reached the herd. He didn't appear to be hurt much, a few skinned places, and a little limp, but he could still run about sixty miles an hour! We decided to let him go for the day, as the old pickup was sure getting hard to steer. We headed in to the motor pool to let Harry, the ranch mechanic, take a look at our shaking pickup.

Raising the pickup on the grease rack, Harry looked at the damage.

"What the hell have you guys been doing? Looks like you either ran over a buffalo or this pickup is growing hair under here!" he commented as he surveyed the damage.

The arrangement at Tucumcari wasn't working out very well. We stopped taking them down there and the numbers sure seemed to increase fast over the next couple years. We had roped and hauled around one hundred and fifty without getting any cowboys or buffalo killed and had had a lot of excitement along the way!

Fish Camp, on Philmont, before flood of 1965. Flood took kitchen off
south end of lodge

Cabins at Fish Camp, Philmont. Flood washed cabin in back ground away.
Jack Rhea is fishing off bridge.

Bob Knox riding Bill, during filming of movie, backing up muzzleloader
buffalo shooter. Philmont Scout Ranch, early 1960s

Buffalo. Philmont

40

Buffalo

The buffalo herd had increased to nearly three hundred head. They were breaking out of their pasture pretty regularly, and we had given them about all the country we could. Bill Littrell and I agreed we were going to have to build a set of corrals that we could pen them in and try to sell some.

Bill, Ray Kinerd, the maintenance foreman for Philmont, and I decided to go up to the big buffalo roundup and sale at Custer State Park, in South Dakota. Custer State Park had over a thousand head of buffalo and we figured we might get some ideas on what to build and how they worked the big herd of buffalo through the corrals.

We drove into Custer, South Dakota, and were met by roadblocks set up all over the small town by State Police and National Guard. They stopped us and informed us that all businesses in the town were shut down due to an Indian disturbance the night before. We would have to go somewhere else for the night, as nothing was open in Custer. The State Police were expecting more trouble in Custer that night, but thought Rapid City would be safe from any disturbance. We headed on up to Rapid City, not wanting to get caught up in this problem.

After checking into a nice hotel, we had a good dinner, and decided to wander around and checkout the night life in Rapid City. Everything seemed quiet and peaceful.

We were sitting in a nightclub, enjoying a drink, relaxing after spending the day driving. We didn't pay much attention to the bartender when he ran over to the front doors and dropped an iron bar across the doorway, locking the doors. There were a couple young ladies on stage doing a very interesting dance, and they pretty well had our full attention!

We could hear some banging on the front door and people yelling and hollering outside. We just figured they wanted in to enjoy the atmosphere. The small window in the front was pretty high and you couldn't see out very well. Of course we weren't looking out the window!

"This is the State Police! Open this door now!" an angry voice demanded, outside our barricaded door.

The dancers gathered up their clothes and hurried off stage. The bartender peered out the window, satisfied it was really the State Police, he opened the door. Two State Policemen, in full battle gear stormed in.

"We have had a riot outside, and you people have five minutes to clear out of here and get off the street!" the big policeman said.

They looked pretty serious so we put down our drinks and walked out into the battle ground.

Police cars, ambulances, all with their flashing lights on, seemed to be everywhere. The sidewalk was covered with broken glass, blood, and all sorts of debris. Several people were lying face down in the street, hands handcuffed behind them. The medics were helping injured, bleeding people into waiting ambulances. State Police and National Guardsmen were loading the handcuffed people into a couple police vans.

As we hot-footed it down the street to our hotel, we noticed most of the businesses along the street had the front windows broken out. Seems the Indians had rioted, breaking out windows, dragging people out of the bars and restaurants and beating the stuff out of them. We were thankful our bartender had a good solid bar on the door where we were! No one was killed in this melee, but the hospital sure had a run on the emergency room, patching up the wounded.

We made it into our hotel rooms without incident, and were setting there talking about how lucky we were to have missed this fracas.

"I better call my wife (Billie) and tell her I'm all right!" Bill said.

"Bill, it's 1:30 in the morning! Billie doesn't know anything about this deal. You're just going to worry her about nothing. Besides, you have had too much to drink to be calling her this time of night!" I argued, trying to talk him out of calling her.

"No, I got to tell her the Indians didn't get me!" Bill insisted.

"What have you been drinking!?" we could hear Billie's voice over the phone as Bill tried to assure her he had escaped the Indians.

Of course Billie called Bettye and Ray's wife. We were all in trouble right quick. They all figured we had got into a fight with some Indians and they weren't very happy with their spouses. Later that morning on the Good

Morning America TV program there was a big story about the Indian riot in Rapid City, so then they were all worried about us!

We left the battle ground of Rapid City with scalps intact, and headed for the round up and auction at Custer State Park. State Police were set up along the road, expecting more trouble at the auction, but there wasn't any trouble, and the sale went off pretty smoothly. We took lots of pictures and got some good ideas on handling buffalo and what it took to hold them. As soon as the auction was over we headed back to the quiet of Philmont.

We designed a set of corrals, and the fence crew and maintenance crew built a double stout set of corrals out of railroad ties. We bought a big squeeze chute, designed to handle buffalo. We were well pleased with the new working facilities. The buffalo had never been in a corral and the first time we used it, it sure got a good test.

We had several buyers come to get the buffalo they had bought, and we got the herd culled down to the number we wanted. One of the volume buyers was a lawyer from Albuquerque. He bought a couple truck loads and took them to his place, which was close to the International Airport in Albuquerque. A few days later on the six o'clock TV news, we got to see our buffalo on television! Not exactly how we would have liked to have seen them, but there they were. Seems they had broken out of their new home and wandered onto the landing strip at the airport! The security people and city police weren't having much luck driving the buffalo with their honking horns and flashing lights. Several plane landings and takeoffs had been interrupted until they were able to get the buffalo off the runway.

◊   ◊   ◊

The Colfax County Fair Board raffled off a beef every year at the County Fair and Rodeo in Springer. The ranches around Colfax County took turns donating a beef for this raffle. It was a good source of income for the Fair Board. It came Philmont's turn to donate a steer. Beef prices had finally climbed up over twenty-five cents a pound, and Bill Littrell sure didn't want to donate a big steer now that they were worth something!

"What do you think about donating a buffalo instead of a steer?" Bill asked me.

"That would probably work. Sure be something different anyway!" I said.

The County Fair Board agreed to try it one year. I guess the novelty of winning a buffalo had a certain amount of allure to it, 'cause they sure sold a bunch of raffle tickets.

The day after the drawing, a young man who worked in the bank with Buddy, my brother-in-law, called me on the phone.

"Boy, my dad is the luckiest guy I know! He won the buffalo!" he exclaimed.

I congratulated him, wondering if maybe I should be offering my condolences. He was going to build a small corral to keep him in while they fattened him up. They wanted to come over the next Saturday and pick up their lucky prize. I assured him their prize would be ready to pick up then.

This was in September and we didn't have any buffalo in the corrals. I asked Bill if maybe this was range delivery? They could just go catch them one.

"Hell no! This wasn't a range delivery deal! You have to get one in the corral for them!" he said in a rather loud voice.

I got the message, so the next morning I saddled my good horse, Bill, and went by and picked up Boss Sanchez to help me load this winner's prize. We hadn't been feeding the buffalo through the summer and I didn't figure we could entice them onto a feed ground to rope one with the pickup and some cake.

We drove out to the buffalo herd and they didn't pay any attention to us. I cinched Bill up pretty tight, picked out a good-sized young bull, eased him out of the herd and built to him. I roped him, and Boss and I got him loaded and hauled him to cattle headquarters. He was pretty wild and I hoped they had built a pretty stout pen to keep him in. He was ready for the lucky winner to come claim his prize.

The young man and his dad drove into headquarters Saturday morning, grinning all over, excited about their good fortune. They had a pretty flimsy looking set of stock racks on their pickup. There was a spare tire mount welded in the back of the pickup bed and I figured we could probably get the buffalo snubbed down to this and hopefully it would hold him.

We got an old rope on the buffalo's horns and got him snubbed up pretty close to the spare tire rack. Looked like it would hold him. They were surprised he was so wild, but thought he would settle down when they got him home. They were sure excited as they thanked us for getting their prize loaded. As they drove off, the buffalo kicked the top boards off one side of the stock racks. We pretended not to notice.

A week or so later, I saw the young man and asked how he was getting along with his buffalo. That was the wrong thing to ask about!

"That S.O.B.!" he exclaimed. "He had damn near kicked the stock racks off our pickup by the time we got out to my dad's place. We backed up to our new corral to unload him. We had to cut the rope to get him loose from the tire rack. Then he just busted all the boards on one side of our new corral and took off, headed east. He busted through our fence, then across the neighbor's place, busted his fence and kept going!"

Dad hollered, "Go get our deer rifles!"

"We loaded both guns and jumped in our pickup and took out after him. We chased him about three miles. He just kept busting through fences, and we finally got close enough to shoot him! I doubt if the meat will be much good, 'cause he sure got hot from all that chasing and running. I had to take two days off from work to go fix all the neighbor's fences he tore down! I sure hope my dad never gets lucky and wins another raffle for a buffalo!"

The County Fair Board wrote to Bill, thanking him for Philmont's generous donation, and asked him not to donate another buffalo! Guess they had talked to the lucky winner!

◇   ◇   ◇

We had a bunch of yearling buffalo in the corral, getting them settled down and used to being in a corral, about ready to take them to Tucumcari. Ben Vargas was working with us, and he noticed one of the yearlings didn't seem as wild as the others. He got him in a small pen and started feeding him by himself, trying to get him gentled down a little. He named him Jake.

Jake sure liked cake and was eating from Ben's hand, getting pretty gentle. Jake would follow Ben all around, looking for a handout of cake. Ben soon had a halter on Jake and had him broke to lead. Jake got to be a one man buffalo, as no one else messed with him. He was sure growing fast, got fat, and Ben had him pretty gentle.

I wasn't too surprised when I drove up to the corrals one morning and saw Jake wearing a saddle. Ben said he just as well be broke to ride. I agreed, just don't ask me to ride him!

Ben made Jake a little bridle with a snaffle bit. Jake did a pretty good job of bucking the first few times Ben got on him, but Ben was a good rider and he managed to get Jake rode. After a few saddlings, Jake quit bucking. Ben rode him everyday, trying to get Jake to turn and stop.

Jake didn't have much of a stop or turn on him, but Ben had been sitting on him every day and figured Jake was ready to go outside, snubbed to a horse.

Lee Merriott, a horseman from Oklahoma was working with us. Lee was sure a nice kid and was making a hand at roping. Ben told him to saddle his heading horse and he could snub Jake for him, as they ventured out of the corral for the first time with Ben riding Jake.

Ben took a long lash rope off one of the pack saddles, took the cinch off and put a big snap in the end of the lash rope. Snapping the long rope into Jake's halter, Ben handed Lee the big coil of lash rope. Lee dallied Jake up pretty close to him as Ben stepped up on Jake. Lee led Jake around the big corral a couple times, Jake leading right along beside Lee's horse.

"Okay, let's go see the world! Keep him snubbed pretty close," Ben said.

Lee headed out into the big adjoining pasture, Jake walking along beside his horse, leading real nice.

"Let's trot a little. Give him a little slack," Ben said.

Lee gave Jake some slack as they trotted across the pasture.

"Give him a little more slack," Ben said.

Jake had broke into a little stiff legged lope, Lee's horse was in a fast trot as they moved out pretty smooth. Lee had taken all his dallies off the saddle horn, as his horse broke into a lope along with Jake. Ben was pulling on first one rein, then the other, trying to get Jake to respond a little to the reins, but Jake didn't seem to notice he had a bridle on.

Lee kicked his horse up into a fast lope, trying to keep up with Jake. I guess Jake remembered getting roped as a youngster, or maybe the call of the wild took over. Whatever it was, he decided to leave there in a hurry.

Jake ducked off to the right and took off as fast as he could run. Ben was really pulling back on the reins, but to no avail. Lee made a quick stab at his saddle horn, trying to get Jake snubbed up again. He missed his dally and dropped several coils of rope in the process, giving Jake about all the slack he could want! Jake and Ben were flat out carrying the mail. Lee took after them, trying to gather up enough rope to get a dally. Lee's horse gained a little on Jake, and Lee gathered up a coil of rope and stuck it on that saddle horn like Jake Barnes at the National Finals, and turned off.

"Don't turn off!" Ben yelled, as he looked back and saw what was about to transpire.

Too late. Lee was a little upset with himself for missing his dallies and dropping his rope when Jake had started running. He had a good wrap now and he figured to put a stop to this runaway! Which he did.

Jake was headed south at roughly sixty miles an hour. Lee turned north and was up to about fifty miles an hour when Jake hit the end of the rope. This was kinda like popping a long bull whip, with Jake and Ben serving as the popper on the end!

The sudden change in direction shot Ben into orbit. Ben made it through lift off real well. His flight was long, high and pretty smooth. Reentry was good, but the actual landing lacked a little in finesse! Ben plowed up a big chunk of real estate as he finally came to a stop.

Jake didn't fare much better. He landed flat on his side as Lee's horse drug him along until they could all get stopped. Jake and Ben had the wind knocked out of them and a skinned spot or two but nothing serious. Lee had sure put a stop to that runaway! They all came back to the corral at a nice slow walk.

Ben decided Jake needed a little more corral work. He kept working with Jake, but he just wasn't cut out to be a reining buffalo. He never did get much of a rein or stop on him. He didn't get rode outside any more either!

We had a young wrangler working with us, Kevin, who sure wanted to ride Jake. Kevin wasn't much of a hand and Ben hadn't let him get on Jake.

Ben had Jake saddled and tied to the corral fence. Kevin kept pestering Ben to get on Jake so Ben finally gave in and told Kevin to go ahead and get on him while he was tied to the fence. Jake had about three foot of slack in the halter rope, and as Kevin walked up to him, Jake stepped back to the end of the lead rope.

Kevin jobbed his size fourteen foot in the stirrup and started to get on in first-class dude style, left hand on the saddle horn and his right hand on the cantle. As he got about halfway on, Jake made a big high jump forward.

The cantle of the saddle hit Kevin squarely in the seat of his pants, sending Kevin screaming over the front of the saddle. In sheer panic, Kevin grabbed at what ever he could grab. He managed to grab Jake around the neck with both arms, the saddle horn dangerously close to his butt. His head hanging down under Jake's horn with his eyeball about an inch from Jake's eyeball.

Jake had only made one jump, but that was enough! Jake stood perfectly still, staring at Kevin's closed eye. Kevin finally realized he wasn't moving and slowly opened his eyes to see if he recognized where he was. When he opened his eyes, all he could see was Jake's eyeball staring into his own!

Kevin let out a blood curdling scream as he frantically went to struggling and kicking, trying to push himself away from Jake. He finally fell free, landing halfway under Jake. His left foot was still in the stirrup. Jake reached around and was rooting Kevin around with his nose, checking to see if he might have a little cake in his shirt pocket. Kevin continued screaming and kicking, trying to get away from Jake's wet nose. Ben stepped up and twisted the stirrup around so he could get Kevin's foot out of it. Kevin crawled across the corral on his hands and knees as fast as he could go.

"That was a hell of a ride there, Kevin! Now don't be bugging me about riding Jake anymore." Ben said, as Kevin finally got to his feet, brushing the dirt off his dirty Levis, trying to regain his composure.

About that time, a writer and photographer from the Denver Post came to Philmont to do a feature article about the ranch. They heard about the buffalo Ben was breaking to ride and came up to the horse barns to get some pictures and interview Ben. The writer was a young, pretty good looking gal, and Kevin sure perked up when she came into the corrals. He figured that if he could ride Jake, he would sure make a favorable impression on this young lady.

Ben saddled Jake, and rode him around the corral as they took their pictures.

"Can I ride him Ben? Can I ride him?" Kevin kept asking, as Ben tried to ignore him.

Kevin was sure giving the young lady his best cowboy smile as he kept asking Ben, "Can I ride him? Can I ride him?"

The young lady didn't seem very impressed with Kevin. He knew if he could just get to ride Jake, she would really notice him. They were about to finish their interview with Ben, Kevin kept on with his "Can I ride him?"

Ben finally gave in to Kevin's constant plea to ride Jake. Holding Jake, Ben told Kevin to come and get on. Kevin gave the young lady his biggest smile, as he wallered up on Jake. Ben stepped back away from Jake, turning him loose. The photographer had some pretty fast film in his camera, but I don't think it was fast enough to capture Kevin's ride on Jake.

When Ben stepped back, Jake went straight up, like a hairy rocket, sucked'er back, and Kevin landed flat on his back in front of the young lady. He didn't smile. He looked like a fish out of water, the way his mouth was working, trying to get a breath of air.

Jake rushed up to the flattened Kevin and started licking and rooting him around, searching for a piece of cake. Kevin just laid there, making funny noises. Old "One Jump Kevin" had done it again.

"Is he all right?" the young lady asked Ben.

"Oh yes Ma'am, he does that all the time!" Ben answered, trying to keep a straight face and not bust out laughing.

Kevin managed to set up as the writer and photographer thanked Ben for his time and left the corral. Kevin didn't manage much of a smile for her as they walked away.

"Well, I guess you answered you're own dumb question, "Can I ride him" didn't you?" Ben said as he unsaddled Jake. Kevin had enough buffalo riding and never asked his question again!

Jake continued to grow and had gotten pretty big. He never did get to where he would turn or stop very well. He lost his respect for fences and seemed to be more trouble than he was worth, so he got a one way ticket to Tucumcari.

41

Bearskin Rug

Fall sure was in the air as I rode down from prowling the cattle in Miners Park and Crater Lake. I turned and rode up the high ridge between Lovers Leap and Uracca Canyon. There was a good dirt tank that had caught quite a bit of water up there, and some cattle had been using this high ridge. I noticed a bumper crop of pinon nuts and had seen a lot of bear sign around some of the pinon trees.

I crossed the head of a real deep little canyon that cut its way down through the rough rocky ridge top. Across this narrow deep canyon I spotted a real nice brown bear digging around under some pinon trees.

He was sure fat and slicked off. I pulled my horse up and sat there watching the bear as he dug around searching for pinon nuts. He hadn't got scent of me and didn't look up in my direction so I watched him undetected for a little while. He was pretty good sized and I wished I had a rifle with me, as it was bear hunting season.

I rode on in to headquarters that evening and kept thinking about that fat slick bear. That night after supper I decided to see if I could make a little deal with Bettye.

"Honey," real innocent like, I asked, "Would you like to make love on a bear skin rug?"

She looked at me like I was some kind of a nut. But having lived with me a long time, it would take more than this little proposition to throw her.

"Sounds interesting!" she answered, giving me that cute little smile. "You get me a bear skin and we will just try it and see how it is!"

All right! That bear didn't know it, but he was doomed. His fate was sealed right then!

I had bought a new pair of Donner hiking boots in preparation for the up-coming hunting season. What better way to try out these new hiking boots than to go bear hunting? The next day I came in around noon and turned my horse out. Put on my new hiking boots and told Bettye I was going out to get her a bear skin rug. My dog Cowboy and I loaded up in the old pickup and drove up close to Lovers Leap and looked this big ridge over. Sure seemed bigger and higher now that I was afoot instead of horseback! Ah, but the rewards would sure be worth it, so I slung my .270 rifle over my shoulder and started hiking up this big high ridge.

The new boots felt good as Cowboy and I slowly made our way up the ridge. We climbed steadily for about an hour. As we got nearer to where I had seen the bear the day before I started getting a little excited.

Sure a lot of "What Ifs" start going through your mind! What if I can't find him? What if I miss him? What if he comes after us? What if I just wound him and he gets away? What if . . .

I stayed on the north side of the real deep narrow canyon where I had seen the bear. I stopped and sat down on an old log, figuring out where I should go to find the bear. I had no more than sat down when this big fat bear comes walking out of the brush directly across the canyon from me! My heart jumped up in my throat. I could hardly believe the bear was really right there! He walked over to the Pinon tree he had been digging under yesterday, and started digging around in the soft dirt under the tree. It was the same bear, only he looked bigger now that I was afoot!!

I eased around behind the log, and jacked a shell in my .270. Cowboy had spotted the bear and was really watching him. The hair on the back of his neck and shoulders was sticking straight up as he let out a low growl, staring at the bear. I squeezed off a shot, the bear whirled around, made a roar and a loud growl. He seemed to curl up in a big ball then started rolling down the steep mountain side. He was crashing through the brush and rolling rocks as he tumbled farther and farther down the steep hill. Finally, he came to a stop a good two hundred yards down in the bottom of the deep canyon, out of sight. The oak brush was pretty thick down where I had seen the bear disappear. I couldn't see any movement and all was pretty quite, except for the loud banging my heart was doing against the front of my jacket. Cowboy was crowding up against my leg, whining and growling as he looked down into the bottom of the canyon.

I started easing down, watching the brush where the bear had gone. No movement, but I figured he was waiting in the brush to ambush me when I got closer! What if! What if!! Using an old cowboy trick I had picked up somewhere, I said, "Go get him, Cowboy!" Without a moments hesitation, Cowboy tore off down the canyon and rushed into the brush where the bear had gone. Then I felt a little guilty, sending Cowboy in there after the bear! I rushed down through the brush and rocks. I was scared to go and scared not to! I didn't want Cowboy to get ate by this big bear!

Suddenly, Cowboy went to barking and growling like he was in a sure enough fight! I hollered for him to get back, but I could tell from his growling and barking he wasn't about to give up this fight. As I got closer I could see Cowboy right on top of that big bear. He was flat eating him up!

I rushed up to them, ready to shoot the bear again when Cowboy stopped his bear killing and ran up to me, jumping and wiggling all over. The bear was as dead as he was going to get, and Cowboy was taking full credit! He was one excited Australian Sheppard! I was pretty excited myself as I congratulated Cowboy on his successful bear hunt!

Well, like they say, the fun ends and the hell begins! How you going to get your bear out of this deep canyon I asked Cowboy? He looked at me like to say, I got the bear, you get him out of here! Well, I got the bear by a foot but I saw right quick I couldn't drag him out of that canyon bottom. He was sure a nice big bear.

The canyon was too steep and narrow to get a horse down into and pack the bear out. I thought back to my motivation to come up here on this ridge and get a bear in the first place! It was for a rug! I sure didn't want the meat.

I set about skinning the bear down there in the canyon bottom. Cowboy watched every move I made and stood ready to grab the bear and kill him again if need be. I got the bear skinned in good shape, leaving the head and feet intact. I could hardly pick up the hide! This was one big sucker! I rolled the hide up lengthwise and managed to get it up around my neck and shoulders. Bear's head hanging down past my waist on one side and the hind feet down around my knee on the other. With my rifle slung over my shoulder, I started climbing and crawling up the side of the canyon. About two hundred yards up the canyon side the slope became less steep and I was able to stand and walk upright without doing so much crawling on all fours! I was sure glad there weren't any other hunters around as I crawled up the side of that canyon with that bear hide over my back and draped around my neck!

The sun was fast slipping down toward Trail Peak and I was glad to get out of that canyon before it got dark. I was coming down the last part of the ridge, above the road, as darkness settled down on us. I came out on the road pretty close to the pickup and put my rug in the back and started home. Cowboy jumped in the back of the pickup, keeping a watchful eye on the bear.

I noticed a set of headlights coming up the road toward us as we were driving toward Headquarters. I had told Bettye where I had planned on going bear hunting and figured the lights I saw were probably her, coming to see if I needed any help.

I pulled the pickup over to the side of the road and went to the back and spread my new bear skin rug out in the back of the pickup. Sure enough, it was Bettye coming up looking for me. As she pulled up to my pickup I told her to go on by and turn her car around so the lights would shine in the back of the pickup.

"I got something for you, Honey!" I beamed, trying not to sound too anxious!

"You got to be kidding!" she giggled as she jumped out of the car and ran up to look in the back of the pickup.

"I filled my end of the deal!" I said, "There is your bearskin rug!"

I didn't hold her to the bargain that night.

I sent the bear skin to Jonas Bros. Taxidermy in Denver. They did an excellent job in making a nice bear skin rug. Our bear skin rug sure looked good on the floor at Cattle Headquarters. If you don't have a bear skin rug I would highly recommend that you get one! They are hard to beat for those more amorous occasions!!

The kitchen in our house had a counter that separated the kitchen from the dining room. Had a couple stools at the counter and made a nice coffee drinking spot.

Bettye was in the kitchen fixing supper one evening, and I was sitting at the counter drinking coffee and just visiting about the events of the day. I noticed the bear skin rug on the floor and I got one of those more brilliant ideas I come up with every now and then.

I slipped off the stool and went over to the bear rug. Getting down on my hands and knees I pulled the rug up over my back with the bear head on the back of my head and the legs hanging down over my shoulders.

Crawling on my hands and knees, I crawled around the corner, coming out of the dining room into the kitchen. Giving it my best bear growl and roar I made my entrance into the kitchen!

I damn near got hit in the head with a hot skillet! Bettye screamed like a bear was about to get her and went straight up in the air! I got out from under the bear hide and assured her it was only me! Then I helped her climb down off the top of the refrigerator. She decided maybe the best place for the bear rug was nailed solid to the wall after that. I had sure messed up a good deal for some of those amorous evenings though!

42

Lee

Philmont had leased the Ute Creek Ranch and I was working up there with a couple of cowboys putting in a new set of corrals and a livestock scale. I got an urgent call on the radio that Bettye needed me to get home as soon as possible. Sounded pretty urgent. The girl at the office who had called didn't know what was wrong, but she said Bettye sounded pretty serious.

Well, I couldn't imagine what was so important. I knew Bettye wouldn't have the office call me if she didn't have an emergency, so I jumped in my pickup and headed home, all kinds of things running through my mind as to what could be so important to call me in.

I drove up to the house, no other vehicles around, and I rushed in, to see what was wrong. There stood Bettye with a puzzled, bewildered look on her face, talking to a tall, long-haired, scraggly-looking kid.

"Honey, this is your son, Lee!" Bettye said.

You talk about getting caught off guard and left speechless, that was me! I had known I had a son, but had never seen him, and to suddenly have a young man say "Hi, Dad" just about knocked me over.

Shortly after graduating from high school I had rushed into a marriage with Mary Alice Dulmage, a girl from Colorado Springs. We were a couple of young kids who thought we were in love. We didn't stay married very long, both of us realizing we weren't ready for this kind of commitment. We ended up getting an annulment shortly after the marriage. I went down to New Mexico, punching cows and she moved out to California. We lost track of each other. I had heard she had a baby but never saw her or the baby so guess I kind of put it out of my mind. Mary Alice had called me two or three years before and told me we had a son and he wanted to meet his father. I had told her he would be welcome if he wanted to come out to New Mexico, but I didn't really think he would!

I guarantee it came back to mind in a big hurry when Bettye said "Honey this is your son!!" Here he was for real, eighteen years old.

Little Bob and Myrna were about as shocked as I was when they came home from school and met their half-brother whom they didn't know they had! This was kind of an awkward time in our lives, to say the least.

Bettye took Lee into Cimarron the next day and got him a haircut, cowboy hat and boots, new shirt and Levis. I went to work the next day trying to figure out what I was going to do with this new addition to our family. I took Lee around with me to work and sure got some surprised reactions from people when I introduced Lee to them as my son!

Lee wanted to stay with us, and Little Bob was sure glad to have a brother and they formed a close bond right quick. Myrna wasn't too sure she needed another brother, but she and Lee got along pretty well, too. I was sure proud of Bettye and the kids, the way they took Lee in and made him a part of our family.

Lee hadn't had any experience at hard work or ranch life, being raised in the city. He wanted to get a job and stay on the ranch. So I got him a job on the fence crew, and he pitched right in and made a hand. When we could, we would take him with us horseback. He hadn't ridden before, but was a fast learner and sure liked the riding part of ranch life. He and Little Bob rode a lot together and Lee soon became pretty good help horseback.

Lee stayed with us a little over a year. He learned to work and got enough taste of ranch life living with us that he wanted to continue working on a ranch. When he left Philmont he got a job up in Colorado working for a ranch in South Park. He worked several ranches up in that part of the country and made a good hand wherever he went.

Finding cowboy wages pretty slim, Lee went to work for the railroad. He worked his way up through the ranks to become an engineer. He now has a little place up near Edgemont, South Dakota, where he has some horses, and a little bunch of long horn cows. I'm glad the exposure to ranch life he got with us stayed with him! He has sure made me proud. He has grown into a fine young man with a lovely wife, Chris. Lee and Chris have a lovely daughter, Laura, along with two teenage boys. Laura is sure a sweet addition to my granddaughters.

Lee, Chris and Laura visited us the summer of 1999 and it was sure a good time getting to know his family. I hope to meet the boys this coming summer.

Grandson Lee in front, RC and Bob, sure looks like a happy crew!

Sons RC and Lee with Bob 1999. I'm pretty proud of both of these boys!

43

Larry

Larry Mesaric was a young cowboy who had drifted over to the Cimarron country from Arizona. He went to work for the UU Bar and I got to know him as a sure enough good hand. When his job played out at the UU Bar, Larry came to work with the horse department at Philmont.

Larry had just gotten married to a real sweet girl named Louise from Cimarron. They moved up to Ponil to run the horse string there. Louise liked to ride and would go out on the horseback rides with Larry and the scouts most of the time.

Larry had a horse in his string called Coco, a good looking chestnut, with a strange quirk. He loved to buck and could darn sure do a good job of it. Coco had bucked off about everybody who had tried to ride him. He had a bad reputation.

But Larry figured him out. He would saddle Coco, then tie his bridle reins around his neck and turn him loose with the empty saddle. Coco would put on one of the finest bucking horse exhibitions you could hope to see! Bucking and bawling, really wiping up the corral, Coco would do his thing a couple laps around the corral, then quit and never offer to buck again no matter who rode him! He darn sure had to get it out of his system though and if he didn't get it out with an empty saddle he would sure get you when you tried to ride him!

Louise loved to ride Coco and it was sure funny to watch the reaction from the scouts getting ready for their horseback ride, when Larry would saddle Coco, tell every one to get on the fence out of the way, then turn Coco loose. Coco would buck and bawl, popping the stirrups up over to the seat of the saddle as he put on his show. When he quit bucking Larry would catch him and lead him over to Louise to ride.

"I'm mad at my wife today!" he would say as Louise would climb up on Coco! Coco would just walk off like an old broke saddle horse. He never did buck with Louise.

Larry transferred over to the cattle department after his summer at Ponil, and we worked together several years. He was sure a good cowboy and we became good friends through the years. Larry was in his early twenties and still had a lot of kid in him. He and Li'l Bob became great buddies, keeping me on my toes to keep up with those two! Larry would do about anything needed doing and was always happy go lucky. He was tougher than an old boot, standing about 5'11" weighing in at probably 160 pounds.

A business in Raton was opening a new branch office in Cimarron and for some of their grand-opening celebration they were sponsoring a foot race from Raton to Cimarron, forty-five miles! They were offering a grand prize of $100.00 to the winner; big bucks to a working cowboy. Of course Larry entered this race.

The race favorite was a Golden Glove champion boxer, a local hero from Raton. He was in training for boxing and had gotten a lot of publicity prior to the race. Undaunted by all this newspaper hype, Larry got ready for the big race by buying a pair of tennis shoes. At least he wasn't going to try this race with his boots and spurs on!

The race started in front of the business in Raton, amidst a lot of cameras and a big V.I.P. send off. Of course the boxer took the lead, smiling and waving to the crowd, as a large number of runners followed him out of town, Larry in the pack.

The business had support vehicles that followed the runners, offering drinking water, snacks and picking up the runners that started dropping out after several miles. The boxer took a commanding lead and as the miles clicked off, no one challenged him for the lead.

Larry hung in the race, keeping the boxer in sight as they headed down the long road to Cimarron. The boxer would stop and rest and as Larry would get close to him he would take off again, never relinquishing his lead. More and more runners dropped out, and as they neared Cimarron it was down to Larry and the boxer. Larry just couldn't pass him, although he had tried a couple of times. Finally, as they came into the edge of town, Larry figured he was just going to have to settle for second.

About a half a block from the new business and the finish line stood the old Cimarron movie theater. Large plate glass windows across the front offered a good mirror. The boxer couldn't resist stopping to look at himself and make sure his hair was just right for the cameras waiting for the winner at the finish line.

Larry couldn't believe this boxer had stopped to comb his hair! Not worrying about how pretty he was, Larry gave it all he had and ran past the movie theater as fast as he could manage. The surprised boxer hollered at Larry and took after him as fast as he could run. Too late! Larry beat him across the finish line!

There was a big crowd of the boxer's fans standing at the finish line cheering their hero in and wondering where the hell this cowboy had came from! It was plain that Larry had won the race, but the boxer challenged the finish and ended up taking a swing at Larry, which he quickly returned! The officials broke up the fight and then refused to pay off the $100.00 prize because of unsportsmanlike activity! We all knew Larry had won the race, in spite of what the judges said Larry was still our hero!

◇　　◇　　◇

We had most of our cattle up in the high country for the summer, and Larry had moved up to Bonita Cow Camp looking after the cattle. I had a couple of saddle horses at Bonita and would go up and prowl with Larry two or three times a week.

While riding up Bonita canyon one morning Larry and I came upon a big steer calf that had been killed and about half eaten. Looked like the steer's neck had been broken and it was obvious that a bear had been feeding on the carcass. We wondered if maybe a bear had killed the steer. Or maybe the steer had died from some other cause and the bear was just feeding on the carcass. So we didn't get very concerned.

A few days later Larry found another dead steer, same deal as the first one. Neck broken and about half eaten up. We started getting a little more concerned, especially when the boss wanted to know what the hell was killing these big steers!

One morning Larry came driving his old yellow Army surplus pickup into headquarters about sixty miles an hour.

"It's a bear all right and he killed another one right down by the corrals!" he hollered as he scrambled out of the old yellow pickup.

Larry had ridden up on the old bear just as the bear jumped this big calf and busted the calf's neck. Larry hadn't wasted any time getting in old yeller and heading down off the mountain. He was sure spooked and excited about seeing this big bear.

We talked to the boss and decided we would trap the bear with a leg trap. I went back up to Bonita with Larry and we got the trap set next to the fresh killed steer. I left my old 30-30 rifle with Larry so if he caught the bear in the leg trap that night he would have something to shoot him with.

I rolled out pretty early next morning and headed for Bonita, wondering how the bear trapper had fared. As I drove up to the corrals and the dead steer, I could see the old yellow pickup backed up to the dead steer. No Larry. I walked around behind the pickup and there laid the great big dead bear with one foot still in the trap. I could see a big bullet hole in his shoulder where he had been shot. The tailgate of the pickup was down and the bear was laying behind the pickup. Looked like the bear had been trying to get in the pickup. I looked in the cab of the pickup and there on the seat laid my 30-30. No Larry. Now what the hell, I wondered? Where had Larry taken off to leaving the 30-30 and the bear ready to load?

"Hey Larry!" I hollered.

No answer.

"Hey Larry!" I hollered a little louder.

Nothing. I reached in and honked the horn on old yeller. The sound vibrated through the quite aspens, but still no response from Larry. Our saddle horses came trotting up to the corrals from the adjoining horse pasture. Hearing the horn honking they were all coming in for a little breakfast. They were all present and accounted for so Larry hadn't gone somewhere a horseback.

"HEY LARRY!" I bellowed in my loudest cow calling yell.

Nothing. Just the echo bouncing down the canyon.

I went around and got in my pickup and drove down to the gate going into the horse pasture and headed around the bend up the road to the Bonita Cow Camp. The camp was about a quarter of a mile from the corrals where the bear and old yeller were. A little finger of aspen and blue spruce protruding out into the edge of the meadow kept the view of the camp concealed from the corrals.

As I drove around the edge of the timber and the camp came into view, I thought I saw some movement at the kitchen window. Sure enough, the curtain moved back again and there was Larry peering anxiously out the window.

Now what the hell was he up to, I wondered as I drove up to the camp and started getting out of the pickup. Slowly the door opened and a sheepishly looking Larry stepped out on the porch with a silly grin on his face.

"Did you see the bear any place?" he asked, his voice kinda shaky.

"What's going on?" I answered. "The bear's down at the pickup deader than hell!"

"He is? Dead? At the pickup! You sure?" he sounded pretty doubtful.

"Man yes! You nailed that big bugger!" I answered.

"I did? You sure he is dead?" sounding a little better but still not really convinced.

"Yeah, but what's the matter? You sure look shook up. What are you doing up here at the camp?" I asked.

"Well, I went down to the trap and there was the bear with his foot caught in the trap. I jumped out of old yeller and shot the bear. Man I thought he was dead. I backed yeller up to him to load him and bring him in." Larry was explaining as he puffed on his cigarette. "I laid the 30-30 on the seat of the pickup and I backed up to the bear. I couldn't drag him in so I got astraddle of him and tried to lift him up in to the back of the pickup. When I lifted up on him that's when he started making this funny noise! I thought he had came back to life and started growling!"

Larry was pacing up and down the porch smoking cigarettes as fast as they would burn, as he told me what had happened.

"When that big S.O.B. growled at me, I thought he had me!" Larry was really getting excited now as he lit another cigarette. "I dropped that damn bear and hauled ass up here to the camp. I don't know which way the bear went!" a pale and shaken Larry continued.

"I've been watching out the window for an hour and I haven't seen him any place, you sure he is down there dead?" he asked again.

I was about to bust out laughing by then imagining Larry astraddle this big bear and thinking he had came back to life as the air rushed out of the bear when Larry picked up his shoulders and head and put him down on the tail gate, forcing the air out of the bear. I would liked to have seen Larry hot footing it up the road to the camp thinking that bear was in hot pursuit! Bet he would have outrun that Golden Gloves boxer in that race!

We had a cup of coffee and another cigarette and headed back down to see if the bear was still there. Larry was sure pleased when he peeked around the back of old yeller and saw his big dead bear laying where he had left him!

"Hell, he could have came back to life." Larry said as we got him up in the back of old yeller and headed into headquarters.

I called Littrell on the radio and told him Larry had got the bear that had been killing cattle and that we were on the way in with him. Larry was quite the hero around the office as we drove in with the cattle killing bear. We skipped some of the details in retelling the story. It wasn't near as funny, but what the heck, Larry got himself a big bear and saved some more cattle from getting killed! The bear was an old boar that had lost most of his teeth and had turned to killing cattle and needed to be done away with.

Larry Mesaric with big bear trapped at Bonita, Philmont Scout Ranch

44

Lifeguards/Hunters

July's usual summer rains hadn't shown up yet, as Larry Mesaric, Li'l Bob and I were prowling the cattle on Deer Lake Mesa. We were sure hot and dry. The big, persistent deer flies were about to eat our horses alive as we rode up on the natural lake from which the mesa got its name. The lake had a good deal of water in it, covering several acres. It had a good solid mud bottom in it and cattle could wade out into the water to drink with out bogging down. It was shallow for about thirty feet or so then dropped off into deep water for several hundred yards across. There was an abundance of water grass and moss growing well out in the water.

We had caught and doctored several big calves that were showing signs of pink eye. There was a bunch of cows and calves there at the lake as we rode up. We split up and started easing through the cows looking for pink eye or anything else that might need doctoring. We didn't need much of an excuse to rope some thing! We had been going to Cimarron two or three evenings a week and team roping. Larry and Li'l Bob were all cocked and primed to catch anything, whether it needed doctoring or not!

Li'l Bob and Larry were pretty close to each other, and I noticed them both taking their ropes down so I knew they had found something to rope. I rode back toward them to see if they had found something that needed doctoring. They both got off their horses and began tightening up their cinches. They were grinning like two kids that had found a prize.

"That big heifer sure has a bad eye!" Larry said, unable to keep the pleasure out of his voice.

I saw the big heifer calf he was pointing to, her eye was squinted shut and she needed a little doctoring. He was right and I agreed, as he and Li'l Bob mounted up and shook out their loops.

"You found her so you get first shot" Li'l Bob said, "Turn her back and I'll double hock her!"

Larry built to the heifer and she took off like a spooked deer. Larry made a big circle after her and finally got close enough to throw his loop, which sailed over her head. Li'l Bob was hot on his heels and quickly fell in behind the running heifer. He stood up in his stirrups and threw a pretty horn loop, catching the heifer around the top of the head. Only problem was the heifer didn't have any horns!

Larry laughed with glee as he quickly fell in behind the heifer again. The heifer was getting pretty tired by then and in desperation turned out toward the lake. Larry threw his loop as the heifer got to the edge of the water. His loop fell in the mud.

Larry and Li'l Bob sat there on their horses at the edge of the water watching the heifer swimming out into the lake. They were undecided whether or not to ride in after her. They both had enough kid in them to recognize a good opportunity when they saw one.

"Hell, she's going to drown!" Larry hollered as he turned his horse away from the edge of the water. "Come on Li'l Bob, let's go get her!"

Larry jumped off his horse and started taking his chaps and spurs off. Then came his shirt and Levis! Li'l Bob caught on to what Larry was up to and he quickly started getting his clothes off too! Sure didn't take those two long to get stripped down to their shorts!

"What the hell you two yoyo's doing?" I asked as I rode up and they were headed for the lake.

"That heifer is going to drown if we don't go save her!" Larry exclaimed.

"Oh B.S." I answered, "You two couldn't catch that calf on a bet. Leave her alone and she will swim back out."

"I don't think so," Larry insisted, "we better go save her!"

"Yeah Dad, we better go get her." Li'l Bob joined in.

Well I figured it would be a good opportunity for these two to cool off so I sat back and told them to be careful and not get out too far.

They hit the water laughing, running and jumping like two big pups getting to go play in the water. I had to admit it did look kind of refreshing, as hot as it was that day. The thought even crossed my mind to join them!

Li'l Bob wasn't a very good swimmer. When the water started getting deep he stopped and headed back to shore, leaving the life guard duty to Larry. Larry was a good swimmer and as the water got deeper he swam with a strong stroke in hot pursuit of the heifer. The heifer had turned and was wanting to head back to shore, but when she saw Larry coming after her she turned and started swimming for the opposite shore.

Larry started tiring, finally gave up on saving the heifer and started back to shore where Li'l Bob and I were waiting. He would swim a little ways, try to float, then dog paddle as he headed back. I could see he was getting pretty tired and was trying to float to conserve his energy. Then he went under, disappearing under the murky water. With a lot of splashing he came back up and started hollering.

"Hey Bob!" blub, blub. "Hey Bob!!" cough, blub, sputter.

"Yeah!" I hollered back.

"Hey Bob!" cough sputter, "Maybe you better throw me a rope!" Cough, blub, sputter. I could hear a little panic creeping in his voice as he disappeared under the water again.

I was riding Danny and turned him into the water, as I built a loop in my rope, and headed for where I had last seen Larry. The water was well up on Danny's sides as he splashed out into the lake. Larry suddenly popped up again and I threw my loop at him. It landed just in front of him and he managed to grab it as he was going down again. I turned Danny for the shore and we came out pulling Larry like we were trying to get him up on water skis! I drug him through the mud and up onto the grass. I jumped off Danny and ran to Larry as he was emptying his belly of about twenty gallons of muddy lake water.

He coughed and sputtered, cussing a little. Finally getting his breath he decided he was going to live.

"The damned moss and weeds tangled my legs and I couldn't keep going!" he gasped. "Let me catch my breath and I'll go get that heifer!"

"You just stay here and get your air back!" I told him. He had scared me pretty good when he went under out there in the lake, and I was sure glad to get him up on the grass.

I left Larry and Li'l Bob drying off in the hot sun and rode around to the other side of the lake where the heifer had swam out. I caught and doctored her and went back to my swimmers. They had recovered by then and were laughing and joking about saving the poor little heifer!

◊   ◊   ◊

Philmont's North Ponil Canyon had an abundance of grass, the creek was running good, and it looked like it might be a good winter home for a hundred cows. Larry got the job of taking care of this bunch of cows. There was an old set of corrals at Old Camp with a small horse pasture. Larry kept his saddle horses there and drove back and forth from headquarters two or three times a week.

Bill Littrell was still our boss then and he decided Larry should camp at Old Camp and not be driving back and forth. The cows were calving and needed to be seen every day. Only problem was there wasn't a camp at Old Camp! Just the name! There was a windmill near the corral where Boy Scouts got water in the summer. Larry balked at the idea of staying in a Boy Scout tent!

Philmont had a bunch of Army surplus equipment and vehicles. Among them was a big Army ambulance, with a big red cross painted on the side. Bill came up with the bright idea of taking the back of this ambulance off the truck bed it was mounted on and making it into a cow camp for Larry!

It was a big metal box about eight by ten feet and the top was about six foot high. Being a true optimist, Larry figured it would be easy to keep warm and didn't have much floor space to sweep!

We hauled the ambulance box up to Old Camp and got it set up near the windmill. Put in a little stove, a couple of folding bunk beds along one wall, a little table, one chair, and Larry was fixed up! Pretty close quarters but Larry wasn't too hard to please. He soon had the little box fixed up and made livable.

The cows had wintered good and Larry had moved them into North Ponil Canyon, between Old Camp and Indian Writings.

Larry's old yeller Ford pickup didn't have four wheel drive, but as fast as Larry drove, he just hit the high spots and didn't get stuck very often!

One morning, I thought a tornado was coming down the road headed for cattle headquarters, but as it slid around the corner on two wheels, I saw it was Larry and his yellow pickup. He jumped out, grinning all over, making it hard to chew him out for driving so damn fast.

"What's the big hurry!?" I asked trying to look like a boss and not be taken in by his grin and obvious pleasure at just being alive.

"Boy we really got trouble at Old Camp!" Larry exclaimed. "There's a big hound dog up there killing all my calves!"

I had a quick flashback to the bear trapping incident at Bonita the summer before!

After a couple cups of coffee, I finally got Larry settled down enough to tell me what was going on. Seems a stray hound dog had moved in near Old Camp and had been chasing some newborn calves, killing one. Larry had seen the dog chasing calves but had not been able to catch him. He had tried feeding the dog so that he might catch him, but the hound wouldn't let him get close. Larry had a good description; big black and tan, long-eared hound. Had a leather collar around his neck with some tags on it.

I gave Larry my old 30-30 and told him that if he saw the hound chasing calves again to shoot him. I called several hunters and guides I knew who had hound dogs, trying to find the dog's owner. No one was short a dog and my efforts didn't turn up anyone who claimed this renegade hound dog.

Early the next morning, there wasn't any question whether it was a tornado or Larry coming down the road! A tornado didn't travel that fast! In a big cloud of dust, Larry jumped out of Old Yeller.

"He did it again! Killed another calf last night! I found him with blood all over him, eating my calf!" Larry yelled, really worked up.

Took a little more coffee this time to settle him down. The hound had killed another calf on the feed ground below Old Camp. When Larry drove up, the hound ran off up into the timber and brush, and Larry hadn't got a shot at him. He had hunted around the area, looking for the hound, but hadn't seen him again.

Li'l Bob heard Larry and me talking about this hound dog and he sure wanted to go up and help Larry get this calf killer. Larry said he would pick Li'l Bob up after school that evening, and he could go up and spend the weekend with Larry at Old Camp.

They figured to sit in Old Yeller on the feed ground that night and when the hound dog came up they would jump out and shoot him. Knowing these two, I had a few doubts about this plan.

"What could go wrong with a fool-proof plan like this?" they both asked me.

"Well, other than you shooting each other, a couple cows and a calf, I guess not much!" I replied.

So the plan was set in motion. Larry picked Li'l Bob up after school and in a cloud of dust they headed for Old Camp. I had the feeling I could hear them laughing above the roar of Old Yeller as they took off down the road.

They got into Old Camp that evening and cooked up a little supper, making plans for the night and how they were going to get that hound dog. Darkness settled pretty early into North Ponil Canyon.

Some snow drifts were scattered around the frozen feed ground. The temperature dropped well below freezing when the sun disappeared. With a little wind blowing, it was a lovely night to sit in Old Yeller with the windows rolled down, the motor turned off, no heater, just waiting for this killer dog!

The only sound was the wind hurrying by and the chattering of teeth as the two fearless hunters waited for their quarry. Couldn't talk above a low whisper because the hound had real good ears, and he would hear them and not show up. The comforting 30-30 was loaded and ready, barrel pointed down at the floor and the stock sticking up between the hunters. Larry was sitting behind the steering wheel. Li'l Bob, with his eagle eye, in the passenger seat. They both were peering out into the moonless black night, trying desperately to see the phantom killer sneaking into the feed ground.

Cows and calves bedded down nearby, all quiet. A couple old smelly saddle blankets the boys had retrieved from the back of the pickup were pulled up under their chins. Even the old stiff saddle blankets didn't seem to help the shivering much, as they stared out into the darkness. Around midnight it was sure getting hard to stay awake. A good sign of when you are freezing to death is when you can't stay awake so they figured they were getting close to the end of the trail!

As the big hound walked up to the yellow pickup, he could hear a strange chattering sound coming out of the cab. Curious as to what was making this chattering sound, he walked up to the driver's side, stood up on his hind legs and stuck his head in the open window.

As is normal for this breed of dog, he was kind of panting with his mouth open. The chattering sound was coming from under the cowboy hat right there in front of the hound's nose! He leaned in closer to get a smell.

When the hound's hot breath hit Larry on the neck, he awoke in time to see this huge head just inches away from his chattering teeth! With a scream that would scare the devil himself, Larry exploded out of the driver's seat and made a head-first dive for the open window on the passenger side. Li'l Bob liked to crapped his britches when this blood curdling scream jarred him out of his nearly frozen slumber. Not waiting to see what had got his partner, he jerked the door handle back, opening the door to escape. As Larry dove at the open window the door swung open and Larry's head and shoulders made it out the window with rest of him falling into Li'l Bob's lap.

In the dark Li'l Bob couldn't tell for sure what was happening, but he knew from the way Larry was hollering, something had him and was fixing to get him, too.

Fighting his way out from under the discarded saddle blankets and Larry's kicking legs, Li'l Bob finally managed to dive head first out the open door. As he landed on his head on the frozen ground, a yelling Larry fell back out of the open window, landing on top of a struggling Li'l Bob. They were both rolling around in the darkness on the frozen ground, kicking and punching, trying to get away from whatever it was that was about to get them. Before either one got seriously hurt they figured out they were struggling with each other.

Larry jumped up and grabbed the 30-30, which had gotten knocked down to the floor of the pickup. Jacking a shell into the chamber Larry cautiously eased around the pickup. No hound dog in sight. Just to make him feel better Larry fired a couple rounds up into the cold dark sky.

"Bet that will keep him away!" Larry said, "Let's get the hell out of here!"

They headed back to camp to build a fire and try to warm up and compare notes as to just what had happened.

Guess the hound dog figured that it was too dangerous for him, some thing might fall out of that yeller pickup and hurt him. So he headed out for another hunting ground. He was never seen in North Ponil again! Li'l Bob and Larry had some strange scrapes and bruises when they came down from Old Camp and it was a while later before they were willing to talk much about their night hunting the hound dog.

Best I could tell they hadn't killed any cows or calves, and Old Yeller didn't seem to have any new holes in it. Li'l Bob and Larry were both all right, and the hound dog had left, so I figured they had done a good job!

45

Taos

Li'l Bob and Myrna were in high school and thinking about maybe going to college. Working for Phimont, at that time, sure wasn't very profitable for a cow foreman. The thought of putting two kids in college on my wages was a little scary!

Bettye's brother Fred was working in the bank in Springer and while we were visiting with him about how broke we were and the kids talking college, he told us about a business opportunity open in Taos that we might be interested in. Fred's friend, Pat Marker from Springer, had a big motel, bar and restaurant in Taos and he was wanting to lease the bar and restaurant to someone. With Bettye's experience waiting on tables in restaurants and my experience in bars, it looked like it might be a good opportunity to make more money than by cowboying. One little problem with this business venture was all my experience in bars had been on the wrong side of the bar, I really didn't know anything about the business!

We went up to Taos and met Pat Marker and his wife, a real nice elderly couple. They showed us all around the place, went over the books, told us all about how easy it was to make a lot of money. Bettye and I agreed we ought to give it a try, so we signed a two-year lease on the bar, restaurant and package liquor store. Boy! What an education these two old country kids did get in those two long years!

Bill Littrell asked me to stay with Philmont until the spring branding was finished and I agreed. Bettye and Myrna moved to Taos and took over the Indian Hills Restaurant, bar and package liquor store. Li'l Bob stayed with me and helped through the branding. This was a pretty tough time for Bettye, taking on this big job alone and I was sure anxious to get up to Taos to help her.

I was about as handy as nothing when I arrived to help Bettye. We had a bartender, Joe, who had been there quite awhile. He worked nights so

I took the bar in the afternoons learning the business of bartending, then helped Joe at night.

One afternoon while I was bartending alone, a customer came in cussing a blue streak. Seems his car had broken down across the street and he couldn't get it started. Telling me all about his car not starting, he asked me for a screw driver. Being the old helpful bartender, I pulled a catch-all drawer open and searched around for a screwdriver!

"Don't seem to have a screwdriver, would a pair of pliers or crescent wrench help you?" I asked.

He looked at me like I was some kind of a nut.

"What the hell are you talking about?" he asked. "I just want a drink! Can you fix me a screwdriver or not!?"

I had a lot to learn about being a bartender! I did pretty good if no one was in the bar, washing and polishing glasses just like Joe did. But when people started coming in, I felt like an old wild cow that had been corralled for the first time! Just looking for a hole to duck into and get out of there!

I finally got over being so shy about people. Made some pretty classic mistakes, but with the help of my little bartender's guide book on mixing drinks, I got to where I was running the bar at night, when Joe quit and moved on.

Bettye sure had her hands full trying to keep the kitchen staff and waitresses lined out. Myrna hated being penned about as much as I did, but she soon began to enjoy the tips she was making waiting tables. She sure made a good waitress.

It was pretty tough for Li'l Bob, but he pitched in washing dishes, throwing trash and was our number one gopher! He helped with the cooking and anything else we needed him to do. We all missed the quiet life we had known on the ranch, but the allure of getting rich kept us plugging away, making the best of our situation.

We had brought a couple of horses over to Taos from Cimarron, renting a little pasture for them. A rodeo came up in Questa, around twenty-five miles from Taos. Li'l Bob and I got to sneak out for the day and go to the rodeo. We entered the team roping and got lucky and won it. We were feeling pretty good about winning the roping.

I got back to Taos that evening, changed clothes, put on my white shirt and necktie, and started bartending. Some of the cowboys who had been to the Questa rodeo came in and were having a few drinks. I over heard one of them talking about the team roping. Seemed a couple sure enough toughs from Cimarron had came up to Questa and won their roping. They were sure upset about these toughs and thought they might try and keep them from coming back to Questa! I just kept polishing glasses and put on my best bartender smile. They never did recognize me. Li'l Bob and I sure got a good chuckle out of that. We had never been classified as "toughs" before!

One of my frequent bar patrons was Poncho, an active member of the Taos County Sheriff's Posse. The Taos rodeo was coming up soon and Poncho was telling me about how the Sheriff's Posse rode in the rodeo parade.

"Have you ever ridden a horse?" Poncho asked me one evening.

I kinda hesitated and said, "Yes, a little I guess," not knowing just how to answer this question.

"I could give you some free riding lessons and maybe you could learn enough to ride with us in the parade," Poncho said.

Not knowing how to get out of this very gracefully, I told him I appreciated his offer but didn't think I would have time to get away from the bar to take riding lessons!

The Sheriffs Posse made their grand ride in the parade without me. Li'l Bob and I got in the team roping, placing second. Poncho came up to me at the rodeo, about half mad.

"Why didn't you tell me you were a cowboy? Trying to make me a fool!?" he exclaimed.

"No Poncho, you asked me if I had ridden before and I told you yes, a little, that was no lie, I've ridden a little!" I replied.

He had to laugh then and said he was glad he didn't have to give me riding lessons. We went on to become pretty good friends while I was in Taos.

We leased a ten-acre tract from Hugh Littrell, (Bill's father). Had a nice big house, barn and good pasture. I bought ten head of roping steers and life became a little more bearable! Got a small roping club started, and Bettye found it pretty hard to keep me corralled at the bar and restaurant. I helped the Sheriff's Posse build a new rodeo arena and we sure had a good place to rope.

I had a good friend, Gary Rickman, who was the game warden in

Taos. Bettye liked Gary, but she wasn't too happy when he showed up because she knew I was fixing to slip out again! Gary came by the bar and drank coffee with me pretty regularly. He always seemed to be going somewhere I hadn't been and welcomed my riding around with him. I sure enjoyed getting out and seeing some new country and getting some fresh air with Gary. He filled in as bartender a few times when I needed extra help, and was sure a good bouncer when we had a dance! I wasn't much of a fighter, but the way the booze would change customers' attitudes I found myself in several scrapes. Bettye sure made a hand at riot control!

I was sitting in the restaurant, grabbing a quick bite to eat one evening, as "Happy Hour" had just ended and the crowd had thinned out.

There was an arched, open entrance between the bar and restaurant. Bettye was tending bar for me. A fight broke out at the bar. One guy grabbed up one of the bar stools, fixing to hit another guy over the head with it. Bettye grabbed a black jack I kept behind the bar, and came around the end of the bar, to join in the festivities.

Lifting a bar stool over his head, the fighter swung the stool at the other guy, but the long stool hit the vega in the ceiling, and he dropped it. As he reached for another bar stool Bettye lowered the boom on him. Holding the blackjack in both hands, she hit him across the arm as he grabbed for the bar stool, making a nice clean break in his wrist! Needless to say he dropped the stool! Cussing and crying, he cradled his broken arm to his chest as his friends rushed him out the door, heading for the hospital. I came charging in to help Bettye.

"Go finish your supper, Honey!" she smiled sweetly at me. "Everything is fine in here!"

You just don't mess with this little cowgirl!

◊   ◊   ◊

Bettye and I bought a nice home on the outskirts of Taos and had a good five acres for a horse pasture. The five acres was fenced around the outside perimeter, with the house setting inside the fenced area.

There was a hippie colony up the road a mile or so from our place and it was pretty common to see the hippie vans going up and down the road.

One night, after I came home from closing the bar, around 1:30 in the morning, Bettye and I were sitting in our living room talking. All the lights were off, except for a small lamp near the couch. No TV or radio going, just a quiet time that we were enjoying together. Li'l Bob and Myrna were both gone for the night, so we were alone.

As we sat there in the near dark, talking, we heard a noise; sounded like glass cracking and breaking. We stopped talking and peered down the hall, toward Myrna's room, where it sounded like the noise had came from. Crack!, crash, the sound of falling glass was clearly coming from Myrna's room. I figured some hippies were breaking into the back bedroom.

I got up and hurried into the room where I had my gun case. I could hear the sound of more breaking glass and a soft brushing sound. I grabbed my 30:06 out of the gun case and loaded a shell, ready to confront these hippies breaking into the house! I eased out into the hall and started toward Myrna's room. Bettye was setting on the couch, wide-eyed, with her hand over her mouth, fearing what I was getting into.

As I tiptoed down the hall the brushing sound was louder, combined with more breaking glass. I could picture someone brushing the broken glass off the window sill as they crawled in through the broken window.

Reaching into the dark bedroom, I flipped the light switch on ready to go to war.

"You big black S.O.B.!" I hollered, with the 30:06 up to my shoulder.

When she heard me holler, Bettye screamed, expecting to hear the 30:06 start talking. The big black S.O.B. was "Crow" my big black rope horse! He was rubbing his rear end up against the house and had got over a little too far and pushed the bedroom window in! The brushing sound was his butt rubbing on the window sill! I damn near shot him anyway! Boy he did give us a good scare and a pretty good laugh after we got our blood pressures back down!

◊　　◊　　◊

Bettye had to have the restaurant open at six each morning, seven days a week, and I was bartending until 1:30 or 2:00 in the morning. We weren't exactly having much of a life together! The restaurant crowd Bettye knew were completely different people than those I knew from the bar, so we didn't have much going on in common.

Li'l Bob excelled in sports, becoming the second athlete in school history to receive a varsity letter in five major sports, football, track, basketball, baseball, and wrestling. We were sure proud of him.

Myrna did well in school, but this was a tough environment for pretty blondes! Taos has a big Fiesta, where they select a young lady from each of three ethnic groups, Spanish, Indian, and Anglo, to reign over the celebration and festivities, as princesses. Myrna won the honor as Anglo princess. Myrna too, had sure made us proud and made a lovely princess! Of course old Dad thought she was the prettiest!

Li'l Bob and his girl friend, Trudy Valerio, told us they were going to get married. Well of course I threw a hissy fit, kinda like Fred had done when I told him Bettye and I were going to get married. My fit did about as much good as Fred's had done. Li'l Bob and Trudy got married while both seniors in high school. They graduated together and decided to move to Phoenix, where he was going to enroll in a electronics school. They left with Bettye and my blessings, and moved to Arizona.

Bill and Billie Littrell would come by to visit and have dinner with us about once a month, so I kept informed as to what was going on at Philmont. On one of their visits, Bill told me that Philmont wanted to incorporate the horse and cattle departments into one unit. He offered me the job as livestock superintendent, to help implement this new plan. The job sounded good to me, I was ready to get out of Taos.

Our lease was nearly expired and we had to decide whether to renew it or not. Didn't take long to make that decision! Bettye, Myrna and I packed up and headed back to Philmont. Cowboy wages weren't so bad after all! We found there was a lot more to life than money!

Myrna, Princess of Taos Fiesta 1970

Myrna with Princess Court, Taos Fiesta 1970

46

New Job

Putting the cattle and horse departments together was a smooth merger. Boss Sanchez and Leo Martinez were still the men running the horse department. We had been friends for several years and worked well together combining the two departments. Larry Mesaric had been running the cattle department while I was in Taos, and he had decided to move back to Arizona.

I found myself in a completely new role. Instead of being one of the cowboys or horsemen, I was suddenly the guy who was doing the hiring and firing!

Looking through the big stack of applications for wrangler and horsemen, it seemed that everyone wanted to be a wrangler, and darn few had the least bit of experience around horses! Some of the more experienced had ridden a horse once on their grandpa's farm!

We couldn't ask for a picture of the applicant nor could we ask height, weight, nationality. For all I knew I could be hiring a guy that was eight feet tall and weighted 350 pounds! We didn't have a horse on the ranch that could pack him around! Fortunately I never hired one who was physically unable to do the job as a wrangler.

Boss and I picked through the stack of applicants and hoped we could live with what we had chosen. We sure got some dandies once in a while, but most of the kids we hired made the grade and we didn't have to send very many home early.

Boss was good at giving these green kids a two-week crash course in horseshoeing, saddling, and riding and caring for the horses. We usually had two or three boys coming back that had a year or so experience and were capable of taking on the responsibilities of horseman. They were a lot of help in teaching the new kids the ropes.

♦   ♦   ♦

Leo Martinez was sure a good hand and a pleasure to work with. He had worked for the government when they were trying to eradicate the outbreak of hoof and mouth disease that was threatening to come into the country from Mexico. He could sure tell you some hair raising experiences of riding down in Mexico on that job!

The adult training center at Philmont offered a horseback ride for the smaller kids who weren't old enough to go out on the trail as explorer scouts. They rode out of Headquarters, making a big circle up on the side of Urraca Mesa, then back across the open, flat Bull pasture, on into headquarters.

Leo, along with two wranglers, had about thirty-five of these little riders out one afternoon, when a real bad thunderstorm came rolling in off the mountains. They were about half way across the Bull pasture, not a tree or bush anywhere around, when the hard rain turned into good sized hail.

Leo knew the little kids couldn't handle their horses as the hail began beating down. He had them ride around in a tight circle and all the kids jump off their horse's and hold on to their bridle reins. Leo and the wranglers quickly ran to each horse, jerked the saddle off and gave the frightened rider his saddle pad. They slipped the bridles off and turned the horses loose. The kids layed down and curled up under their saddle pads as the hail stones became bigger. The loose horses stampeded off toward headquarters.

When this bunch of loose horses suddenly came running into the corrals at headquarters in the hard driving hail storm, we knew Leo needed help right quick! Boss and I jumped in our pickups and headed up toward the Bull pasture and Uracca Mesa. As we turned up the road going through the Bull pasture, we could see someone out in the middle of the pasture.

We drove up to Leo and his clumps of wet, scared, crying little kids, who were all huddled under their saddle pads, shivering and cold. About four inches of hail covered the ground. We called in to headquarters for some transportation for these kids and started loading saddles in our pickups. Thanks to Leo's quick thinking, none of the kids were hurt. They did get a little scared and got a good soaking though.

Leo transferred from the horse department to become the head of

Philmont security. We missed him in the livestock department, but he was still around to shoot the breeze with occasionally.

◊　　◊　　◊

The cavalcade's had been dropped by the Philmont camping department by the time I came back and got involved in the horse department. I visited with Lloyd Knutson, director of camping and Bill Littrell, ranch manager, about what a good program it had been. They weren't very excited about it, but I kept talking it up. Finally they agreed to let me present it to the Ranch Committee, Philmont's governing body. They were pretty supportive of the idea of offering a ten-day horseback trip around Philmont, so the cavalcade came back into being.

The next summer, after buying a good number of horses, gear, and hiring more wranglers, figuring out the itinerary for the trip, etc., I figured we were ready to launch my new idea.

When the first cavalcade was preparing to leave headquarters, I was right in the middle of everything, making sure my new idea went off smoothly. I knew a lot of people were waiting for the results and I sure wanted this cavalcade to be a success.

The pack horses were packed, the kids were all mounted, and ready to go, with a hand-picked crew to take them out. They left headquarters, crossed the road and headed for the trail around the end of Tooth of Time Ridge.

I drove out on the road and watched from my pickup as they rode off toward the ridge. The trail skirted around the end of the ridge, winding by large oak brush thickets, which were favorite places for deer to lay up during the day.

I pulled off to the side of the road, where I could see the long line of riders across the field. I was feeling pretty good as I watched my bright idea becoming a reality.

The horseman, leading one pack horse, was in the lead as they rode by a large stand of oak brush beside the trail. Suddenly the fourth horse back in the line spooked out of line, downed his head and went to bucking, sending his rider off into the wild blue yonder. The next horse spooked and broke into a runaway, his rider falling off. The next horse back took off bucking after his partner, the rider hanging on for dear life, riding him about three jumps before hitting the dirt. Two more horses took off running, their riders falling off, as I sat there wondering if I was having a bad nightmare!

Seemed like every horse over there was either bucking or running off! Best I could tell we had four or five riders on the ground. The loose horses, along with those that still had a rider, were balled up in a milling throng in the corner of the fence down below the trail. The horseman and wranglers were trying to keep the spooked horses in the corner.

I left a nice black donut on the pavement as I peeled out and headed to the nearest gate to get over to the scene of the wreck. The horseman and wranglers had the horses and riders pretty well calmed down by the time I got over there.

I drove up to one of the kids who was sitting on the ground holding his arm and crying. I loaded him in my pickup and went on down to check the others. No one else was hurt very badly, just a little shaken up and scared.

Seems a little bunch of deer had picked that spot of oak brush, along side the trail to take their siesta in. As the string of saddle horses and laughing riders came by the deer couldn't stand all that company and jumped up, spooking the horses as they went by, causing a mini stampede!

After we got everyone calmed down, they all wanted to continue. We got all the riders mounted again and they started on down the trail. I took the little injured rider over to the Health Lodge, where it was quickly determined he had broken his wrist in his fall from his horse. They loaded him up in the ambulance and took him to Raton to get the broken wrist set.

Knutson heard about the big wreck and came rushing into the Health Lodge as the ambulance was leaving. I gave him the details of what had happened.

"That's just great, Knox! You got any more bright ideas?"

Guess I hadn't impressed Knutson with this new program!

I went over to see my little injured rider that afternoon, when he came back from the hospital. He had a nice new cast and was in good spirits. I felt bad about him getting hurt so I offered to take him with me to Clarks Fork where the Cavalcade was spending their first night. He wanted to go and the doctor said it would be all right, so we went up to have supper with his crew.

He was welcomed like a wounded war hero and got all the crews' signatures on his cast. He had a great time.

I wanted to keep in close contact with the horseman on this first cavalcade, so every afternoon I went by the Health Lodge to pick up my new friend, and we went out to have supper with the cavalcade and sit in on the campfire program at each camp.

"This is great, Mr. Knox! I get to be with my crew for supper every night, go to all the campfires and best of all I don't have to ride that dumb old horse!" he told me one evening, as we were headed back to the Health Lodge.

The cavalcade program went on to be one of the most popular programs offered and we didn't have any more casualties.

◊   ◊   ◊

I had approached Littrell with the idea of building a roping arena at cattle headquarters. Bill said no way could he justify building an arena on Philmont. Ben Vargas, Boss and myself had gotten bitten by the roping bug and we were hauling our horses into the rodeo grounds at Cimarron a couple times a week to rope.

With the success of the cavalcade program, I used a little different approach on Littrell. I explained to Bill that the kids needed a place to have a little fun on horseback. They were all ready for a chance to try out their newly learned skills of horseback riding. After riding mostly single file over the Philmont trails, they were ready to get a little faster!

Bill listened to my sales pitch, as I explained how we could always use the extra corral space, as a good place for the wranglers to ride the dude horses before the scouts rode them. The horse department had been moved down to cattle headquarters. The big new corral could be well utilized by the combined livestock operation. Bill was sold on the idea.

We got Ed Mondragon, the farm boss and a good blade operator, to level off a large piece of ground adjoining the back corral at headquarters. The fence crew helped us put up a good stout fence and we had a pretty good place for the cavalcade riders to have their barrel races, pole bending, and other games horseback. It just happened to be the right size for a roping arena!

Having got the ground work laid, I went to work on Littrell, again, explaining what a good idea this was to put in roping boxes, chute and return alley. Might be able to work it into the Cavalcade program? All we needed was a few steers and I just happened to know where we could buy some real cheap! Almost guaranteed to make money!

"Knox, you should have been a politician, the way you manage to work things around!" Bill said, as he finally approved our grandiose plans.

The new arena was sure worthwhile, affording the cavalcade riders an excellent place to try out their new skills a horseback. We had two caval-cades out on the trail at the same time and on their final day they came into headquarters together. This afforded some pretty intensive competition be-tween the two groups. They all had a lot of fun and some of them were handling their horses pretty well.

The summer wranglers had a good place to ride all the horses, and tuneup their skills, while working the kinks out of some of the dude horses. Of course the cowboys working full time thought they had died and gone to heaven! An arena in their backyard with plenty steers to rope! Did it get any better than this?

Several young men who got their start in this arena went on to be-come sure enough tough ropers. Ben Vargas and his son Shawn, Rod Tay-lor, Leo Martinez, and Chuck Enloe just to mention a few, come to mind as good ropers that got most of their practice and skills in this arena.

Most of the wranglers wanted to rope, but seldom did we find one who was ready to ride a horse well enough, let alone rope a steer. They had to put in a lot of time on the roping dummy before we let them get horse-back. Finding gentle horses that these kids could ride and rope off of was a trick in it's self.

◊   ◊   ◊

As the new wranglers were checking in at headquarters, we looked them over pretty close. You can tell a lot about a fellow by his hat and boots. One young man showed a little promise as he picked out a bunk in the remodeled bunkhouse. His boots were pretty scuffed and his hat wasn't brand new, it had a good sweat stain that you don't buy in a store.

He introduced himself as Jim Taylor. I had his name on the list of new wranglers so I checked him in. This new wrangler pulled a well-used rope out of his bag and stepped up to our roping dummy. He shook out a loop and stuck it on those horns like he knew what he was doing.

It was late afternoon and Ben and I were getting ready to rope a little.

"We are fixing to run a few, like to join us?" I asked Jim.

"Don't know of anything I'd rather do!" Jim answered.

We mounted Jim on a pretty good horse and he sure showed us this wasn't his first time to back up in the box! He was a good roper, handled a horse real well. I wondered how I had gotten lucky to pull his name out of that big stack of applications!

A big part of the first two weeks for the new wranglers was spent learning to shoe horses. Hard work, anyway you cut it. Since Jim was a pretty fair horseshoer he was getting more than his share of a pretty good work out.

I started pulling Jim out of the horseshoeing pen and taking him with me to help me doctor some cows and calves with bad eyes we had in the pasture below headquarters. Jim sure didn't complain about this extra duty as he would sure rather rope and doctor cattle than shoe horses! He was sure good help and we had some good times roping together.

We sent Jim up to Beaubien for the summer, and on his days off you were sure to find him around the arena ready to rope.

The health lodge called one evening (they never called with good news) saying they had a wrangler from Beaubien in the ambulance on the way down. They didn't know who it was or what was wrong.

I finished supper right quick and headed over to the health lodge, wondering. Who? What? and How bad?

The ambulance was backed up to the door as I drove up and I hurried inside. Looking in the emergency room I saw Jim lying on the examination table, looking like he had been run over by a truck!

He wasn't very talkative as the doctor finished up his examination. He didn't appear to have anything broken but the doctor thought he ought to go into Raton for some X-rays.

I finally got the story out of him. Seems the cavalcade had come into Beaubien that afternoon. They had a spotted mule, Pepper, they were packing. He was a little spooky and during the conversation with the cavalcade wranglers something was said about betting on whether anyone could ride

Pepper. The bets were placed and Jim was the designated rider. He got his saddle on Pepper and stepped on. Pepper was a pretty good pack mule, but no one had ever tried to ride him. He sure didn't want anyone getting the idea he was broke to ride!

Pepper got pretty high as he bucked across the corral, giving Jim about all he could handle. Pepper was bucking toward the pole corral fence and he tried to jump it. He managed to get almost over the top pole, but came crashing down on his side, with Jim under him and the broken poles. Pepper came out of the wreck in better shape than Jim!

Jim's X-rays showed no broken bones. He had a badly bruised leg and some pretty sore cracked ribs, but not bad enough to keep him from roping with us on his next day off! I never knew who won the bet!

47

Wrangler Tricks

One of the programs offered to the campers at Clarks Fork was black powder rifle shooting. A couple staff members well trained in black powder shooting and safety showed the campers how the old muzzle loaded rifles were loaded and fired. The staff put on a good demonstration loaded the muzzle loaders, and let the campers shoot at targets with the old black powder rifles.

We also had a string of saddle horses at Clarks Fork. A horseman and three wranglers that took out two rides a day. One of these wranglers decided to celebrate the Fourth of July in grand style by making his own special firecracker. He got into the black powder used for the muzzle loaders and wrapped some powder in paper, folding and sealing it pretty tight. He left a short piece of string sticking out of one end to light.

I learned of his smart trick when the health lodge called me, telling me they had brought a wrangler in with bad burns on his hands.

I went over to the health lodge to see how bad the situation was. One of the wrangler's hands was burned pretty badly, seems his fuse was too short, and his firecracker had gone off before he could throw it. He was lucky he hadn't lost a finger or two. I gave him a pretty good lecture and no sympathy as I took him back to Clark's Fork. The horseman there figured he could find something for the wrangler to do even with his heavily bandaged hands. I gave all the wranglers a good pep talk about making fire crackers with the black powder!

About a week later I got an urgent call from Clarks Fork to come up there ASAP!

I happened to be near by and drove on up to the camp to see what opportunity awaited me there! Better not be another firecracker, I thought.

Several staff members were standing outside the cabin door that went into the kitchen. Black smoke was slowly drifting out of the open door. My firecracker wrangler was standing there with the other staff. I noticed he didn't have his hat on and he looked rather pale. He was really looking hard at his scuffed boots, not looking up at me, as I approached the smoking cabin.

"Now what the hell did you do?" I asked the wrangler.

"He blew up our stove!" the camp director exclaimed, more than a little excited.

As the smoke had cleared out enough so we could see some of the damage, we walked into the kitchen. The wood-burning cook stove sitting there had an odd shape to one side of it. Looked like a pot bellied cook stove! The left side was rounded and stretched out of shape. The back of the stove had a big bulge in it. The oven door was against the wall across the room. All the lids were gone from the top of the stove, and were scattered around on the kitchen floor. The stovepipe was lying on the floor behind the stove. The ceiling of the kitchen had several big black holes in it where the flying stove lids had tried to escape and the smell of gunpowder was pretty strong in that smoky kitchen.

I stepped to the door and not very ceremoniously I hollered at my bandaged wrangler to get his $#@^%*!$&& in there right now!!!

"You got any ideas about what happened here?" I asked. Well . . . seems the horseman sent him down to the camp to see if he could help the staff there. With his burned hands he wasn't much help to the horseman and wranglers. The camp director told him to go into the kitchen and get a fire going in the stove so they could warm up the coffee and get ready to cook their evening meal. It had been raining and their firewood was pretty wet making it hard to get a fire going. After several futile attempts at getting the fire started, this super smart wrangler remembered the black powder! He remembered my telling him not to make any more firecrackers. Following my instructions, he didn't make a firecracker, he just took a can of black powder and poured it all over the wet wood in the firebox of the stove!

Putting the lids back on the stove, he closed the small door in the front of the firebox, slid the small damper control on the side of the stove open and struck a kitchen match. As the match flamed to life he stuck it in the small air hole.

The ample amount of back powder blew up, sending the stove lids almost through the ceiling and stretching the stove into a new shape. Again the wrangler was lucky! He didn't get hurt in the explosion or start the cabin on fire! At this point I figured I had better do something with this young man before he burned or blew Philmont up so I sent him home a little early.

◇　　◇　　◇

That same summer, Uncle Bob had been packing the mule string at Crater Lake. Philmont had put a bunch of burros at Crater Lake for the campers to pack as they hiked into the back country. We had a bunch of burros at Abreu also. Campers could pick up their burros at Crater Lake and leave them at Abreu, when they finished their trek, or vice versa.

One of the summer staff was the burro wrangler, whose job was to give the campers instructions on how to pack their burros. This wrangler sure wanted to learn how to rope, and had bought a rope. Bob was a good teacher and before long the wrangler could rope a post and started roping burros in the corral. The used rope he had bought had a horn knot tied in the end of it. Bob had cautioned him not to put the horn loop on his saddle horn because he could sure get in a storm.

One afternoon the burro wrangler saddled a gentle horse, tied his new rope on his saddle and went over to Abreu. He had called Abreu on the radio and told them he would be there that afternoon. It was about an hour's ride over to Abreu.

The trail to Abreu wound around through thick, tall, stands of oak brush. Lots of scattered pine, pinon and cedar trees were along the winding trail as it wandered around for about three miles through the Crater Lake horse pasture. All the loose burros, pack mules, and saddle horses were turned out in this pasture. Various sized malpai rocks were scattered all through the grassy openings between the oak brush and trees.

Several hours later, Abreu called Crater Lake on the two-way radio, asking if the wrangler had changed his plans, as he hadn't arrived there yet. Bob was a little concerned, so he saddled his horse and headed out through the horse pasture to see if he could find any sign of him.

Bob rode up on the loose saddle horses in a small grassy opening and saw the missing wrangler's saddled horse, grazing with the other horses. Bob noticed the wrangler's rope was missing. Catching the wrangler's horse, Bob led him along, as he rode on looking for the burro wrangler.

A little further along the trail, Bob saw someone afoot who appeared to be wandering around, seemingly confused and disoriented. Riding up to him, Bob saw it was the missing wrangler. He had a big knot on his forehead, his face was skinned up and pretty bloody. His shirt was torn down the front, and he had lost his hat.

"What the hell happened to you?" Bob asked as he rode up to the wounded warrior.

"I guess I got knocked out! I don't remember very much," the confused wrangler answered.

Bob got off his horse and went to the wrangler's horse where a boy scout canteen of water was hanging from the saddle horn. Giving the wrangler a drink and splashing a little water in the kid's face, he got the story.

"I had my rope down, practicing roping rocks, when I rode up on the bunch of burros. I decided to try to rope one from my horse. I remembered what you told me, not to put the horn loop around the saddle horn. I put my belt through the horn loop of my rope! The burros started running and I managed to get close to one and threw my loop. I caught him! My horse stopped. The burro didn't. I remember getting jerked out of the saddle and hitting the ground. I hit a big rock with my head and the rest of it's kinda fuzzy. I don't know where my horse went, or the burro. I did just like you told me, I didn't put the horn loop on my saddle horn!" the kid explained to Bob.

"I'll be damned! Guess I never thought of that!" Bob answered.

Getting the wrangler back on his horse, Bob found the grazing burros near by. One of them was dragging the wranglers rope and the busted Philmont belt, securely held by the tightened horn loop. Bob caught the burro and retrieved the wrangler's rope and belt.

"Maybe you better stick to roping afoot," Bob suggested.

◇   ◇   ◇

One morning at headquarters, Ben Vargas was taking out a group from the training center on a horseback ride. With his wrangler, Dennis, a young green kid, they had all the riders mounted and ready to leave the corrals. Ben told Dennis to go in and close the back door to the saddle room before they left.

The back door to the saddle room opened to the outside and had a latch on it. Latched back to the side of the building, the wind wouldn't blow it shut. The door was painted brown and the outside of the building was a faded yellow.

Ben waited and waited for Dennis. The riders got impatient, ready to start their horseback ride.

"Hey Dennis! Come on, let's go!" Ben hollered.

No Dennis.

After several minutes Ben decided he better go see if Dennis had fallen asleep or what had happened to him.

"We'll be ready in just a minute," Ben told the riders as he got off his horse and went looking for Dennis.

"Dennis, what the hell are you doing?" Ben hollered as he went into the saddle room.

"Somebody ripped off our door, Ben!" Dennis exclaimed.

"What the hell do you mean!?" Ben said.

"The door! Somebody stole it! It's gone!" An excited Dennis said.

Ben stepped outside and there was the door, latched back against the wall. Ben looked at Dennis in disbelief.

"Did you look around good for it Dennis?" he asked.

"I've been looking every place for it, Ben. I think somebody stole our back door!"

"I'll look out here, Ben," Dennis said as he started walking around the big corral, searching the ground like he was looking for a lost contact lens. Ben let him wander around the corral, kicking horse manure around, searching for the missing door.

"Dennis, come here!" Ben said in a nice calm voice.

Dennis walked back to where Ben was standing by the open doorway. Grabbing Dennis, Ben spun him around with his face toward the door. "What the hell do you think that is!?" Ben yelled in Dennis's ear as Dennis's hat fell on the ground.

"Oh! here it is Ben!" Dennis replied, pleased that he had finally found the door! "I didn't know it latched back like that!"

Ben said the scary part of that deal was that Dennis was going into West Point to become a military leader! Now that was a scary thought!

That summer, we were getting the new wranglers introduced to the fun task of shoeing horses. Eight or nine of the new wranglers each had a horse tied to the fence around the large corral. Ben was busy going from one to another helping them figure out how to get the shoe nailed on without crippling the horse or themselves. One kid had his horse's foot rasped and fairly level, ready for the shoe. With the horse's foot between his knees, every time he started to drive the nail with his hammer, he would hit it wrong, bending the nail.

He pulled the nail, dropping it on the ground in a little pile of bent nails. As Ben came by to see how he was doing, he noticed the pile of slightly bent nails.

"When you get a slightly bent nail like that, don't throw it away. Just put it on the shoe and straighten it out with your hammer," Ben told this wrangler.

Moving on to the next wrangler needing some help Ben heard a loud exclamation, "Ow!" That was a fairly common thing to hear around there. "Ow!" "Ow!" along with quite a bit of cussing, and other expletives!

Looking back at the wrangler with the pile of bent horseshoe nails, Ben saw the problem and the source of all the "Ow's!"

This kid with the pile of bent horseshoe nails was kneeling on one knee with the shoeing hammer in hand, straightening the bent horseshoe nails by putting the nail on top of his foot, then hitting the nail a good lick with the shoeing hammer! This was causing the loud "Ow" as he hit the nail on his size 14 boot!

Ben informed the wrangler he meant him to straighten the nails on the horseshoe, not the wranglers shoe!! This wrangler was probably going to be a famous politician!

It took a lot of patience to teach some of these kids. They had to learn that the curb strap didn't go over the horse's nose, the saddle pad went under the saddle, not on top of it, and a horse didn't open his mouth for the bit when you asked him to say "Aww!"

48

Nicky / Baldy

Ben Vargas, Bob Ricklefs and I had gathered a bunch of cows and calves out of Ute Gulch and were moving them down to the Webster Pasture. Ben was riding a little brown horse called "Nicky" that was pretty bronky. Nicky sure liked to buck and he had made Ben pull a little leather when he had blown up and done a pretty good job of bucking that morning. It was about all Ben could do to get him rode. Nicky kept it in mind all day, grabbing his butt and looking for another excuse to blow up! Ben was sitting pretty tight on him, not doing any unnecessary moving of his arms or feet.

We had to go by Webster Lake, a big man-made lake with a high dam on the east and south side. The cattle were hot and dry, and as we passed by the lake the cows tried to get to the edge of the lake, crowding and pushing to get a drink. We were pretty busy, trying to push them on past the lake as we didn't have far to go and didn't want to stop and water the herd there.

Ben was on the lake side of the cows, trying to keep them moving. Bob and I had our ropes down, popping the cows on the rump to encourage them to go on. Ben hadn't taken his rope down as Nicky was sure enough scared of a rope and Ben didn't want to push his luck. He was trying his best to get along with Nicky.

The cows had balled up along the edge of the water. Out of frustration Ben took his bridle reins and, hollering right loud, slapped his reins on the leg of his chaps. That was about the first time Ben had moved his hand very far and the loud slap was all Nicky had been waiting for!

Nicky blew up like he was coming out of the bucking chutes at a rodeo! Nicky ducked back and to the left, made his first jump straight up, out into the lake. He still had pretty good footing after his first jump and took his second jump pretty high into the air. Nicky wasn't very good at walking on water so when he came down he disappeared under the water! The water came up to Ben's shirt pockets and his eyes were about as big around as saucers. Nicky came up out of the water like a submarine surfacing. Ben was looking around for a lifeboat, not sure what to do next. He looked like he was about to abandon ship.

"Stay with him!" I hollered at Ben.

"Jump off!" Ricklefs hollered.

Ben started looking over the side, deciding which way to jump.

"Stay with him, Ben!" I hollered again.

Ben got back in the middle of Nicky, hanging on for all he was worth.

"Jump off!" Ricklefs hollered.

Ben started to bail out, then grabbed the saddle horn, and got back in the middle of Nicky when I hollered, "Stay with him!" He started to jump off when Ricklefs would holler, "Jump off!" He just wasn't too sure of what was best, as this was a rather new experience for him. With all the expert advice he was getting from his cheering section he wasn't sure which route might be the best.

Nicky did a good job of swimming, making a little circle out in the lake, finally heading back to shore. Ben had decided to ride him in to dry land.

The lake was real mossy and had a lot of long seaweed growing in it. Nicky came out of the lake looking like a brown and green creature coming out of the blue lagoon! Long green seaweeds hung over his neck, and Ben's feet looked like he had a pair of long green tapaderos on his stirrups, the green weeds dragging on the ground on either side.

Ben was one wet, pissed off young cowboy as Nicky reached the edge of the water. He hadn't drowned and just figured he had about all of Nicky's B S he could handle for one day. Spuring Nicky up one side and down the other, he took his long wet bridle reins and warmed Nicky's rear end. Nicky looked like a half drowned rat as Ben proceeded to show him the rewards of bucking off into the lake with him. With his long wet bridle reins, Ben gave Nicky a little "over and under" as he rimmed Nicky back and forth along the lake shore. Nicky soon forgot the long weeds hanging off Ben's feet.

After Ben figured Nicky had pretty well gotten the message he pulled up and stepped off near a big rock. Sitting on the rock Ben held first one foot then the other up so he could pour the water out of his boots. Nicky shook like a wet dog, trying to get the water and weeds out of his ears and nose.

"Damn that water's cold!" Ben said as Ricklefs and I congratulated him on his ride. "I didn't know whether to stay on or get off! You guys were sure a lot of help! Jump off, stay on, jump off, stay on. Hell, I didn't know what to do!"

After that, Nicky sure had a change in attitude and didn't mind at all when Ben slapped his reins on his chap leg. We started the cows on past Webster Lake!

A neighboring ranch was looking for some broke ranch horses. When their cow boss asked us if we had any horses for sale, we told him about Nicky. We told him that he was a pretty fair horse but he did like to buck. He said he didn't mind a little bucking and had some cowboys who could ride him.

Well, it wasn't long before he found out that his hands weren't getting Nicky rode very well. He decided to bring Nicky into the rodeo on the Fourth of July. He got a couple rodeo hands to make exhibition rides on Nicky. Nicky bucked them off in grand style and the stock contractor bought Nicky and put him in the bronc string. At last, Nicky got to do what he liked best, bucking cowboys off!

◊　　◊　　◊

I had bought several horses at the La Junta, Colorado, horse sale, a big stout sorrel horse among them. Jim Byrd was working with Bob Ricklefs and me at the time and sure liked the looks of the new sorrel horse, named "Baldy". He liked the fact that he had a lot of chrome on him, a big bald face and stocking legs. Jim rode him for the first time when we brought a bunch of cows and calves into the Vega below headquarters.

It had been a long, slow, hot drive and our horses were sure thirsty. We paired up everything and rode over to a dirt tank on the edge of the Vega to give our horses a drink. This tank was a big pit dug out with a dragline years ago, and the subterranean water kept it full all the time. There were several of these pit tanks throughout the Vega and they all stayed full from the underground feed. The bottoms of these tanks were pretty boggy so we had to keep an eye on them when we had livestock in the Vegas. An animal could safely water at these tanks if they didn't get out in them very far.

My horse and Bob's had been at this tank before and stopped at the outer edge, stretching their necks out to get a drink of the clear cool water. Jim rode in between Bob and me on Baldy. Baldy was pretty hot and he walked right out into the water, stirring up the mud and turning the water black around him.

Jim pulled him up and got him stopped, leaning over his neck as he gave him a little slack so Baldy could get a drink.

"That's pretty boggy, Jim," I mentioned as Baldy started pawing the water. "I think he wants to lay down, you better get out of there!" I added.

Jim jerked Baldy's head up and tried to turn him around. Baldy slung his head back and forth as he lunged straight ahead out into the pond. He started bogging down and gave a big jump, straight out into the middle of the pond. As Baldy flopped over on his side and went down, Jim scrambled off, into the black water. Jim got a pretty good soaking and as he stood up discovered the water was just over waist deep.

Baldy had the constitution of a dying sheep. He just groaned right loud, didn't even try to get up as his head disappeared under the water. Jim floundered around in the muddy black water and managed to get his bridle reins and pulled Baldy's head up out of the water. Baldy blew a big wad of black mud and water out of his nose, blinked his eyes, looked around, moaned real loud again and dropped his head back under the water, just like a sheep headed to the last roundup.

The clear looking water had turned as black as ink and smelled like a long neglected septic tank! Made us wonder just where this pond was getting the steady inflow from.

Bob and I jerked our ropes down and pitched our loops out to Jim. Jim and Baldy were out in the tank far enough that we had to ride into the edge of the water for Jim to reach our loops. He managed to get Baldy's head up enough to get our loops over his head and we turned our horses back to the bank trying to drag Baldy out of the boggy mess.

Our horses couldn't get any footing and we couldn't budge Baldy. About all we accomplished was giving him a pretty good choking! When we gave him some slack, Jim got our muddy ropes off Baldy's head and he dropped his head back under the water. Jim got his head out of the water again but every time he let go of this reins Baldy dropped his head under the black muddy water. This old horse really had a lot of try in him! Trying to die!!

"Go get Harry and the Blue Goose!" I hollered at Bob. "Hold his head up, Jim!"

The Blue Goose was a great big Army surplus winch truck with a long telescoping boom mounted on the back. It was painted a bright blue, powered by a large Mack diesel, and had about ten or twelve wheels on it. Quite an impressive rig, that Harry, the ranch mechanic loved to drive. Harry had an assortment of air horns on this rig and he could play a pretty good rendition of some popular tunes on them. Well he played them loud anyway!

We were about a quarter of a mile from the motor pool garage where Harry and the Blue Goose were. Bob took off like a pony express rider going for help as Jim held Baldy's head up out of the water. I sat there on my horse offering Jim encouragement and commenting on how smart old Baldy was. I tried to stay up wind of them as the smell coming from the black water was getting stronger.

We soon heard a crude rendition of Jingle Bells being played on the air horns and knew the Blue Goose was on the way! Bob came loping back about the time Harry arrived.

Harry wanted to visit and asked us how we liked his musical talents. We stressed the fact that the damned horse was about to drown and maybe the cowboy, too; could we please talk later?

Harry backed the Blue Goose up to the edge of the pond and ran the boom out toward Jim and Baldy. Jim got the cable around Baldy's head and motioned for Harry to start pulling him out of the mud. Harry engaged the winch and as the loop tightened around Baldy's neck, Harry stopped the winch.

"This might choke him!" Harry exclaimed.

"Good!" we all answered in unison.

"Pull that S.O.B. out of there!" I demanded of Harry.

Harry started the winch again and Baldy started coming out of the bog as Jim splashed away from him, scrambling for dry land. Harry stopped the winch and shifted gears, driving straight ahead dragging the choking struggling Baldy to dry land. His eyes were bugging out and his tongue hung out about a foot. It looked like we may have helped Baldy along with his death wish! Bob and I quickly got the cable off Baldy's neck and he got some air back in him. He lay there like he was dead. His "want to" had got up and gone. I walked around him, and not so gently, kicked him in the butt. He raised his head and looked around, kinda confused. He slowly got to his feet, coughing and blowing mud and water out of his mouth and nose.

Jim came wading out of the inky black mud and water, trying to keep the mud from sucking his boots off. His tan colored elk skin chaps had turned a sickly looking dark blue, almost black. His saddle was a big mud ball on Baldy and it was a shade darker in color than Jim's chaps. Jim and Baldy both smelled like a sewer.

We thanked Harry for his help, mounted up and headed for head-quarters. The melodious notes of Jingle Bells drifted across the Vega as Harry disappeared in a cloud of dust. Baldy's bright white bald face and stocking legs were a weird blue color and his mane and tail hung down in thick black muddy strings. The bright chrome was pretty tarnished! He looked like a refugee from a flood. Jim wasn't very talkative and Bob and I kept our distance, as the smell was pretty strong coming from Jim and Baldy!

We got into headquarters and Jim rode up to a faucet and hose next to the saddle room. He unsaddled Baldy, had a few more words of praise for him and he turned him out. He turned the hose on his saddle and chaps trying to wash the mud out of them. With a stiff brush Jim scrubbed and washed his saddle and chaps cussing Baldy all the while.

The next morning when we opened the saddle room it smelled like a sewer leak in there! Jim scrubbed his saddle and chaps several times after that but never did get rid of the smell. He finally sold his chaps to a wrangler and traded his saddle off for another one that didn't smell quite so bad. Baldy got cut back to the dude string and Jim never rode him again.

Jim Byrd, Bob Ricklefs, Bob Knox, Philmont cowboys 1971

49

Some Top Hands

I guess one of the most rewarding parts of my job was seeing some of the young wranglers really catch on and become good hands. Many of them became horsemen, running the horse camps and training new wranglers under the watchful eye of Boss Sanchez. Many of them came back for several summer seasons. While they were working with us we gave them all a taste of cow punching. Several of them went on to cowboying jobs, making good hands on ranches around the Cimarron country and beyond.

Some who come to mind as I write this were; Ben Vargas, Bob Ricklefs, Chuck Enloe, Rod Taylor, Doug Johnson, Leo Martinez, R.W. Hampton, Jim Rice, Rankin Wolf, Jim Taylor, and others I'm afraid I can't recall!

Ben was born and raised on Philmont. I had worked with his Dad, Tom, for many years. I knew that being Tom's son, he had been started right. Ben came to us fresh out of high school, wanting to work with horses. He didn't think much of cows, his interest was in the horse department, but he quickly learned to make a hand with the cow work and went to work full-time in the livestock department.

Jim Byrd was working with me then, and when Ben informed us he was planning to get married, Jim and I set out to give this youngster all the advice and wisdom the two of us could come up with! Fortunately, Ben didn't pay any attention to us, and has had many happy years of marriage to Marilyn! They have a lovely daughter, Kelly, and a fine son, Shawn. Shawn grew up in the roping arena at Philmont and if you are looking for a good partner in the next big roping, hook up with Ben or Shawn as they would sure be hard to beat! Ben is now the horse foreman at Philmont. Boss Sanchez left some big boots to fill and Ben has sure done an excellent job filling them.

I believe Bob Ricklefs came out as a wrangler while still in high school. He quickly showed he was capable of running a horse string and was a mainstay at Ponil for several summers.

Bob got his degree from the University of Wyoming and wanted some practical ranch experience. We were glad to give him a permanent job in the livestock department, where he made us a good hand. Bob learned the cattle operation real well and with his education, moved into the ranch superintendent job when I left Philmont. He is doing a good job for Philmont in this position.

Rod Taylor came to work for Philmont as a western lore program counselor. He was pretty handy with a guitar and entertained campers with his playing and singing and teaching western lore. He was at one of the horse camps and got to helping the wranglers with the horse rides. He was a better hand than some of the wranglers we had, so we hired him as a wrangler!

Rod came to work for me at the UU Bar, several years after I left Philmont. I remembered him as a pretty good hand with horses and gave him a cowboy job. He sure didn't disappoint me. The old kid was a darn good cowboy! Philmont had a job opening in the cattle department, while Rod was working with me at the UU Bar, and he decided to go back there. This was a good move for Rod as it gave him the opportunity to further his musical talents. He has cut several records and has made a good name for himself in the western music field. He is presently holding the job of cow foreman for Philmont.

Chuck Enloe came to Philmont like so many wranglers, a little green, but wanting to learn. He was the kind of kid that caught on real quick and soon had established himself as one of the better horseman to work the horse strings at Philmont. He liked to rope about as much as Ben and I did, and soon became pretty good at turning a steer back for you. Boss and I were always glad to get Chuck back to run the horse string at Ponil Camp as we knew he always did an excellent job.

Chuck moved on from Philmont's summer job and worked several years for the Moore Ranch near Raton. I was at the UU Bar when Chuck left the Moore ranch and came to work with me at the UU Bar, where we worked together several years. Chuck became my right-hand man. We shared a lot of good times and a few tough ones. He was always a top-notch hand, really intelligent and understanding the more complex challenges we faced at the UU Bar. Chuck along with several others of us got hit pretty hard when the UU Bar sold and we found ourselves turned out to pasture.

Chuck landed on his feet, though, and is working again for Philmont.

Guess this speaks pretty well of the ranch where four green kids can work up from wranglers to the management positions they all hold today. My hat's off to all of you! You have made me proud!

Doug Johnson was a natural when it came to working with horses and cattle. He made us a top hand, a good leader among the younger wranglers, whom they all looked up to. Doug cowboyed for several big ranches around Cimarron; the UU Bar, WS, and the TO out of Raton. He built a good reputation as a top hand, knowledgeable, dependable and honest as they come.

Doug got married to a swell gal, Rhonda, while he was working for the UU Bar. They moved up to the Cottonwood camp, about twenty-five rough miles from Cimarron. Bettye and Rhonda had become good friends and of course I sure enjoyed visiting with Doug. Many a night Bettye and I would bounce up that long rough road to eat supper, visit and play cards with Doug and Rhonda. Rhonda had worked miracles in fixing up the old Cottonwood camp and making it home. They are sure good kids, and Bettye and I had some good times sharing with them, while Doug and I taught Rhonda and Bettye the finer points of playing pitch!

At this writing Doug is using his cowboy talents working for the Vermejo Park Ranch, helping care for Ted Turner's buffalo herd. They sure got a good man when they got Doug!

I almost missed a bet on R.W. Hampton. The program office handled all the job applications and separated them into various departments hiring summer staff. R.W.'s application went to the program department as a western lore program counselor, because of his musical talents. I didn't hire staff for this program so I didn't see his application when it came in. He was not selected for employment, so his application went into the stack of rejects.

During the summer I started having trouble with the crew I had at Clarks Fork. I had tried to get them to do their job but they were causing a lot of trouble and I was sure getting a lot of complaints about the horse rides out of their camp. Things just got worse and I ended up having to fire the whole crew and send them home. I was sure needing some wranglers right quick.

I was talking to Betty Brown, the gal who handled the applications in the camping headquarters office, and told her my predicament. She called me and told me one of the applicants for the western lore program who hadn't been hired might be a candidate for a wrangler. She told me he was at Philmont, on the trail with a group of scouts. I went by her office and looked over this application. It looked like he would be worth talking to. I got the itinerary his group was on and drove up to the camp where they were going to be that night.

The little skinny kid that the scout master introduced as Dick Hampton was sure a nice kind of boy. He was polite, a big grin on his face and seemed honest as a dollar, and eager to be a wrangler.

I talked with him about being a wrangler and learned he had ridden some, knew which end of a horse to put the bridle on at least! His expertise was with a guitar and singing, and I figured I could put up with a little music if he could saddle horses and take out rides. He told me that he had to go home with his crew, but assured me his dad would bring him right back!

Dick was back in a few days from his home in Texas and I put him at Clarks Fork with the new wrangler crew. He had missed all the early wrangler training, but caught on right quick. He sure made a good hand for the rest of the season. He could sure play the guitar and sang old cowboy songs with a lot of feeling. After hearing him play and sing I figured maybe I wouldn't try to talk him out of that idea after all! He was one of the first ones hired the next year and he worked for us several summers. Dick took over Clarks Fork as horseman, doing a good job.

Dick went on to cowboying in Texas after his stint at Philmont. I heard about him occasionally, that he was no longer called Dick, but was known as R.W.! I wasn't too surprised when I learned R.W. was appearing in several western movies and was quite successful as a recording artist. The kid could darn sure sing and play his guitar, and he was sure cowboy enough to put some authenticity in a western movie!

Needless to say, I was sure pleased when R.W., his lovely wife Lisa, and there three young sons, joined us in church here in Cimarron. They have bought a small place over near Miami, N.M., and attend church with us when his busy schedule allows. They are a welcome addition to the church and this part of the country.

Rankin Wolfe came up from Arizona. He had a little more experience than a lot of the kids with horses and quickly made one of our top hands. Rankin ran the horse string at Clarks Fork for several seasons and made it one of the better programs on the ranch.

Rankin picked a Philmont girl for his bride, Lisa Mondragon, the daughter of my good friend Ed Mondragon. Ed ran the farm operation for me at Philmont. A better man you couldn't find.

After leaving Philmont, Rankin and Lisa ran a big ranch near Santa Fe for several years, and then moved to another ranch in Texas. They are back in the Cimarron country now. Rankin is running the Red River ranch near Springer and Lisa is working for the Cimarron Schools. Rankin always has a big smile under his big moustache, and has sure made a good hand wherever he goes.

Leo Martinez, the son of my good friend Leo Sr., came to work with us while still in high school in Cimarron.

Leo followed in his dad's footsteps and sure made a good hand right quick. He wasn't very big, but what he lacked in size he made up for in "want too"! He took to team roping like a duck to water and sure got to be a good roper.

Leo attended New Mexico State University and his summers he spent punching cows for me at the UU Bar. Sure a good cowboy. He decided to put his education to work and is now teaching school in Cimarron. He still manages to get in a lot of ropings around Cimarron and wins his share. His lovely wife, Lynn, whom he managed to catch while attending college, is also teaching in Cimarron. Leo always has a big smile and never a bad thing to say about anyone or anything! I'm sure my old friend Leo Sr., would be mighty proud of this young man.

Jim Rice worked several summers for me at Philmont; pretty green kid when he started, but one of those kind of kids who had a lot of "want to" about him and made a good hand at what ever job he was given. Always had the biggest smile in the country, and with his winning ways at team roping as a heeler he had plenty to smile about!

Jim worked for me at the UU Bar, where he sure was a good cowboy. He got a job as livestock inspector for the state and was brand inspector at Taos for several years. Jim is back in Cimarron at this writing, working in construction.

Jim Taylor gave up mule riding, and was one of the better hands I had the privilege of working with. He married a Philmont girl, Robin Taylor, and they worked several years with me at the UU Bar. Jim quit cowboying when he left the UU Bar and is now living in Cimarron. He commutes to Santa Fe, where he is a sales representative for a large company. The cowboy world lost a good cowboy when Jim hung up his saddle.

Boss Sanchez and Bob Knox roping arena, Philmont Scout Ranch

Bob Knox heading, Boss Sanchez getting ready to rope heels

Boss Sanchez and Bob Knox, looks like they got the job done

Cavalcade at Crater Lake, Philmont 1950s

Cavalcade packing up at headquarters, Philmont 1979

Cavalcade horses coming in at Philmont

Bob Knox riding by Cimarroncito Lake 1975

Wranglers 1979: Bottom row: (left to right) Bob Knox standing, Paul Tweed, Lynn Willow, Angel Neives, Paul Kitterman, Bill Stansfield, Ted Bettary, Andy Knutson, Keith Hocutt, Garry Hakenson (standing). Back row: Dean Davis, Keith Newbill, Leo Martinez, Steve Cummins, Mark Pigg, Chuck Enloe, Alan Flurkey, Robert Anderson, Richard Lassiter, Frank Antos, Mark Steele.

50

The Big Bear

I had hauled my horse up to the Webster corrals at Philmont, in the fall of '75, unloaded and made a pretty good circle up through the Brush pasture. I was riding a pretty good young horse we had just bought. He was a good looking buckskin, and we called him Buck. He was a little snorty, but not bad, just needed some miles put on him. As I rode on up into the upper Clarks Fork country I noticed a lot of bear sign and tracks. There was a good crop of acorns that fall and the bear were sure working this area.

I had bought a deer and bear hunting license in preparation for the up coming hunting season. I was carrying a .41 Magnum pistol that I had been shooting quite a bit. It was sure a hard hitting pistol and I had gotten pretty good with it. Even though I could shoot this pistol pretty well, I sure hadn't planned on going bear hunting with it!

As I was riding down the trail coming out of Clarks Fork I saw something running up ahead of me through the brush. I couldn't tell for sure what it was because the oak brush was pretty thick. Buck sure got to snorting and looking all around kinda spooked when, up ahead of me about seventy yards, a real nice black bear broke out of the brush and ran up to a big pinon and started climbing up the tree. Buck spotted him about the time I did and we came to a sudden stop. When the bear had climbed up the tree a little ways he stopped, looking all around. He spotted me and down the tree he came, disappearing into the brush again.

Seeing this bear really got my interest up. I thought if he had just stayed there in that tree a little longer I might have got a good shot at him! The more I thought about it, the more I figured I could have gotten that bear with my pistol. If I had just had a little more time. I got myself pretty worked up over this bear and really started looking for bear!!!

Buck had gotten a good smell of the bear and he was sure paying attention to every dark spot and shadow around. He was looking for bear too, but not for the same reason I was! My dog "Boots", a tough Australian Sheppard, was with me and he could smell bear all around us and seemed a little excited, too. The sun was still an hour above the mountain tops to the west and I figured the time was just about right to find me a bear!

I rode off the ridge headed down to the Cimarroncito Creek. I came to the trail the horseback riders used in the summer, taking Boy Scouts on horseback rides out of Clarks Fork. This trail wound around the side of a pretty steep hill. I decided to drop on down in the bottom of the canyon and follow the creek down toward where I had left my pickup and trailer. There were a lot of old Cottonwood trees and lots of oak brush along the canyon floor. Off to my right I had a pretty good view of the steep hill side and figured I might get lucky and see a bear up on the side hill.

Buck had relaxed and was traveling along real good, Boots right at his heels. I rode out into a little clearing where I could see the hillside. I couldn't believe my eyes! My heart jumped up in my throat, I thought I was hallucinating! There he was, biggest brown bear I had ever seen, walking down off the steep hillside, headed to the canyon bottom. He hadn't seen me and I whirled Buck back into the cover of the thick oak brush. I jumped off and tied him to a solid oak tree.

My heart was beating about a hundred and ten miles an hour as I jerked my pistol out of the holster and ran back to the edge of the clearing where I could see the bear. Boy was he big! He still hadn't picked up my scent or seen me, as he walked straight down the hillside toward me. He was about seventy five yards away moving steadily down toward some thick brush. There wasn't anything to get a good rest on to shoot, so I sat down flat on my butt, resting my arms over my knees, and drew down on this big bear. When I sat down I realized he was going to be out of sight in just two or three more steps as he was nearly to the stand of oak brush. I pulled down on him, aimed right behind his shoulders. From the angle I was sitting all I could see was the top of his shoulders and back. I had to hurry a little more than I would have liked to, but I knew it was now or never!

The .41 Magnum roared and the bear whirled around and did his own little bit of roaring too! He rolled over and disappeared into the oak brush. I felt sure I had hit him, just didn't know how badly he might be hit. I stood up so I could see better. I watched a minute or two, Boots whining at my side, when I spotted the bear moving out pretty fast along the trail headed east. He disappeared down the trail. Well crap, I was pretty sure he was hit and I sure hated to have a wounded bear get away from me.

I rushed back to Buck, who was snorting and getting a little jumpy from the loud report from the .41 Magnum. I rode up through the brush to where I had seen the bear go down. I found where he had tumbled down the hillside and there were a few drops of blood. Well, this was good and bad! Good I had hit him. Bad, he had gotten away, wounded.

I turned Buck down the trail the way the bear had gone. Hurrying along, I looked for blood or tracks. A couple hundred yards along the trail I couldn't find any blood and the trail was hard packed, not showing any tracks at all. I was really looking hard at the trail when suddenly Buck snorted and jumped to the side like he had seen a bear. Hell, he did! There that big bugger was! Standing between a couple pinon trees about fifty yards off the trail! He was standing there broadside to me, watching us. I baled off and whipped a little fast draw McGraw on that bugger! There wasn't anything to tie Buck to and I didn't have time anyway! I stepped out to the end of my bridle reins, took a quick unsteady aim at the bear and fired. Blew dirt all over that bear! Fired again, as Buck took flight, and I have no idea where that shot hit! Buck nearly jerked away from me and I stumbled, nearly going down. I hung on to those bridle reins for all I was worth. I sure didn't want to get left afoot right then. Buck drug me down the hillside a little ways before I finally got him stopped. He was sure shook up this time! Seeing the bear so close and the two shots were a little more than he could stand!

I finally got Buck pulled around so I could get on him again and rode back up to where I had last seen the bear. I found his tracks where he had peeled out after I blew dirt on him, but I saw no blood. I soon lost the tracks on the hard ground, and the bear wasn't leaving tracks or blood that I could follow. I rode back and forth, up and down, criss-cross, really getting desperate, as I tried in vain to find a track or drop of blood. No sign of that big bugger, and I had no idea which way he might have run, while Buck and I had waltzed down the hillside.

Got desperate. As the sun by now was getting closer to setting behind the mountains, I sure wasn't ready to give up on this little deal. I decided to ride on up to the high peak above where I had first seen the bear. It offered a good view of all the surrounding area. Off to the south, toward the Tooth of Time ridge, was all open country where I knew I could see the bear if he headed that way. I had scared him off from the east so I figured he had to go back west or north down into the canyon from where I had shot the first time.

I rode up to the top of this high peak and the view was sure good. I was right above where I had gotten my first shot. Back to the east I could see where I had gotten my second shot. Wide open pasture land to the south and the Clarks Fork pasture to the west, I had a good view of all of it. No bear! Buck, Boots and I were all searching the country around us for any sign of anything moving. Nothing! The sun was just a whisker above the mountain top. I was really feeling bad.

About a half mile up west, in the Clarks Fork pasture, was a big dirt tank about half full of water. As I looked at this dam I thought I saw something moving at the edge of the water.

I kept watching the edge of the water and suddenly what should come walking out of the water but my big bear! I almost let out a yell I was so excited to see him again! I spurred Buck down off that peak like the devil was after us. I loped up to the gate going into the Clarks Fork horse pasture, and headed for the dam, which was about a hundred yards above the gate. As I rode around the point of the dam I could see the bear walking off into a big thick stand of oak brush a couple hundred yards ahead of me.

I rode Buck off to a big tree and got off and tied him. Boots and I headed for the brush where I had seen the bear go in. It was sure thick in there; I couldn't see the bear. My pulse rate was going up pretty fast! The more I peered into that thick brush the smaller my pistol seemed to get! I got down on my hands and knees, trying to see under the brush. But all I saw were just a lot of suspicious shadows and all kinds of boogers! Nothing to shoot at and I was starting to get a little jumpy, wondering if this was really what I ought to be doing! Then it dawned on me what to do!

"Go get him, Boots"! My buddy Boots didn't hesitate. He took off into that thick oak brush ready to catch himself a big bear! Boots no more than got out of sight than I heard him bark and then yelp, as I heard the bear growl pretty loud! Here came Boots, flying out of that brush like a bear was after him! Hell, he was after him!

Boots and I threw a stampede out of there. I outran him a little ways, but Boots soon passed me! I looked back over my shoulder and couldn't see the bear any place so I finally stopped. I was afraid my heart was beating so hard it was going to knock the pocket off my shirt! Boots came back to me, sat down and looked at me as if to say, next time, you go get him! I checked Boots over, and he wasn't hurt, so guess the bear hadn't slapped him. His tongue was hanging out and he was breathing about as fast as I was. We regrouped and headed slowly back to the brush thicket with mixed emotions!

I took my chaps and spurs off. They weren't helping my running any, and started sneaking back to where I thought the bear was. As I got closer to the brush where I expected him to be, I caught a glimpse of something going up the hill on the other side of the brush. There he went! Just walking away like he didn't have a care in the world. He disappeared again, out of sight over the ridge, heading for the open country south.

The sun had given it up for the day, sliding down the back side of the mountains, and I was fast running out of daylight.

"Come on Boots," I said, as we picked our way through the oak thicket. "Let's get that big bugger!"

We came out of the brush and headed up the hill the way the bear had gone. We charged that hill like the Seventh Calvary! My pistol sure didn't give me much confidence, but I had such an adrenaline rush I probably would have charged that hillside with a willow switch in my hand! Boots beat me to the top of the ridge. I saw him stop all at once, growling. He looked back at me, to see if I was coming. I didn't know if that was a good sign or not! Why did you stop, Boots? I rushed up to the top of the ridge, breathing like a wind broke horse!

There he was! Biggest bear I had ever seen, about fifty yards in front of me! He had stopped and turned broadside to me, growling, the hair on his back and neck sticking straight up! I didn't take time to look at the sights on my pistol. I was so excited I just raised my pistol and fired, purely by instinct. The bear dropped like a sack full of old laundry! I couldn't believe this! I didn't even get to aim at him and there he was, flat on the ground! I figured it was an old bear trick and he would jump up any minute and have me for supper! I held the pistol on him, but not even a wiggle. I knew what to do next, though!

"Go get him Boots!" I said. He didn't hesitate, ran as fast as he could and jumped right in the middle of the bear! Biting and growling, Boots was sure killing this big bear! I eased up to them, still not convinced this bear was dead, expecting him to jump up any second. Nudging the bear with the toe of my boot and getting no response, it finally soaked in that we had got our bear! I let out a war hoop, laughing and hugging Boots! He was nearly excited as I was. He ran around and around the bear barking and jumping up and down, grinning all over! We acted like two kids, hugging each other and congratulating each other. We were sure pumped up and were really celebrating!

I couldn't find where I had hit the bear to drop him in his tracks like he fell. I looked him over pretty well, in the fast fading daylight, but couldn't find a bullet hole. I wondered if maybe I had just scared him to death!?

After checking one last time to make sure that big bugger was really dead, Boots and I headed back over the ridge to where I hoped Buck was still tied. He was still there. I got my chaps and spurs back on and we headed out for the pickup which was about three miles from where we were.

It was getting dark by the time we got to the pickup. I unhooked the trailer and tied Buck to it. Boots and I got in the pickup and headed back to get our bear. I had the bear's location pretty well in mind and after a little driving around we came up to the bear. I felt a great sense of relief when the bear showed up in the lights from the pickup. I backed the pickup up to the bear and got out to load him. Wrong again! I could hardly budge him! Boots wasn't any help. He sat there in the back of the pickup as if to say, I got him, you load him!

I had a two-way radio in the pickup, and I called to anyone who might hear me. Leo Martinez, the security man for Philmont, answered my call. I told Leo I had a big bear down and couldn't load him by myself. I asked him to call Bettye and have her come up to the Brush pasture and give me a hand. He answered that he would come himself so I gave him directions to where I was. I was sure glad to see the lights of Leo's pickup appear a short while later.

"That's the biggest bear I ever saw on Philmont!" Leo exclaimed.

I told him about my hunt and how Boots and I had finally gotten the bear.

"I'll be damned!" Leo exclaimed. "Are you sure you don't have a rifle around here somewhere? I sure as hell ain't going bear hunting with a pistol!"

We pulled and strained, and got that big rascal in the back of the pickup. We both guessed at what we thought he might weigh, but decided to take the bear to the livestock scales at cattle headquarters to weigh him. Lloyd Knutson, director of program at Philmont, had heard the conversation between Leo and me on the radio. He wanted to know where we were with the bear, as he wanted to see it. We told him to meet us at cattle headquarters. We figured we could use a little help unloading and loading this bear!

"Knox, you are one gutsy S.O.B., or dumber than I thought you were, to go hunting a bear this big with a pistol!" Knutson remarked as he looked the bear over.

We rolled the bear out onto the livestock scales. After weighing him in @ 525 pounds, Lloyd and Leo helped me skin the bear that night in the back of the pickup. The hide covered the bed of the pickup.

As we were skinning him we kept looking for a bullet hole. We found a flesh wound in his hip, my first shot as he was coming down the hill. My shot had been a little high and sure not near fatal. The bear was so fat where the bullet hit I could see why there never was any blood trail. He just hadn't bled from that wound. As the skinning got up near his head we finally found the fatal shot. It had hit him right behind the head, broke his neck, killing him instantly. Pretty lucky shot. Good thing I hadn't aimed at him! I'd probably missed him, as excited as I had been.

Knutson took most of the meat. We shipped the hide to Jonas Bros. in Denver to have it tanned. It was sure one big rug! Last I knew, it graced the floor in front of the big fireplace in the main living room at the Villa Philmont. Lots of people have gotten to see it but not very many know the story behind the bear. He could have had Boots and me for supper if he had wanted to. Maybe he just figured it was his time. I never went bear hunting with a pistol again!

Bob riding Crow, in the high country at Philmont

Bettye riding Sandy at Lovers Leap Spring, Philmont

Bettye in Bonita Canyon, Philmont

Bettye at Bonita Cow Camp, on cowboy vacation

Bob with big bear taken with pistol, Philmont

Bob riding Buck, his bear hunting horse

Bettye on her mare Misty at Cattle Headquarters, Philmont

51

Cutting Down

One of the best times at Philmont, was the cattle drive, around the first of June. The calves had been branded and worked, the cows sprayed or dipped, and ready to go to the high country for the summer. We would have around three hundred fifty to four hundred pairs gathered into the Bull pasture, a few days prior to the drive.

We used all the Philmont cowboys plus a few of the summer horsemen for this annual twenty mile trek to the mountains. It was usually a hard, but fun time, not a very good place for dudes.

Bettye seemed to enjoy doing her part in this endeavor by fixing a big cowboy breakfast for the entire crew. Hot biscuits and gravy, fried eggs, bacon, sausage, hash browns and plenty of hot strong coffee to wash it down with. The crew enjoyed this and Bettye liked to feed them. A lot of biscuits and sausage found their way into a chap pocket for later.

The Bull pasture was just across the road from cattle headquarters, and we would ride into it just before daylight. I would get a count on the cattle as they moved out of the Bull pasture, and the cowboys strung them out, heading west. I always said, "Don't let the sun catch us in the Bull pasture!" Better be out and on our way as the sun came up, or we were late and it would get hot before we got into the higher, cooler country.

Crossing the small Uracca Creek, we picked up the dirt road that we would follow to Crater Lake, passing the Stockade, Lovers Leap, and slowly climbing up into the mountains. Traveling early in the morning, we seldom had any vehicle traffic, and the cattle would string out along the road.

We figured to get to Crater Lake, which was around eight miles, before 10:00 AM. There was a small holding trap just above the camp, at the foot of the steep stock drive, where we dropped the cattle and let them rest for about an hour. This gave the cowboys a chance to refuel on coffee with the summer staff at Crater Lake.

Leaving the trap was "where the fun ends and the hell begins" as we had left the road and started up the old stock drive. This stock drive was about as steep as a cow could climb, a series of winding stock trails snaking their way up the mountain side through the tall timber. Given a little time and a lot of cussing, the cows would slowly work their way up.

We broke the herd up into small bunches of forty or fifty head, with a couple cowboys behind each bunch and kept them strung out and climbing. I would get ahead of the lead cows as they topped out at Fowler Pass, opening the gate and counting them through.

It was all down hill from there, as the stock drive dropped off the mountain into Bonita Canyon. Always a pretty sight, open canyon bottom, with a lot of green grass and a nice stream winding down through it. Surely looked good to the cow herd as well as the cowboys.

The cows went to work on the tall lush grass as if they had better eat it all today as it might be gone tomorrow! The calves thought it looked like an ideal place to rest and take a siesta, while the cowboys got a chance to do what the calves did.

After the calves had rested an hour or so they would start thinking about momma and looking for a little milk. We would get busy, mothering up everything, as the calves would sure leave there if they didn't find their mothers, and go back to where they had came from.

After everything was paired up, the cowboys went up to Bonita Cow Camp, about three miles up the canyon. Fixing a good supper and seeing who could tell the biggest windy was a good time as we spent the night at Bonita. The next morning we prowled through the cows, making sure everything was settled, then ride on down to headquarters.

One year, Joe Clay, who was in charge of programs, asked me if we would take the western lore program kid with us on the stock drive. Joe thought the hands on experience would help him in being more authentic in his program for campers going thru Beau Bien.

I wasn't overly excited about this deal, but finally agreed to let the kid go with us.

He showed up at my house, in the slow rain, around four in the morning, ready to go. He was wearing a poor imitation of a cowboy hat, light jacket and a big pair of snow white batwing chaps, furnished by the program department. He had on a size fourteen hiking boot. He said cowboy boots hurt his feet. Looked like I sure had a winner.

The cowboys kept giving me questioning looks as we ate breakfast. Our program man said it was too early for him to eat, would just like some orange juice, please, thank you.

He had his official boy scout sleeping bag with him, that he needed to take, so Ben helped him roll it up and tied it behind his saddle. We mounted him on an old gentle dude horse and headed out for the Bull pasture.

As we rode into the Bull pasture, it started raining a little more. All the cowboys had slickers on. The program boy didn't have a rain coat or slicker and we didn't have an extra, but he said he didn't need one.

We got out of the Bull pasture in good shape as the cows strung out on the road. The cattle were moving out in this rain and mud, making better time than usual. I dropped back just below Lovers Leap, to see how the drags were doing and our program boy.

"That damned kids causing more trouble than he's worth!" one of the cowboys said as I rode up. "He keeps crowding the drags, causing calves to break back and he won't stay back".

About that time I saw what he meant as the program kid crowded into the drags, hollering and slapping his white chap leg with his bridle reins. I guess he had seen too many western movies.

"Hey, get your @$#%$ over here" I hollered at him.

I rode up beside him and reached over and took his bridle reins out of his hand. Tying a knot in them, I dropped them over his saddle horn.

"Don't touch them damned reins again until I tell you to!" I gently coached. "Put your hands in your pockets and leave them there until we get to Crater Lake."

I rode off, moving up the flank of the herd, and left him back there to think about it for awhile. A couple miles on up the road I got a chance to drop back to the drags again to see how things were going.

Right up in the middle of the herd was the program boy, his old horse plodding along at the same pace as the cows. The cowboys were driving him along like one of the herd. I figured that was a good place for him as the cows had seemingly accepted the old dude horse as one of them. His reins were still over the saddle horn and his hands were deep in his pockets.

Crater Lake was a welcome sight. We dropped the cows in the holding trap and rode down to the cabin to refuel on coffee. Our program boy came with us, looking a little worse for wear. His cheap hat looked like the sun bonnets my grandma had worn, drooping over his head. His new blue jeans had soaked up the rain, and turned the white chaps a peculiar shade of blue. He was pretty well soaked to the bone.

One of the Crater Lake staff loaned him a boy scout poncho. A square piece of material with a hole in the middle to stick his head through, as it draped over him like a mini-tent.

We made it over the top to Bonita in good shape, rain still coming down. We bushed up under a big fir tree and got a fire going to warm up and dry out a little. Program boy decided to leave us and ride on up the six miles or so to Beau Bien, where he was to work that summer.

Our little camp site was on a hillside. Program boy started to get on his horse, with the horse uphill from him. I started to holler at him but figured he was there to learn, so I didn't tell him to turn his horse around. Surely he could see that wasn't going to work!

He stuck his size fourteen hiking shoe in the stirrup and started the long climb up. He had his left hand on the saddle horn, his right trying to get a hold of the cantle. His bonnet was drooping down in his face, hindering his vision. As he struggled up, his leg hit the sleeping bag tied to the back of his saddle, and he fell backward. He landed in a wet pile under the old dude horse, his foot stuck all the way in the stirrup, his poncho covering his head. I jumped up to grab the horse, but the old pony just stood there looking down at the struggling program boy, wondering what the hell he was going to do next.

We managed to get his foot out of the stirrup, turned his horse around and got him mounted and sent him on his way, thankful for gentle dude horses. The next morning as we rode by Beau Bien, the program boy was out on the front porch trying to wash the blue out of his pretty white chaps. We didn't take anymore program counselors on the cattle drive!

◊   ◊   ◊

The Philmont Ranch Committee had determined that the cow herd on Philmont was larger than necessary and made the decision to cut the numbers from around five hundred mother cows down to one hundred twenty five. This was sure a disappointment to me. I argued against it, but to no avail. Camping for Scouts was Philmont's number one priority and it seemed they just had too many cows. Several of the members wanted to get rid of all the cows completely. Seems some of the summer campers had stepped in some cow manure and they had complained. When Waite Phillips, donor of the property, had given the ranch to the Boy Scouts, he had stipulated that the ranch would keep and maintain a cow herd so Philmont would always be known as a working ranch. They had to keep some cows.

I argued that on a hundred and thirty seven thousand acres there ought to be plenty of room for five hundred cows and the scouts too, mentioning the fact that if they were going to hike on a ranch they should expect to step in a little cow manure once in a while! If they didn't like a little cow manure they could hike on scout camps instead of a scout ranch! My comments went over kinda like a big loud burp at a formal dinner.

Since the cattle department had been incorporated into the livestock department, it was financially supported by the B.S.A. and didn't have to pay it's own way, as we had in the past, so that was a futile argument too.

We went through the cow herd, cutting the top end off to keep and around three hundred and fifty cows were sold to the WS Ranch (Vermejo Park). Bob Ricklefs, Ben Vargas and I drove the cows across Nash Draw to the WS fence, where Philmont and the WS joined.

We were met there by Freddie Martinez, cow boss for the WS, and his crew of cowboys. Freddie and I counted the cows through the gate, agreed on the number, shook hands and they were WS cows.

Bob, Ben and I sat there on our horses a few minutes and watched the end of an era move slowly over the hill. We turned our horses toward headquarters, not having much to say as we rode home. Nothing stays the same.

52

Moving On

After getting married in Taos, and graduating from high school, Li'l Bob and Trudy moved down to Phoenix, where he enrolled in an electronics training school. This didn't last too long. They came back to the Cimarron country and Li'l Bob went to work for Judd Knight at the Vermejo Park Ranch. He had too much cowboy in him to settle for city life.

Myrna finished high school in Cimarron and shortly after graduation, married a young cowboy, Coy James. He and Myrna had finished high school together. Coy was sure a good saddle bronc rider, and he and Myrna seemed destined for a cowboy lifestyle.

Li'l' Bob and Trudy, Coy and Myrna had worked together for Judd Knight at Vermejo Park for a while. I'm sure there are some wild stories they could tell about their times there. It didn't seem like too long ago that I was riding for Judd at the Ring place, and I wondered if my kids had had to ride that crazy little mule to jingle horses on; the one that I used to dread getting on in the dark every morning!

Coy and Myrna moved on to Texas, working different ranches, while Li'l Bob and Trudy moved down by Wagon Mound, working for the Diamond A Ranch. Coy and Myrna were hard to keep track of for a while, working for a lot of different outfits. They moved down to Arizona, punching cows for some big outfits there. They seemed to like Arizona pretty well and never came back to the Cimarron country to work. They had two little girls, Lisa and Shanna, whom Bettye and I didn't get to see near enough! They were needing some spoiling from Grandma and Grandpa.

Myrna sent some pictures of them occasionally. Grandma Bettye couldn't stand being so far from those kids, so we made a trip to visit them when we could. Myrna's directions to Bettye, then relayed to me as to how to find the cow camp where they were living, gave us a lot of interesting miles prowling around ranches, looking for a cow camp that might have our granddaughters in it! We had some good times, though, and saw a lot of new country.

Li'l Bob and Trudy also did their part in making Bettye and me grand-parents. They had a little boy, Lee, and a little girl, Felice. They were sure cute little kids. As Lee was my only grandson, I was a little partial to him. I figured he sure needed a grandpa to get him started cowboying. Of course his dad was giving him about all the cowboying a little kid could handle!

The summer of 1979, Li'l Bob and Trudy and the two grand kids had came up to spend the weekend with us. One of the cavalcades had come into headquarters the day before and were having their Gymkhana the next day. We went down to the new arena to watch the scouts do their thing; barrel racing, pole bending and a lot of horseback games. This, after all, was how we had managed to get our roping arena so we made a big produc-tion of this Gymkhana. We gave prizes to the winners, redeemable at the ranch trading post and ice cream stand. We made sure everyone won at least an ice cream. We figured we would have a little jackpot team roping after the Gymkhana. Lee really perked up when he saw all these kids riding around having so much fun and he wanted in on this deal.

I still had my rope horse, Crow. Bettye rode him when she rode with me, and Myrna had run the barrels and poles on him when she was still at home in high school. I put a little kid's saddle on Crow, and set Lee up on him. He looked like a big horsefly on Crow, as I turned them loose in the arena. Crow was sure a good baby sitter. He would turn and stop for Lee and only go as fast as he felt Lee could stay on. If he felt Lee slipping, he would slow down and seemed to try and get back under his little passenger.

Lee had his dad get the Cavalcade schedules and tried to time his visits to when we were having a Gymkhana. It was funny to see the expres-sions on the scouts faces as I would have Lee give them a demonstration on how to run the barrel and pole bending patterns. Lee was around five or six then, and he and Crow would sail around the arena like a couple of old pros.

◊   ◊   ◊

I had been promoted to the job of ranch superintendent. With that nice big title, came an office and a pretty easy job. My saddle horses were getting fat and lazy, not getting ridden much. Most of my time was being spent in the office or a pickup. We had only a little over a hundred head of cows, and it sure didn't take much riding to look after them. Cowboying had kinda gone down hill.

Then I noticed an add in the West Texas Livestock Journal for a cow boss on a big ranch in Northern New Mexico. I perked up right quick and made a couple of phone calls to find out where this ranch was located. To my surprise, it was Philmont's neighbor, the UU Bar Ranch.

I was familiar with this ranch, having known and neighbored with them for many years. I knew Ed and Howard McDaniels when they had the ranch back in the fifties and sixties and I had met the new owners, Bill and Harriet Faudree, who bought the ranch in 1970.

Li'l Bob had been cowboying for several big outfits and had gone to work for the UU Bar. We got to visit pretty often since he and his family had moved back to the Cimarron country. Some of the stories he had to tell about what they were doing at the UU Bar were hard to believe. I told him I was thinking about applying for the cow boss job there, and he said I was out of my mind! They had a ranch manager from South Africa and he was running all the cowboys crazy with his ideas and stuff he had them doing.

I went ahead and sent in my application. I figured I didn't have much of a chance to get the job, as I was starting to get a little long in the tooth. But to my surprise they called me and set up an appointment for an interview with the ranch manager, Rosy DuToit, and the ranch consultant Alan Savory. They were interviewing twenty some applicants, so my hopes didn't get very high.

I met with them at the Casa del Gavilan (The Nairn Place), the big fancy home the owners used when they were on the ranch. I had banged up my back the day before my scheduled interview, so I couldn't straighten up very well and if I sat down I could hardly get up! I was really in great shape for a cowboying job interview. Fifty years old and crippled up in the back! I tried to assure them that this was just a temporary little thing, that I would probably be fine in the morning!

The interview was interesting. Both these men were from South Africa and their English was a little hard to understand at times! They explained that they were implementing a new concept into ranch management and cattle grazing and needed a young man that they could train, one who was open minded to new ideas. They gave me a quick overall idea of what they were doing with the ranch and from what they told me it made sense. I told them I might be an old dog, but I could still learn new tricks!

They thanked me for my time and interest and said they would be in touch. As I climbed back into my pickup and drove off, I figured that was the last I would hear from those two guys.

Bettye was having some pretty serious medical problems and had made an appointment to go through the medical clinic in Lubbock, Texas, where a friend of ours was on staff. She needed to spend a week there so I had taken off a week to go with her. It had been over a week since I had gone for the job interview and I had pretty well put it out of my mind.

At the clinic, Bettye was going through every kind of test they could think of. On the third day we were there, one of the nurses came to me and said I had an important phone call. I wondered what had come up at Philmont. I had left the hospital number at the Philmont office in case of emergency.

I nearly fell over when I heard that strange accent. It was Rosy, telling me I had been selected for the cow boss job and could I start to work in the morning! I tried to explain that I was in Texas, that my wife was sick; also explained that I had to give Philmont at least a two-week notice. No, I couldn't be at work in the morning! I thanked him for the opportunity and assured him I would be there soon as possible.

I don't think Bettye had figured I would get the job. When I told her Rosy had called and we were moving to the UU Bar, she wasn't exactly over joyed! She had always supported me in anything I dreamed up and she tried to sound enthusiastic as we talked about this move. The UU Bar sure didn't have a very good track record when it came to keeping employees around very long, but I assured her we could make the difference in turning this outfit around and make it a good place to work.

I guess I was trying to convince myself as much as her! I had seen this ranch struggle through the years with many managers and cowboys coming and going. If someone worked there over a year he was considered an old timer!

I had often wondered if I could run a big cow outfit. Philmont with its five hundred head had been fun and easy. But now, with just over a hundred cows, there just wasn't much cowboying left to do. I guess I still had the cowboying bug, because I was sure anxious to give the UU Bar a try.

I turned in my resignation to Philmont with mixed emotions. Philmont had been home for a long time, but I felt it was time to move on; I just wasn't cut out for all the office work that went along with my job. Paul Claussen was Philmont general manager then, and Paul and I had become good friends. He sure didn't want me to leave, but gave me his best wishes and we parted with no hard feelings.

This was a pretty tough time for Bettye. Just getting home from the clinic in Lubbock and having to pack up and move. We made it through the move and tried to get settled in the huge house at the Cimarron Place that we called home for the next fourteen years.

Bob on Bill, Grandson Lee on Crow, Philmont 1979

Grandson Lee riding Crow, tuning up for Gymkhana, Philmont 1979

Lee showing how to turn the poles, Gymkhana at Philmont 1979

Lee crossing the finish line, Boss Sanchez with flag, Philmont

53

Cowboy Up!

The first of March, 1980, I was suddenly busier than a one-armed paperhanger! I had nine cowboys working out of six cow camps, scattered over two hundred and ten sections. It was forty-five miles from Cottonwood camp on the north end to Sweet water camp, on the south end. The ranch had around 2300 mother cows, plus bulls and replacement heifers. I couldn't complain about not having enough cowboying to do!

Rosy called an all hands meeting at Rayado, where I got my first chance to meet with the full crew to see if anyone had any urgent needs. The cowboy at Cottonwood camp said he was loosing quite a few calves and had lost several cows, too. I told him I would be there next morning to see if we could determine the cause of the problem. The rest of the crew didn't seem to be having any major problems. Calving season was in full swing, and everyone was busy feeding and calving.

I drove into Cottonwood just as the cowboy there was finishing breakfast. I drank a little coffee then headed out to see his cattle. I couldn't believe the condition this bunch of cows was in. I thought I had seen some poor cattle before but never had I seen anything like this. They were young cows, so poor and weak a lot of them could hardly walk. What few calves that were with them were doggied, the cows not giving any milk. I started getting a little upset with this deal right quick. The cowboy explained what had happened.

He had asked for some hay and cake for the cattle. Rosy hadn't been to Cottonwood, but looking at his map in the office it was obvious they shouldn't need any hay. The map showed lots of open land that should have lots of grass on it. This looked like a good place to use protein blocks instead of cake. He told the cowboy where to put out the protein blocks, which he did. Only problem was, he was told to put the cattle in Metcalf Canyon and the protein blocks in Cook Canyon! The poor cows were flat starving to death! Their food supply consisted of oak brush and pine needles, not the best feed for calving cows on.

The cowboy had tried to explain the problem to Rosy, but had been instructed to do as he was told and not to question management decisions. I was pretty upset with both parties about then, but figured getting mad wouldn't help the cows. They sure needed some help!

The UU Bar didn't have any corrals up in this north country. All the cattle were trailed in, coming across Philmont. I knew this bunch of cows was too weak to make the long drive out of there. Philmont had an old set of burro pens at Old Camp, a few miles down the canyon from where most of the cattle were. This was the camp where Larry and Li'l Bob had their encounter with the hound dog. Philmont said we could use their pens.

I got a cowboy from Rayado who could drive the old ranch bobtail truck and I hooked onto a gooseneck trailer. We pulled out around 4:00 AM and headed for Old Camp. The three of us started gathering cows into the burro corrals. We were bringing in only what we could haul, as the pens were pretty small and not very stout. We started hauling cows down to Sweet water, forty-five miles south. I got home about nine that night.

"Some man called looking for a job this morning around six," Bettye said as I was eating a late supper. "He called again this evening around eight, I told him to try tomorrow."

The next day was some more of the same, only I got home at nine thirty.

"That guy called again, still looking for a job, just after five this morning. He called from a pay phone and didn't leave a number to call him. Then he called a little while ago, and I told him maybe he could get you tomorrow!" Bettye told me as I was crawling into bed.

We were making to trip a day to Sweet water and were getting the worst end of the cows out of Old Camp and onto some feed. The hours were pretty long but we were getting the job done without any serious problems.

"The same guy called again at five this morning and at nine tonight. I told him you were pretty busy, but just to keep trying. He finally said that on second thought, with the hours that outfit works, he didn't think he much wanted to work here anyway, so just forget it!" Bettye said. "Wonder why he wouldn't want to work here!" We both had to laugh.

My going to work for Rosy at the UU Bar caused him some confusion when he suddenly had two Bob Knoxes working for him. Li'l Bob had outgrown that name long ago and was known as Bob. But Rosy figured out that the way to tell us apart was by renaming Li'l Bob, "RC", as his name is Robert Charles. He sure didn't want to be called Robert or Charles so he agreed to switch over to RC. It took quite a while for those who knew him to change over but it was a good handle and has stuck with him ever since.

We had the wreck at Cottonwood under control when spring branding time rolled in along with a few scattered showers we were glad to receive. The cattle were pretty well scattered around the ranch so the branding location moved every few days. With six branding camps we did a lot of traveling. We branded over 2000 calves. It was sure a good time!

We had a good cowboy crew, everyone knew what needed to be done and how to do it. It was a fun time for all of us. We had a few wrecks, some pretty good bronc rides and a few classic buck offs.

Harriet Faudree, the mainstay in the ranch ownership, found out when the branding was going to start and moved out to the ranch from her home in Midland, Texas. She took up residence in her ranch home at the Casa del Gavilon. She loved being part of the ranch branding and prepared some of the best food, which she brought out to wherever we were branding right around lunch time. She could sure do a fine job of feeding this big hungry crew, and the single boys nearly foundered on her good cooking.

Rosy never came out to any of the brandings. He spent all his time in the office planning pasture layouts on the ranch maps. Nearly all the existing fences were being taken out from the Cimarron Place to Rayado. These old fences were to be replaced with electric fencing, enabling us to put around forty thousand acres into the new grazing use plan.

As soon as the branding was over and the cattle put on summer pastures I went to my first school on the Savory Grazing Method. I had told Allan Savory that this old dog could learn some new tricks, and he was sure teaching some new tricks! What he was teaching sure went against the grain of the old traditional ranching practices.

His teaching sure made sense though, when you understood it, and before long I was ready to put it into practice. This new program was met with various reactions from the cowboy crew. A few wouldn't try to learn; they quit and moved on. Several decided to stay around to see if it would work, and a few were real interested and wanted to learn more.

The coffee shop talk around Cimarron was about the crazy guy from South Africa who was ruining the UU Bar with all the little pie shaped pastures and electric fences! After two years of this grazing program the range land was definitely improved from when we started. Our neighbors, who thought we were crazy, could sure see the improvement in the overall range conditions and soon adopted this grazing method into their own ranching programs. The negative coffee shop talk soon died down. Maybe that crazy South African had something going after all!

The cattle market had been in a long slump in 1983. The owners of the ranch decided to sell the cowherd and stock the ranch with yearlings during the summer season. I talked them out of selling all the cows, so we kept around eight-hundred head and sold the rest. We put the cows we kept down in the Sweet water country. We brought in around 4500 yearlings for the summer grazing season. We sure had good weight gains on the yearlings, so we had the best of both worlds!

54

Summer Cattle

We got in a bunch of long-eared Brahma type steers for the summer. They were pretty good to handle on the open country, but when they got up into some rocky, brush covered rough country, they seemed to loose their minds! Sure got a little "trotty!"

We had several hundred head of these "trotty" steers in South Lake pasture. Getting close to shipping time, we were gathering them and putting them down in the shipping Vega. This was a little wild and fast. Quite a few of them had to be roped, tied down, loaded into trailers and given a free ride to the Vega. There were four or five steers left in South Lake that we still needed to pick up. One of these was a big long-eared brindle steer that had managed to escape a couple of times. He sure wasn't about to get gathered.

Bear hunting season had started and the ranch had allowed a local guide and outfitter to hunt bear on parts of the ranch. The outfitter and his girlfriend had brought a hunter down to the north end of the South Lake pasture. They planned to unload their horses and their hunting dogs there and hunt the north end of South Lake, up past the old Goat Camp, and on up to the top of Ortega Mesa.

They unloaded their horses, got the hunter mounted on a mule, girl friend on a big paint horse and the guide let the dogs out of the front end of the horse trailer. As he stepped up on his horse the hunting dogs ran around a large thicket of oak brush near by and started barking up a storm. The guide hollered at the dogs to get back but they were barking treed on the other side of the thick brush and wouldn't come to the guide. Riding around the brush to see what they had treed, he saw that the dogs had the big wild brindle steer at bay in the thick brush. The dogs still wouldn't come back to the guide, so he got off his horse and tried to catch and neck the dogs together with a big snap between their collars. While busy trying to calm and catch the excited, barking dogs he had dropped his bridle reins.

Old brindle saw his opportunity and charged out of the brush at a dead run straight for the guide and the barking dogs. With his head down low, he bowled dogs in several directions. The guide dropped all interest in catching dogs and took off running. Brindle quickly caught up with him and gave him a not so gentle boost in the rear end, sending the guide head over heels into the thick oak brush. The guide's saddle horse didn't want any part of this argument and ran around the thicket to the girlfriend and the hunter who were sitting on their mounts. The dogs followed the guides horse in a big hurry.

"What's going on?" asked the confused hunter.

"I don't know, but we better get the hell out of here!" the girlfriend exclaimed as she saw old brindle zeroing in on them as he came flying around the oak brush, dogs barking and running all around.

She smacked old paint across the rump and spurred him out of there as fast as he could go. "Look out!" she hollered over her shoulder to the bewildered hunter. The hunter's mount, an old gentle mule, didn't get in much of a hurry. He was watching the barking dogs and when old brindle broadsided him he was a little surprised to say the least! Old brindle knocked the mule and the hunter about ten feet. The mule landed flat on his side. The hunter hit the ground, free of the mule, and scrambled to get out of this rather strange predicament. Stepping up their barking when they saw the mule go down, the dogs turned their attention to the kicking, struggling mule and hunter.

Old brindle figured he had made his point, about getting gathered.

With the dogs in hot pursuit, he took off up the draw looking for something else to whip. The girlfriend and old paint had made a little circle out of harm's way and came riding back as the hunter was brushing the dirt off his new "Eddie Bauers".

"What the hell was that cow's problem!" he demanded, not very happy with his bear hunting trip so far.

"Where did that crazy S.O.B. go?" the guide asked as he came creeping around the oak brush, holding together the pieces of his shirt that he hadn't left hanging on the oak brush.

"He headed up toward the old camp," the girlfriend told him.

"I hope we have better luck with a bear than we did with that damned cow!" the hunter said as he climbed back on his mule.

The dogs had given up the chase and came back, proud of themselves for chasing off the steer. Necking the dogs together, the hunting party rode on up the draw. And keeping a wary eye out for this unsociable steer, as they approached the ruins of what had once been the Goat Camp Cow Camp they spotted old brindle. He had gone into the nearly fallen down barn and was standing in the sagging doorway looking out at them. He pawed the ground and shook his head in defiance as they rode up. They rode well out around the old barn and let old brindle have his shed, as they rode on up to Ortega Mesa.

◊   ◊   ◊

We had put one hundred fifty of these long-eared Brahma steers on Sweetwater Mesa. Sure a rough mesa, covered with malpai rocks, mostly on edge! Oak brush was about six feet tall and thick as it could get. A few scattered pine and pinon trees and a few small open meadows with pretty good grass and water sure made it a good place for these brahma cross steers to get wild.

We went up there with several cowboys to gather the mesa, but came down with only around twenty-five head. Our second gather wasn't any better, coming down with around ten or twelve. The three or four miles of washed out, rock filled road up the mesa made it next to impossible to pull a trailer up there. Several steers had been roped, but we had two good saddle horses crippled from running over the sharp, jagged edges of the malpai. We decided we had to do something a little different to get this bunch of steers off the mesa.

The main cowherd was down a few miles below Sweetwater. We went through them, cut around thirty head of pretty gentle cows and drove them up to the top of Sweetwater Mesa where this bunch of wild steers was. In spite of the loud complaining from the man camped at Sweetwater, I had him start taking a little jag of cake up to the top of Sweetwater Mesa every day and call the cows in and feed them.

He had a four-wheel drive ranch pickup and he sure needed it to getup there! The old road sure washed out badly so it was a slow rough trip.

At first a few steers peeked out of the brush and trees to see what the cows were doing as the cake was poured out to them. Starting to leave, the cowboy saw some of the steers creep out of the brush, to grab a bite of cake. After a few days of this more and more steers got the word and were hanging around the cows waiting for the free hand out. After several days of feeding it looked like we had the whole hundred head of steers eating cake and not running off when the feed truck drove up.

I had told Rosy of the trouble we were having, gathering these steers. Looking at the map, he just couldn't understand why we hadn't gathered the steers! Rosy had never been on the mesa and never had been horseback on the ranch. But all at once he wanted a horse and insisted on going with us when we went to try and bring the steers down. I tried all my diplomatic skills, trying to talk him out of this idea, but he insisted on going with us. Since he was the ranch manager, I couldn't hardly tell him he couldn't go. So we got an old gentle horse we figured he could ride. He borrowed a pair of chaps and was ready to go.

Against my better judgment we loaded Rosy and his horse and met the rest of the cowboys at the bottom of the mesa, where the road came down into the valley leading to Sweetwater and the shipping pens. We left most of the crew at the bottom, as we knew there would be a horse race there if we got the steers that far. Rosy, George, RC, Grandson Lee and I rode up to the top of the mesa.

The load of cake in the pickup had gone up ahead of us, hopefully calling the cows and steers into the feed ground. We eased up through the brush and trees to where we could see the feed wagon and a big bunch of steers and cows around the pickup. We planned to call the cows down off the mesa with the cake and pickup, figuring the steers would follow along, too.

There were a couple of springs back to the north. I told George and RC to make a circle back that way in case there might be some steers that hadn't come into the feed ground. Lee went with his dad and I circled to the west to make a little circle. Rosy followed along behind RC and George. They jumped five or six head of steers and built to them. It didn't take long to leave Rosy alone and lost. Lee finally turned back and pulled up in an open meadow, listening for his dad. Rosy rode up to Lee, glad to find someone.

"Where's your dad? Where's George? Where are the cattle? Where are we? Where's Bob?" Rosy was hollering at Lee.

Lee didn't think about being polite to the big boss right then. "If you would be quiet, I could probably hear my dad and know where he was!" Lee said to the stammering Rosy.

Rosy wasn't used to being told by a ten year old kid to be quiet! But before they could get into an argument, Lee heard RC holler off in the distance. He wheeled his horse around and took off at a run headed for the sound of his dad's voice.

"Wait! Wait! Lee don't leave me! Wait!" Rosy yelled as Lee disappeared into the brush.

The steers RC and George had jumped ran into the feed ground with the others. RC and George pulled back into the brush out of sight of the feed ground. Lee rode up to them and said Rosy was back in the brush somewhere looking for them. RC rode back and found a lost and confused Rosy and brought him out.

I gave the signal to start out with the feed truck. We stayed back out of sight, steers falling in behind the cows, following the honking pickup. The cowboy driving the feed truck stuck his head out the window and did his best imitation of a cattle call. We knew that if the steers saw us horseback they would scatter like a bunch of quail. So we stayed back out of sight as the herd started down off the rim rock along the steep rutted road.

We were pretty proud of our little plan. It looked like it was going to work. We followed along, keeping the cattle in sight, staying well back, and not posing a threat to the steers.

Rosy didn't like being back so far from the cattle and decided he would ride down the other side of the large hill the road went around. He wanted to go down to the bottom and let the guys there know we were coming with the cattle and steers. I told him to just go straight down and stay away from the road. He dropped off and disappeared into the brush and we could hear him going down the mountain side.

The road was pretty steep and had several switch backs in it. As we looked down on the long string of cows and steers going around the bend of the switch back below us, who should come busting out of the brush, right on the turn in the road, but our fearless leader, Rosy! Yelling in his best Zimbabwe yell, slapping his reins on his chap leg to hurry the steers along he sure blew our little plan all to hell!

The cows and calves were first in line following the pickup with the steers right behind them. Rosy hit it just right! Right behind the cows, turning the steers back in one big first class stampede! The steers made a run to get back to the safety of the mesa top, scattering up the mountainside. There was no turning them as they came charging back toward RC, George, Lee and me.

We turned a few back and bunch got around us! A little bunch of five or six turned off and headed for a little break in the rim rock to the south of the road. RC made a run to get ahead of them, trying to turn them back. He got into a big boulder slide and jumped off his horse and scrambled over the boulders, trying to keep the steers from getting to the rim rock. Standing on a big boulder, hollering and cussing waving his hat at the charging brahma steers, he looked like Utah Carrol trying to turn the stampede! These goofy buggers weren't about to turn and RC saw they were calling his bluff. He dove behind a big boulder just as the lead steer, making a frantic jump to get back up on the rim rock, sailed over him. The other five steers followed their leader and all managed to make the jump over RC and get back on top. George and I didn't have any better luck as the whole bunch got back and disappeared over the top of the mesa. RC came riding up, pretty well covered in fresh manure as the steers had pretty well plastered him as they jumped over him. He was lucky none of them had fallen back down on top of him!

The vote was unanimous; four in favor, none opposed, to killing that damned Rosy when we found him again! When we got to the bottom the other cowboys had the cowherd held up waiting for us to bring the steers down. When we told them what happened they were all in favor of just having a lynching right there.

Rosy came riding up. Everyone was watching me to see if I would take my rope down for the hanging. We didn't hang the boss, even though we wanted to. I let him know he had sure blowed the hell out of our plan. He halfway apologized, saying he didn't realize the cattle were that wild. He knew he had a pretty hostile bunch of cowboys there and didn't have anything else to say. We took the cows back up on top, and with much cussing and belly aching, the hauling of the cake was started again.

Shortly afterward, Rosy called RC into the office. "Look at this, RC, I've figured out how we are going to gather the steers off Sweetwater Mesa!"

Rosy exclaimed as he spread several sheets of blue prints out on the conference table.

"We are going to build our own helicopter!" Rosy announced.

RC looked at him like he was some crazy South African set loose on the ranch to destroy all the cowboys. Seeing Rosy was serious as he could be, RC got himself a cup of coffee and sat down. He began studying the plans for the helicopter, stalling for time until he could make his escape from the office.

I saw RC later that day. He said "Dad, you better watch that Rosy! He's crazier than hell! He wants me to help him build a helicopter!"

Luckily, Rosy left the ranch before his helicopter could become a reality. The cowboys were all mad at RC for not helping Rosy build his helicopter! They figured that would have been a quick easy way to get rid of him.

Then in about a week we got the steers down without Rosy knowing.

The road going into the shipping corrals at Sunnyside was sure getting rough. It needed to be graded, as it had lots of big chuckholes. The road down to Sweetwater needed some blade work, too. I mentioned this to Rosy at one of our weekly meetings. I got a nod like he might have heard me.

A few days later I went by the office. Rosy peered over the top of his glasses at me from around a big stack of catalogs.

"Come in", he said, as I walked up to the coffee pot.

"Which of these do you think would be the best?" he asked as he tossed an opened catalog across his desk to me.

The catalog was open to a variety of wheelbarrows, small, big and bigger. All size and shapes with different kinds of tires. I wondered if maybe he was going to take up gardening! What the heck did he want with a wheelbarrow?

"What are you planning to do with a wheelbarrow?" I asked in all my innocence.

"I'm not going to do a damned thing with a wheelbarrow, but those cowboys are! No need to send the road maintainer to those camps. The cowboys have plenty time in the evenings. In their spare time they can shovel some dirt into their wheelbarrows and fill in the chuckholes!" Rosy said.

I damned near choked on my coffee! He was serious! RC was right. Crazier than hell!

Seemed like I spent most of my time serving as a buffer between Rosy and the cowboy crew. Rosy was a real smart man, just didn't have a lick of common sense. He had been born and raised in South Africa and to him the cowboys were just like the natives he had been used to working over there. After about a year, the owners asked Rosy to leave and he made the long journey back to South Africa.

He had lost his ranch there in a civil war prior to coming to the USA. The last I heard he was working as a carpenter in Cape Town. It had certainly been an experience working for him!

55

Frog Honey and Grandkids

Frog Honey was a small Dunn gelding in the ranch remuda. He had sure got a heck of a name hung on him from somewhere. Good little cow horse, but hard to find a cowboy who much wanted to ride him; as he was about the size of a Welch pony.

Grandson Lee was getting big enough to start riding quite a bit with the cowboys, and Frog Honey was just his big. Frog was pretty gentle, but wouldn't put up with much messing around. Lee had to pay attention while he was riding him. Lee got to rope and drag some calves to the branding fire on Frog. They made a good pair.

Lee was helping me and a couple of cowboys move several hundred head of steers out of the Porter pasture. We had moved a bunch earlier that morning, and by the time we got to the Porter bunch, the day had gotten pretty warm. The main water for these steers was at the bottom of a small mesa, and they were sure wanting to get a drink. We were doing some pretty rapid riding, hollering and cussing, trying to drive them up this hill, away from the water. It was kinda like what one of the cowboys said, "This is like trying to sweep water up hill! It just keeps coming back on you!"

Lee and Frog were right in the middle of it all, really getting after the steers. I guess Lee, in his anxiety, spurred Frog a little too far back. Whatever touched him off, Frog downed his head and blew up big time. Lee didn't last long as Frog bucked down through the bunch of steers, scattering them in every direction. Lee hit the ground pretty hard, and finally quit rolling, coming to a stop near where I was. I rushed over to him as he was trying to sit up. He didn't seem to be hurt much, but sure had gotten scared. He had fallen off a few horses, but this was the first time he had been on a sure enough bucking horse and he was a little shook up.

Lee was kinda biting his lower lip, trying not to cry in front of me and the other cowboys. Big tears in his eyes as he shook his head in answer to my questions as to what was and wasn't broken. One of the cowboys had caught Frog and came leading him back to where Lee and I were sitting on the ground.

"I brought your horse back for you," the cowboy said to Lee.

"I ain't never going to ride him again!" Lee exclaimed.

I tried to reassure him that Frog would be all right. Maybe he had gotten a little heavy with the spurs in the heat of battle. Besides, a cowboy always gets back on when he gets thrown! Right?

"Hell No! I ain't never going to ride him again! I don't care what cowboys do, I ain't getting on him!" Lee answered, in no uncertain terms.

"It's sure a long walk back to camp from out here," I said, using a little different strategy.

"I don't care. I ain't riding that sucker again! Grandpa, can I ride your horse and you ride Frog?" Lee asked, big tears in his eyes.

Well heck, what are Grandpas for anyway?

I was riding Mescalero, a big, stout Grulla horse. He was pretty gentle and I figured Lee could probably ride him. I pulled my saddle and put Lee's small kid saddle on Mescalero. He looked a little strange, this great big horse with a little kid saddle on him. But not any stranger looking than Frog, when I threw my saddle on him, my stirrups hung down below his belly.

I got a lot of kidding from the cowboys as I rode this little kid horse! Lee sure liked Mescalero and wanted to make it a permanent trade, but Grandpa finally had to say no! A few days later Lee was ready to ride Frog again. He was just a little more careful of how he used his spurs.

Lee spent some time up in the high country, camped with Chuck and Leo at LaGrulla cow camp. They didn't cut him any slack and made him carry water and chop fire wood and help with other chores around camp. Lee's threats to tell his grandpa about being made to work around camp didn't help him a bit. Chuck and Leo told him to just go ahead and tell your grandpa. He will tell you that you have to work if you are going to stay up here with us. Lee never did say anything to me. He made a pretty good hand, with just a little grumbling!

◇   ◇   ◇

I had taken over as ranch manager after Rosy left. Shortly after, RC moved up to the job of wildlife manager for the ranch, overseeing all the extensive hunting and fishing programs. Booking hunts for antelope, deer, elk, bear and turkey, he also directed and helped with the guiding during the actual hunts. This was right up his alley. He sure stayed busy through the fall and winter with the hunts. Spring and summer kept him busy with the fishing program offered at several high country lakes. Stocking the lakes with large trout, taking reservations for fishermen and keeping them happy while at the ranch kept him jumping.

I sure missed him as a cowboy, but he managed to give us a hand with the cattle works whenever he could. We were always glad to have him riding with us. He had the best of both worlds, as he loved cowboying, as well as hunting and fishing.

It was a sad time for all of us when he and Trudy decided to split up. Trudy moved back up to Taos with Lee and Felice. RC stayed on with the ranch and tried the bachelor scene for a while. Lee came back to stay with his dad after about a year, and Felice came back a while later. The kids had two homes, juggling back and forth between Trudy and RC.

RC got lucky and met a real sweet young lady from Clayton, LeeAnn Harris. She was teaching school in Cimarron, and having been raised on a ranch, she and RC seemed to hit it off pretty well. Bettye and I knew LeeAnn, and were sure happy when she and RC started going together. We were really pleased when they told us they planned to get married!

LeeAnn really turned out to be someone special! She fit right into the family and was sure a big helpmate to RC. Lee and Felice finished up high school living with them.

Trudy met and married a real nice man, Ed Healy. They have a nice home near Taos and are happily married.

RC and LeeAnn were blessed with a little girl, Brooke, and a couple years later, another little gal, Jamie. Bettye and I have really gotten into this Papa and Grandma bit! These two little girls have sure been a blessing and a joy to spoil!

We just wished our grandkids and greatgrandkids in Arizona lived closer. We sure enjoy them when we do get to see them.

56

Winding Down

I had put a good cowboy crew together and we settled down to a pretty good working operation. One thing about it, they were sure well mounted. Faudree's sure liked good horses and didn't cut any corners keeping the best saddle horses available for the cowboys to ride. We had a good roping arena at Rayado and always had plenty of roping steers.

We had a band of around twenty top broodmares and bred them to the best stallions we could find. One of our leading sires was Mr. B Jack, a son of the famous Two Eyed Jack. The cowboys sure liked riding his colts, as they had a world of cow in them; they were natural athletes and had gentle dispositions.

Leroy Webb was riding Mr. B Jack, showing and roping on him at quarter horse shows around the country. He was the champion heading horse in New Mexico in 1984, reserve champion heeling and calf roping horse. He had qualified to go to the World Quarter Horse Show in Oklahoma City in all three events heading, heeling and calf roping. Looked like he had a good shot at the all-around horse award.

Leroy had brought him back to the ranch after qualifying him for the World Show, and we had him turned out with a little band of mares. To our dismay, he turned up with a broken hind leg! Of course we were all devastated and rushed him to Dr. Truman Smith in Raton. Truman is one of the best vets in the country, and we knew if anything could be done for Mr. B Jack, Truman would know what was best. Truman's Xray showed a clean break just below the hock. He recommended taking him to Fort Collins to have surgery done there.

After a successful surgery and a steel plate screwed into his leg we brought Mr. B Jack back to Raton. Truman had a large horse swimming pool at his facility in Raton. We left B Jack in Truman's care while his leg healed, so B Jack got a daily work out in the swimming pool and his leg healed up real well. This accident happened in mid August and the World Show was the first of November.

Mr. B Jack sure had a lot of heart and Truman thought he was sound enough to try the World Show. We entered him in the heading and heeling but felt the hard stop called for in the calf roping might reinjure the broken leg so didn't enter him in that event.

I took RC, Chuck Pledge, CD Garcia with me to Oklahoma City to watch Mr. B Jack compete in the World Quarter Horse Show. He was competing with the top horses in the world and we were sure proud to see him in this exclusive competition. He sure didn't disappoint us, winning fourth in the heading and sixth in heeling. Not bad after having a broken leg such a short time before the show.

I bought one of his colts, Two Eyed Domino, and had Leroy break him and show him along with B Jack at several shows as a three year old. He did very well, winning the junior horse championship at Denver and Tucson. Bettye and I got to go watch Domino at a few shows and were proud of this big colt. We found out pretty quick that this could get expensive pretty fast and decided to retire Domino from the show ring! I went to riding him on the ranch and he was probably the best horse I ever had the privilege to throw a saddle on. I rode him many years and he just got better with age. I'm glad he is in semi-retirement on good pasture and being well cared for.

The UU Bar ownership was having difficulties with family differences. The ranch was solid, financially, but the owners decided to sell the ranch to settle their personal conflicts.

I kept thinking they would workout their differences, but when the asking price for the ranch was agreed on with a buyer, they sold out in October, 1994.

We have a house in Cimarron, so we had a place to go. We had a huge yard sale, packed up, and moved to town.

Bettye and I had fourteen good years with the UU Bar. The many years spent at Philmont were rewarding and that ranch was a good place to raise our family. The good Lord has sure blessed our lives, and for this we are most thankful.

Retirement really wasn't what I had been looking for, but I found myself suddenly retired! Needing something to do, I started writing some of my cowboying life stories for my kids, grandkids and greatgrandkids. The results are what you have just about finished reading. Maybe it has brought you a smile or maybe a chuckle. I hope so.

In my lifetime I have sure got to cowboy with some good hands, made a lot of friends, rode some top flight horses, and got to live the life I chose, as I was "Growing up to Cowboy!"

Adios!

RC, Lee and Bob in Garcia Park, UU Bar Ranch

Grandson Lee, Granddaughter Felice with Bob at UU Bar Ranch

Grandson Lee riding Frog Honey UU Bar Ranch

Bob and Lee roping calves at branding, UU Bar Ranch

Lee brought calf to flankers, UU Bar Ranch

Bob Knox, CD Garcia, David Fernandez, Chuck Enloe, on
Rivera Mesa, UU Bar Ranch

Gathering cattle off Rivera Mesa, after early snow, UU Bar Ranch

Gathering cattle off Rivera Mesa, after early snow, UU Bar Ranch

Bob on Mescalero, RC on Tumbleweed at La Grulla Cow Camp
on UU Bar Ranch

Bob and RC at La Grulla Cow Camp

RC, Bob and Lee, ready to rope, at Cimarron Place, UU Bar Ranch

Domino. Horses don't get much better than this one

Bob roping on Domino at Rayado, UU Bar Ranch.
With Chuck Pledge on gate

57

Remembering

Glad this is the last day of shipping at Sunnyside. We've been hitting it every day for five days. Shipping six hundred fifty head a day. We finish up the thirty-nine hundred today move down to Sweetwater in a couple of days. Got twenty-five hundred down there to ship. Be glad for the change of scenery. Have to drive twenty miles further. Get up a little earlier.

Domino greets me with a soft nicker as I go into the corral and flip the dim light on over the saddle room door. I pour him a can of grain in his feed tub. As he eats his breakfast, I brush him off. Throwing my saddle on him, he threatens to nip me if I cinch him too tight. Buckle on my spurs, hang my chaps and bridle on my shoulder, as I untie his halter lead rope and lead him out to the trailer. He is anxious to get in; 4:30 A.M., right on schedule. Three miles up to the pavement, see the headlights of another early bird on the road to Springer. Cimarron seems to be still asleep as I drive through town. Six miles south, slow down a little going past Philmont. Lots of deer around here, don't need to hit one this morning. Going up the long hill past Philmont, I can see the flicker of headlights coming up the road from our Abeyta cow camp to the east. Must be George.

Seven more winding miles. Can't get anything on the radio this morning. Dropping off the hill at Rayado, I see the headlights coming up the road from the south. Must be CD and David coming up from Sweetwater.

Turn off the pavement, bounce over the rough cattleguard headed east toward Sunnyside. See Chuck has already left as I pass the Rayado corrals. Three miles of rough road, I come up on a long line of ten semi-trucks pulled over and parked beside the road. Drivers trying to catch a little catnap, waiting for us to get the cattle in and ready to load.

Driving past the corrals, I see several saddled horses in the light from the Sunnyside saddle room. Chuck and his partner's horses are tied to the horse trailer and nicker a greeting to Domino as I pull up out of the way and park. Domino is anxious to get out of the trailer; he snorts and looks around for any boogers that might be lurking in the darkness.

Walking into the Sunnyside bunk house I'm met with the aroma of boiled coffee. Sure smells good. Several cowboys setting around the table in various stages of sleep and awake. Some smiles, some rather blank looks. George, CD, and David come in. Get a cup of coffee. Pulling on chaps, a little good natured kidding. "Still want to be a cowboy?" Chuck asks David and Billy, the two maintenance men for the ranch that have been recruited to help with the shipping. They are both a little saddle sore, not used to riding. "Not very damned romantic", David comments. Billy is all smiles, really eating this up. Coming from New York, he is probably getting to live a childhood dream.

"Okay boys, let's get'em", I say, rinsing my coffee cup and heading for the door. Everyone follows suit, the jingle of spurs rings out into the darkness as the cowboys head over to their horses. I take the lead as we hit a long trot down the rocky lane leading to the Vega shipping pasture. The only light in the darkness is the faint glow of a couple cigarettes, and the occasional spark flying off a rock as the shod horses pass by. A couple of horses a little humpy yet, but no bronc rides this morning. Pretty dark yet, just a faint promise of light starting to show on the eastern horizon, as we pull up at the gate going into the four section shipping pasture.

"Chuck, take three men and gather the mesa and south side across the bog. David, go up the long neck on the southwest corner, then help Chuck. CD, take three men and work the north side across the creek, couple of guys come back up the creek through the willows. The rest of us will go to the back side. We need them all this morning, men. Chuck, go with me through the gate when we get there, we'll try to keep them from running when we hit the lane. Let's get'em!"

We all lope off into the dark in different directions. Around two miles to the back side, scattered steers move out of the way as we lope past. Not much talking, the sounds of the horses blowing, spurs jingling, saddle leathers slightly squeaking. Pretty chilly this morning. Riding at a lope helps warm a guy up a little.

Getting light enough to tell a steer from a bush as we ride up to the backside fence. Spread out and start back, throwing everything together and drifting them west toward the gate. Pick up those coming up out of the creek. Light enough to see that Chuck has a good sized bunch coming down the draw from the mesa. Steers sure feeling good this morning, some of them wanting to run. Got several hundred head together.

Sun made it up again! Sure feels good on my chilly back. The mountains to the west sure look good with this first morning light hitting them. Sky couldn't get any brighter blue. CD rides up, his big contagious grin showing bright under his black hat. We both pause and look around us. The rising sun, clear bright blue sky, green grass, the sound of the clear water rushing by in Rayado Creek, the feel of a good horse under me, several hundred fat steers moving out ahead of us, cowboys on both sides of us, the honest smell of horse sweat.

"Don't guess it gets any better than this, does it Bob?" CD says.

I sure think he was right.

Cowboying!! I feel fortunate that I can say I've been there and done that. It sure was a good ride!

GLOSSARY

Words and terms used by the author

BLM: Burea of Land Management- Government Agency.

Bronc: Wild, unbroke horse.

Bronky: Wild acting, unbroke.

Cake: 3/4" by 2-3 inch cubes of grain and hay. (Not for your birthday party)

Cinch: Mohair girth that goes under horses belly to cinch saddle on. (Not like a royal flush in a poker game!)

Dally: To take a wrap around saddle horn with rope. (Watch your fingers and thumb!)

Dallied: Rope wrapped around saddle horn. (Preferably without fingers or thumb under rope!)

Diamond Hitch: Rope tie used to secure pack on packhorse or mule.

Double Hock: To catch both hind feet. (Hopefully!)

Dude String: Gentle saddle horses for dudes to ride!

Flanked: Having flank strap tightened around horse or bulls flanks.

FlankStrap: Leather strap tightened around flank to encourage high kicking while bucking. (no, it doesn't hurt the animal!)

Flankers: Men (and some tough girls) a foot that throw calf down and hold on ground to brand. (Real glamourous job.)

Flank Cinch: 2-4 inch leather back cinch on most stock saddles.

Flank cinch hobble: Short leather strap connecting front and back cinches. (Better hope yours don't break!)

Handle: Horses response to rider. (Good, bad and not worth a damn!)

Heading Horse: Horse trained to rope heads or horns on. (Rider actually does roping, not the horse!)

Heeling Horse: Same as above only other end!

High Lope: In fancy language thats a canter or gallop

Hobble: Soft rope or strap to tie horses front feet together (Like trying to run with your pants around your ankles!)

Homestead: To live on designated land given to individuals by Government to help settle the wild and wooly west. Usually 640 acres.

Homestead, Proved up: Build a house (more or less) and live off land designated length of time, usually one year minimum, to get title to land.

Hoolihan: Throw rope overhand without twirling to catch horses in corral. (Not as easy as it looks)

Horn knot: Knot tied in rope to put over saddle horn. (Don't have to worry about getting dallies, plenty other things your going to have to worry about if you make a catch!)

Long in the Tooth: Getting a little old. (Don't worry, your times coming!)

Mavericks: Wild, unbranded, unmarked. (Like you were before you got married!)

Muggers: Guys afoot that try to hold wild cow as partner trys to milk her. (Kinda like guys you read about in town looking for tourists)

Mother up: Make sure calf is with his mother after they have been separated. (Not referring to your Mothers softball team)

Paired up: Cow and calf are together. (Or catch an Ace when you have one in the hole!)

Neck rein: To turn horse with rein pressure on neck. (Some times a club helps!)

N. Porter: Old time saddle maker from Phoenix, Az. (No, it isn't the night porter on the train.)

Panniers: Large canvas bags designed to hang on pack saddle. (Fancy name for canvas bags!)

Pull the well: To pull the sucker rod or pipe out of a well. (Not a cowboys favorite chore! Most of them don't know what it means either!)

Quicked: To rasp or drive horse shoe nail into tender area of horses hoof. (Like when you trim your toe nails to short!)

Section: Area of land one mile square, 640 acres.

Tied hard and fast: Rope tied solid to saddle horn. (Cause of a lot of wild wrecks!)

Slick forked: Old style saddle with no rider support in front of saddle. (Hard to ride a bronc in one of these!)

Turning the crank: Term used to describe a hard bucking horse. (Not guiding your mother-in-law!)

Trotty: Wild cattle, prone to run. (Not like those people you see in their little shorts going around the track!)

Waspy: Wild, hard to ride. (How things get when your horse kicks over a hornets nest!)

Printed in the United States
863400001B